D1564700

Language Intervention Series
Volume IX

TEACHING
FUNCTIONAL LANGUAGE

TEACHING FUNCTIONAL LANGUAGE, edited by Steven Warren, Ph.D., and Ann Rogers-Warren, Ph.D., is the ninth volume in the **Language Intervention Series**—Richard L. Schiefelbusch, series editor. Other volumes in this series include:

Published:

Volume I **BASES OF LANGUAGE INTERVENTION** edited by
  Richard L. Schiefelbusch, Ph.D.

Volume II **LANGUAGE INTERVENTION STRATEGIES** edited by
  Richard L. Schiefelbusch, Ph.D.

Volume III **LANGUAGE INTERVENTION FROM APE TO CHILD**
  edited by *Richard L. Schiefelbusch, Ph.D., and John H. Hollis, Ed.D.*

Volume IV **NONSPEECH LANGUAGE AND COMMUNICATION**
  Analysis and Intervention edited by *Richard L. Schiefelbusch, Ph.D.*

Volume V **EMERGING LANGUAGE IN AUTISTIC CHILDREN**
  edited by *Warren H. Fay, Ph.D., and Adriana Luce Schuler, M.A.*

Volume VI **EARLY LANGUAGE** **Acquisition and Intervention**
  edited by *Richard L. Schiefelbusch, Ph.D., and Diane Bricker, Ph.D.*

Volume VII **DEVELOPMENT LANGUAGE INTERVENTION**
  Psycholinguistic Applications edited by *Kenneth F. Ruder, Ph.D., and Michael D. Smith, Ph.D.*

Volume VIII **THE ACQUISITION OF COMMUNICATIVE**
  COMPETENCE edited by *Richard L. Schiefelbusch, Ph.D., and Joanne Pickar, M.A*

In preparation:

COMMUNICATIVE COMPETENCE **Assessment and Intervention**
  edited by *Richard L. Schiefelbusch, Ph.D.*

Language Intervention Series
Volume IX

TEACHING FUNCTIONAL LANGUAGE

Generalization and Maintenance of Language Skills

Edited by

Steven F. Warren, Ph.D.

Assistant Professor
of Special Education and Psychology
Peabody College of Vanderbilt University
Nashville, Tennessee

Ann K. Rogers-Warren, Ph.D.

Associate Professor
of Special Education and Psychology
Peabody College of Vanderbilt University
Nashville, Tennessee

University Park Press · Baltimore

University Park Press
International Publishers in Medicine and Allied Health
300 North Charles Street
Baltimore, Maryland 21201

Sponsoring editor: Janet S. Hankin
Production editor: Megan Barnard Shelton
Cover and text design by: Caliber Design Planning, Inc.

Typeset by: BG Composition, Inc.
Manufactured in the United States of America by: Halliday Lithograph

Library of Congress Cataloging in Publication Data
Main entry under title:
Teaching functional language.
   (Language intervention series ; v. 9)
   Bibliography: p.
   Includes index.
   1. Language disorders in children.   2. Children—
Language.   I. Warren, Steven F.   II. Rogers-Warren,
Ann K.   III. Series.
RJ496.L35T43   1984   618.92′855   84-20998
ISBN 0-8391-1798-1

We are, first and foremost, what our families have taught us to be.

This book is dedicated to Jim Kaiser, who is a constant reminder of the importance of early speech and language intervention with the handicapped, and to James V. Warren, whose lifetime work has improved the lives of hundreds of handicapped children in rural Nebraska.

contents

Contributors   ix
Preface   xi
Foreword   xiii

Section I   Current Perspectives on Language Remediation

chapter 1   **Teaching Functional Language:** An Introduction
Steven F. Warren and Ann K. Rogers-Warren   3

chapter 2   **Communication Intervention:** A Selective Review of What, When, and How to Teach
Joe Reichle and William J. Keogh   25

Section II   Functional Language Training: Applications

chapter 3   **Naturalistic Language Training Techniques**
Betty Hart   63

chapter 4   **Language through Conversation:** A Model for Intervention with Language-Delayed Persons
James D. MacDonald   89

chapter 5   **Communication in Autistic Persons:** Characteristics and Intervention
Cathy L. Alpert and Ann K. Rogers-Warren   123

chapter 6   **Communication Intervention for the "Difficult-to-Teach" Severely Handicapped**
William J. Keogh and Joe Reichle   157

Section III   Facilitating and Measuring Generalization

chapter 7   **Clinical Strategies for the Measurement of Language Generalization**
Steven F. Warren   197

chapter 8   **Enhancing Language Generalization Using Matrix and Stimulus Equivalence Training**
Howard Goldstein   225

chapter 9   **Training Techniques That May Facilitate Generalization**
Kathleen Stremel-Campbell and C. Robert Campbell   251

Section IV   Utilizing Significant Others

chapter 10   **Programming Peer Support for Functional Language**
Linda Paul   289

chapter 11   **Programming Teacher Support for Functional Language**
C. Robert Campbell, Kathleen Stremel-Campbell, and Ann K. Rogers-Warren   309

Index   341

Cathy L. Alpert, Ph.D.
Department of Special Education
Peabody College of Vanderbilt
    University
Nashville, Tennessee 37203

C. Robert Campbell, Ed.D.
Rainbows United, Inc.
2615 Wellesley
Wichita, KS 67220

Howard Goldstein, Ph.D.
Department of Communication
University of Pittsburgh
Pittsburgh, Pennsylvania 15260

Betty Hart, Ph.D.
Bureau of Child Research
University of Kansas
Lawrence, Kansas 66045

William K. Keogh, Ph.D.
Center for Developmental
    Disabilities
University of Vermont
Burlington, Vermont 05401

James D. MacDonald, Ph.D.
Nisonger Center
Ohio State University
1580 Cannon Drive
Columbus, Ohio 43210

Linda Paul, Ph.D.
Suffolk Child Development Center
Hollywood Drive
Smithtown, New York 11787

Joe Reichle, Ph.D.
Department of Communication
    Disorders
115 Shevlin Hall
University of Minnesota
164 Pillsbury Drive, S.E.
Minneapolis, Minnesota 55455

Ann K. Rogers-Warren, Ph.D.
Department of Special Education
Peabody College of Vanderbilt
    University
Nashville, Tennessee 37203

Richard L. Schiefelbusch, Ph.D.
Bureau of Child Research
University of Kansas
Lawrence, Kansas 66045

**Kathleen Stremel-Campbell,
M.A.**
Teaching Research Division
Oregon State System of Higher
    Education
345 North Monmouth Avenue
Monmouth, Oregon 97361

Steven F. Warren, Ph.D.
Department of Special Education
Peabody College of Vanderbilt
    University
Nashville, Tennessee 37203

Over the years, there have been many books written that are relevant to language remediation. Most of those books have addressed the *bases* of language intervention: the logic of intervention, the theoretical framework for intervention, specific experimental studies of limited interventions, assessment strategies, and comparisons between the development of normal and language-deficient individuals. The contributions of this rich and varied literature have been numerous, yet surprisingly few volumes have focused specifically on the question that is of primary interest to language interventionists: How do you teach functional language to children with major communication deficits? *Functional language* in this case means language that is used to communicate in everyday settings with adults and peers. Implied in the definition of "functional language" is the assumption that training has produced a generalized repertoire of forms that can be used effectively outside the training context.

The question of how to teach functional language is not a new one. For almost 20 years, researchers, clinicians, and teachers have offered curricula that attempted to answer the question. Many of those curricula were primarily based on the "best guess" of their authors and only secondarily based on empirical research. Entering our third decade of language intervention, we still do not have complete, data-based answers, but progress in research and training has occurred. In this book, we have attempted to translate recent empirical and theoretical knowledge on teaching functional language into a form that can be readily used by therapists, teachers, and parents. The result of our efforts is not a cookbook of procedures, but a synthesis of techniques into a conceptual framework and sets of guidelines for intervention. Given the complexity of the communication system and the heterogeneous nature of language deficits, a "cookbook" approach would have been misleading and of little real use in teaching truly functional skills to a range of students.

This volume emphasizes principles and procedures of intervention. The therapist or teacher must still conduct assessments, develop individual child programs, and select content. This book will help answer the crucial questions of how to teach, where to teach, who to have teach, when to teach and when not to teach, how to organize content to facilitate generalization, how to reinforce, what criterion to set for success, and how to determine if the training is working.

Each of these issues is addressed from the perspective of facilitating generalization. Generalization has been the major problem in effective language intervention. At this point in the development of intervention strategies, teaching procedures that do not produce generalized use in natural settings can no longer be considered effective. Generalization from training is likely to be the outcome of incorporating generalization-facilitating techniques into several components of the training process. Thus, each aspect of training must be considered from the perspective of how it will influence initial learning and generalization of new skills.

Although several theories of child development and human behavior have influenced aspects of this book, the perspective of most of the contributing authors is clearly behavioral. However, it is more useful to characterize the book in terms of its recurrent themes rather than its theoretical perspectives. These themes include: inclusion of parents and teachers as primary trainers, utilization of incidental teaching techniques, emphasis on training in conversational contexts, promotion of the child's social and communicative initiations, following the child's lead, utilizing naturalistic functional reinforcement, and always approaching training with the goal of facilitating acquisition and ensuring generalization to the child's functional repertoire.

Finally, a word about the individual authors is warranted. Each author brings to his or her chapter skills as a researcher and as a practitioner. In almost every case, the proposed guidelines for intervention are based on empirical evidence (frequently research by the authors themselves) and the authors' experiences in language intervention with children who have serious communication deficits. The blend of research and clinical skills characteristic of the contributors has resulted in a volume that we believe will have both scientific and clinical validity. We are immensely grateful to the contributors. Working with them in the process of developing this book has broadened our empirical and practical knowledge of the essential strategies for teaching functional language. We hope this volume will do the same for our readers.

Steven F. Warren
Ann K. Rogers-Warren
May, 1984

Children's language is functional when it is used in environments with peers and adult companions to affect their behavior. Functional language plays a prominent part in the daily life of the developing child. When the child's language deficiencies do not allow for communication with the adults and peers who provide stimulation and learning opportunities, there must be a program of functional language training. Such programs should be based on some simple concepts about functional language development.

Typically, the first words a child uses are embedded in play or in frequently repeated family routines such as greetings or goodbyes. Those words are a feature in an often-repeated social exchange and are keyed to familiar and regular contexts. Those words allow the child to participate in social rituals. In the beginning stages of language development, language is embedded in social participation. Social interaction keys language use and provides the context for language learning. As the number and variety of contexts the child experiences increase, so do the functions of language.

The notion of function occurs in several aspects of the communication system. Language functions are the social basis of linguistic behavior. Linguistic behavior varies according to social functions (Whitehurst and Zimmerman, 1979). In behavioral terms, *function* describes the relationship between stimulus and response events. Language is *functional* if it mediates subsequent events. When language use increases as a result of change in the environment, it then can be assumed that language is functional in the new environment.

The term *function* is also used in communication theory to explain a language event, as in speaking of an expressive function (an act of speaking) or a listening function (discrimination of meaning or the perception of phonemes). Again, the functions of language influence the child's language performance.

When we focus on language forms, we deal with syntax. Schiefelbusch, Ruder, and Bricker (1976) pointed out that "a sentence of the form subject-verb-object typically serves the function of expressing semantic relationships existing between agents (mapped in the linguistic form as grammatical subject), action (verb), and objects or recipients of the action (object of the sentence)." In like manner, past tense and plurality mark particular functional semantic relations. Their linguistic forms are the morphological markers *-ed* and *-s*. The term *function* in this context refers to linguistic effects and is part of a total theory of language. In designing intervention plans, we must consider *both* the semantic and the social aspects of language.

The authors of this volume are experienced language intervention scientists and clinicians who have woven a range of intervention strategies into a functional plan. To fully appreciate this plan, the reader should visualize the everyday settings in which children communicate. Those settings comprise the field of social interaction in which handicapped children must learn to participate. The target language for training *functional* language must serve the child-user in these multi-featured contexts.

"Functional" describes a qualitative aspect of language use. Specific language can be more or less functional. Almost every form trained in language intervention may be somewhat functional, but what we want to do is to make newly trained language as functional as possible. We want to teach language in a way that it will produce expected social or mediating effects under normal conditions. That is the focus of naturalistic training.

Most experimental work on training functional language has occurred in the area of language *generalization* research. The designs and strategies for facilitating generalization involve parents, teachers, and peers as an instrumental part of the intervention procedures. This book more than any current or previous book explains how interventions can be engineered within the daily environments so training for language use is congruent with the social experiences of children and generalized use of new forms is ensured. The fusion of research method and clinical experience presented in this volume predicts an important future for *functional language intervention*. It also predicts more effective developments in language intervention programs nationwide.

R.L.S.
May, 1984

REFERENCES

Schiefelbusch, R. L., Ruder, K. F., and Bricker, W. A. 1976. Training strategies for language deficient children: An overview. *In* N. G. Haring and R. L. Schiefelbusch (eds.), Teaching Special Children. McGraw-Hill, New York.

Whitehurst, G. J., and Zimmerman, B. J. 1979. The Functions of Language and Cognition. Academic Press, New York.

acknowledgments

We wish to thank several individuals for the important contributions they made to this volume. For their invaluable help in preparing the manuscript we would like to thank Patsy Horner and Mary Beth Johnston of the University of Kansas, and Gayle Hawkes and Dali White of Vanderbilt University. Marilyn Fischer of the University of Kansas acted as technical editor for the manuscript and made important contributions to the readability of each chapter. For their input and advice prior to and during the early stages of the project, special thanks go to Drs. Donald M. Baer and Joseph E. Spradlin of the University of Kansas. Finally, we wish to thank Richard L. Schiefelbusch, Director of the Bureau of Child Research at the University of Kansas, for his support and knowledgeable advice during all stages of the project.

Section

I

Current Perspectives on Language Remediation

chapter 1

Teaching Functional Language
An Introduction

Steven F. Warren
and
Ann K. Rogers-Warren
Department of Special Education
Peabody College of
Vanderbilt University

contents

WHAT IS FUNCTIONAL LANGUAGE?   6

**ACQUISITION AND GENERALIZATION—
A PERSPECTIVE**   7

     What Is Taught   8
     Who Teaches   9
     How Skills Are Taught   10
     How the Student Is Reinforced   10
     Where Teaching Occurs   12
     How the Content of Training Is Organized   12
     What Criteria for Learning Are Applied   13
     How the Effects of Training Are Measured   14
     How Responsive and Supportive the Child's Environment Is to New
       Learning   14

THE SUPERSTRUCTURE OF LANGUAGE TRAINING   15

     The Parent   16
     The Teacher   17
     The Therapist   18
     The Program Administrator   18
     The Training Programs   18
     Can the System Respond?   19

PLAN FOR THE BOOK   19

OVERVIEW   21

REFERENCES   22

Teaching functional language to developmentally delayed children is one of the primary goals of most special education efforts. Regardless of the specific reasons why children fail to fully acquire a communication system, language training likely will be a basic component of their education. Many handicapped individuals require intensive language training throughout their educational years, whereas their nonhandicapped peers succeed in acquiring functional language during their preschool years with little perceivable effort. Delay in acquiring a functional language system necessarily alters an individual's entire educational curriculum and, frequently, the course of his or her entire life.

Given the importance of language, the goals of language interventionists and reseachers must be to develop highly effective and efficient language remediation systems for those who have difficulty learning language (Schiefelbusch, 1983). These systems should be implemented as soon as a serious language delay is identified. Normal infants and toddlers seem to acquire new communication and language skills every day during the first years of their lives. By age 5, normal children have acquired communication skills that make further cognitive, social, and linguistic development possible during childhood and adolescence. Hence, with the delayed child there is no time to lose. A responsive education system that is not constrained by restrictive policies (e.g., minimum age requirements) is essential. However, a set of responsive policies is not sufficient. Therapeutic strategies must be effective and cost efficient in terms of time, personnel, and other required resources. No matter how hard we try nor how theoretically correct and elegant the intervention model is, if the therapeutic strategy does not result in the child's acquiring a generalized communicative repertoire, we have failed (or at least have not yet succeeded).

We have not yet developed an optimally effective and cost-efficient language remediation system. On the other hand, definite progress has been made during the past 20 years. Many researchers and clinicians are convinced that the traditional therapeutic model characterized by an adult working with a child a few minutes a day in an isolated context can never result in acceptable generalization. Training lexical items and syntax separate from their communicative functions is considered a poor strategy. Furthermore, these professionals believe that generalization can be affected either positively or negatively by a range of variables implicit in training. Therefore new training strategies have been developed in the natural environment to enable the child to generalize from training and to acquire new forms of communication. New training models have been conceptualized to incorporate these techniques in systematic ways. A great deal of research remains to be done on these models

---

Throughout this chapter, "he" and "she" are used interchangeably to describe parents, teachers, children, students, and therapists. No sex bias is intended.

and techniques. Nevertheless, it is critical that these recently developed techniques, strategies, and procedures for teaching functional language reach therapists and teachers now. This volume is an attempt to provide some of this information in a format that is usable in interventions.

In this chapter, we present our perspective on teaching functional language. We discuss nine elements of language training that affect generalization and acquisition and present a superstructure for therapy that is compatible with the proposals made by our other contributors. Finally, there is a brief overview of the remainder of the book, including the purpose of each chapter and section.

WHAT IS FUNCTIONAL LANGUAGE?

Language is a symbol system that constitutes one means of communication. Communication can occur in various modalities including listening, speaking, reading, writing, looking, signing, and gesturing. To be *functional,* language must be used in a communicative interaction, and it must affect the listener in specific intended ways. Functional language *communicates.* There is no way to tell a priori whether a given lexical syntactic or pragmatic form will be functional for a child. Use and functions for forms are established by the child experiencing the consequences that result from using that word or form. That is, the child learns to control the environment (to cause certain consequences) by using certain sounds and combinations of sounds. This process possibly begins in the first weeks of life when the child begins to use different cries that result in particular consequences (e.g., food, being picked up, clean diapers).

The function of a word or sentence is established when the child directly experiences the consequences for its use. The child must find those consequences reinforcing if she is to continue using that word or sentence. Fortunately, there is a broad range of consequences that are likely to be reinforcing for the child. The successful experience of controlling the environment may in itself be a reinforcing event. Truly reinforcing consequences are the key to functional language training. This premise has many implications for how language training should be conducted. For instance, language training will be most effective when the teacher has the child's attention and interest (Hart and Rogers-Warren, 1978). This does not mean necessarily that the child should be seated, looking at the teacher, and waiting for her to speak (as is often recommended in the traditional one-to-one training situation). The situation can also be that the child wants something (a reinforcer) that she cannot obtain without using language as a mediator. The reinforcer could be an object, an action, or someone's attention. The key is that the child has initiated contact in a communicative way to obtain this end. In situations like this parents frequently interpret the child's request, model an appropriate verbal response for the child or expand on the child's statement, and fulfill the request (Bruner et al., 1980). When the child is interested in obtaining a particular end, she is likely to pay close attention to the behavior of the parent and the parent is likely to have an opportunity to effectively teach language (Bloom and Lahey, 1978). Training techniques in which teachers follow the child's lead (that is, pay attention to the child's specifications of her reinforcers) should be most effective because teaching occurs when the child is attending and because the language being taught to the child is a positive consequence. Such teaching should be functional.

Who should do language training? To ensure that the language being trained is functional and, therefore, most likely to be generalized, language training should be conducted by those who spend the most time communicating with the child. Typically, these are the child's parents and teachers. These people normally spend several hours every day with the child in situations in which language is very functional—eating, dressing, toileting, playing games, getting in the car, and so forth. With normal children language is often taught during such routines (Snow, 1977). To teach language effectively during these routines, parents and teachers themselves must be taught techniques that can be used "incidently."

Although naturalistic training will occur in the same types of routines in which normal language learning occurs, specific alterations in the interaction will be required to ensure that language-deficient children will learn from these interactions. When parents or teachers proceed in interactions with delayed children in the same way they would proceed with a normally developing child, the cues, prompts, and consequences for language may not constitute sufficiently discriminable conditions for learning. It is not that parents or teachers of handicapped children are deficient in their interactions with the child. Rather, different, more discriminable, and more frequent teaching strategies may be needed for learning to occur. In particular, the history of parent-child interaction may have been one in which the parents' previous, natural attempts to teach language have not been successful, subsequently causing both parents and child to interact less frequently and to be less responsive to each other. Training parents and teachers will consist not only of teaching them specific prompting techniques, but also of supporting their efforts with children who may have a history of not responding to such teaching efforts. This in turn implies a new and important role for speech therapists as teacher and parent trainers.

ACQUISITION AND GENERALIZATION—
A PERSPECTIVE

The goal of language remediation is to improve students' abilities to communicate. This goal can be accomplished in two ways: by ensuring that students generalize what is taught to their actual usage repertoire and by enhancing students' abilities to acquire language independently. Accelerating natural acquisition and ensuring generalization from training are the results of many variables in the training process. It is important to understand and to accommodate for the fact that almost all aspects of the remediation process may affect the outcome of training. A fundamental tenet of the perspectives presented in this book is that generalization is not an outcome of any single variable but, rather is the cumulative result of many components of training. Therefore, each aspect of training must be considered in terms of how it may ultimately influence acquisition and generalization.

Learning may be characterized as consisting of three overlapping levels. First is the acquisition level where the child learns the basic response or skill (for example, the word *ball* is associated with a spherical object). Language training typically concentrates on this level by teaching simple form-event relationships and teaching new skills as soon as the student evidences associative learning. Next is the generalization level when the student begins to use the response under a variety of conditions. She may overgeneralize or undergeneralize use of the response as she explores its potential functions and discovers its essential attributes and delimiters. This level of language learning frequently is ignored in language training. Finally, the student attains competence in using the response. At this point, the student may approximate adult competence in the use of the response. She knows when to use it and when not to use it. The response is integrated with other communicative responses in her repertoire; it is used generatively. This level, although obviously the desired outcome of intervention, usually is ignored completely in training.

The three levels of learning are interrelated. If teaching at the basic acquisition level produces a tightly discriminated response (e.g., the student learns to associate the world *ball* with only one or two particular balls) generalization is unlikely unless it is subsequently programmed. If generalization is restricted or fails to occur, the child will have no basis for attaining competence. An effective language remediation approach must ensure that learning occurs across all three levels.

Many variables may affect the outcome of training. At least nine basic variables clearly can make a significant difference. These include: 1) what is taught, 2) who teaches, 3) how skills are taught, 4) how the student is reinforced, 5) where teaching occurs, 6) how the content of training is organized, 7) what criteria for learning are applied, 8) how the effects of training are measured, 9) and how responsive and supportive the students' environment is to new learning.

What Is Taught

The content of training can be conceptualized on many levels. Students must be taught more than just words and sentences, they must be taught the functions of language and a strategy for learning new language (McLean and Snyder-McLean, 1978). Functions and strategies may be the most important "content" of language training. Functions and strategies are taught as a result of the combined components of training (who teaches, how teaching is done, and so forth). Specific forms (words and sentences) are also important. The forms must be ones that are *likely* to be functional for the student immediately. He must be able to use them to make requests, describe things and answer questions. Labels should name objects that are important to the student and frequently found in his environment. Sentence forms should map pragmatic functions the student has already acquired. New forms should be only slightly more complex than the ones he presently uses to express that function. For example, Warren and Rogers-Warren (1983) reported that severely retarded children may not generalize trained forms that are much more than a morpheme longer than their normal mean length of utterance (MLU) no matter how thoroughly longer forms are trained.

The distinction between what students *can* learn in one-to-one training and what they functionally *use* for communication is especially important. The content of training should be just slightly more complex than the student's current functioning level and should represent objects and functions that are important to the student. Specific content, in the sense of which words or sentence forms should be trained, is rarely mentioned in this text. [Selection of forms that are likely to be functional is assumed.] Instead, the chapters deal primarily with the process of teaching and how teaching can be most functional for the child.

Who Teaches

In many ways, parents and teachers are ideal language trainers because of their relationships with the student and the amount of time they spend with her. It simply makes no sense from the perspective of facilitating acquisition and generalization for a therapist who sees a child once or twice a week to be entirely responsible for teaching language. However, enthusiasm for parents and teachers as primary trainers must be tempered by a realistic examination of the multiple demands placed on them in relation to the education and care of the handicapped child. Parents are natural language teachers of their children and to expand this role by training them to use some special teaching procedures is logically reasonable (Spradlin and Siegal, 1982). Parents of handicapped children (particularly mothers because they are almost always the training parent), like parents of normal children, serve many functions in the family unit, and teaching is only one of them. The increased stresses and time demands that are typically associated with caring for a handicapped child (Gallagher et al., 1983) further reduce parents' flexibility in assuming new or expanded roles as teachers or therapists. Including parents as therapists, when there are effective training strategies, clear targets for intervention, and a support system to encourage the parents, is appropriate and can make a tremendous difference in the child's language learning. However, not all parents can assume this role, and no parent should be *required* to serve as a primary teacher for her child.

A similar point applies to teachers. With adequate support in a classroom that is well managed, a teacher can be a primary language trainer, but assuming that a teacher can or wishes to take on this function without training and support is unwise. If parents and teachers are to be effective language teachers, they will need to learn special techniques for interacting with the child. The therapist should be responsible for teaching them these techniques, for monitoring child progress, and for conducting assessments. This multiple—therapist model of intervention is discussed more extensively later in this chapter. Such a model is implicit in the proposals of Hart (Chapter 3) and of MacDonald (Chapter 4) and compatible with other proposals made in this book.

How Skills Are Taught

Teaching is interacting with the student. Mothers of normal children appear to teach by following the child's lead, carefully maintaining an optimal communicative match, and reinforcing function rather than form (Moerk, 1977). Mothers appear to be most focused on keeping the child's interest (Schachter, 1979). They provide expanded models and try to get the child to produce a response slightly above his current competency level. This process is described in detail by Bruner (1978). A number of techniques for teaching language to handicapped children can be abstracted from descriptions of this natural teaching process. MacDonald (Chapter 4), and Hart (Chapter 3) to a lesser extent, have both done this. However, the special problems of handicapped children sometimes make "normal" teaching models insufficient or ineffective. Accordingly, Alpert and Rogers-Warren (Chapter 5) and Keogh and Reichle (Chapter 6) describe procedures developed by applied behavior analysts (as were Hart's, in spite of their apparent similarity to "normal" teaching models) for use with autistic and severely retarded children. The issue of how to teach in terms of the techniques incorporated into the training process to ensure generalization is the focus of both Stremel-Campbell and Campbell's (Chapter 9) and Goldstein's chapters (Chapter 8). These authors discuss a range of techniques (from matrix training models to "loose" training) that have been shown by applied behavior analysts to facilitate language generalization in handicapped children.

How the Student Is Reinforced

Reinforcement is one of the most important processes in language acquisition and in remediation; it is also one of the most misunderstood. Word and sentence forms derive their functions from their reinforcement histories (Skinner, 1957). A child uses the statement "I want a drink" because it usually works to obtain water or juice; that is, it is reinforced. It is possible to understand the importance of reinforcement and still fail to apply the principles of reinforcement in training.

Children who fail to learn language in the natural environment may do so for a variety of reasons. One reason is that the consequences for their communication attempts are not sufficiently reinforcing to them to result in an increased rate of communication. Alternatively, they may fail to associate the consequences with their response. In planned language intervention, events and objects known to be reinforcing to the student are used to establish the initial performance of communicative responses. Exaggerated praise, food, physical contact, and other preferred events may be presented contingent on utterances that, in fact, specify a different sort of reinforcer (for example, the child is taught to say "red ball" in response to the presentation of a relevant stimulus but is reinforced with the presentation of bits of candy, rather than being given the ball).

Although use of primary reinforcers in training may be necessary to establish responding in severely delayed children, consideration must also be given to introducing the child to the consequences available for the linguistic response in everyday conversation. Essentially, there are two lessons to be learned in language training: how to produce a response, and what its associated consequences will be. For language to generalize, it must be reinforced by the naturally occurring consequences. Establishing naturally occurring events as reinforcers for the severely handicapped child may be in itself a training goal. By pairing naturally occurring consequences with consequences known to be reinforcing to the child, the trainer is able to condition the natural consequences or at least to introduce them under conditions that will favor their establishment as reinforcers.

Conditioning naturally occurring events as reinforcers may be essential to teaching functional language with some children. Establishing some functions may require teaching when the student is not reinforced by natural consequences or does not systematically notice the association between the behavior and its consequences. Events and objects are reinforcers only when their presentation results in an increase in the preceding response. It is the relationship between response and consequence that is essential, not the consequence per se. To depend on naturally occurring events to suffice as reinforcers for new or emerging language without at least an observational analysis of the actual reinforcing qualities of the consequence for the particular student is a risky choice. This is especially true for more severely handicapped students who have failed to learn functional communication skills in an environment filled with these particular natural contingencies.

Eventually, for most people, communication itself is a natural reinforcer for language. However, initially one cannot assume that communication success is sufficiently reinforcing to ensure learning or generalization. In general, planning a systematic introduction of natural reinforcing contingencies must be a central part of the training process (see Stremel-Campbell and Campbell, Chapter 9). The more severely delayed or deviant a child's skills are, the more systematic the transition from known primary reinforcers to naturally occurring social contact reinforcers may need to be. To depend on natural contingencies is just as unwise as continuing to use bits of candy as a consequence for language.

Where Teaching Occurs

Language should be taught where it is to be used. Teaching should occur at home and in the classroom, particularly within the daily routines where language is functional. Parents rarely spend time just sitting around talking with their child or specifically teaching language. There are too many other things to be done. Language is taught in the course of eating, dressing, toileting, bathing, and various transitions when language typically needs to be used. These situations are good occasions for language remediation because both the child and the adult may benefit from the child's use of language. For example, at lunch effective language on the part of the child can mean the difference between too much or not enough ketchup on one's hamburger. For the adult, functional language can mean the difference between telling the child to get the milk and having to get up and get it oneself. Language should be taught where it is to be used to do the things it most needs to do.

How the Content of Training Is Organized

One implicit goal in language training is efficiency: maximum learning from minimum training. Some ways of organizing the content of training are more efficient than others. For example, to train noun-verb combinations, one might devise a matrix with noun examples on one side and verb examples on the other. By systematically training key noun-verb combinations, generalization to all other possible noun-verb pairs can be achieved without direct training. The matrix training format is clearly more efficient than training each novel noun-verb combination. However, Goldstein (Chapter 8) demonstrates that it is even more efficient in terms of expected generalization to train down this matrix in a stepwise fashion than in a diagonal manner. That is, training two overlapping examples in each of two successive categories of noun-verb combinations (*push car, push truck; pull truck, pull cup*) is more effective than training one noun-verb combination in each category (*push car; pull truck*). Students abstract the rule for noun-verb combination with less training if this overlapping examples method of organizing the training content is used.

Goldstein also discusses stimulus equivalence training as another means of enhancing training efficiency. Much of language, particularly referential language, involves equivalences among stimuli. Equivalence implies that one stimulus can be substituted for another. Different referents, symbols, and linguistic responses can be substitutable members of a stimulus class, such as car (i.e., many types of cars as well as pictures of cars, emblems, trademarks, and model names that all denote "car"). This tendency of humans to form stimulus classes can be utilized to make language training more efficient. For example, if a child understands the equivalence between the spoken words for cars and pictures of cars, and between the spoken words and written words for cars, then the relationships between pictures of cars and the names of cars can be taught and will generalize from just a few (perhaps only one or two) examples of this relationship. Goldstein provides numerous applications of this approach. In each case, the flexibility of the stimulus equivalence paradigm allows the intervener to take advantage of those equivalences already known by the child to easily teach new equivalences and relationships that are important to communication.

Stremel-Campbell and Campbell (Chapter 9) offer several suggestions about organizing training to maximize generalization. These suggestions center on the systematic use of carefully selected multiple training examplars, the loosening of stimulus control after the student provides evidence of initial acquisition of a response, and the introduction of natural maintaining consequences for language use into the training context. The application of each of these tactics is based on evidence of initial acquisition of a response under tightly controlled stimulus conditions and frequent reinforcement. Such conditions facilitate efficient initial acquisition, but may subsequently restrict generalization. The procedures discussed by Stremel-Campbell and Campbell promote generalization, but retain efficient initial training techniques.

What Criteria for Learning Are Applied

One frequent error in language training is to claim success prematurely. That is, it is often assumed that students have learned a language structure or function because they can accurately display the response on 80% of the posttraining probe trials. Probes may not correspond to the communication conditions found in the student's everyday environments. Anything less than a demonstration by the student of the trained language under the conditions imposed by the everyday environment is potentially misleading. An example of the discrepancy between probe and naturalistic performance is reported in a longitudinal study of language generalization by Warren and Rogers-Warren (1983). They studied six severely retarded children who had reached "criterion" on 71 two-, three-, and four-word forms during training. Even though subjects could respond correctly on posttraining generalization probes across settings, trainers, and objects, they actually used only 43 (or 61%) of these forms in their everyday environments.

Training criteria will affect not only what procedures will be used for training and generalization facilitation, but also how thoroughly the training impacts the student's communication system. Applying more stringent criteria, particularly including evidence of generalization as a condition for completing training, may be one of the most straightforward ways of increasing the impact of training. This issue is discussed by Warren in Chapter 7.

How the Effects of Training Are Measured

Because language is a basic skill that interfaces with cognitive and social development, language training may have a range of effects beyond those directly planned. Training can affect the student's cognitive and social skills. When a child learns names of objects in the environment, she may acquire content for social interchange. For example, she may initiate communication to peers by requesting a particular toy by name. Acquiring labels may also assist the child in forming concepts about objects (Anglin, 1977). Furthermore, an increasing language repertoire allows the child to learn from linguistic description as well as from direct experience with objects and events. The effects also may be varied within the domain of language. Training could affect the student's lexicon, syntax, grammar, receptive skills, pragmatic functioning, and frequency of speech as well as the conditions under which he uses these skills. Selecting targets to measure as outcomes of training should be based on the student's most pressing needs. For example, changes in overall responsiveness and frequency of verbalization may be more relevant measures of the effectiveness of language training than a change in MLU for a student with very limited skills.

In most cases, few resources are devoted to measuring the effectiveness of training. When the effects of training are not determined empirically, ineffective training strategies may be employed at considerable expense for lengthy periods of time before the lack of desired impact on the student's communication is noticed. To ensure functional language training, an appropriate measurement strategy must be adopted to qualify and quantify changes in student behavior resulting from training. Measurement strategies and their implications are discussed by Warren in Chapter 7.

How Responsive and Supportive the Child's Environment Is to New Learning

One way to program for generalization is to introduce a new skill to its natural community of reinforcement (Stokes and Baer, 1977). The natural community is an environment where the newly learned response will be functionally reinforced when it occurs. Under these conditions, new responses are maintained. As a child acquires new skills and her behavior changes as a result of language training, the environment must respond in ways that support this change if it is to be maintained. During normal development, an adaptation naturally occurs in mother-child interaction. Mothers are aware of their children's improved skills because they are in close contact with the children and *expect* the children to change (Newport, 1976). With handicapped children, adults sometimes lose the expectation that the child will change and thus, fail to respond differentially when change and growth do occur.

Peers and teachers (as well as parents) can make the environment more responsive to the student's new language skills. Section IV of the book contains two chapters that address these issues. Paul (Chapter 10) discusses programming peer support for functional language and offers several suggestions based on experimental research. Campbell et al. (Chapter 11) offer suggestions for programming support by classroom teachers. Each of the nine issues discussed above are important in facilitating acquisition of new skills and generalization. The language trainer must consider them when designing an intervention program, and be aware that they play a role in the remediation process even if—or especially if—they are ignored.

THE SUPERSTRUCTURE OF LANGUAGE TRAINING

The suggestions made throughout this book for addressing these nine issues imply a major change in the superstructure of language training. New roles are suggested for parents, teachers, and speech therapists that may be difficult to execute in the traditional administrative structure of language remediation programs. If language training is to be effective, the superstructure must accommodate and support these new roles.

Before the passage of PL 94-142, most speech therapists working in the schools dealt primarily with specific speech disorders (e.g., stuttering) afflicting children who were otherwise normal or moderately language delayed. Children were referred to the therapist, who worked with them individually for a short period of time once or twice a week. Therapists often had caseloads of 40 to 60 such children, frequently located in several schools. This model of therapy was an accepted standard. Since PL 94-142 was passed, therapists have found themselves with a clientele that increasingly consists of mentally retarded children, some of whom do not have even a rudimentary communication system.

The change in clientele and concomitant shift from emphasizing speech therapy to language intervention has caused something of a crisis for speech clinicians. In recognition of the changing demands on professionals and the increasing emphasis on language intervention, the American Speech and Hearing Association changed its name to the American Speech-Language-Hearing Association a few years ago and has increasingly focused on issues related to language intervention. Clinician training programs are becoming more oriented to the problems of language remediation (Muma et al., 1983). As clinicians receive more training in language intervention, the emphasis in public school speech-language services will undoubtedly change. However, the service delivery systems must also change to incorporate a more broadly based model of intervention such as the one proposed here if the effectiveness of language training within the schools is to improve. Change at the systems delivery level would enhance further the development of more appropriate therapist training programs because the skills necessary to operate effectively in the new system will be somewhat different from those needed in the current one. The needed changes can be exemplified best by describing the roles and responsibilities of parents, teachers, therapists, and program administrators in the emerging language intervention model.

The Parent

Parents will play a major role in the remediation process. Parents are in a unique position to shape their child's language because of the nature of their relationship with the child, the amount of time they spend with the child in routine communication situations (i.e., eating, toileting, dressing) where functional language can be easily taught, and their intimate and up-to-date knowledge of the child's skills (Costello, 1983). An increasing role for parents in their child's language remediation program should not place unreasonable demands on parents (Wulz et al., 1983).

The parent should not be expected to sit down with the child and conduct training sessions, but, with training and support from professionals, parents can teach language in the context of conversational interactions by using relatively simple techniques such as those described by Hart, MacDonald, and Stremel-Campbell and Campbell in this volume. Parents may assist in tracking their children's generalization using simple techniques, such as those described by Warren. To assume this new role parents must receive a great deal of support and training from the speech therapist (ideally on a weekly basis). Parent training should be initiated as soon as a student's language deficiency is identified. It is hoped that early involvement of parents will allow them to begin training their children before the normally facilitative parent-child interaction patterns have been severely disrupted by a long period of little or no development.

This new role places greater responsibility on the parents in the short term, but, if it leads to much greater long-term gains for the child, both parents and child will ultimately benefit. It is important to assess the family situation, demands on the parents, and parent skills and interest before initiating a therapy program that depends on intense parent involvement. Although every parent may be involved in his or her child's language training, specific roles for parents should be tailored to individual families' needs and preferences.

The Teacher

The classroom teacher is the second primary source of training. Again, involvement of teachers is recommended because teachers spend large amounts of time with students in functional contexts for learning language. The techniques discussed here by Hart and by Stremel-Campbell and Campbell were developed for classroom teachers and are especially appropriate in this context. The teacher can also utilize peers to support child language, following the suggestions of Paul (Chapter 10).

The teacher will continue to conduct group language-oriented activities, as many currently do, but will also be involved in taking regular data on the child's acquisition and generalization in cooperation with the speech therapist. The classroom teacher should receive training in millieu techniques from the speech therapist. Generally, classroom teachers should work hand-in-hand with the therapist to address the communication needs of the child. In cases where a parent cannot play a major role in the remediation process, the teacher may be a primary source of training. This training will go on in the context of traditional classroom activities, especially during snacks, toileting, free play, and transitions in and out of the classroom.

Some of the same cautions regarding level of involvement that were mentioned in reference to parents should be considered when recommending teachers as primary interveners. Many teachers do not have a background in language and without specific training will not have the skills to initiate language training. Teachers may see language intervention as a topic outside the realm of their skills and responsibilities.

Also, special education teachers typically are responsible for a wide range of educational tasks in addition to direct teaching (for example, serving on screening and assessment teams, conducting parent groups, and consulting with regular education teachers who have handicapped children mainstreamed in their classrooms). Requiring these teachers to assume additional responsibilities related to language intervention further increases the demands on their time and skills. However, since language can be integrated into the classroom curriculum, these teachers are in an excellent position to teach new language. In any case, they should be provided with specific, intensive, and continuing support from the speech therapist. In-service programming, weekly conferences, and assistance with implementing and evaluating classroom-based interventions should be expected of the speech staff.

The Therapist

In many respects the largest change must occur in the role of speech-language therapists. To institute the model proposed here, the therapist must become primarily a parent and teacher trainer. She may still conduct one-to-one therapy as need arises. She will still do diagnostic assessments, be primarily responsible for tracking child progress, and determine the content of training, the procedures to be used in training, and the time to make changes in the training programs. She will do less direct training and invest more time in parent and teacher training. Her overall caseload may remain at a relatively high level, such as 20 to 30 children and their families (no therapist should have a caseload larger than that regardless of the system being used). In the proposed model, the speech therapist is cast in the role of expert, consultant, and case manager. These new responsibilities will require that she release some of her former role-based tasks and become fully integrated with the educational systems.[1]

The Program Administrator

If this system is to work it must have the support of the program administrators, including principals and directors of special services. These individuals must understand the utility of the consultant-therapist approach and facilitate the necessary administrative changes to accommodate it. Often, therapists and teachers have recognized alternative ways to deliver language remediation, but the needed changes were difficult to make in rigid administrative systems.

One way to initiate change in service delivery systems is through the Individual Education Programs (IEPs) that are required for all handicapped children. The means for achieving the educational goals specified as part of the IEP can be written to reflect the changes in service delivery suggested here. However, in the long run system-wide change will be necessary if this model is to be used efficiently. Changes may include specific training for therapists to assist them in developing their skills as consultants, use of computer-based data systems to facilitate processing of assessment and training data, functional recognition of parents as partners in the educational process, and the further incorporation of language use as a classroom curriculum domain in special education and resource classrooms.

The Training Programs

University training programs for speech-language therapists must continue to change in the direction of providing therapists with skills to work with

---

[1]A "consultation model" for speech and language intervention has been described in detail by Frassinelli et al. (1983).

severely language-delayed children and to train parents, teachers, and other adults. Either training programs can be reactive to changes in the education system or they can take the lead in promoting these changes by training a new style of therapist with these skills. In order to make these changes, therapist training programs must be open to input from researchers and practitioners in special education and psychology who have been working with developmentally delayed children in an experimental tradition that has emphasized treating the needs of the individual. Truly interdisciplinary training efforts are much needed for both speech therapists and special education teachers.

Can the System Respond?

Intervention systems must be functional for the individuals they serve (Schiefelbusch, 1983). Knowledge of how to teach functional language to handicapped children has increased significantly in recent years and will continue to expand. The design of intervention systems must change as treatment models improve. Even now professionals find themselves in the uncomfortable position of knowing how to teach a student, being mandated to intervene with that student, but being restricted from providing the best possible intervention by the limits of the service delivery system (i.e., not enough time to thoroughly train the student; insufficient access to classrooms where generalization might be facilitated; insufficient resources to collect generalization data). When this dilemma arises in the field of medicine, the system usually responds quickly because the issues can be literally matters of life or death. Efficient and effective language remediation is equally important in many respects. An inefficient language intervention program can mean the difference between an individual's attaining reasonable independence (i.e., being able to hold a job) and his remaining dependent because of gross communication deficits. Ultimately, the issue is not whether the service delivery system can change, but what must be done to facilitate this change.

PLAN FOR THE BOOK

In a field as rich and rapidly developing as language remediation, no single text is truly comprehensive on any issue, and so it is with teaching functional language. Researchers and practitioners in speech therapy, special education, and psychology are currently working on ways to teach functional language. Much of their work is represented here. We have attempted to present the most recent procedures and ideas from applied and basic research to address the nine issues concerning language remediation raised in this introduction. The reader must integrate this information with presentations by others in the field that also may be useful in maximizing generalization and acquisition effects (see other books in R. L. Schiefelbusch's *Language Intervention Series*).

Each chapter in this book was solicited to fulfill a specific function in relation to the overall goal of the volume. Chapter 2, by Reichle and Keogh, provides a selective review of research on what, when, and how to teach language. In some respects this chapter provides a baseline against which it is possible to evaluate the procedures and ideas offered in other chapters throughout the book. Together with the present chapter, Chapter 2 forms a general introduction to the issues involved in developing an empirically tested technology of language remediation.

Section II consists of four chapters, each of which proposes a form of functional language training. These chapters cover techniques appropriate for children ranging from mildly and moderately retarded (chapters by Hart and by MacDonald) to severely autistic (Alpert and Rogers-Warren) and severely retarded (Keogh and Reichle). Hart presents several naturalistic language training techniques that mimic normal mother-child interaction at various stages. These techniques have been subjected to many experimental analyses in recent years. As a group, the proposed techniques have been referred to by various authors as "milieu teaching" strategies (meaning environment based) and as "incidental teaching" strategies. MacDonald presents a comprehensive model of intervention based on training parents to teach language through conversational interactions. His model reflects recent research on mother-child interaction and owes much to the influence of Jerome Bruner and others. MacDonald's approach shares many tenets with the techniques described by Hart.

In Chapter 5, Alpert and Rogers-Warren address the problems of one of the most difficult language-delayed populations, autistic children. The characteristics associated with autism are so disruptive to learning and to effective communication that a range of behavioral techniques must be applied in language intervention with autistic persons. Alpert and Rogers-Warren provide a detailed review of what is known about the communication deficits of autistic children and a comprehensive set of suggestions for designing effective interventions.

Finally, Keogh and Reichle take up the issue of the "difficult-to-teach" severely handicapped child. These are children who are so severely retarded that most remedial approaches do not succeed in teaching them new language or communication skills. Keogh and Reichle outline a prelinguistic curriculum designed to teach these children the prerequisites necessary to learn at least a rudimentary communication system.

Section III consists of three chapters that address issues of measuring and facilitating generalization from training. The techniques and suggestions presented here can be used in the context of traditional language training or in combination with the techniques suggested by Hart and by MacDonald. In Chapter 7, Warren proposes clinical strategies for measuring language generalization resulting from training. The techniques he suggests are specifically applicable to the needs and concerns of special educators and speech therapists working in schools without significant external resources or uncommitted time.

Goldstein (Chapter 8) presents two well-researched approaches for facilitating generalization using matrix and stimulus equivalence training procedures. These procedures are particularly applicable for training two- and three-term structures and have been designed to ensure economy in training.

In Chapter 9, Stremel-Campbell and Campbell present several techniques that can be incorporated into training to increase the likelihood of generalization. The effects of each technique have been experimentally demonstrated, at least under some conditions. Like the techniques proposed by Goldstein, the techniques presented by Stremel-Campbell and Campbell can be applied with children ranging from mildly to severely delayed in language development.

Section IV of the book was designed to assist the reader in implementing the strategies suggested in earlier chapters and to ensure that the environment in which training will occur or in which generalization is expected will be responsive to and supportive of emerging language. The chapter by Paul (Chapter 10) reviews research on utilizing peers to facilitate language use. The chapter by Campbell et al. (Chapter 11) addresses issues related to training teachers and involving them in the language remediation process. Campbell and colleagues present three different models of teacher involvement, discuss the pros and cons of each, and then propose various ways to ensure that teachers acquire the skills necessary to be effective language and communication facilitators.

OVERVIEW

Language remediation represents a complex and challenging enterprise that must be individualized for each child to be successful. No single curriculum can cover the needs of all children. For this reason, therapist, teacher, and parent must learn principles and procedures that can be used to teach a range of content and skills. Persons who attempt to teach language must understand the process by which language is taught and its generalization facilitated. They must also be able to apply the principles derived from this process to enhance the child's language development.

We are at the point in the development of technology of language remediation where a general clinical approach is emerging from the diversity of theoretical views. The techniques described by Betty Hart are an excellent example of this. These techniques mimic interaction processes identified by cognitive psychologists working from a starting point in the Piagetian tradition, yet they were developed by applied behavior analysts working from the Skinnerian tradition. The theorists and researchers who influenced this book include Skinner, Piaget, Bruner, Moerk, Nelson, Baer, and Bijou. Aspects of these diverse views become palatable when one asks the question, "How can I teach functional language?" Theoretical purity becomes less important in this context than does the answer to the question.

It has been said that the ultimate test of any theory of human development is its ability to explain language acquisition (Dale, 1976). If this is so, then for our purposes the empirical proving ground of such a theory will be its ability to "predict" procedures that will promote language acquisition and generalization by language-deficient persons. To date, useful procedures have been derived from several theoretical approaches. This suggests two things. First, theorists must continue to integrate their works until a more unitary description is empirically verified. Second, those of us concerned with remediation should continue to develop techniques that teach functional language, regardless of their theoretical origin.

REFERENCES

Anglin, J. M. 1977. Word, Object, and Conceptual Development. Norton, New York.

Bloom, L., and Lahey, M. 1978. Language Development and Language Disorders. Wiley, New York.

Bruner, J. 1978. Learning the mother tongue. Hum. Nature 1:42–48.

Bruner, J., Roy, C., and Ratner, N. 1980. The beginnings of requests. In K. E. Nelson (ed.), Children's Language, Vol. 3. Gardner Press, New York.

Costello, J. M. 1983. Generalization across settings: Language intervention with children. In J. Miller, D. E. Yoder, and R. L. Schiefelbusch (eds.), Language Intervention. American Speech-Language-Hearing Association, Rockville, MD.

Dale, P. S. 1976. Language Development. Holt, Rinehart, and Winston, New York.

Frassinelli, L., Superior, K., and Meyers, J. 1983. A consultation model for speech and language intervention. ASHA 25:25–30.

Gallagher, J. J., Beckman, P., & Cross, A. H. 1983. Families of handicapped children: Sources of stress and its amelioration. Except. Child. 50:1–19.

Hart, B. M., and Rogers-Warren, A. 1978. Milieu teaching approaches. In R. L. Schiefelbusch (ed.), Language Intervention Strategies. University Park Press, Baltimore.

McLean, J. E., and Snyder-McLean, L. K. 1978. A Transactional Approach to Early Language Training. Charles Merrill, Columbus, OH.

Moerk, E. L. 1977. Pragmatic and Semantic Aspects of Early Language Development. University Park Press, Baltimore.

Muma, J. R., Pierce, S., and Muma, D. L. 1983. Language training in speech-language pathology: Substantive intervention. ASHA 25:35–40.

Newport, E. 1976. The speech of mothers to young children. *In* N. J. Castellan, D. B. Pifoni, and G. R. Potts (eds.), Cognitive Theory: Vol. II. Earlbaum, Hillsdale, NJ.

Schachter, F. F. 1979. Everyday Mother Talk to Toddlers: Early Intervention. Academic, New York.

Schiefelbusch, R. L. 1983. Language Intervention: What is it? *In* J. Miller, D. E. Yoder, and R. L. Schiefelbusch (eds.), Language Intervention. American Speech-Language-Hearing Association, Rockville, MD.

Skinner, B. F. 1957. Verbal Behavior. Appleton-Century-Crofts, New York.

Snow, C. 1977. The development of conversation between mothers and babies. J. Child Lang. 4:1–22.

Spradlin, J. E., and Siegal, G. M. 1982. Language training in natural and clinical environments. J. Speech Hear. Disord. 47:2–6.

Stokes, T. F., and Baer, D. M. 1977. An implicit technology of generalization. J. Appl. Behav. Anal. 10:349–367.

Warren, S. F., and Rogers-Warren, A. K. 1983. A longitudinal analysis of language generalization among adolescents with severely handicapping conditions. J. Assoc. Persons Severe Handicaps 8(4):18–31.

Wulz, S. V., Hall, M. N., and Klein, M. D. 1983. A home-centered instructional communication strategy for severely handicapped children. J. Speech Hear. Disord. 48:2–10.

2

Communication Intervention
A Selective Review of What, When, and How To Teach

Joe Reichle

Department of Communication Disorders
University of Minnesota
Minneapolis

and

William J. Keogh

Center for Developmental Disabilities
Department of Special Education
University of Vermont
Burlington

contents

WHAT TO TEACH   28
    Communication Prerequisites   28
    Establishing Word Use   31
    Establishing Multiword Utterances   36

SEQUENCING COMMUNICATION OBJECTIVES
  (WHEN TO TEACH)   39

HOW TO TEACH   43
    Less Intrusive Strategies   44
    More Intrusive Strategies   47
    Integration of Incidental and More Intrusive Formats   49
    Other Issues in Program Implementation   50

SUMMARY   52

REFERENCES   54

Most children acquire sophisticated communicative behavior without any special assistance. However, some children require some level of organized instruction before they are able to utilize a functional repertoire of communicative behavior. Fortunately for teachers and therapists working with communicatively handicapped individuals, there are many intervention programs available. This chapter discusses the strengths and weaknesses of a representative sample of these programs relative to what is currently known about acquisition and intervention.[1] The purpose of this critique is to provide a baseline analysis that can be used to guide us in both current and future program development and application efforts.

In our attempt to examine programs designed to teach a basic communicative repertoire to severely handicapped children, we were challenged to select an organizational framework for these programs. Historically, the distinction between remedial and developmental approaches has been used for categorizing communication intervention strategies (Guess et al., 1978; Siegel and Spradlin, 1978; Williams and York, 1977). Although this may be a convenient way to identify the *prevailing* character of a particular program, it implies that a program must be one type and not the other. To the contrary, most programs represent a "blending" of approaches. Some of the most widely used "developmentally based" curricula (Bricker et al., 1977; MacDonald and Horstmeier, 1978; Miller and Yoder, 1973) rely heavily upon contributions from the remedial literature, just as interventions characterized as "behavioral" have embraced contributions from the developmental literature.

Hart (1980) suggested that the shrinking gap between developmentalists and behaviorists in part may be due to the recent emphasis upon pragmatics as a basis for early communication intervention. Ervin-Tripp (1971, p. 37) defined pragmatics as "saying the right thing the right way at the right time . . ." Hart (1980) pointed out that both behaviorists and developmentalists view pragmatics as "observable behavior performance in relation to context . . ." A closer scrutiny of the area of pragmatics suggests that one cannot adhere to Ervin-Tripp's definition without discussing three topics: 1) the behavior's topography (i.e., what to teach); 2) when to teach it (i.e., the sequence to follow); and 3) how to teach it. Similarly, by definition, pragmatics encompasses aspects of stimulus and response generalization (Rogers-

Preparation of portions of this article was supported in part by contract No. 300-82-0363 awarded to the University of Minnesota from the Division of Innovation & Development, Special Education Programs, U.S. Department of Education. The opinions expressed herein do not necessarily reflect the position or policy of the U.S. Department of Education and no official endorsement should be inferred.

[1]We have reviewed and critiqued aspects of 10 organized curriculum or treatment programs for the severely handicapped child. In addition we have reviewed a wide range of relevant research with both normal and handicapped children.

Warren and Warren, in preparation). Clearly, pragmatics is a thread that runs through the entire cloth of a communication program. Because of the importance of pragmatics to functional communication skills, we will use it as the topic that binds the package of what to teach, when to teach, and how to teach.

At the outset of this chapter, we suggest that several critical points of inquiry are required of any author of a language intervention curriculum. First, if the author has chosen to teach behaviors because normal children acquire the behaviors we ask: Is there any empirical evidence to suggest that 1) the skills being taught have redeeming qualities of their own or 2) the skills are prerequisite to later acquired skills? Second, if the author presents a hierarchical skill sequence to be acquired we ask: Is there any evidence to support other methods of sequencing, and if so, why did the author select a particular one over another? Finally, we must turn to specific instructional procedures suggested and ask: 1) Is there any empirical evidence to support the procedure chosen; 2) Can the procedure be practically used given a variety of service delivery models in operation; and 3) Are there logical procedural alternatives that may provide the same result? We suspect that most of these questions cannot be clearly answered, but instead will serve to focus our discussion.

WHAT TO TEACH

Communication Prerequisites

Most communication intervention programs attempt to answer the question of what to teach without fully coming to grips with the need to teach the child why he should learn to communicate. Keogh and Reichle (1982) have suggested the importance of initially teaching the child that symbols can mediate access to desirable objects and events. We have described procedures that teach children to use a simple "want" symbol as a tool to request goods and services. Consequently, the earliest phase of intervention does not require a discrimination among objects' names. Instead, the child learns that the only method of obtaining desired objects and events out of his grasp is to use the symbol "want." Once he can use a symbol to request, he must secure the attention of an adult if his utterance is to impact his listener.

Obtaining another's attention prior to making a request is one example of communicative referencing. Communicative referencing requires that the child first obtain the listener's attention before conversation proceeds. This skill is particularly important for communication board and sign users. These two modalities, because of their "silent" aspects, require an overt attention-getting response as part of a communicative initiation. Unfortunately, most intervention programs place the child in the role of a responder throughout training. This intervention strategy places the child at a distinct disadvantage when he needs to engage a nonattending communicative partner.

McLean and Snyder-McLean (1978) suggested that there are several social prerequisites to early pragmatic skills such as referencing. Although these bases have not been delineated fully, they probably include being reinforced by social attention, enjoying the presence of others, relying on others for assistance, showing objects to others, offering objects to others, and participating in reciprocal exchanges.

Cromer (1976) suggested that cognitive landmarks such as means-end, causality, object permanence, and symbolic play *may be* necessary (but not sufficient) to account for language acquisition. Several investigators have examined Cromer's hypothesis. Chapman (1980) found that these cognitive skills did not correlate with language comprehension after age was partialed out of the analysis. In terms of communicative production, however, Bates et al. (1979) reported a close relationship between early vocal/gestural production and means-end skills. Additionally, they reported that imitation and symbolic play skills were also good predictors of productive language acquisition. Earlier, Harding and Golinkoff (1979) found a correlation between causality and the onset of intentional vocal behavior for a group of 36 normal children. Finally, Nicholich (1977) reported a correlation between symbolic play, vocal imitation, and language production in normally developing children. Generally, a number of investigators have reported the emergence of word production during sensorimotor Stage 5 (Bates et al., 1979; Ingram, 1977; Moerk, 1975). It should be noted that these findings are only correlative and do not demonstrate any causal relationship between cognition and communication.

Empirical evidence suggests that mentally retarded children often follow the same general sequence in cognitive acquisition as their normal counterparts (Rogers, 1977; Woodward, 1959). A few investigators have examined the relationship between cognitive and communicative skills among handicapped populations, particularly Down's syndrome children. Results of some of these studies suggest that correlative relationships exist between the exhibition of behaviors reflective of means-end and communicative production (Reichle and Yoder, 1979). Moore and Meltzoff (1977) found a correlation between object permanency and mean length of utterance (MLU) in Down's syndrome children to be significant. More generally, Kahn (1975) studied 16 severely retarded individuals and reported a significant correlative relationship between expressive language and sensorimotor Stage 6 across the cognitive domains of means-end, causality, imitation, object permanency, and space.

The literature cited above suggests some possible relationships between cognitive and communicative development, but these relationships are far from being fully delineated. The correlative data suggest that certain cognitive skills may *facilitate* communication acquisition.

Cognitive prerequisites are directly, or implicitly, addressed in a number of communication curricula. For example, in teaching motor imitation, Kent's (1974) strategy and content deviate somewhat from a normal developmental model. In her curriculum, new motor behaviors not necessarily in the child's repertoire are recommended as initial actions to be taught. In contrast, a developmental perspective suggests selecting behaviors that are in the child's repertoire but not yet under imitative control.

In some instances, Kent's curriculum is inconsistent with both remedial and developmental perspectives. For example, the value of examining a child's vocal frequency is not stressed even though both developmental and remedial perspectives suggest initially increasing vocal frequency prior to the initiation of a vocal imitation program. Once a child's rate and diversity of spontaneous vocalizations approximates what could be called "elicited babbling," a developmental perspective suggests training the child to engage in vocal turn-taking sequences. During these sequences, the child vocalizes and the adult imitates the child; then the child reproduces his or her original sound. These turn-taking sequences may function to get the temporal aspects of sound imitation under instructional control. Bricker et al. (1976) specifically addressed the need to strengthen a child's spontaneous vocal output and vocal turn-taking as part of the intervention process. MacDonald and Horstmeier (1978) suggested a vocal training strategy similar to that proposed by Bricker et al. (1976). They noted that actions that are visible to the child may be slightly easier to imitate than those that are not. As part of this assessment process, the child is tested to determine his or her ability to imitate behaviors that are visible as well as those that cannot be seen when imitated correctly. MacDonald and Horstmeier (1978) attempted to bridge the gap between motor and vocal imitation by suggesting that action-sound combinations (e.g., making an Indian call by yelling while hitting one's hand on one's mouth), often used by children while playing, be trained as well.

The likely importance of object permanence in the acquisition of communicative behavior is reflected in many intervention programs. For example, Kent (1974) offered an object permanence training sequence where objects were placed under a covering and the child was asked to find one or more of them. In a subsequent task, two boxes were placed in front of the child, then an object was placed in one of the boxes and the child was required to find the hidden object. Bricker et al.'s (1976) program was accompanied initially by a sensorimotor curriculum that used a variety of stimulation techniques to encourage improved cognitive performance across object permanency as well as other cognitive domains.

Causal relationships are taught in the section of the Bricker et al. (1976) curriculum intended to teach functional object use (how socially to make an object work). MacDonald and Horstmeier (1979) trained causal relationships at a more representational level by requiring the child to chain several actions together to represent a short theme (e.g., pouring imaginary tea into a glass and offering the glass to another).

There is some modest evidence correlatively linking cognitive development and communicative acquisitions in both normal and handicapped populations. Consequently, we support the view that intervention efforts must consider cognitive attainments—a view consistent with many widely used intervention programs. However, the interventionist has a responsibility to offer a logical basis for including cognitive tasks in his respective program. If it can be shown that teaching and including a particular set of tasks results in greater teaching efficiency, the relationship of this task to the normal developmental process is moot. Unfortunately, many interventionists leave it up to the teacher and/or clinician to formulate a program logic that relates any given cognitive task to its communicative counterpart. Teaching the child to rake objects toward himself using a tool, or to pull objects out from underneath coverings, may be inappropriate unless these skills can be tied logically to functional daily events. For example, using a "want" symbol involves a task that requires the use of a tool (the symbol) that satisfies teaching the use of an object and at the same time fulfills a functional communication objective. Current data do not support teaching cognitive skills just for the sake of cognitive advancement.

Establishing Word Use

Most communication curricula that we have thus far referenced provide the user with examples of vocabulary for use in program implementation. Unfortunately, these examples are often used without consideration of the individual child's needs. Several general suggestions for an initial vocabulary to teach have been offered (Bloom and Lahey, 1978; Bowerman, 1978; Keogh and Reichle, 1980). Bowerman (1978) and Keogh and Reichle (this volume) have suggested that object names that are taught should correspond directly to the objects that they represent (e.g., "cookie" is a better word to use to represent a cookie than a more generic word like "food"). Keogh and Reichle (this volume) reason that if the child initially calls a cookie by the name "food," he may be confused subsequently when he is taught to refer to hamburger with the word "food." An even greater confusion could result when the child is taught the words "cookie" and "hamburger." Keogh and Reichle (this volume) further suggested that double-function words like "drink," which can be used as either an object or an action, can be more specifically represented by "milk," "orange juice," and so forth.

Frequently, intervention programs are criticized for their failure to emphasize the relational semantic functions such as rejection and recurrence.

A relational term is one that can be used across a variety of persons, objects, or actions (for example, a child can reject almost any object). Rejection is one of the earliest functions expressed, yet is rarely found in the early phases of an intervention program. One reason for this omission may be that the initial meaning applied to "no" is rejection. The most pragmatically appropriate method to teach "no" involves the use of an avoidance paradigm (negative reinforcement). For example, if some undesired substance is offered and the child says "No," he avoids it. However, if he fails to reject the substance, it is forced upon him. Many interventionists are reluctant to use an avoidance procedure because of the inherent disadvantages of negative reinforcement and punishment paradigms.

A second basis for the limited treatment of relational semantic functions involves generalization. By definition, the use of a relational semantic function necessitates stimulus generalization. Often interventionists assume that these generalization demands may preclude extensive use in the early phases of a communication program. However, this view is inconsistent with the early developmental data reporting extensive use of functions such as recurrence.

Sometimes teachers and therapists force unnecessary discriminations among relational vocabulary words when there is no need. For example, the opportunity to observe or elicit recurrence is totally dependent upon the saliency of the object or event that was originally requested. Consequently, it is redundant to teach the child additional vocabulary (e.g., "more") to serve the special function of recurrence when the word "want" can serve both the initial request and the recurrence function. Whenever possible, redundant vocabulary should be avoided and words in the child's repertoire should be matched with as many different semantic functions as possible.

The selection of vocabulary for augmentative systems necessitates some additional criteria. Most interventionists agree that the initial trained vocabulary should consist of words that sound dissimilar. This rule is applied easily to both signs and the graphic stimuli used on a communication board. Assuming that the child can imitate motorically (for signing) and graphically match to sample (for communication board use), it is possible to verify whether the child can discriminate perceptually different symbols prior to training. Unfortunately, matching-to-sample procedures rarely are implemented in intervention programs.

Motor imitation programming is addressed frequently in signing programs. There is a need to extend the use of a motor imitation paradigm to assess the child's ability to produce a variety of prehension patterns (e.g., squeeze, palmar, pincer) and unilateral/bilateral hand use positions (e.g., bilateral symmetrical to midline). Determining whether the learner produces these patterns (in the context of sign production) can assist the teacher in defining a response criterion. Dennis et al. (1982) have suggested sampling the child's daily activities to determine whether prehension patterns required in signs already exist as part of the child's repertoire of motor skills used to interact with objects.

One additional consideration in the selection of communication board or signing vocabulary involves iconicity. Siple (1978) described the iconic aspect of sign as a "picture-like quality." Iconic signs may be easier for intellectually delayed, autistic, and normal children to learn (Brown, 1977; Griffith and Robinson, 1980; Konstantareas et al., 1978). This may be because iconic signs place less of a demand on representational skills (Skelly et al., 1974). Unfortunately, many commonly used signs are not iconic.

The majority of intervention programs aimed at establishing an initial repertoire of semantic relations have several weaknesses. No single program addresses the breadth of decision rules that should be considered in selecting vocabulary to teach. Even curricula that do not explicitly dictate individual vocabulary words can be misleading. For example, MacDonald and Horstmeier (1978) suggested "drink," "orange juice," and "milk" as an early vocabulary. In order to acquire the meaning of these words, the child must be able to classify both orange juice and milk as subclasses of drink (Bowerman, 1978). This discrimination may be too subtle for some children to make (at least during the early phases of intervention). Even after word meanings have been taught, most language intervention programs do not address efficiently the use of those meanings to express a variety of communicative intents (e.g., requesting and commenting).

The acquisition of early production of discriminative demanding and commenting, in many instances, may be thwarted by existing language intervention programs. McLean and Snyder-McLean (1978) have made this point through the use of an elegant example. The teacher holds up a comb and says "What do you want?" The child (who does not really want the comb) says "Comb." If the teacher then hands the learner the comb, there is a pragmatic mismatch because he did not want the comb. If, on the other hand, the teacher simply gives praise (but not the comb) there is also a pragmatic mismatch because the question form assumed that the child's response was a request.

Keogh and Reichle (1982) suggested initially teaching the use of a "want" symbol each time that a request is made. Conversely, object names would only be used to comment. For example, if a child wanted juice he would either encode "want" or "want juice" (depending upon his word combining skills). If he produced "Juice," the utterance would be treated as a comment (i.e., it should not be reinforced by giving the child juice).

Attention to early pragmatics has focused primarily upon the intent of isolated utterances. Much less attention has been given to the maintenance and extension of a conversational topic across speaking turns. Once children are participating in communicative exchanges, they are faced with the responsibility that Rees (1980) referred to as "keeping the meaning going." This requires the initiation and maintenance of topics. Keenan and Schieffelin (1976) suggested that to establish a discourse topic the speaker must do several things: 1) obtain the listener's attention; 2) provide enough information to enable the listener to identify critical objects, individuals, or ideas; and 3) provide sufficient semantic and contextual information for the listener to determine the relationship between the referents used. The listener, on the other hand, must attend, identify referents and relations among the referants, and request clarification. Our current knowledge regarding intervention techniques in this area is limited. However, MacDonald (this volume) discusses several intervention techniques that have great potential for stimulating conversational exchanges.

When a communication failure occurs, total responsibility cannot rest with the speaker. If the listener has not received sufficient information to allow a continuation of the interaction, he must be able to request additional information. Guess et al. (1978) described a task to stimulate the child to first ask for information and then subsequently use the information that had been retrieved. The teacher selected a vocabulary that contained some objects that the child could label and other objects that the child could not label. When a known object was presented, the child was reinforced for the correct production of a label corresponding to the object. When an unknown object was presented, the child was reinforced for asking "What's that?" After the unknown objects had been labeled for the child, he was reinforced only for a correct label of the object during subsequent trials. Unfortunately, few intervention programs attempt to teach information recruiting behavior in a functional context.

From the standpoint of language comprehension, most curricula rely heavily upon a traditional two-choice discrimination task to teach word meanings. However, the intervention literature provides well-documented alternatives. For example, Striefel and Wetherby (1973) demonstrated the feasibility of initially accompanying a verbal instruction with a controlling prompt (physical guidance). During successive training opportunities, the controlling prompt was systematically eliminated, resulting in the eventual transfer of instructional control to a verbal instruction. Although this procedure was implemented with adolescents, it has great applicability to younger handicapped individuals. Ratner and Bruner (1978) have described redundantly cued games played between adults and their children. After repeated participation, children were reported to begin anticipating portions of the game.

Once such participation is established in handicapped populations, the interventionist can focus on whether the child's anticipations were under the instructional control of gestures and/or verbal utterances associated with the game. If the learner is not under verbal control but consistently relies on the teacher's gestural cue to perform, the controlling cue (gestural) can be paired with the noncontrolling cue (verbal). Gradually, the gestural cue can be faded so that, eventually, the learner responds to the presentation of the verbal cue. For example, suppose that a preschooler participates in the hand-clapping portion of Patticake only when his hands are pushed together in a clapping motion. Over several Patticake opportunities the teacher systematically pairs the verbal instruction "patticake" with the physical prompt. Next the teacher begins to gradually eliminate her physical assistance while continuing to offer the verbal instruction "patticake" at each game opportunity. Eventually, the learner will clap his hands together in response to the word "patticake."

Of course in our example, the spoken word "patticake" is usually offered in a characteristic singsong fashion. It is possible that the intonation of the phrase results in the learner's correct performance. This can be tested if on some opportunities to play Patticake no singsong information is used, and the teacher very matter of factly says "patticake." Once several different game performances are under the instructional control of a spoken word or words (e.g., "get you" = chase game; "peek-a-boo" = hands over eyes), the interventionist can rightly claim the establishment of simple language comprehension.

When children participate in a vocabulary comprehension task they must utilize two different but highly interrelated skills. After hearing the spoken vocabulary, the child must comprehend the words and then subsequently he must search for the requested objects. For many children, the searching function is particularly difficult when children initially begin to acquire vocabulary comprehension skills. Consequently, the early corpus of the vocabulary should include items that are located in a highly predictable place (e.g., hand, glasses) in the natural environment.

Observations presented thus far suggest that early comprehension training should not necessarily require the child to travel to locate the object requested. Keogh and Reichle (1982) suggested that the aspects of searching can be delineated further. It is possible to determine whether the child may have difficulty remembering the object name on his way to retrieve it by implementing a variation of a matching task. The interventionist first gives the instruction (e.g., "Find milk"), pauses for several seconds, and then presents the choices.

An additional criterion in the selection of comprehension training vocabulary focuses upon whether to select actions that the child can perform on himself or actions that can be applied to an object. Choosing actions that can be done by oneself (e.g., singing, dancing, jumping) may seem easier because they require a minimal search for a stimulus object. However, performing an action on an object may allow the object to be used as a mediator during the early phases of training. MacDonald and Horstmeier (1978) and Keogh and Reichle (1982) chose labels that corresponded to actions previously taught in functional object use programs as the content for action comprehension training. Their rationale was based on the logic that these objects may serve as an initial controlling stimulus during teaching. For example, the child sees the object and hears the action name almost simultaneously. At first, the sight of the object may control his response. Over successive trials, however, the object presentation can be delayed so that the action label is provided and the learner must select an object from an array to use in performing the action.

In summary, more attention should be placed on specifying criteria for the selection of vocabulary for initial comprehension and production intervention. These criteria must promote a clear match between word (symbol) and referent. We are only beginning to address the area of pragmatic skills used with initially acquired vocabulary. Production programs must more precisely overlay the discriminative use of demands and comments with the new word meanings taught to learners. In the domain of language comprehension, more attention must be devoted to alternative strategies for the establishment of early comprehension skills. Additionally, more attention must be given to the environmental context in which initial instruction-following skills are taught. This attention must include a careful consideration of the searching and memory skills involved.

Establishing Multiword Utterances

Bloom's (1979) premise that, during the early portion of the child's language development, cognitive, semantic, and syntactic constraints coact to limit the child's language is now widely accepted by language interventionists. This discussion focuses on extended word meaning within multiple-word utterances in terms of production and then comprehension.

Miller and Yoder (1973) proposed one of the initial semantically based syntax training programs. They operated on the premise that a language intervention program could modify behavior through the manipulation of the child's environment (by emphasizing the use of the techniques of expansion and semantic modeling). Their program had three principles: 1) reduce syntax to telegraphic speech when talking to the child; 2) expand and model utterances produced by the child; and 3) talk as much as possible about things happening at the moment.

Stremel and Waryas (1974) described a language intervention program that was very similar to Miller and and Yoder's program in its theoretical basis but covered a greater range of syntactic skills with greater specificity. Their program is best described as a series of sequential language-training procedures for children who display delayed or deficient language structures. The Stremel and Waryas program is administered in a more rigid instructional format than Miller and Yoder's (1973). It utilizes an innovative cluster approach that readily allows the teacher to simultaneously program semantic as well as related syntactic skills.

A second innovative feature of the Stremel and Waryas program involves the training of forms such as pronouns on the basis of their semantic content. Discrimination of semantic features of pronouns, including human/nonhuman and male/female, are established in the early phases of training. Additionally, the same stimuli are used in the training of question comprehension (i.e., the child is taught to discriminate between "who" and "what" by pairing "who" with humans and "what" with nonhumans).

A third innovative feature of this program is its reliance on the natural environment to complete training. For example, after comprehension training, pronouns are taught productively in isolation unless the child demonstrates production at 50% criterion level on the first two sets of items in comprehension training. In this case the natural environment is relied upon to complete teaching.

Most intervention programs address the production of multiple-word utterances through three-term semantic functions. Guidelines for selecting two- and three-word constructions have been offered by several interventionists. McLean and Snyder-McLean (1978) suggested initially targeting two-word utterances that mark action sequences (e.g., *boy hit, hit ball*). MacDonald and Horstmeier (1978) suggested a similar strategy. They recommended early two-word combinations that consist of agent + action and action + object. These were the two most frequently occurring combinations in the speech of 40 normal preschoolers examined by MacDonald and Horstmeier (1978). McLean and Snyder-McLean also suggested targeting two separate but successive two-word utterances that, when taken together, more completely describe a referant situation (e.g., *boy hit–hit ball*).

Keogh and Reichle (1982) suggested that initial two-word strings used to demand should consist of "want + object." If the child is demanding an object, he must communicate "want + object." If, on the other hand, he is commenting on an object, he may communicate "object." This contrast may provide an easier introduction to the basis for lengthening one's utterance in order to be better understood (e.g., if the child was demanding and simply uttered "want," the interventionist would give him a puzzled look and prompt "want + object"). Keogh and Reichle (1982) also suggested that the severely handicapped child stands to benefit more from spending a greater proportion of his time learning new vocabulary to pair with "want" than from learning to chain action and object utterances together. For example, if the child wants a cookie, one can assume that he plans on eating it. Consequently, "eat cookie" provides more redundant information and is somewhat less informative given that the listener has the advantage of context to decode the speaker's message.

At about the same time that two-word utterances are introduced, many curricula begin to teach the names of locations and attributes (Guess et al., 1978; Kent, 1974; MacDonald and Horstmeier, 1978). This general sequencing phenomenon is supported by Bloom and Lahey's (1978) observation that the use of attributes at the single-word utterance level is rare. MacDonald and

Horstmeier (1978) suggested that, at the two-word stage of production, the child can be taught to pair attributes that include *big*, *my*, *more*, *nice*, *gone*, *hot*, *wet*, and *dirty* with object names. Kent (1974) focuses on attributes that include *big*, *little*, color, and numeration (1–5) in both comprehension and production tasks. However, most programs minimally address cognitive facilitators for these vocabulary classes. In this respect, Kent's (1974) program is one of the more comprehensive because she first teaches children to sort based on the attribute feature that subsequently will be taught in comprehension and production training. These efforts ensure that the child is at least capable of visually discriminating the attribute that is about to be named.

Just as utterance length represents a critical production variable, it can also have a significant effect upon comprehension. For example, comprehending the utterance "get milk" does not ensure that the child will comprehend lengthier versions (e.g., "get the milk right now"). Keogh and Reichle (1980) suggested specific intervention programs for teaching children to abstract critical bits of meaning from lengthier sentences.

Instruction-following skills that require the child to retrieve two unrelated objects (e.g., "Find cup and ball") are often taught prior to sentence comprehension training. Keogh and Reichle (1980) suggested that the child be provided with an initial opportunity to discriminate between verbal instructions that randomly request a single object and on other trials request two *related* objects (e.g., Trial 1: "Find towel"; Trial 2: "Find toothbrush and soap"). This strategy ensures that the child will discriminate between an instruction that contains one critical bit of information and an instruction that contains two such bits of information. This strategy also avoids teaching the child to follow instructions that he is unlikely to ever need to perform (e.g., "Get toothbrush and ashtray").

Once the content of the syntax training program has been determined the teacher must make sure that the construction being taught is functional in normal conversation as well as in the training context. If the teacher is attempting to stimulate the child to produce the subject + verb + object construction, it is important that none of the information contained in the message is already known to the listener. The following examples demonstrate a situation in which subject + verb + object is obligatory and one in which the subject construction is not obligatory.

Example 1: Teacher looking		*Example 2: Teacher blindfolded*	
Teacher shows child a picture of a dog and says, "What's the dog doing?"	Child says, "Biting man."	Teacher shows child a picture of a dog biting a man and says, "What's happening?"	Child says, "Dog biting man."

In the first example, the topic "dog" could be presupposed because both speaking partners know that the dog was the topical focus. In the second example, the presupposition is not as clear-cut. Because it is not, the subject marker becomes more necessary. Unless context is considered when teaching syntactic constructions, the child runs the risk of learning how to use a construction without knowing exactly when or even why to use it.

Teaching children to comprehend and produce syntactic constructions requires the delineation of skills that serve as a bridge from the pragmatic and semantic domains. Syntactic intervention programs must not only strive to teach syntactic construction but must also attend to the contexts in which their production is required.

SEQUENCING COMMUNICATION OBJECTIVES (WHEN TO TEACH)

Given that many language-delayed children follow an acquisition pattern similar to that in normal children (Miller and Yoder, 1974) and that there is an increasing understanding of normal acquisition processes, normal children's behavior may provide functional treatment guideposts. However, as we have learned more about normal development, it has become apparent that pinpointing precise language landmarks is not as straightforward a task as once believed. Furthermore, circumstances do exist that bring into question the appropriateness of using developmental data for guiding *all* intervention decisions—particularly when the following factors are considered:

1. Significant individual differences occur in language acquisition among normal children.
2. Normal children appear to acquire different classes of communicative behavior simultaneously.
3. When an augmentative system for communication is used much of what we know about normal language may not apply.
4. Empirical evidence has demonstrated that some intervention sequences are successful even though they contradict normal developmental sequences.
5. Many children show such deviant behavior patterns that normal developmental guideposts may be entirely inappropriate.

Each of these issues is addressed briefly below.

Chapman (1980) observed that there are individual acquisition differences in a significant proportion of communicative behaviors acquired by normal children. These differences are seen in the rate of overall acquisition across all parameters of language comprehension and production. Table 1 provides some examples of these differences. Unfortunately, most communication curricula follow a strict vertical hierarchy and do not allow for individual acquisition patterns.

Table 1.   Examples of variability in the age at which normal children acquire communicative skills

Age Range (months)	Skill	Source
8–12	Repeats vocalization upon being imitated	Uzgiris and Hunt (1975)
10–18	Requests for object or attention	J. Miller (1980)
16–31	Production of modifier + noun (±1 standard deviation)	J. Miller (1980)
16–34	Production of "What's this?", "What's that?" (±1 standard deviation)	J. Miller (1980)
16–41	Marking of yes/no questions only by rising intonation (±1 standard deviation)	J. Miller (1980)
28–45	Production of "when" questions (±1 standard deviation)	J. Miller (1980)

It is generally recognized that normally developing children acquire
some important communicative behaviors simultaneously. However, most
communication curricula attend only minimally to this phenomenon (e.g.,
Guess et al., 1978; Kent, 1974). Although the traditional hierarchical
sequencing may be the easiest for teachers and clinicians to implement, it may
create more problems than its simplicity would imply. For example, a strict
hierarchical approach forces the teacher to train providing information prior to
demanding. That is, virtually all intervention programs first teach the child to
produce object names to supply information. From a developmental perspective, however, this skill could be trained simultaneously with a demanding
function. Similarly, most intervention programs imply that a child should not
be taught to make requests until he is able to vocally imitate and comprehend
object names. However, normal children often simultaneously acquire these
skills.

Many communication programs assume that developmental models can
be overlayed onto augmentative systems. This logic may be faulty. First,
some of the necessary skills required to use augmentative systems deviate
from those required to communicate in the verbal mode. Second, an augmentative response mode may effect the most efficient sequencing of communication objectives. Third, the rate of acquisition may significantly differ when
using an augmentative system.

A direct selection communication board requires the child to select a
symbol by pointing to it with his finger, hand, headstick, or eye gaze. This
skill requires that the child be able to: 1) point to a discrete target; 2) rapidly
make successive points to targets that cover a significant range of motion, and
3) turn a page (if numerous symbols will be on the learner's board). When
children are unable to produce a symbol selection response solely of their own
volition, a scanning board is frequently used. For example, the child might
move a light cursor from symbol to symbol by activating a switch that can be

mechanically or electrically interfaced with the board. To utilize an electronic scanning board, the child must perform several behaviors, including activating a cursor and making it pause on the symbol that he wishes to communicate. Although developmental data provide some relevant information regarding the child's ability to use communication aids, they are not sufficient to allow sequencing of all subskills that are needed.

With communication boards, it is important to remember that changing from a verbal to a graphic response mode may affect the overall training sequence. Communication intervention programs frequently recommend training comprehension prior to production. However, there may be some basis for suggesting that production be taught first, or at least simultaneously with comprehension, when using a communication board. Keogh and Reichle (1982) suggested that object name production using a direct selection communication board is practically the same as performing a nonidentical match to sample (e.g., teacher holds up a real object and asks "What's that?"—child matches the real object to a graphic symbol on his board). On the other hand, such a comprehension task requires a cross-modal match between the teacher's spoken word and the child's selection of a graphic symbol. Keogh and Reichle (1983) speculated that for many learners a within-mode matching task is easier than a cross-modal matching task. Additionally, there are some data to suggest that in the graphic mode there is a modest savings in training trials by first teaching communication board production and subsequently focusing on comprehension (Reichle et al., 1984). This finding has also been reported in vocal mode training. Guess et al. (1978) and more recently Cuvo and Riva (1980) demonstrated that severely handicapped children can successfully be taught productive vocabulary use prior to comprehension. Furthermore, Cuvo and Riva (1980) reported bidirectional generalization, suggesting that "production first" training was as efficient as the traditional developmental sequence. Until more definitive work is completed regarding the production versus comprehension issue, we suggest that intervention may logically be implemented in either mode provided generalization probes are administered in the remaining mode. Similarly, in terms of content, there is no reason why intervention could not proceed simultaneously in both modes.

The traditional relationship between comprehension and production in many communication intervention procedures exemplifies the influence of early descriptive studies. More recently, developmental language data suggest that comprehension of any given word does not always precede productive use of that word (Miller, 1980). Unfortunately, many communicatively handicapped learners may be "pigeonholed" into prerequisite comprehension programs that postpone needed production training.

The fact that we are constantly learning more about normal development and that this information, in at least some cases, may contradict earlier developmental findings has led many interventionists away from a strictly developmental model of communication intervention. These interventionists have suggested specific intervention strategies that may be more efficient and effective, although they contradict current developmental data. For example, Keogh and Reichle (this volume) have suggested that with some handicapped children it may be more efficient to make some pragmatic functions specific to word class. Using this logic, the child would be taught to demand by emitting "want" and to comment by emitting a name to signify an object, action, location, or attribute. A demand for an object or event would not be accepted unless accompanied by a "want" symbol. A second example applies to teaching question comprehension. Chapman (1974) reported that initial question forms acquired by children included yes/no, "what," "what doing," and "where." Stremel and Waryas (1974) pointed out that there is a clear-cut semantic contrast between "what" and "who" questions because one involves nonliving objects and the other involves living things. Consequently, "who" represents one of the initial question forms that Stremel and Waryas (1974) addressed, even though a strictly developmental sequence might suggest otherwise.

Another program sequencing issue involves the relationship between learning to comprehend the names of objects and actions. Most intervention programs suggest that object comprehension is easier to teach than action comprehension. This assumption is based upon the belief that object name comprehension emerges earlier in normal-developing populations. However, upon closer scrutiny, the developmental literature discusses early comprehension of relational semantic functions such as rejection ("no"), and recurrence ("more"). These words, like action words, specify relationships with objects rather than labels for objects. At present we know little about the comparative difficulty between early semantic functions expressed by normal populations. We know even less about the relative difficulty among these functions for learners with severe handicaps.

Many handicapped children have communicative repertoires that deviate significantly in quality or quantity from those of normal children. In part these differences may be accounted for as the result of a narrowly focused intervention procedure, (e.g., an intervention program that focused nearly exclusively on object name comprehension and little else). Communicatively handicapped children often display a mismatch between their pragmatic and semantic/syntactic skills. For example, Fay (1975) and Fay and Butler (1968) reported that autistic learners were more apt to emit echolalic verbal behavior when information was requested that they were unable to supply. Other investigators have described the use of echolalia to introduce a new topic (e.g, the learner says "Mr. Bill Show" in the middle of a bath because he wishes to watch TV). Unfortunately, many intervention programs have focused on reducing the frequency of echolalia and other deviant speech patterns without necessarily focusing on the communicative context in which the behavior was emitted. These behavior deceleration programs were done presumably because of the lack of description in the normal acquisition literature of the transition of these behaviors into more socially acceptable communication strategies. In normal-developing children the initial expression of communicative intent is often accomplished using unacceptable or marginally acceptable behaviors. Fortunately, persons in the learner's environment shape those behaviors. However, with handicapped learners we frequently punish, timeout, or extinguish not only those behaviors but their pragmatic intent as well. More programming attention must be given to the communicative intent of behaviors already in the handicapped learner's repertoire.

Other deviances exhibited by handicapped learners in the motor and vocal modalities may be beyond the learner's control. For example, in the motor domain, normal developmental motor data may be irrelevant in training a cerebral palsied child to sign. Vocally, the conditions of dysarthria and apraxia may limit significantly the usefulness of normal phonological data in the development of vocal modality skills. Extinction of communication attempts represents a constant threat for these learners because of their limited intelligibility. Care must be taken by the interventionist not only to address the establishment of sign or speech approximations but also to make frequent objective appraisals of the learner's intelligibility with both familiar and unfamiliar individuals.

In summary, there may be many paths that lead to communicative competence. While adhering to a normal sequence may be desirable when possible, there are numerous examples where a normal model fails to enhance the discrimination being learned either by providing intermediary steps that may not be needed or by failing to provide intermediary steps when they are needed. In addition to the need for more finely sequenced paths, there is a growing literature suggesting that the use of nondevelopmentally sequenced communication objectives can result in learning that is just as efficient as that which occurs when developmentally sequenced objectives are utilized (Umbreit, 1981). Interventionists are only beginning to examine critical issues that pertain to the sequencing of communication objectives.

HOW TO TEACH

Although there is an extensive technology that describes "how to teach," many communication intervention programs have placed significantly more emphasis on "what to teach." Fortunately, there are several innovative intervention programs and techniques that integrate current technology with current programmatic content. Most interventionists agree that training in the natural environment using relatively unobtrusive instructional procedures represents the most desirable treatment conditions (Spradlin and Siegel, 1982).

The least intrusive intervention strategies focus on the use of naturally occurring discriminative stimuli and reinforcers, and are exemplified in curricula described by Hart and Risley (¹975), Neel (1982), and MacDonald (this volume).

Less Intrusive Strategies

The systematic use of naturally occurring discriminative stimuli, varied adult prompts, and functional reinforcers has been described as incidental teaching (Hart and Risley, 1975; Keogh, 1980). Because an incidental teaching episode is normally child initiated, all of the stimulus conditions (both antecedent and consequent) are optimal for functional language learning at the precise moment when the child is attending to an object, action, or other person. For example, if the teacher is engaged in a small group activity organized around self-help or motor skills training, and one of the students climbs in a wagon and gestures to the teacher that he would like to be pushed, the teacher could ask the child, "What do you want me to do?" If the child does not respond to the adult's question, a prompt may be given to imitate the word "push." The natural consequence for such an attempt is a (it is hoped) delightful push around the play area by the attending adult. Thus, the integrity of the antecedent condition (climbing into the wagon and gesturing), the prompted language response, and the consequence of getting a ride all occur within the context of a naturally occurring classroom event.

Hart and Risley (1975) suggested that the overall effectiveness of communicative intervention may be enhanced if the handicapped child's environment is organized carefully so that the skills being taught in formal sessions may be reinforced as they occur under differing stimulus conditions. The rationale for this approach has been outlined by Keogh (1980) and rests on two assumptions: 1) by identifying forms and functions that are useful to the child in a particular set of circumstances, the chances for motivated learning are greater than when arbitrarily imposed responses are chosen by the teacher; and 2) by identifying naturally occurring reinforcers available in the child's natural environment, newly developed communicative responses may show greater generalization and maintenance.

Hart and Risley's (1975) incidental teaching model was developed in a preschool classroom for disadvantaged children. Although the nature of individual language problems may differ between disadvantaged children and other handicapping conditions, the fundamental tenets of the incidental teaching process remain the same. The attending adult must make a series of decisions. The primary decision concerns the form of language response to be prompted. This decision is based on the adult's prior knowledge of the child's existing level of language competence. Next, the adult must decide if a prompt should be given to set the incidental teaching episode into motion, and, if so, another decision must be made concerning the sort of prompt that would be most appropriate under the specific circumstances.

Hart (this volume) suggests that incidental teaching may be of value not only from the standpoint of training the child, but also in terms of sensitizing parents and teachers to their child's communicative behavior. This latter aspect may be particularly important because initially parents and teachers may have a difficult time identifying and acting upon incidental teaching opportunities (Stremel-Campbell, personal communication, January 1984).

One strategy for selecting instructional procedures for use in natural environments is to choose ones that may already be in the parents' or teachers' repertoire but not efficiently used. This strategy allows a shaping paradigm to be used in perfecting a parent's or teacher's instructional behavior and is consistent with Stokes and Baer's (1977) conclusion that one of the most dependable generalization programming techniques is the use of natural contingencies that operate in the child's environment.

Numerous investigators have focused on the characteristics of adult speech to children (Broen, 1972; Ferguson, 1964; Garnica, 1977; Phillips, 1973; Snow and Ferguson, 1977). These studies suggest that adult language patterns are varied significantly in their phonologic, semantic, and syntactic patterns dependent upon (at least) the chronological age of the normal learner.

Ferguson (1964) and Garnica (1977) reported that pitch used by mothers while interacting with 2-year-olds was significantly more variable than the pitch used with 5-year-olds. Similarly, with the younger children mothers' content words were longer in duration and mothers used two primary stresses (rather than one) in sentences. Chapman (1980) suggested that the differential use of certain prosodic characteristics during interactions with young children represents an effort to "get and keep the child's attention. . . ." Keogh and Reichle (this volume) recommend using prosodic features as part of the discriminative stimulus in early imitation tasks. They suggest that, with learners who fail to imitate phonemes, it may be desirable to use loudness, pitch, and duration as stimulus dimensions. Both the normal child development literature and the intervention literature suggest that prosodic features represent stimulus dimensions that are easy to highlight and subsequently fade, and that appear to facilitate the establishment of communicative behavior.

Broen (1972) compared the language behavior that mothers addressed to their own 2- and 4-year-olds. She found that mothers used significantly slower speaking rates with 2- than with 4-year-olds. She also observed that, with young children, adults used very predictable pause patterns (there were nearly always pauses after each sentence or single-word remark). Finally, mothers were extremely redundant in their interactions with younger children. All of these strategies suggest viable stimulation techniques that could be incorporated into environmentally based language comprehension programs.

Brown and Bellugi (1964) initially described an adult behavior referred to as "imitation with expansion." For example, the child says "Doggie," to which the adult says "Doggie run" (presuming the dog is running) or "The doggie is running." Expansions may be used to extend either the child's semantic or syntactic skills. Although initial attempts to demonstrate the instructional utility of expansions were not highly successful (Cazden, 1965; Feldman and Rodgen, 1970), more recent investigations (Branston, 1979; Malouf and Dodd, 1972; Nelson et al., 1973; Schumaker, 1976) have reported the successful use of expansions in establishing repertoires of semantic and syntactic behavior. Ratner and Bruner (1978) described the emergence of games such as Peek-a-Boo and Show and Give at an early level of interpersonal interactions. They suggested that these games rely heavily upon repetition and may stimulate increasing lengths of interactions between adult and child. Ninio and Bruner (1978) reported that repetition is very prevalent in labeling games that occur between mothers and children of ages 8 months to 1.6 years. The repeated game format described by Ninio and Bruner includes four components. Initially, a mother requests her child's attention (e.g., "Look"). Next, they ask, "What's that?" The third component involves the production of a label. Chapman (1980) pointed out that the vocabularies that mothers select as targets involve a "clear use of detailed knowledge" with respect to what words their children had previously heard and/or objects that the children frequently use. It is possible that these sequences are important in the establishment of early communication turn-taking.

Chapman (1978) described a variety of cues emitted by the adult and used by the child that give the illusion of comprehension. Typically, these cues involve attending to the adult's eye gaze, pointing, and direction of ambulation. For example, suppose the mother wants the child to pick up a pea that has dropped on the floor during dinner. She elicits the child's attention, says "Get the pea" and at the same time points to the floor. The child obligingly picks up the pea *not* because he understood the spoken word but because he understood the gesture. Using the technology of stimulus fading, the mother could teach her child to understand the spoken instruction "Get the pea." It is interesting that few language curricula attempt to teach early comprehension skills through the management of stimulus properties. Instead most seem to rely heavily on response prompts.

There seems to be an abundance of prompts that can be used in the natural environment. Some of the prompts that have been identified here may be particularly fruitful for use by parents. Because there is a high probability that parents already use these prompts to some degree, the interventionist's job focuses on establishing the generalized use of these prompts as well as the means of systematically reducing the child's dependency on them. Mac-Donald (this volume) describes a parent-based paradigm for teaching language using conversational tasks. MacDonald's efforts represent a compilation of some of the explicit teaching technology that also has a level of environmental validity.

Despite the potential of intervention procedures that rely on natural interaction patterns, some cautions are necessary. Spradlin and Siegel (1982) suggested that too little is known about natural prompts used in incidental teaching procedures. Hart (this volume) acknowledges the lack of empirical studies that thoroughly evaluate environmental influences as part of a language intervention paradigm. She adds that the credibility of incidental teaching is strongest in making language more socially appropriate. The skepticism expressed by Spradlin and Siegel (1982) seems well advised until a stronger data base for incidental formats can be generated.

More Intrusive Strategies

More intrusive intervention strategies are those that involve the implementation of a predetermined schedule of training opportunities. In more intrusive intervention strategies, each training opportunity is teacher instigated, whereas during the implementation of less intrusive strategies each training opportunity is learner instigated. Intervention strategies such as those described by Kent (1974), Stremel and Waryas (1974), Fredericks et al. (1976), Williams and Fox (1977), and Guess et al. (1978) represent some of the most intrusive. These intervention procedures specify verbal instructions and training environments and suggest the use of specific materials.

One criticism of the most structured programs is that they focus so heavily on enhancing the discrimination to be acquired that they may sacrifice promoting generalization. The phenomenon of generalization applies to both stimuli and responses. Stimulus generalization traditionally has referred to the emission of a trained response in the presence of novel persons, settings, and/or stimulus objects. Response generalization, on the other hand, has referred to the emission of responses that are functionally similar to a trained response. Warren and Rogers-Warren (1980) pointed out that most communication intervention programs do not program for extensive stimulus or response generalization.

Efforts to establish response generalization have been less prevalent than attempts to address stimulus generalization. Warren and Rogers-Warren (1980) reported the results of a longitudinal analysis of response generalization after implementation of the Guess et al. (1978) and Stremel and Waryas (1974) training programs with severely handicapped learners. Each learner was observed regularly for at least one year. Verbatim speech records were made in classrooms, homes, or other living settings. The results suggested that the use of specific syntactic forms (e.g., noun-verb-adjective-noun) did not generalize thoroughly. However, the results did suggest that simple syntactic relationships (noun-verb) did generalize when multiple examplars were trained across increasingly complex steps (noun-verb, noun-verb-noun). The best examples of response generalization seem to occur with respect to semantic function. Warren and Rogers-Warren (1980) suggested that this is because direct reinforcement in the natural environment is contingent on the function that language serves.

Another form of response generalization involves transfer from comprehension to production. Most intervention programs appear to assume that a form and function taught in comprehension will not necessarily generalize to production. Several investigators (Guess, 1969; Ruder et al., 1974, 1977) have explored this aspect of generalization. Guess (1969) studied two severely retarded adolescents who, after being taught to comprehend the plural morpheme, failed to generalize to productive use during an elicitation task. More recently, however, Kohl et al. (1979) demonstrated that a group of severely handicapped learners generalized from comprehension to production in an augmentative communication program that involved signing. Additionally, Cuvo and Riva (1980) found bidirectional response generalization from comprehension to production and vice versa in a severely handicapped population.

Many structured programs treat stimulus generalization unevenly. For example, several programs (Stremel and Waryas, 1974; Williams and Fox, 1977) attend to the transition from real objects to pictures as stimuli and from a two-choice to a three-choice discrimination. However, none of these programs examines the generalization from simple comprehension in a short sentence to comprehension in a multiple-word sentence (e.g., "Get juice" versus "Get me the juice right now").

Another important aspect of language generalization is the self-initiated use of communicative forms and functions. There are very few available intervention programs that specifically address self-initiation. Twardosz and Baer (1973) taught two severely handicapped adolescents to ask questions. These investigators demonstrated that, by using verbal prompts and reinforcement, both learners began asking questions about probe objects. The Guess et al. (1978) curriculum is one of the few curricula that directly address teaching learners to functionally request and then subsequently use information. Unfortunately, this curriculum does not program the extension of question asking to self-initiated use.

For users of augmentative communication systems, generalization involves the transfer to communicative production in one modality (i.e., signing) to another modality (i.e., verbal). Despite several reports of training transfer using structured procedures (Creedon, 1976; Miller and Miller, 1973; Schaeffer, 1980; Stremel-Campbell et al., 1976), the base of available data is often overrepresented. Most often these reports are anecdotal rather than data based. This "cross-modal" aspect of generalization deserves more direct attention than it has thus far received.

The limited programming of stimulus and response generalization in structured intervention programs has resulted in the equation of structured programs with a failure to establish generalized behavior. Fortunately, generalization and structured programming need not be incompatible.

Integration of Incidental and More Intrusive Formats

In many instances, the communication interventionist faces a dilemma. From the standpoint of promoting generalized communicative behavior, incidental teaching seems ideal. However, some handicapped children may initiate communication so seldom that the incidental teaching strategy is neutralized by insufficient training trials. Even if sufficient training opportunities can be generated by teacher prompting, cue subtleties in the natural environment may obscure the discrimination being taught. Several investigators (Bricker et al., 1976; Keogh and Reichle, 1982; MacDonald and Horstmeier, 1978) have suggested using a combination of structured one-to-one or small group training sessions (to develop the topography of the language behavior) in combination with the incidental teaching method (to promote generalized and spontaneous use of newly developed behaviors). Recently, several investigators have operationalized strategies that maximize the advantages of less intrusive as well as structured teaching formats.

Holvoet et al. (1980) proposed an instructional environment designed for severely handicapped students in which tasks are arranged so that events in the natural environment serve as discriminative stimuli for the emission of a target behavior. Their training format concurrently clusters skills so that the first skill member (e.g., saying "Toast") serves as the discriminative stimulus for the emission of the next target behavior in the cluster (e.g., placing bread in a toaster). A cluster is usually described as a group of 2 or more behaviors that are sequenced so as to replicate their order of occurrence in the natural environment. For example, consider a behavioral cluster in which: 1) the teacher asks the student to get the juice; 2) when he returns, she asks him what he has; and 3) the teacher pours the student a small drink. After the student has consumed the juice, sometimes he is asked if he wants "juice" and other times whether he wants some undesirable object. In this particular example, comprehension and production programming are integrated logically into a functional activity that focuses upon the retrieval of a desired object. During isolated trials within the cluster, the student has an opportunity to follow a verbal instruction, produce the label of the critical object named in the teacher's instruction, and produce words to accept or reject a named object. The Holvoet et al. (1980) proposal clearly represents an attempt to maintain a structured intervention session while stimulating integration of skills that could be typically encountered in the natural environment.

MacDonald and Horstmeier (1978) allowed for structured as well as unstructured opportunities for incidental teaching in their intervention program. They recommended conducting training in small-group structured sessions and simultaneously running small-group play sessions that provide the opportunity for incidental instruction.

A critical need exists for carefully executed studies aimed at evaluating the relative effectiveness of strategies such as those delineated by Holvoet et al. (1980) and MacDonald and Horstmeier (1978). If communication intervention programs are to be ecologically valid, the integration of structured and incidental teaching formats must become a major focus of future research.

Other Issues in Program Implementation

Some factors are critical to efficient intervention regardless of whether a highly structured protocol is used. These issues involve determining the role of stimulus and response prompts, mastery criterion, and the number of exemplars to be taught simultaneously.

Stimulus control as defined by K. Miller (1980) is the "increased probability of a discriminated behavior that is produced by some stimulus." Stimulus prompts are defined as any environmental feature occurring prior to the opportunity to respond that increases the probability that a given response will occur. Striefel and Owens (1979) referred to the transfer of stimulus control as involving procedures that "systematically pair previously neutral stimuli with stimuli that already control a specific response so that the previously neutral stimuli also control the response" (p. 2). Usually the controlling stimulus is eliminated by fading it from the stimulus array.

Spradlin and Siegel (1982) noted a lack of well-documented procedures for effective stimulus fading programs. One stimulus fading strategy has been referred to as time delay. In this procedure the time between the presentation of a controlling and a training stimulus is lengthened. Time delay has been used to teach instruction-following behavior (Striefel et al., 1974), verbal object naming (Risley and Wolf, 1967), sign comprehension (Smeets and Striefel, 1976), and more recently sign production (Snell and Gast, 1981). Striefel and Owens (1979) summarized the advantages of time delay: 1) it requires no special materials; 2) it can be taught to relatively untrained personnel; and 3) it results in low error rates. Snell and Gast (1981) described three types of child errors that occur in a time delay procedure. These include no response, failure to wait for the support stimulus, and errors made while waiting for the support stimulus. We know very little about the prevention of these error patterns. However, time delay is a promising strategy for which a great deal of additional research is needed.

Shaping is a technique in which successive approximations of a response are reinforced. Snell and Gast (1981) have reported that shaping is being used less and less by teachers because it is time-consuming. Nevertheless shaping remains one of the primary methods of initiating production training in the vocal mode. In part the increasing proliferation of instructional strategies in augmentative systems that do not require extensive use of shaping may be affecting the popularity of shaping as an instructional procedure.

Once an instructional strategy is selected it must be integrated with the exemplars to be taught during any given session. The literature suggests three methods of selecting the number of vocabulary words that can be simultaneously introduced during any given phase of training. These include serial, concurrent, and mixed ordering training. In serial training, each item is trained to criterion before a new item is introduced. In concurrent (or simultaneous) training, more than one item is trained in each session. A study of mixed ordering by Cuvo et al. (1980) demonstrated that the latter two strategies were more efficient than serial training in vocabulary acquisition. Most communication programs utilize concurrent training.

MacDonald and Horstmeier (1978) used a format in which the first six object comprehension vocabulary items were taught concurrently. After acquisition, 10 new words are to be taught concurrently (although enough previously taught words are to be included to ensure 50% correct responding). Bricker et al. (1976) concurrently taught the comprehension of five object labels. Kent (1974) trained only one new item at a time while concurrently maintaining previously trained behaviors for most behavior in her program. Not all programs are consistent in the formula used to combine vocabulary words in a concurrent training paradigm. For example, Bricker et al. (1976) suggested that the teacher teach one sound at a time imitatively even though in their early word recognition program they taught up to five words concurrently. Unfortunately, empirical data suggesting a range of exemplars to teach concurrently are sparse. Well-controlled studies that critically examine the relative efficacy of various concurrent mixes of training stimuli are needed.

Of course, the distinction between mixed and concurrent training depends largely on the acquisition criteria used. A review of a number of intervention programs suggests a wide range of criteria. A number of interventionists (Frederick et al., 1976; Guess et al., 1978) require criterion performance during a single session but also allow the opportunity to mix previously acquired items into training trials for new vocabulary. The effect allows the gradual elimination of discrete training trials.

The specific criterion level for program steps varies tremendously across curricula. MacDonald and Horstmeier (1978) and Miller and Yoder (1974) offered suggestions for assessment probe criterion but left the actual determination up to the interventionist. Kent (1974), on the other hand, required a uniform 90% mastery level. There is a critical need to set criteria for mastery performance based on individual student needs. Individual students may require different quantities of trials under differing density schedules to successfully acquire vocabulary. A logical selection strategy would involve the scrutiny of a student's past performance to determine a functional criterion level.

The preceding issues are important regardless of the intrusiveness of the curriculum's format. Careful attention to some of these variables may have significant effects upon not only acquisition but generalization and maintenance as well.

SUMMARY

The past several years have produced a number of communication intervention programs aimed primarily at the establishment of an initial repertoire of communicative behavior. Virtually all of these programs reflect components of both developmental and remedial intervention models. The infusion of cognitive research findings into communication intervention programs has increased steadily. This may reflect more logic than good empirical research, because there is very limited evidence suggesting causal relationships between cognitive landmarks and language acquisition.

At present, there is a notable absence of programs that address the pragmatic aspects of communicative behavior. Only recently have McLean and Snyder-McLean (1978) and MacDonald (this volume) presented intervention models that attempt to keep pace with the growing proliferation of data on the development of these skills. In addition to the influence on program content, pragmatics had (or should have) a significant effect upon program sequencing and instructional strategies. Too many intervention programs lock the child into a strict vertical sequence of skills in which Skill A may not serve as a prerequisite for Skill B. In order to utilize the program clustering strategy suggested by Holvoet et al. (1980), more attention needs to be placed on clustering communication skills that can be practically used together.

It is obvious that an incidental teaching paradigm is most desirable from a pragmatic standpoint. With in vivo training, there is a much greater opportunity to teach language with a normal conversational flow (see chapters by Hart and by MacDonald, this volume). Additionally, the opportunity to learn generalized functional uses of language is maximized. However, some students may not benefit significantly from incidental teaching alone. For these students an effort must be made to include desirable features of incidental instruction in a more highly structured environment. MacDonald and Horstmeier's (1978) efforts for combining structured with less structured training formats represent a step in the right direction.

Failure to attend to functional aspects of the natural environment has resulted in a somewhat dismal treatment of generalization. Efforts must be made during acquisition to plan for stimulus and response generalization. Further aspects of generalization that involve transfer from comprehension to production and from an augmentative mode to a speech mode must be more thoroughly addressed. One bright spot in the treatment of generalization has been the focus on the establishment of self-initiated forms of communicative behavior (Halle et al., 1979; Warren and Rogers-Warren, 1980).

Some deficiencies in current programs exemplify how quickly the area of communication intervention is changing as some of the most readily used communicative curricula only marginally address augmentative systems. Largely as a result of our treatment of younger and more severely handicapped children, there is a growing need to establish a strong base of empirically supported programs to teach initial access of augmentative systems (particularly communication boards).

There are many questions facing researchers that should be addressed if the field of communication intervention is to smoothly advance.

1. What facilitating effects do certain cognitive skills have on handicapped learners? If there are such facilitating skills, can they be practically taught using functional, age-appropriate activities?
2. What communicative behaviors actually serve as prerequisites for the establishment of other communicative behaviors in any given language intervention curriculum?
3. What is the relationship between comprehension and production skills? More specifically, what is the influence of response mode (vocal, communication board, signing) or level of language (semantic or syntactic) upon this relationship?
4. What critical variables should be considered when selecting an augmentative communication system?
5. How does one efficiently teach a variety of pragmatic skills? More specifically, can pragmatic skills be efficiently addressed in both incidental and more intrusive curricula?
6. What is the relative effect of traditional discrete trial training compared with the programming models derived from Holvoet et al. (1980) and Hart and Risley (1975)?
7. Under what conditions is any given learner most apt to benefit from the use of response prompts, as compared to stimulus control procedures such as time delay?

In addition to the questions above, there is a critical need for generators of widely used communicative curricula to conduct longitudinal investigations to demonstrate that a learner could be taken from point "A" through point "Z" in a curriculum. Too often communicative curricula are field tested cross-sectionally. Cross-sectional designs fail to generate data that speak to the sequenced continuity of a program.

Not all of the responsibility for more efficient communication programming can be placed on the researcher. Teachers and speech pathologists must make every effort to update their skills. These skills revolve around content knowledge (what to teach) and instructional technology (how to teach). Up-to-date and highly skilled teachers and speech pathologists are wise consumers of information. They are in a position to use a communication curriculum that is thoughtfully selected from a menu of existing programs. This skill is critically important if one believes, as we do, that no single communication curriculum currently available can meet the needs of all children that the teacher or speech pathologist is likely to encounter.

We conclude our review of intervention programs on a positive note. It is clear that communication programs of the seventies and eighties are much more sensitive to skill functionality than are earlier programs. It is also clear that most communication programs have attempted to integrate emerging content and technological advances into their curricula. We have come a long way and still have some distance to go. Although we cannot yet see the light at the end of the tunnel, we have reason to believe that, when we do, it will not be an oncoming train.

REFERENCES

Bates, E., Benigni, L., Bretherton, I., Camaioni, L., and Volterra, V. 1979. Cognition and communication from 9–13 months: Correlational findings. *In* E. Bates (ed.), The Emergence of Symbols: Cognition and Communication in Infancy. Academic, New York.

Bloom, L. 1970. Language Development: Form and Function of Emerging Grammars. MIT Press, Cambridge, MA.

Bloom, L., and Lahey, M. 1978. Language Development and Language Disorders. Wiley, New York.

Bowerman, M. 1978. Semantic and syntactic development: A review of what, when and how in language acquisition. *In* R. L. Schiefelbusch (ed.), Bases of Language Intervention, pp. 97–189. University Park Press, Baltimore.

Branston, M. 1979. The effect of increased expansions on the acquisition of semantic structures in young developmentally delayed children: A training study. Unpublished doctoral dissertation, University of Wisconsin, Madison.

Bricker, D., Dennison, L., and Bricker, W., 1976. A language intervention program for developmentally young children. MCCD Monograph Series, No. 1. Mailman Center for Child Development, University of Miami, Miami.

Broen, P. 1972. The verbal environment of the language learning child. ASHA Monogr. 17.

Brown, R. 1977. Why are signed languages easier to learn than spoken languages? Paper presented at the National Symposium on Sign Language Research and Teaching, Chicago.

Brown, R., and Bellugi, V. 1964. Three processes in the child's acquisition of syntax. Harvard Educ. Rev. 34:133–151.

Cazden, C. 1965. Environmental assistance to the child's acquisition of grammar. Unpublished doctoral dissertation, Harvard University, Cambridge, MA.

Chapman, R. 1974. Strategies that simulate language comprehension. Unpublished manuscript, University of Wisconsin, Madison.

Chapman, R. 1978. Comprehension strategies in children. *In* J. F. Cavanaugh and W. Strange (eds.), Speech and Language in the Laboratory School and Clinic. MIT Press, Cambridge, MA.

Chapman, R. 1980. Language comprehension and cognitive development. *In* A. P. Reilly (ed.), The Communication Game: Perspectives on the Development of Speech, Language and Nonverbal Skills. Johnson and Johnson, Skillman, NJ.

Creedon, M. P. (ed.). 1976. Appropriate Behavior Through Communication. Dysfunctioning Child Center Publication, Michael Reese Medical Center, Chicago.

Cromer, R. 1976. The cognitive hypothesis of language acquisition and its implications for child language deficiency. *In* D. M. Morehead and A. E. Morehead (eds.), Normal and Deficient Child Language. University Park Press, Baltimore.

Cuvo, A., Klevans, L., Borakove, S., Van Laiduyk, J., and Lutzker, J. 1980. A comparison of three strategies for teaching object names. J. Appl. Behav. Anal. 13:249–257.

Cuvo, A., and Riva, M. 1980. Generalization and transfer between comprehension and production: A comparison of retarded and nonretarded persons. J. Appl. Behav. Anal. 13:315–331.

Dennis, R., Reichle, J., Williams, W. and Vogelsberg, R. T. 1982. The selection and use of signs with severely handicapped learners: A review and discussion of motor criteria. J. Assoc. Severely Handic. 7:20–32.

Ervin-Tripp, S. 1971. Sociolinguistics. *In* J. Fishman (ed.), Advances in the Sociology of Language. Mouton, The Hague.

Fay, W. 1975. Occurrence of children's echoic responses according to interlocutionary question types. J. Speech Hear. Res. 18:336–345.

Fay, W., and Butler, B. 1968. Echolalia, IQ, and the developmental dichotomy of speech and language systems. J. Speech Hear. Res. 11:365–371.

Feldman, C., and Rodgen, M. 1970. The effects of various types of adult responses in the syntactic acquisition of two-to-three year olds. Unpublished manuscript, University of Chicago, Chicago.

Ferguson, C. 1964. Baby talk in six languages. Am. Anthropol. 66:103–114.

Fredericks, H. D., Riggs, C., Furey, T., Grove, D., Moore, W., McDonnell, J., Jordan, E., Hanson, W., Baldwin, V., and Wadlow, M. 1976. The Teaching Research Curriculum for Moderately and Severely Handicapped. Charles C Thomas, Springfield, IL.

Garnica, O. 1977. Some prosodic and paralinguistic features of speech to young children. *In* C. E. Snow and C. Ferguson (eds.), Talking to Children: Language Input and Acquisition. Cambridge University Press, Cambridge, England.

Griffith, P., and Robinson, J. 1980. Influence of iconicity and phonological similarity on sign learning by mentally retarded children. Am. J. Ment. Defic. 85:291–298.

Guess, D. 1969. A functional analysis of receptive language and productive speech: Acquisition of the plural morpheme. J. Appl. Behav. Anal. 2:55–64.

Guess, D., Sailor, W., and Baer, D. 1978. Children with limited language. *In* R. L.

Schiefelbusch (ed.), Language Intervention Strategies. University Park Press, Baltimore.

Halle, J., Marshall A., and Spradlin, J. 1979. Time delay: A technique to increase language usage and facilitate generalization in retarded children. J. Appl. Behav. Anal. 12:431–439.

Harding, C., and Golinkoff, R. 1979. Origins of intentional vocalizations in prelinguistic infants. Child Dev. 50:33–40.

Hart, B. 1980. Pragmatics: How language is used. Anal. Intervention Dev. Disabil. 1:299–313.

Hart, B., and Risley, T. 1975. Incidental teaching of language in the preschool. J. Appl. Behav. Anal. 8:411–420.

Holvoet, J., Guess, D., Mulligan, M., and Brown, F. 1980. The individualized curriculum sequencing model (II): A teaching strategy for severely handicapped students. J. Assoc. Severely Handic. 5:352–367.

Ingram, D. 1977. Sensorimotor intelligence and language development. In A. Lock (ed.), Action, Gesture and Symbol: The Emergence of Language. Academic, New York.

Kahn, J. 1975. Relationship of Piaget's sensorimotor period to language acquisition of profoundly retarded children. Am. J. Ment. Defic. 79:640–643.

Keenan, E., and Schieffelin, B. 1976. Topic as a discourse notion: A study of topic in the conversations of children and adults. In C. Li (ed.), Subject and Topics. Academic, New York.

Kent, L. 1974. Language Acquisition Program for the Retarded or Multiply Impaired. Research Press, Champaign, IL.

Keogh, W. 1980. Incidental teaching procedures. Excerpts from a grant application submitted to the Bureau of Education for the Handicapped. University of Vermont, Burlington.

Keogh, W., and Reichle, J. 1980. Excerpts from the Vermont Early Communication Curriculum. Unpublished manuscript, University of Vermont, Burlington.

Keogh, W., and Reichle, J. 1982. Excerpts from the Vermont Early Communication Curriculum. University of Vermont, Burlington.

Kohl, F., Karlan, G., and Heal, L. 1979. Effects of pairing manual signs with verbal cues upon the acquisition of instruction-following expressive language with severely retarded children. AAESPH Rev. 4:291–300.

Konstantareas, M., Oxman, J., and Webster, C. 1978. Iconicity: Effects on the acquisition of sign language by autistic and other severely dysfunctional children. In P. Siple (ed.), Understanding Language Through Sign Language Research. Academic, New York.

MacDonald, J., and Horstmeier, D. 1978. Environmental Language Intervention Program. Charles Merrill, Columbus, OH.

McLean, J., and Snyder-McLean, L. 1978. A Transactional Approach to Early Language Training. Charles Merrill, Columbus, OH.

Malouf, R., and Dodd, D. 1972. Role of exposure, imitation and expansion in the acquisition of an artificial grammatical rule. Dev. Psychol. 7:195–203.

Miller, A., and Miller, E. 1973. Cognitive-developmental training with elevated boards and sign language. J. Autism Child. Schizophrenia 3:65–85.

Miller, J. 1980. Assessing Language Production in Children: Experimental Procedures. University Park Press, Baltimore.

Miller, J., and Yoder, D. 1973. A syntax teaching program. *In* J. McLean, D. Yoder, and R. L. Schiefelbusch (eds.), Language Intervention with the Retarded. University Park Press, Baltimore.

Miller, J., and Yoder, D. 1974. An ontogenetic language strategy for retarded children. *In* R. L. Schiefelbusch and L. Lloyd (eds.), Language Perspectives: Acquisition, Retardation and Intervention. University Park Press, Baltimore.

Miller, K. 1980. Principles of Everyday Behavior Analysis. Brooks/Cole Publishing, Monterey, CA.

Moerk, E. 1975. Verbal interactions between children and their mothers during the preschool years. Dev. Psychol. 11:788–795.

Moore, M., and Meltzoff, A. 1977. Imitation of facial and manual gestures by human neonates. Science 198:75–78.

Neel, R. 1982. Teaching autistic children: A functional curriculum approach. Unpublished manuscript, University of Washington, Seattle.

Nelson, K., Carskaddon, G., and Bonvillian, J. 1973. Syntax acquisition: Impact of experimental variation in adult verbal interaction with the child. Child Dev. 44:497–504.

Nicholich, L. 1977. Beyond sensorimotor intelligence: Assessment of symbolic maturity through analysis of pretend play. Merrill-Palmer Q. 23:89–99.

Ninio, A., and Bruner, J. 1978. The achievement and antecedent of labeling. J. Child Lang. 6:1–6.

Phillips, J. 1973. Syntax and vocabulary of mothers' speech to young children: Age and sex comparisons. Child Dev. 44:192–195.

Ratner, N., and Bruner, J. 1978. Games, social exchange and the acquisition of language. J. Child Lang. 5:391–401.

Rees, N. 1980. Pragmatics of language: Applications to normal and disordered language development. *In* R. L. Schiefelbusch (ed.), Bases of Language Intervention. University Park Press, Baltimore.

Reichle, J. 1982. Teaching action comprehension prior to object comprehension. Department of Communication Disorders. Working Paper #1, University of Minnesota, Minneapolis.

Reichle, J., Rogers, N., and Barrett, C. 1984. Establishing pragmatic discrimination among the communicative functions of requesting, rejecting and commenting in an adolescent. J. Assoc. Severely Handic. 9:31–36.

Reichle, J., and Yoder, D. 1979. Assessment and early stimulation of communication in the severely and profoundly mentally retarded. *In* R. York and E. Edgar (eds.), Teaching the Severely Handicapped, Vol. 4. American Association for the Education of the Severely/Profoundly Handicapped, Seattle.

Risley, T., and Wolf, M. 1967. Establishing functional speech in echolalic children. Behav. Res. Ther. 5:73–88.

Rogers, S. 1977. Characteristics of the cognitive development of profoundly retarded children. Child Dev. 48:837–843.

Rogers-Warren, A., and Warren, S. F. Pragmatic and generalization. *In* R. L. Schiefelbusch (eds.), Communicative Competence: Assessment and Intervention. University Park Press, Baltimore.

Ruder, K., Herman, P., and Schiefelbusch, R. L. 1977. Effects of verbal imitation and comprehension training on verbal production. J. Psycholing. Res. 6:59–71.

Ruder, K., Smith, M., and Herman, P. 1974. Effects of verbal imitation and comprehension on verbal production of lexical items. *In* L. V. McReynolds (ed.), Developing Systematic Procedures for Training Children's Language. ASHA Monogr. 18:15–29.

Schaeffer, B. 1980. Spontaneous language through signed speech. *In* R. L. Schiefelbusch (ed.), Nonspeech Language and Communication Analysis and Intervention, pp. 421–446. University Park Press, Baltimore

Schumaker, J. 1976. Mother's expansions: Their characteristics and effects on child language. Unpublished doctoral dissertation, University of Kansas, Lawrence.

Siegel, G. M., and Spradlin, J. E. 1978. Programming for language and communication therapy. *In* R. L. Schiefelbusch (ed.), Language Intervention Strategies. University Park Press, Baltimore

Siple, P. (ed.). 1978. Understanding Language Through Sign Language Research. Academic, New York.

Skelly, M., Schinsky, L., Smith, R., and Fust, R. 1974. American Indian Sign (Amerind) as a facilitator of verbalization for the oral verbal apraxic. J. Speech Hear. Disord. 39:445–456.

Smeets, P., and Striefel, S. 1976. Acquisition and crossmodal generalization of receptive and expressive signing skills in a retarded deaf girl. Am. J. Ment. Defic. 20:197–205.

Snell, M., and Gast, D. 1981. Applying time delay procedure to the instruction of severely handicapped. J. Assoc. Severely Handicapped 6:13–14.

Snow, C., and Ferguson, C. (eds.). 1977. Talking to Children. Cambridge University Press, Cambridge.

Spradlin, J., and Siegel, G. 1982. Language training in natural and clinical environments. J. Speech Hear. Disord. 47:2–6.

Stokes, T., and Baer, D. 1977. An implicit technology of generalization. J. Appl. Behav. Anal. 10:349–367.

Stremel, K., and Waryas, C. 1974. A behavioral-psycholinguistic approach to language training. *In* L. McReynolds (ed.), Developing Systematic Procedures for Training Children's Language. ASHA Monogr. 18:96–130.

Stremel-Campbell, K., Cantrell, D., and Halle, J. 1976. Manual signing as a language system and a speech initiator for the nonverbal severely handicapped student. *In* E. Sontag, J. Smith, and N. Certo (eds.), Educational Programming for the Severely and Profoundly Handicapped. The Council for Exceptional Children, Reston, VA.

Striefel, S., Bryan, K., and Aikin, D. 1974. Transfer of stimulus control from motor to verbal stimuli. J. Appl. Behav. Anal. 7:123–135.

Striefel, S., and Owens, C. 1979. Transfer of stimulus control procedures: Applications to language acquisition training with developmentally handicapped. Unpublished manuscript, Utah State University, Logan.

Striefel, S., and Wetherby, B. 1973. Instruction-following behavior of a retarded child and its controlling stimuli. J. Appl. Behav. Anal. 6:663–670.

Twardosz, S., and Baer D. 1973. Training two severely retarded adolescents to ask questions. J. Appl. Behav. Anal. 4:655–661.

Umbreit, J. 1981. Effects of developmentally sequenced instruction on the rate of skill acquisition by severely handicapped students. J. Assoc. Severely Handicapped 5:121–129.

Uzgiris, I., and Hunt, J. 1975. Ordinal Scales of Development: Assessment in Infancy. University of Illinois Press, Champaign.

Warren, S., and Rogers-Warren, A. 1980. Current perspectives in language remediation. Educ. Treatment Child. 3:133–152.

Williams, W., and Fox, T. 1977. Vermont minimum objectives system. Unpublished manuscript, University of Vermont, Burlington.

Williams W., and York, R. 1977. Developing Instructional Programs for Severely Handicapped Students. Unpublished manuscript, Center for Developmental Disabilities, University of Vermont, Burlington.

Woodward, M. 1959. The behavior of idiots interpreted by Piaget's theory of sensorimotor development. Br. J. Educ. Psychol. 29:60–71.

Section

II

Functional Language Training Applications

chapter

3

Naturalistic Language Training Techniques

Betty Hart

Bureau of Child Research
University of Kansas
Lawrence, Kansas

CONCEPTUAL AND EXPERIMENTAL BACKGROUND   **66**
   **Experimentally Demonstrated Processes That Facilitate
   Generalization and Acquisition**   **68**
   **Aspects of the Environment That Facilitate Generalization and
   Acquisition**   **79**

SUMMARY AND CONCLUSIONS   **83**

ACKNOWLEDGMENTS   **86**

REFERENCES   **86**

Training techniques are designed to facilitate generalization into nontraining environments, and nontraining environments can be deliberately arranged to promote use of trained language. Language development can be maximized by using techniques that facilitate generalization both in training sessions and in the natural, nontraining environment.

Different techniques (although not different principles) are needed in the nontraining environment because, as a setting, it is quite different from the training environment. The stimuli available are normally more numerous, varied, and complex; a trainer cannot control distractors or what a child will attend to. Also, a trainer often has little control over the behavior of important adults who may or may not be responsive to the child's use of trained language in the nontraining environment. Untrained, busy adults may not hear small approximations, and so may not respond in ways that shape improved language.

Furthermore, the nontraining environment (its people, materials, setting, and routines) may be cueing behaviors incompatible with use of trained language. Children may have learned to discriminate between the training and the nontraining environments: talking is reinforced in one and silence in the other, or eye contact and a recipient-designed response is reinforced in the training environment whereas deviant language patterns are reinforced in the nontraining environment. The training environment may be rich in positive reinforcement, whereas in the nontraining environment the most frequently occurring consequence for the child may be success in driving an adult away, and so discontinuing interaction.

When there is a major mismatch between the cues and consequences of the training and nontraining environments, the nontraining environment may have to be changed. In order that the techniques used to facilitate generalization from training can have an effect on behavior in the nontraining environment, the nontraining environment must provide appropriate cues and positive responses to trained language. Adults may have to be prompted, or trained, to respond to different child behaviors in different ways. Almost certainly, new activity arrangements will be needed.

This chapter is about environmental intervention: arranging nontraining environments to facilitate generalization from training. It is assumed that the techniques described below will be used in parallel with techniques within training sessions, and that the adults in the nontraining environment and the trainers in the training environment are involved in regular evaluation of each child's progress, working together to facilitate generalization and acquisition.

This work was supported by a grant (HD 03144) from the National Institute of Child Health and Human Development to the Bureau of Child Research and the Department of Human Development at the University of Kansas.

65

CONCEPTUAL AND EXPERIMENTAL
BACKGROUND

The goal in environmental intervention (in teaching children to use trained language in nontraining environments) is to teach children to use language just as normal children do. Therefore, teaching language in nontraining environments includes the following goals:

Encouraging direct generalization of trained language
Encouraging direct acquisition of new language structures and vocabulary
Encouraging generalization and acquisition of speech functions
Encouraging increases in verbal responsivity
Encouraging increases in verbal initiation to adults and peers
Encouraging increases in length of verbal interaction episodes

These goals (what the environmental arrangements are designed to effect) may be more extensive than the goals of the training program currently in use. However, the basic principles used in the design of environmental intervention are identical to those used in the design of training:

Arrangement of a stimulus setting that will cue appropriate behavior
Training child attention to appropriate cues
Prompting appropriate behavior
Shaping approximations
Differentially reinforcing appropriate responses

Also the sequencing (the curriculum) within the environmental intervention component is likely to correspond to the logic of the training program. Thus, what is taught within a particular program may be based on developmental logic (see Guess et al., 1978, for definitions and discussion). Children are led to master, for instance, speech functions for requesting as instrumental and regulatory functions (see Halliday, 1975) prior to being taught informing functions. Or a program may be based on remedial logic (Guess et al., 1978), according to which the child's age or stage of development is considered irrelevant (Baer, 1970) and the child is taught both to request and to inform, depending on the availability of reinforcers for each behavior in particular stimulus situations. On the other hand, a program might combine the two approaches (e.g., Bricker and Bricker, 1974).

At present, what tends to differentiate the design of environmental intervention from the design of training programs is the literature on which each is based. Environmental intervention tends to be related to the developmental literature, whereas the design of training programs is based on experimental research.

Most language training programs use the methods of operant conditioning (Guess et al., 1978). They are based on techniques demonstrated to be effective in laboratory experiments where stimulus conditions (setting events and consequences) are carefully controlled. From these experiments, we know the effects on language learning of important aspects of the environment. Differential reinforcement and imitation training lead to generalization across members of response classes (Guess and Baer, 1973). Prompting, shaping, and chaining lead to improvements in the topography of language (Risley and Wolf, 1967).

Outside laboratory settings, however, only a few experimental studies have undertaken to assess environmental influences on language learning. (A distinction is made here between studies of language behavior and studies of language improvement, i.e., changes in the topography of language in the direction of forms designated more socially appropriate.) Rather, environmental intervention tends to be based on the developmental literature that describes the stages and setting conditions of normal language acquisition. Much of this literature is descriptive, either of sequences in the acquisition of language forms and structures or of interactional contexts seen to contribute to progress in acquisition. Environmental influences on progress in acquisition are generally assessed by counting the frequency of occurrence of particular aspects (such as imitation, models, or reinforcement) and correlating that frequency with measures of relative progress in language acquisition (e.g., Carew, 1980, with verbal IQ; Cross, 1978, with age; Ellis and Wells, 1980, with MLU and range and number of meanings).

This literature suggests that the following aspects of the environment contribute to language acquisition:

Stimulation: the richness and variety of objects and experiences provided
Adult-child ratio: the one-to-one nature of early interactions
Topic: child selection of the topic for interaction
Routines: the standardized framework of early interactions
Models: the language the child hears
Imitation: repetition of models by child or adult
Prompts: methods of evoking language from the child
Function: the consequences of language use for the child

Increasing numbers of studies indicate that differences in the frequency with which these environmental aspects occur are correlated with differences in progress in early language acquisition across groups of children. However, the relative contribution of any one aspect is difficult to assess. (For example, see Snow, 1981, for a review of differing assessments of the contribution of imitation to early language acquisition.) Experimental research is needed in order to isolate the contribution of any one aspect from that of all the rest. It is likely to be extremely difficult, however, to separate one aspect from most or all of the other aspects.

It seems possible that environmental assistance to language acquisition does not take the form of distinct setting and/or consequent events, but instead occurs in the form of combinations or patterns of those events. It may not be the frequency with which particular environmental aspects occur that assists language acquisition, but the frequency with which those aspects are embedded within particular language-building processes. This helps to account for the varying strengths of reported correlations between particular environmental aspects and child progress in language acquisition (see, for instance, Ellis and Wells, 1980): at certain times, particular environmental aspects may occur within a language-building process and at other times they may not.

The design of training programs illustrates the importance of process: that language learning is facilitated not so much by particular aspects of the setting or of trainer behavior, but rather by the arrangement of those aspects within a stimulus-consequence paradigm. What makes training programs effective is not the occurrence, or even the frequency, of aspects such as imitation, prompting, or modeling, but the process of which they are a part, the "systematic series of progressive and interdependent actions directed to attaining some end" (*Random House Dictionary*, 1966).

The role of process is borne out by the few experimental studies that have been conducted in natural, nontraining environments. Those studies have shown that language improves in the presence of particular processes that, like the training process, involve systematic arrangement of particular environmental aspects. Furthermore, each of the language-improving processes demonstrated to be effective in nontraining environments seems to be a naturally occurring process, one that occurs with some regularity and generality within the environments of young children acquiring a first language.

The advantage of systematizing, for use in environmental intervention, naturally occurring processes is that generalization seems to be "built in." Because they are "natural," such processes are likely to occur in uncontrolled stimulus conditions, where the properties of stimuli are simultaneously different across exemplars and the same (because they tend to share characteristics of the "home" environment to which young children are usually limited). Interventions designed for the unsystematically controlled stimulus conditions of nontraining environments may be facilitated, therefore, by adapting those language-building processes that occur within natural (highly variable) environments, rather than by trying to design ways to generalize behavior from artificially controlled conditions into more ecologically natural ones.

Experimentally Demonstrated Processes that Facilitate Generalization and Acquisition

Three experimentally validated processes for facilitating language acquisition and generalization are: mand-model, delay, and incidental teaching. Each process is described below, first in terms of reports of observation of the process in use in the natural environment, then in terms of the series of actions specified in the process, with examples of their use. This description is followed by a summary of the experimental demonstration of the effects on language of using the process, and finally, by consideration of the particular end (the behavioral goal) to which the process is uniquely directed.

Mand-Model Bruner (1978) described a type of prelinguistic interaction that seems to occur frequently between mothers and their 12–15-month-old children. First the mother points or otherwise directs the child's attention (as, by saying, "Look"). Once joint attention (topic) is established, the mother asks a question, like, "What's that?" If the child vocalizes, the mother then produces a label (a model). "The almost invariant order [in such interactions is] from a vocative through a question to a. . . label" (Bruner, 1978, p. 208). Across many repetitions of this interaction, parental behavior remained largely the same; however, there was a steady increase in the number of exchanges initiated by the child, and in the child's frequency of responding to the mother's attention-directing initiations.

The mand-model process is a systematization of this naturally occurring interaction. The process specifies the following sequence of steps (Rogers-Warren and Warren, 1980, p. 367):

1. Teachers direct children's attention by providing a variety of attractive materials children want to play with.
2. When a child approaches material (such that joint teacher-child attention is focused on that material as topic), the teacher mands, "Tell me what this is," or "Tell me what you want."
3. If the child does not respond, or gives a minimal response (e.g., one word when the child is capable of using sentences), the teacher provides a model for the child to imitate. The teacher may also prompt within this step, as by elaborating the mand to, for example, "Give me a whole sentence," and then providing a model only if the child does not respond appropriately to the prompt.
4. The teacher praises the child for responding appropriately to the mand, or for imitating, and gives the child the (topic) material.

For example, the teacher in the painting area sets out paints, crayons, chalk, and paste on tables. Each potential activity is set up with all the necessary materials attractively displayed within a separate space, ready for use. All a child has to do is sit down and begin enjoying the activity. The potentially reinforcing aspects of each activity have been made as salient as possible, so that the child will be attracted to participate.

When a child approaches a particular activity, such as the paint, just as the child is about to sit down before it the teacher says, "Tell me what you want." Because the teacher always asks, the mand is likely to have become routine for the child, as much a part of beginning a new activity as is sitting down at a table. The teachers have established themselves as responsive, as people who will help (prompt or model) in order that a child can get what is currently of paramount interest (a reinforcer). As the teacher mands verbalization from the child, the teacher looks, and perhaps gestures, from the activity to the child, indicating nonverbally the joint focus of attention.

The teacher focuses completely and positively on the child. If the child ignores the teacher's focused attention and starts to sit down, the teacher gently lays her hands over the child's hands so as to prevent the chair being pulled away from the table. If the child does not verbalize or make eye contact with the teacher, the teacher may bring one hand to the child's chin and gently turn the child's face in order to make eye contact. The teacher thus tries to make it apparent to the child that access to the activity (the reinforcer) is not being denied; it is simply that there is a part of the routine (a link in the chain) that is so far missing.

If the teacher has to redirect the child's attention from the paint (the topic, the reinforcer) to herself, and thus change the topic of interaction, the teacher ordinarily provides a model immediately, and/or accepts whatever verbalization the child produces. The teacher needs to give the child access to the paint as a reinforcer for attending and responding to the teacher mand while the paint is still a reinforcer (before the child has forgotten about it, or decided it is not worth the effort to get it). The teacher must establish the mand as discriminative, as a part of the routine for gaining access to reinforcers, before she can begin to shape on whatever verbal behavior the child produces.

Once the child has learned the routine, such that when the child approaches the paint and the teacher says, "Tell me what you want," the child says, while sitting down, "Paint," the teacher can begin asking for improved language. For instance, if the child has been observed to produce full sentences on occasion, the teacher may prompt by elaborating the mand, saying, "Give me a whole sentence." If the child is still learning the meaning of this prompt, the teacher immediately provides a model ("I want paint"). Once the child is familiar with the prompt, the teacher can either wait before providing a model, or provide a lesser prompt by partially cueing the verbalization with "I. . ." or "I wan. . . ." Or the teacher can shape descriptive behavior by prompting ("What color of paint do you want?") or elaborating the mand to "I have red paint and green paint. Tell me what color you want."

The particular aspects of verbal behavior that the teacher prompts in the nontraining environment are likely to be those worked on in the training environment. The teachers arrange a setting appropriate for using trained language, and then use the mand-model process to help children generalize trained language from the training setting into appropriate use in the nontraining setting. Teachers are likely to prompt target verbalizations in the same ways and the same sequence that the verbalizations are prompted in training sessions. Then the teachers gradually generalize the target verbalizations to other forms of prompts.

Once the child responds to whatever the teacher has manded (imitates the model "I want paint," or describes "Red paint"), the teacher praises, confirms the correctness of the response, and gives the child access to the reinforcer. For instance, the teacher says, "Terrific, you said, 'I want paint,' and here it is." The teacher is careful to repeat the child's response, both in order to let the child know that she heard and understood it, and as a model of (and cue to) what she would like to hear the child say the next time the child comes to paint.

The effectiveness of the mand-model process was demonstrated using a multiple baseline design (Baer et al., 1968) across three language-delayed children. Each child received approximately 20 minutes of individual language training in a separate room each day during attendance at a laboratory preschool setting. After the mand-model process was introduced to each child in turn within the preschool classroom, not only was there accelerated generalization of trained language items into classroom use, but other aspects of language not subject to nonclassroom training improved as well. Each child's rate of verbalizing increased, as did the frequency with which each child responded to adult requests for verbalization (questions, mands, models). Also, for each child, increases in vocabulary and in complexity of utterances were seen (see Rogers-Warren and Warren, 1980). Thus, even though the mand-model process was targeted on facilitating generalization from training, it produced marked and beneficial effects on general language behavior.

The particular behavioral goal to which the mand-model process is directed (whether used naturally by a parent or systematically by a teacher) is establishing joint attention (topic selection) as a cue for verbalization. A child's communicative behavior not only has to be under stimulus control, but it must be verbal in order for the environment to most efficiently assist development. When a parent can hear the child, the parent can respond much more frequently, on many more different occasions, and in much more varied ways than a parent who can respond only when watching for nonverbal signals. Thus, parents seem to deliberately teach their children the cue of joint attention as discriminative for verbalization.

Establishing stimulus conditions discriminative for verbalization is also a first step in language training programs. Child verbalization is brought under the control of joint trainer-child attention: the trainer presents a stimulus, waits for the child to focus on it, and then asks, "What's this?" In the nontraining environment, adults do not have the option of removing stimuli that may distract the child. They try to establish joint attention by saying, for instance, "Look," or offering a child a novel material, but if the child is uncooperative or uninterested too few occasions of joint attention may occur for adults to establish it as a cue for verbalization. Hence, in addition to directing the child's attention, adults in the nontraining environment follow the child and create occasions of joint attention by adding their attention to whatever the child is attending to. When the child is painting, for instance, the teacher goes to the child, watches a moment, and then asks, "What are you doing?"

However, these conditions of joint attention are adult arranged. The adult either initiates and directs the child's attention in some way so as to establish joint focus, or follows the child and provides joint attention to whatever the child selects. Thus, the child's behavior is under the stimulus control of the adult's presence, and the child may verbalize only when an adult is attending and not otherwise. This means that, as in training sessions, an adult must lead language improvement: if the adult does not set the occasion (ask a question, display a stimulus), language use does not develop.

What is needed (and what occurs in the natural environment) is for verbalization to come under the control of stimuli other than the attending presence of an adult. When a child will respond to an event, and call an adult to attend, the child is creating a teaching moment for the adult. However, the cue for verbalization here cannot be joint attention (the condition created by the mand-model process), or the verbal behavior (mand, question) of the adult. Rather, the child must verbalize in response to a cue other than the adult's verbal behavior. The child must verbalize in order to establish joint attention. What seems to happen naturally is that parents simply wait until the child does so.

Delay   Rather than hovering over their children, instructing them, parents seem to wait for the children to initiate interaction: in-home observations have shown that, from infancy to age 3, 80% or more of all parent-child interactions are child initiated (Carew, 1980; Moss and Robson, 1968; White, 1978). Furthermore, within standardized interactions such as picture-book reading, when children reach 18–20 months of age parents begin expecting (waiting for) more mature forms of behavior. For instance, mothers begin naming what their children point to only if the children do not do so (Murphy, 1978).

The delay process may be seen as a systematization of this naturally occurring interaction. The process specifies the following sequence of steps (from Halle et al., 1979, 1981):

1. An adult is in proximity to a child, looking at the child, perhaps questioningly or expectantly. The adult may be displaying a material the child is likely to be interested in.
2. When the child looks at the adult, the adult does not speak for 15 seconds.
3. If the child does not speak, the adult models the appropriate verbalization (request for material, assistance, permission). The adult may repeat the model twice, each time waiting 15 seconds for the child to speak.

4. The adult gives the child what the child seems to want—whether or not the child has verbalized after the series of three adult models.

For example, the teacher in the painting area has set up the area as described above, with a variety of materials arranged so as to make the potentially reinforcing aspects of each activity as salient as possible. When a child approaches a particular activity (for example, the paint), the teacher focuses fully on the child, looking at the child expectantly.

If the child ignores the teacher and begins to sit down at the table, the teacher puts one hand on the chair to prevent it from being drawn away from the table, and the other hand on the child's chin. The teacher gently turns the child's face in order to make eye contact. The teacher may, as she alternates looking at the paint and then expectantly at the child, also alternate the child's face from looking at one and then the other. The teacher thus tries to make the cue (joint focus of attention) as salient as possible to the child.

If the child still does not verbalize, the teacher models the response, e.g., "Paint, please," or "I want paint." If the child still does not speak, the teacher models twice more. Then, even if the child remains silent, the teacher gives the child access to the paint. The teacher cannot withhold the reinforcer (the paint) or delay it so long that the child loses interest. The teacher must be sure that the basic chain is maintained, so that joint focus of attention remains discriminative for access to reinforcement.

However, if the child spontaneously looks at the teacher while beginning to sit down before the paint (thus indicating that joint focus of attention has been learned as a cue discriminative for access to reinforcement), but still does not speak, even after the teacher models for the third time, special procedures may be needed. The child may need one-to-one training in imitation, or, if the child can imitate, it may be necessary to fade in the delay as was done by Halle et al. (1979). Thus, the teacher would present the model, "Paint," as soon as the child made eye contact with her and the paint, and over time would gradually wait several seconds longer before presenting the model.

Also, in an intervention setting teachers would be likely to fade from the mand-model process into the delay process. Teachers would gradually wait longer, in conditions of joint attention, before presenting the mand, "Tell me what you want," and they would gradually reduce the mand both in loudness and in length. Teachers would also fade to presenting the mand from increased distances from the child. In addition, they would wait to present the mand until the child was looking at the material rather than at them. For instance, when a child came to the paint and looked at the teacher, the teacher might go to the child and stand behind the child. The teacher would then pause (delay just a moment at first), if necessary gently turning the child's face to look at the paint, before saying softly, "Tell me." Thus the teacher would fade in child verbalization relative to a stimulus other than teacher

attention, and then gradually delay the production of the mand, and/or introduce modeling (e.g., "Paint please").

The effectiveness of the delay process was demonstrated by Halle et al.
(1979) with six children in a state institution for the retarded. Delaying giving
the children their food trays at breakfast and lunch led to increases in child
requests for the trays, and such requests generalized across people and mealtimes. In another study (Halle et al., 1981), teachers in a special classroom
presented the delay process in a multiple baseline study across six developmentally delayed children. After the delay process was introduced to each
child in turn, the frequency of vocal initiations increased markedly for that
child not only within experimental contexts (for example, asking for academic
assignment sheets, for play materials, and for snack items) but also in generalization contexts (asking for pencil and paper, for permission to leave the table,
for help in zipping a coat before going to recess). Generalization to nonexperimental contexts relied heavily on the fact that the teachers spontaneously
began to use the delay process in those contexts. Instead of preempting speech
by giving children things they were seen to want or need, the teachers began
waiting for the children to ask.

The particular behavioral goal to which the delay process is directed
(whether used naturally by a parent or systematically by a teacher) is establishing environmental stimuli other than the focus of listener attention as cues
for verbalization. The language a child uses is limited if the stimuli that
control its production are exclusively listener presented. Whatever language a
child may know, the child talks only about those topics, those aspects of the
environment, that adults are interested in talking about and with regard to
which they can elicit verbalizations from the child.

But when a child initiates talk, it is the child who chooses the topic.
Even when the stimulus is another person (or even that person's talk to
someone else), the person is initially attended to as a part of the environment.
When it is the environment that cues talk from a child, the child becomes an
active learner, sensitive to the pressures to learn language in order to inquire
and inform. The child is likely to ask the names of things in order to talk about
them, and to attend to the speech of others as models. The child is likely to do
what normal children do: accompany exploration with quantities of immature
language forms (babbling, mispronunciations, ungrammatical utterances).
Thus, the child creates occasions for language-building processes to occur.
Parents can delay until the child produces more mature forms of language, or
can use incidental teaching to prompt more mature or more elaborate forms.

Incidental Teaching   White (1978) described "brief episodes precipi-
tated by the child rather than the adult" that "seem to us to be the core
teaching situations involved in good development." When the child comes to
the parent and initiates interaction, the parent first tries to identify what the
child wants (the topic).

Once the interest of the child was accurately identified, the adult had what would seem to be the ideal teaching situation—a motivated student and knowledge of exactly what it was the student was focusing on. The adult then responsed with what was needed and generally used some words at or above the child's apparent level of understanding. . . . Once the child showed a lessened interest in the interchange, he was released, allowed to then return to whatever it was he was doing or wanted to do. The entire episode rarely took more than 20 or 30 seconds, although at times there were much longer interchanges. (White, 1978, p. 156)

The incidental teaching process is a systematization of this naturally occurring interaction. The process specifies the following sequence of steps (from Hart and Risley, 1978, pp. 418-419):

1. When a child initiates, the teacher focuses full attention on the child, creating joint focus of attention on the child-chosen topic.
2. The teacher asks for language elaboration. In some cases, the teacher may model the appropriate response immediately prior to asking for elaboration.
3. If the child does not produce an appropriate elaboration, but the teacher has evidence that the child has the response in his repertoire, the teacher prompts. Otherwise, the teacher instructs the child to imitate a model of an appropriate elaboration.
4. The teacher confirms the correctness of the child's language by saying, "That's right," repeating what the child said and giving the child whatever the child initiated about.

For example, the teacher in the painting area has set out a variety of materials as described above, each attractively displayed so as to make its potentially reinforcing properties as salient as possible. When a child enters the painting area, the teacher waits for the child to initiate the interaction. When the child does so by asking to use a particular material (e.g., the paint), the teacher focuses fully on the child and the child-chosen topic. The teacher asks the child to elaborate concerning the paint. The child is very likely to be engaged in sitting down at the table as the teacher asks, for instance, "What color of paint do you want?" Then, as the child names colors, the teacher provides them, each time confirming the correctness of the child's language both by providing the corresponding color and by saying, for example, "Right, blue."

If, after the teacher has provided blue paint, the child says, "I want blue" again, the teacher prompts, pointing to the paint before the child, "I just gave you blue." If the child does not respond with a different color name, the teacher again prompts, by getting another color and saying, for example, "This isn't blue, its. . . ." If the child does not answer or answers incorrectly, the teacher models, "Red." If the child does not imitate the model, the teacher instructs the child, "Say, 'red'," and when the child does so, provides the red paint while confirming, "That's right, red. This is red paint."

When the child begins to paint, the teacher moves away, and then returns periodically to stand for a moment beside the child, watching the painting. Since joint focus of attention has been established as a cue for verbalization for this child, the child is very likely, as the teacher delays speaking, to initiate a comment. For example, the child initiates, "This is a house." The teacher responds by asking for elaboration on the child's topic (the "house," regardless of what the painting may look to be). The teacher asks, for instance, "Who lives there?" If the childs does not answer, the teacher tries once more, asking, for instance, "Is there a mother and father and children?" (The teacher tries to keep the interaction going by asking an easier question, one that calls for only a one-word, yes/no answer). If the child still does not answer, the teacher turns away to do something else; apparently her questions were not related to what the child saw the topic to be. In a few minutes, the teacher should return to present joint focus of attention and hope that the child will initiate another comment so that she can try again.

Teachers use incidental teaching throughout the day in order to ask for elaboration on any and all topics the child initiates. However, they instruct only when they can mediate a reinforcer other than their attention. (If what a child wants is solely attention, more of it is often gotten by doing the "wrong" thing than by doing the "right" thing.) Thus, the nontraining environment is deliberately arranged to provide occasions for use of trained language; for example, it includes numerous examples of materials children have been trained to label and describe. Then, when a child initiates a request for one of those materials, teachers use incidental teaching to prompt or instruct the child in the use of the language trained in the one-to-one sessions. The language learnings targeted, and the prompts used, in Step 3 of the incidental teaching process are likely to be the same as those in Step 3 of the mand-model process.

Unlike the mand-model process, however, the incidental teaching process requires that the teacher wait until the child chooses a topic, and then respond relative to the reinforcer the child names. When a child approaches or looks at a material, the material may or may not be a reinforcer for the child. If a teacher mands the name of the material, the child may respond to the instruction rather than to any reinforcing properties of the material. However, when the child initiates an interaction verbally, the child expressly identifies the topic: the child states what is, for the moment, of prepotent interest—a reinforcer. The teacher can teach relative to that child-identified reinforcer—for as long as it remains a reinforcer. Therefore, the teacher keeps the teaching moment brief, positive, and "easy" for the child. Since the nontraining environment is rich in potential reinforcers for children, a child can readily choose something other than one that requires "hard work" to obtain. However, the richness of the nontraining environment in potential reinforcers also provides teachers with innumerable opportunities for incidental teaching. If a child loses interest and chooses another topic, the teacher can try again.

The effectiveness of the incidental teaching process was demonstrated using a multiple baseline design across three language categories (Hart and Risley, 1974). Incidental teaching was targeted for each of 12 disadvantaged preschool children first on production of nouns (children were asked to name materials they wanted to use during free play), second on production of adjectives (children were asked to describe materials they wanted to use), and third on production of compound sentences (children were asked to say why they wanted to use a material). Among all 12 children, use of each language category increased when, and only when, the incidental teaching process was targeted on use of that category. In another study of incidental teaching (Hart and Risley, 1975), an examination of all the language (excluding that targeted in incidental teaching) that 11 children used during preschool free play revealed that, in the presence of incidental teaching, there occurred major increases in the frequency of general language use and in the production of different words within a 15-minute sampling period (Hart and Risley, 1980). Thus, even though incidental teaching was targeted on a particular form of language, it seemed to produce marked and beneficial effects on general language behavior.

The particular behavioral goal to which the incidental teaching process is directed (whether used naturally by a parent or systematically by teachers) is language elaboration. Teachers always ask children to say more relative to whatever topics (reinforcers) the children choose, and they supply children with appropriate language whenever children seem to need it. Like parents, teachers wait until children express an interest or a need, and teach at the moment when a child is maximally receptive. Because the teaching is brief and positive, the child not only obtains the reinforcer (the topic of need or interest), but is encouraged to express further needs or interests. Thus, the adult becomes a resource as well as a responsive audience: whenever the child becomes interested or feels a need, the state, however transitory, is likely to cue initiation to an adult. In the nontraining environment, there are innumerable stimuli of potential interest to a child, such that the cue is likely to generalize, and the child to initiate interaction concerning a variety of topics.

In normally developing children environmental stimulation seems to "naturally" cue verbal initiation (e.g., babbling or crying), to which parents differentially respond (Goldberg, 1977). When, for whatever reason, this is not the case, a child is likely to need special training not only in terms of the language appropriate to such initiation but in terms of the environmental cues for initiation. To teach the child to respond verbally (rather than nonverbally) to environmental stimuli, adults mand and model such verbalization. They use the mand-model process to establish verbalization as a cue, discriminative for access to reinforcement, then they fade themselves out. They use the delay process to remove listener behavior as a part, or property, of the cue, in order that the child's verbalization comes under the control of the environmental stimulus alone. Then, once the child's verbal behavior is cued by interest in environmental stimuli, incidental teaching can be used to promote generalized responding. When the presence of a reinforcer cues verbal behavior from the child, generalization is likely to be limited only by the variety of the child's reinforcers. As the child initiates talk relative to a variety of environmental stimuli, the child inevitably talks about more different things in more different ways, to more different people, thus creating the conditions for language learning.

Facilitating language acquisition and generalization is likely to involve using all three processes successively, or sometimes simultaneously. Within a particular classroom, for instance, different children may be responding, in different settings, in different ways to different cues. Common to all three processes is the primarily responsive role of the teacher. The teacher adapts teaching in terms of whatever appears to be momentarily a reinforcer for the individual child. When the child initiates interaction, the child specifies what the reinforcer is; until then, the teacher is likely to work at establishing child initiation through manding it relative to what appears to be a reinforcer. Although the classroom has the disadvantage that children can turn away from inept teaching, it also has the advantage that potential reinforcers can be provided, and changed, so as to assure continual variety and novelty for individual children. Thus, all three processes involve teaching relative to powerful and varied reinforcers, and teaching throughout a child's day, since satiation on a limited set of reinforcers does not occur.

Except for the differences in the stimulus variability of the setting, the processes used in teaching within the classroom are not different from those used in training sessions. Even the processes described above have been reported in use previously (for instance, Lovaas, 1966; Risley and Wolf, 1967) in conjunction with training sessions. All three "natural" processes involve use of the prompting and modeling procedures developed for one-to-one language training. All involve differential reinforcement and one-to-one, learner-adapted teaching.

Similar to the training process, the three processes described here involve specification of a series of progressive and interdependent steps directed to attaining a particular goal. It is the fact that they are processes that seems to contribute to their demonstrated effectiveness in producing major and beneficial changes in the language children produce. The important dimension seems to be the deliberate arrangement of a setting–event/consequence relationship designed to shape behavior discriminated to particular cues. The specific aspects of the environment that make up each of the processes (e.g., prompting, modeling, imitation, function) are essentially the same. These aspects of the environment—those likely to be included in almost any language-facilitating process—are considered individually in the next section.

Aspects of the Environment That Facilitate Generalization and Acquisition

A number of aspects of the environment that contribute to language acquisition have been reported in the literature. Among these are: stimulation, adult-child ratio, topic, routines, models, imitation, prompts, function, and rate. The extent of the contribution to language of any one of these aspects is as yet undetermined. It seems probable that the extent of any such contribution may be relative to the process (the setting–event/consequence relation) within which the particular aspect occurs. The aspects of the environment that may facilitate acquisition and generalization of language are discussed individually below, solely for descriptive purposes; it is assumed that the individual aspects are combined within a classroom.

Stimulation   Whether, and how often, a child uses language is likely to be related to the variety of the stimulus setting and how the child interacts with it. Tizard and Rees (1974) found that children who were retarded in expressive language at age 2 no longer showed evidence of retardation after the institution they lived in was changed so as to include (among other things) a greater variety of toys, books, and outings. Play materials can function as reinforcers as well as discriminative stimuli for language use (Hart and Risley, 1974, 1975). Nelson (1973) found a positive correlation between frequency of outings and progress in early language acquisition.

Thus, an important aspect of any environment designed to facilitate language generalization and acquisition is likely to be the kinds and variety of stimuli (both objects and people) made available for children to talk about. Also, it seems important that children get "hooked" on materials. Materials come in so many different forms, appropriate for so many different skill levels and uses, that children are unlikely to become satiated on them as reinforcers and teachers can choose those that are particularly suited to individual skill levels and interests. Through the materials they provide, teachers create the setting events for child initiation, and hence for responsive teaching.

Adult-Child Ratio   Nearly all the literature on mother-infant interaction (see Bruner, 1975, 1978; Schaffer, 1977) describes its one-to-one nature. Snow (1977) observed that mothers talk to their babies most when face to face, and thus chiefly during routine care rather than at other times. The high staff-child ratios characteristic of institutional care have been found to be correlated with language retardation (Schumaker and Sherman, 1978), although, as Tizard and Rees (1974) pointed out, high staff-child ratios are no longer a factor when staff responsibilities are arranged so that staff can get involved in one-to-one interaction with children.

The three processes described in an earlier section, as well as the training process and the mother-child teaching occasions described by, for instance, Bruner (1975, 1978) and Moerk (1972), all involve one-to-one adult-child interactions. This suggests that an environment arranged to promote generalization and acquisition should emphasize free activity periods, when teachers can move from child to child, engaging in numerous brief one-to-one teaching interactions. In such one-to-one interactions, teachers can focus on adapting their behavior to the individual skills and responses of a single child and thus enhance the effectiveness of the teaching moment.

Topic   White (1978) described the most effective mothers as those who adapt their teaching to whatever the child is most interested in at the moment. As a child masters one form of a game such as Peek-a-Boo, for instance, the child becomes easily distracted; the "mother had either to adapt her game to hold him, or lose him altogether" (Ratner and Bruner, 1978, p. 396). "It is the generally accepting mother who appears to be most facilitative" of progress in early language acquisition, although "differential nonacceptance is not detrimental unless it is combined with a general reluctance to accept the child's propositions [topics] and a determination to impose one's own system upon him" (Nelson, 1973, pp. 113–114).

The responsiveness of teachers is likely to be an important factor in language generalization and acquisition. Teachers (or staff) who accept whatever form of language a child produces and endeavor to respond to it in such a way as to increase the probability that its appropriate aspects will reoccur are likely to be more effective than those who do not "hear" such approximations. As in training sessions, teachers teach in terms of what the child is focused on at the moment. Their role is not to attempt to change the topic, once the child has chosen it, but to determine through environmental arrangements what topics the child will choose.

Routines   Bruner (1975) and Ratner and Bruner (1978) noted the relevance to language acquisition of the standardized forms of joint action and joint attention deliberately created by mothers for their infants. These turn-taking routines develop into complex games that increasingly often are initiated by the child (e.g., the picture-book reading routine described by Bruner, 1978). As Bruner (1975) noted, mothers from the beginning accompany action with language, especially at the beginnings and ends of turns. Language behavior thus becomes just another component of learned routines, just another behavior to increase in complexity as the child masters each successive form of the game.

The systematic series of steps specified in a teaching (or training) process makes that process a routine. For instance, when teachers consistently ask (or wait) for a child to speak before contacting a reinforcer, asking becomes as much a part of the routine for getting things as does reaching. Thus in arranging an environment to facilitate generalization and acquisition, teachers are likely to examine closely the schedule of activities, and whenever possible to specify a definite sequence of behaviors, such as for obtaining snacks, going to recess, beginning a new activity, or cleaning up an old one. They may deliberately teach children such routines, both in terms of motor behaviors and in terms of the accompanying language behaviors (for example, see Hart, 1981). Verbalization may thus become a component within a behavioral chain, such that a setting event (e.g., leaving) cues the onset of a chain, after which each member cues that next.

Models   There is considerable literature suggesting the importance to early language acquisition of the speech that children hear modeled by adults. For instance, Moerk (1980) found, in a reanalysis of Brown's (1973) data, that the children studied were likely to produce earlier those forms of adult language that they heard most frequently. Parents adapt their speech to children in ways likely to facilitate language learning: they simplify constructions, stress informational words, and repeat phrases, and they extend and expand child utterances in restatements that model for the children more mature constructions (see Schumaker and Sherman, 1978, for a review of this literature).

This literature suggests the importance of teachers adapting the language they use to the skill level of individual children, and responding in ways that use the children's verbalizations as the basis for modeling more mature forms of language. However, it is likely to be not so much what the teachers do—the forms of language they model—as the interactional context in which the adults' models occur that facilitates children's progress in language learning (Ellis and Wells, 1980). Teachers cannot assume that children will learn language just from hearing other people talk, regardless of how simplified that talk may be. Children are much more likely to learn the language they hear spoken *to them*, and hence adapted to the immediate communicative context (e.g., in the form of feedback relative to the child's topic, or as a directive that facilitates access to something the child wants).

Imitation   There is ample experimental evidence that language production improves when imitation is reinforced (see Schumaker and Sherman, 1978, for review). The frequency with which imitation occurs during normal language acquisition depends on what is defined as an imitation (Snow, 1981), but certainly the occurrence of imitation pervades parent-child teaching interactions (see, for instance, Bruner, 1978; Moerk, 1972). Parents not only cue child imitations, but they imitate too, and the parent's imitation of the child appears to function as a cue for the child to imitate the parent (Folger and Chapman, 1978).

Child imitation of adult models is an important aspect of environmental intervention. Teachers are likely to ask for imitation of deliberately presented models of improved pronunciation, of new labels, and of more complex constructions. They are likely to differentially reinforce successive approximations to more and more accuracy in imitation. Also they are likely to imitate the children's language, both as a cue to the children to imitate them and as confirming feedback concerning the correctness and comprehensibility of the children's speech. Their goal is to reach that "point where the imitations are indistinguishable from an appropriate conversational reply which incorporates words from the partner's previous utterance simply because of topic continuance" (Snow, 1981, p. 211).

Prompts   Prompting, like imitation, is both central to language training and pervasive in early language acquisition. Parents appear to naturally use the levels of prompts described in Hart and Risley (1975): they use *wh*-questions ("What's . . ."), direct instruction ("Say, . . ."), and partial prompts to cue a child to complete a word or an utterance (see, for instance, Moerk, 1972; Schachter, 1979). Also, they emphasize a word in speaking (Bruner, 1978) so as to prompt the child to imitate (Risley and Reynolds, 1970).

In arranging an environment to promote generalization and acquisition, a major focus is likely to be on prompting, because everything in the environment is in fact a potential prompt. Available materials, interesting activities, responsive adults, standardized routines, all serve as cues to action. The prompt value of these aspects of the environment is what teachers can deliberately plan and arrange. Such planning enables them to devote their time to adapting their behavior and prompting relative to the immediate level of skill displayed by individual children. Thus, as in training sessions, the current child response prompts the teacher; the teacher then focuses on the child's topic, and prompts in turn. An effective prompt is one that enables the child to produce an even slightly more advanced skill level; teachers learn what are effective prompts in variable, nontraining, environments by continually trying to get elaborated behavior from children, and by keeping in their repertoire their successes.

Function   The function of language use is its effect on the environment (Hart, 1981; Streeck, 1980). Intentions are learned functions: utterances can thus be intended by a speaker to have predictable effects on a listener. Children learn what language is (i.e., to construct utterances with particular intentions) because of what they have learned that language can do (the effects it has on listeners) (Halliday, 1977). Thus, the language children use is likely to be as varied (or as restricted) as are their communicative needs (the effects they want or need to produce) (Schlesinger, 1974). Function may thus be seen as reinforcement, as the consequences of language use. In natural environments, however, the consequences of language use are considerably more diverse than social approval and/or food. Materials and help are likely to be reinforcers seldom subject to satiation; stimulus change (just making something happen) may be another. For normal language users, however, the most important effect is likely to be the fact that interaction continues (Streeck, 1980). A listener's verbal response serves as a discriminative stimulus for a speaker's next verbalization, such that the class 'verbal response' may acquire reinforcing properties independent of particular utterance content. The only aspect of language use that seems to be deliberately reinforced is "truth value" (Brown and Hanlon, 1970): that is, whether or not a particular utterance is appropriately matched to the context of its use (Hart, 1981). If listeners understand, they respond, and so set the occasion for further talk.

The most important aspect of environmental intervention is thus likely to be its arrangement of consequences for language use. The environment is likely to include as much variety as possible in the effects language use can have, in terms of available materials, activities, and listener responses. Then the teachers can arrange and plan which child behaviors will produce those effects, and how to prompt and shape those behaviors. Since adults can mediate nearly all available environmental effects, they can choose which child behavior, in which individual case and approximation, will be functional in producing a given environmental effect.

Rate   Nelson (1973) found that, at age $2\frac{1}{2}$, talking a lot was positively correlated with all aspects of progress in acquiring language. Among preschool and kindergarten children, talkativeness was correlated with higher performance scores on tests of receptive syntax (Landon and Sommers, 1979). Hart and Risley (1980) found that the more often children talked during preschool free play the more different words they used per 15 minutes; also, the children who talked the most had the largest recorded vocabularies. In home observations, Schachter (1979) found that in linguistically advanced groups, as compared to less advanced groups, both children and parents talked more often.

Apparently, practice can contribute to language improvement. Thus, an important target for intervention in the natural environment is likely to be rate of language use. Teachers are likely to encourage children to talk all the time. They are likely to mand verbalization, delay until children speak, and ask for more talk whenever a child initiates it. Very importantly, teachers are likely to accept every communicative effort a child makes, and use it as an occasion to prompt or shape a more advanced, or more contextually appropriate, topography. The most relevant measure of teacher success is likely to be how much child talk is going on in the classroom because rate is fundamental to generalization. The more children use language, the more they can learn about what it can do.

SUMMARY AND CONCLUSIONS

Many aspects of the natural environment have been discussed that contribute to language generalization and acquisition. These include aspects of the context that cue and support language: the kinds and variety of materials, activities, and events that evoke talk, the availability and responsiveness of hearers, the extent to which the child is interested in the topic for talk, and the existence of routine frameworks for chains of joint action and joint attention. The behaviors of speaker and hearer constitute other aspects likely to facilitate generalization and acquisition: adult models and prompts, and both adult and child imitation. The function (consequence) of language use is likely to be an aspect essential to increasing the rate of language use, and hence, of generalization to an increased variety of objects, people, and situations.

These aspects of the environment are likely to be maximally effective when they are combined in a systematic series of progressive and interdependent actions directed to a particular goal. That is, although each aspect may have its singular influence on language acquisition, it is when aspects are combined within a process that major improvements and generalization are seen. Each of the three processes described above included all of the environmental aspects. In all three processes, teaching took place in a setting rich in stimuli for children to contact. All three required momentary, one-to-one adult-child interaction, and all three focused on the topic the child had chosen as the momentarily prepotent reinforcer. All three processes required teachers to model, prompt, and ask for imitation if necessary, as well as to confirm and give feedback by repeating all or part of a child's utterance. All three processes involved a systematic series of steps specified for teachers, so that a routine, relative to certain cues, could be established. In all three processes, the child's language functioned to gain access to material as well as social reinforcers, and, most importantly, to that reinforcer specified in some way by the child when choosing the topic. Also, all three processes led to increased rates of language use, and to generalization.

The three processes differ primarily in aspects of teacher behavior. This is because they are directed to different ends: each targets a different facet of language use. The mand-model process targets teaching children to verbalize choice of topic. A necessary step in terms of progress in language acquisition is that, in appropriate conditions (e.g., when selecting conversational topics), a child substitutes verbal for nonverbal communication. Until the child does so, the environment cannot shape language as a mode of communication. Therefore, the teacher initiates interaction with the child and mands verbalization. However, for the child with language problems, one who needs specific and systematic teaching in verbalizing topic, the behavior may remain under the stimulus control of the adult's manding behavior.

The delay process is directed to bringing verbalization of topic under the control of environmental stimuli other than an adult's behavior. The adult essentially mands verbalization by delaying the onset of adult behavior (the prompt, mand and/or model), so that the child's verbalizations gradually come more and more under the control of nonsocial aspects of the context.

For language acquisition to progress, it is essential that nonsocial stimuli such as materials and activities evoke verbal behavior: that a child want to talk not just to people, but about *things*. The more things in the environment that the child is interested in talking about, the greater is the pressure to acquire language as a means of communicating perceived properties, actions and relationships.

The incidental teaching process is directed to helping children elaborate language as a means of communicating perceived properties, actions, and relationships. Teachers ask children to say more about whatever topics the children choose to initiate talk about, calling upon the children to draw upon, and perhaps extend, their current repertoires or, if need be, supplying children with appropriate words or expressions. However, the central aspect of incidental teaching is the scheduled reinforcement of rate of initiating relative to nonsocial environmental stimuli. When children have high rates of responding with language to the variable stimulus aspects of the natural environment, this is generalization.

Central to all three processes are 1) their focus on the topic the child chooses, and 2) the one-to-one nature of the interaction. Thus the three processes, like the training process, are based on those conditions most likely to be effective for changing behavior. Teaching occurs on a one-to-one basis, such that the teacher's behavior can be adapted, from moment to moment, to the appropriateness of the child's immediate response. Also, teaching occurs at times when the teacher can mediate a powerful reinforcer. When the child choses the topic, in momentary preference to everything else in the environment, that topic constitutes (for the moment) a reinforcer. The effectiveness of teaching may even be enhanced by the fact of joint attention to the child-chosen reinforcer.

Also, the three processes appear to be ones that occur within the natural environments of children acquiring their first language. Mothers expend considerable effort to get infants to attend to particular aspects of the environment, and initiate interactions about them (Bruner, 1978). Once children are actively exploring the environment, however, mothers tend to wait for the child to initiate interactions. Observations made in children's homes have shown that the children initiate the overwhelming majority of the interactions, to which adults respond with brief, one-to-one attention (Carew, 1980). Differences in progress in language acquisition have been related to how often parents respond to child initiations (Schachter, 1979), and to how well (or if) the parents use the child-initiated topic for a brief moment of teaching (White, 1978).

It is virtually certain that many more than just the three processes described in this chapter occur in the natural environment, because these three processes barely touch on the full complexity of the language learner's task. Further efforts to develop techniques for facilitating the acquisition and generalization of language among children with language problems may thus find profitable the closer examination of the mother-child interaction literature, and the extraction from it, for experimental testing, of other possible processes through which at various stages, ages, or skill levels the natural environment appears to provide assistance to language learners. The failure to learn normal language may be due not so much to a lack of capacity within the child as to a lack of language-assisting processes within the environment.

ACKNOWLEDGMENTS

Much is owed to conversations with Dr. Ann Rogers-Warren, Dr. Steven Warren, Dr. James Halle, and Dr. Todd Risley.

REFERENCES

Baer, D. M. 1970. An age-irrelevant concept of development. Merrill-Palmer Q. 16:238–245.

Baer, D. M., Wolf, M. M., and Risley, T. R. 1968. Some current dimensions of applied behavior analysis. J. Appl. Behav. Anal. 1:91–97.

Bricker, W. A., and Bricker, D. D. 1974. An early language training strategy. In R. L. Schiefelbusch and L. L. Lloyd (eds.), Language Perspectives—Acquisition, Retardation, and Intervention. University Park Press, Baltimore.

Brown, R. 1973. A First Language: The Early Stages. Harvard University Press, Cambridge, MA.

Brown, R., and Hanlon, C. 1970. Derivational complexity and order of acquisition in child speech. In J. R. Hayes (ed.), Cognition and the Development of Language. Wiley, New York.

Bruner, J. S. 1975. The ontogenesis of speech acts. J. Child Lang. 2:1–19.

Bruner, J. 1978. Prelinguistic prerequisites of speech. In R. N. Campbell and P. T. Smith (eds.), Recent Advances in the Psychology of Language: Language Development and Mother-Child Interaction. Plenum, New York.

Carew, J. V. 1980. Experience and the development of intelligence in young children at home and in day care. Monogr. Soc. Res. Child Dev. 45(6–7).

Cross, T. 1978. Mothers' speech and its association with rate of linguistic development in young children. In N. Waterson and C. Snow (eds.), The Development of Communication. Wiley, New York.

Ellis, R., and Wells, G. 1980. Enabling factors in adult-child discourse. First Lang. 1:46–62.

Folger, J. P., and Chapman, R. S. 1978. A pragmatic analysis of spontaneous imitations. J. Child Lang. 5:25–38.

Goldberg, S. 1977. Social competence in infancy: A model of parent-infant interaction. Merrill-Palmer Q. 23:163–177.

Guess, D., and Baer, D. M. 1973. Some experimental analyses of linguistic development in institutionalized retarded children. *In* B. B. Lahey (ed.), The Modification of Language Behavior. Charles C. Thomas, Springfield, IL.

Guess, D., Sailor, W., and Baer, D. M. 1978. Children with limited language. In R. L. Schiefelbusch (ed.), Language Intervention Strategies. University Park Press, Baltimore.

Halle, J. W., Baer, D. M., and Spradlin, J. E. 1981. Teacher's generalized use of delay as a stimulus control procedure to increase language use in handicapped children. J. Appl. Behav. Anal. 14:389–409.

Halle, J. W., Marshall, A. M., and Spradlin, J. E. 1979. Time delay: A technique to increase language use and facilitate generalization in retarded children. J. Appl. Behav. Anal. 12:431–439.

Halliday, M. A. K. 1975. Learning How to Mean. Elsevier, New York.

Halliday, M. A. K. 1977. Explorations in the Functions of Language. Elsevier, New York.

Hart, B. 1981. Pragmatics: How language is used. Anal. Intervention Dev. Disabil. 1:299–313.

Hart, B., and Risley, T. R. 1974. Using preschool materials to modify the language of disadvantaged children. J. Appl. Behav. Anal. 7:243–256.

Hart, B., and Risley, T. R. 1975. Incidental teaching of language in the preschool. J. Appl. Behav. Anal. 8:411–420.

Hart, B., and Risley, T. R. 1978. Promoting productive language through incidental teaching. Educ. Urban Soc. 10:407–429.

Hart, B., and Risley, T. R. 1980. *In vivo* language intervention: Unanticipated general effects. J. Appl. Behav. Anal. 12:407–432.

Landon, S. J., and Sommers, R. K. 1979. Talkativeness and children's linguistic abilities. Lang. Speech 22:269–275.

Lovaas, O. I. 1966. A program for the establishment of speech in psychotic children. *In* J. K. Wing (ed.), Childhood Autism. Pergamon, Oxford.

Moerk, E. L. 1972. Principles of interaction in language learning. Merrill-Palmer Q. 18:229–257.

Moerk, E. L. 1980. Relationships between parental input frequencies and children's language acquisition: A reanalysis of Brown's data. J. Child Lang. 7:105–118.

Moss, H. A., and Robson, K. S. 1968. The role of protest behavior in the development of mother-infant attachment. Paper presented to the American Psychological Association, September, San Francisco.

Murphy, C. M. 1978. Pointing in the context of a shared activity. Child Dev. 49:371–380.

Nelson, K. 1973. Structure and strategy in learning to talk. Monog. Soc. Res. Child Dev. 38(1–2).

Random House Dictionary of the English Language. 1966. Random House, New York.

Ratner, N., and Bruner, J. 1978. Games, social exchange and the acquisition of language. J. Child Lang. 5:391–401.

Risley, T. R., and Reynolds, N. J. 1970. Emphasis as a prompt for verbal imitation. J. Appl. Behav. Anal. 3:185–190.

Risley, T. R., and Wolf, M. M. 1967. Establishing functional speech in echolalic children. Behav. Res. Ther. 5:74–88.

Rogers-Warren, A., and Warren, S. F. 1980. Mands for verbalization: Facilitating the display of newly trained language in children. Behav. Modification 4:361–382.

Schachter, F. F. 1979. Everyday Mother Talk to Toddlers. Academic, New York.

Schaffer, H. R. (ed.). 1977. Studies in Mother-Infant Interaction. Academic, New York.

Schlesinger, I. M. 1974. Relational concepts underlying language. In R. L. Schiefelbusch and L. L. Lloyd (eds.), Language Perspectives—Acquisition, Retardation, and Intervention. University Park Press, Baltimore.

Schumaker, J. B. and Sherman, J. A. 1978. Parent as intervention agent. In R. L. Schiefelbusch (ed.), Language Intervention Strategies. University Park Press, Baltimore.

Snow, C. E. 1977. The development of conversation between mothers and babies. J. Child Lang. 4:1–22.

Snow, C. E. 1981. The uses of imitation. J. Child Lang. 8:205–212.

Streeck, J. 1980. Speech acts in interaction: A critique of Searle. Discourse Processes 3:133–154.

Tizard, B., and Rees J. 1974. A comparison of the effects of adoption, restoration to the natural mother, and continued institutionalization on the cognitive development of four-year-old children. Child Dev. 45:92–99.

White, B. L. 1978. Experience and Environment, Vol. 2. Prentice-Hall, Englewood Cliffs, N.J.

Language through Conversation

A Model for Intervention With Language-Delayed Persons

James D. MacDonald

Nisonger Center
The Ohio State University
Columbus

THEORETICAL, EXPERIMENTAL, AND CLINICAL
  BASES   93
    Communication Theory   93
    Ecological Theory of Child Development   94
    Pragmatics   95
    Functional Analysis of Behavior   96
    General Systems Theory   96
    Summary   97

TREATMENT TARGETS AND TECHNIQUES   97
    Conversation: The First Treatment Target   98
    The Child: The Second Treatment Target   102
    Significant Others: The Third Treatment Target   108

SUMMARY OF DEVELOPMENT PROGRESSION OF
  THE MODEL   115

OVERVIEW   116

REFERENCES   119

For 10 years now, my students and I have struggled with the task of bridging the communication gap between ourselves and handicapped children.[1] Many of these children had some expressive language, but they seemed not to know what to do with it. As we came to know them, we found that these children nearly always knew much more than they communicated. Traditional structural approaches to language severely underestimated their cognitive and social competencies. Until we learned to assess their communication as well as language, we continued to underestimate their knowledge. Our clinical experiences, literature searches, and research program (Almerico and Mac-Donald, 1979; Lombardino, 1978; Lombardino et al., 1981; MacDonald and Blott, 1974; MacDonald and Horstmeier, 1978; MacDonald et al., 1974; Nichols, 1974; Owens, 1979) have led us to the conclusion that if we are to understand and increase children's social, cognitive, and linguistic competencies we must find ways to help them establish conversational systems within which their competencies can be revealed and developed.

In 1971, the language program at the Nisonger Center[2] began to develop assessment and training procedures in response to two basic questions: what kinds of expressive language should be taught first, and how should that teaching take place? We developed an intervention strategy that incorporated a semantic approach to grammar (Brown, 1973; MacDonald, 1978; Schlesinger, 1971) rather than structural (syntax) or conceptual (e.g., color, shape, and size) approaches. The semantic approach offered targets that occurred naturally in the child's sensorimotor and social world. The Environmental Language Intervention (ELI) Program developed from this semantic base and included procedures to teach prelinguistic skills needed for development of the child's early meanings (MacDonald and Horstmeier, 1978).

Our solution to the problem of "how to teach" language included analyses of ways to facilitate generalization to natural settings. When we taught parents skills in language programming, their children showed more generalized gains than did similar children who received therapy in the classroom (MacDonald, 1978; MacDonald et al., 1974; Mechlenberg, 1975; Nichols, 1974). Consequently, Horstmeier and I designed a series of parent-assisted programs to teach initial sentences and prelinguistic skills (Horstmeier and MacDonald, 1978).

During the years that we field tested the language model (ELI) in classrooms and homes, we found that language training effects generalized in

---

[1]Throughout this chapter, "child" refers to any individual whose language and communication performance is at developmental levels between birth and generalized conversational use of sentences. Thus, the model applied to all individuals within this range regardless of age.

[2]The Nisonger Center is one of several university-affiliated programs for mental retardation and developmental disabilities. The programs are funded by the Maternal and Child Health Service of the U.S. Office of Education. Development of the present language intervention model was also funded by a research grant from the Office of Special Education.

some children, but not in others. The discrepancy seemed related to several factors. First, children who showed the most gains were those who had a primary conversational system with their significant others (SOs; parents, teachers, and other adults who play a major role in the child's day-to-day life). Children who lacked a reciprocal turn-taking relationship with others had fewer generalization opportunities in which they would naturally practice their skills.

We observed that didactic, caregiving, and noncontingent parallel patterns often characterized the relationships between handicapped children and their parents and teachers. A behavioral profile of parents and teachers interacting with handicapped children emerged:

They often talk in long sentences, far above the range of their child's communicative competence.

They frequently attempt to communicate without gaining the child's attention.

They communicate "rehetorically," without waiting for or cueing a child's response.

They accommodate to the child's idiosyncratic communication instead of shaping more conventional performance.

Primarily, they have short, "dead end" contacts with the child rather than balanced turn-taking interactions.

They assume that language professionals are in a better position than they are to improve their child's communication.

These behavioral patterns place the child in a noncontingent, receiving role, rather than in the active participant role needed for language learning (Bruner, 1978a; Hunt, 1961). Consequently, we decided that the cornerstone to a new approach would have to be the conversation, that is, the reciprocal and contingent turn-taking relationship that nearly all mothers have with their infants (Lewis and Rosenblum, 1974). As we observed the minimal feedback that adults got from handicapped children, we suspected that these children, in effect, "trained" adults to interact in didactic and caregiving ways.

A second major influence in the model's development was our observation that nearly all handicapped children have an idiosyncratic communication system that is understood by their SOs but not by strangers. In utilizing our earlier programs, we found that we were competing with children's idiosyncratic systems: their existing nonlinguistic and nonvocal communication strategies often work very well. Family and classmates learned to accommodate to these special ways of sending messages. Thus, idiosyncratic communication may be reinforced much more effectively than new skills taught by professionals. So although we were teaching conventional language a few times a week, the child's idiosyncratic communication system was being maintained by regularly occurring, natural reinforcement. Consequently, we began to develop an approach that recognized all behaviors as potentially communicative and that utilized the contingent responsiveness of SOs as part of the treatment.

We found that it was relatively easy to train parents and teachers to carry out didactic lessons, but much more difficult to teach them the incidental training strategies necessary to promote children's generalization. Reviews of pragmatics and parent-child interaction principles resulted in considerable discomfort over the didactic teaching strategies we observed in homes and classrooms. Emerging research and theory argued that much language learning occurred during spontaneous, child-oriented, joint activity routines (Bruner, 1977; Snow, 1972). However, the profession of speech pathology had developed a model of therapy that used a one-to-one brief encounter with one client isolated from his natural environment. That model of therapy may be appropriate for individuals who already have the conversational skills that facilitate generalized use of what is learned in therapy. However, many handicapped children do not have a well-habituated conversational system, and a therapy model that teaches conversational skills in naturalistic interactions was needed.

The remainder of this chapter is devoted to a discussion of the intervention model we are proposing. First, five convergent theoretical perspectives inherent in the model are discussed. These perspectives provide support for the basic premises of the model and implicitly suggest some of our training approaches and techniques. Second, our treatment targets and fundamental treatment techniques are presented in detail. In this section actual procedures are discussed and their relationships to the overall model clarified. The premises and details of the model are presented as concisely as possible. The complete curriculum and further details relevant to assessment, sequence, content, and structure of training modules are available upon request from the author.

THEORETICAL, EXPERIMENTAL, AND CLINICAL BASES

As our overriding goal in the training program became *language through conversation,* we searched for theoretical concepts and research findings that would provide a theoretical bridge to link children's knowledge of language to their uses of it in conversation. Five theoretical approaches were eventually integrated into the content and design of the current model.

Communication Theory

A group of scholars and clinicians (Bateson and Jackson, 1964; Bateson, et al., 1966; Haley, 1962, 1964; Watzlawick et al., 1967) have studied communication disorders in adults for over 30 years. Their theory of communication offers valuable directions for work with children. They offer three theoretical principles:

1. Every behavior, regardless of its form or intention, can communicate; thus any behavior can send a message.
2. Communication is a cybernetic phenomenon, thus communication functions as a feedback loop between members of a dyad who reciprocally affect each other.
3. Expectancy in the form of a self-fulfilling prophecy plays a vital role in determining the way others communicate.

The first principle, *every behavior can communicate,* was the basis for selecting units for assessment and training. Handicapped children frequently send effective messages with primitive signals and behaviors that are idiosyncratic to them. These behaviors are understood by significant others, but may not communicate a message to strangers. When communication is defined in terms of its effect on others, rather than in terms of predetermined structural units, these idiosyncratic communications become a starting point for intervention.

The second principle, *communication is a function of dyadic feedback,* suggested that both children and their SOs should be active clients in the remediation effort. Every child-SO dyad represents a reciprocal feedback loop in which the behavior of each person affects and is affected by the behavior of the other person. Generalized changes in the child's repertoire may not result from training unless his significant others alter their responses to his idiosyncratic behaviors and support newly learned communciation skills.

The third communication principle is the *self-fulfilling prophecy* (Bateson et al., 1966). Parents of handicapped children often act as though they do not expect their child to communicate. Often these parents offer a few cues and leave insufficient time for the child to communicate. If a parent treats the child as noncommunicative the child may get the message and not communicate. A handicapped child's SOs must develop a consistent dyadic relationship that shows acceptance and expectation of the child's communication attempts. Knowledge of the child's initial idiosyncratic communication system is essential if the SO is to shape the child toward utilizing more conventional forms.

Ecological Theory of Child Development

Ecological views of child development and language acquisition (Ainsworth, 1974; Blurton-Jones, 1972; Bronfenbrenner, 1979; Bruner, 1974, 1975, 1978a; Lewis and Rosenblum, 1974; Mahoney, 1975) conclude that children develop language in tandem with their SOs. The dyad's joint activities provide the essential context and contingencies for learning.

Reciprocity of behavior in dyads is widely accepted in theory, but is often disregarded in research and clinical practice. Ecological theory provides two operational principles for therapy. First, clinical treatment must extend beyond the child to include his significant others. Second, if the child develops as a function of his natural learning contexts, then joint activity routines (Bruner, 1975) in conversational contexts are necessary for language learning to occur. An ecological approach requires establishing or ameliorating the conversational context between the child and the SO from which language naturally emerges (Lewis and Lee-Painter, 1974; Snow and Ferguson, 1978).

The work of Ainsworth (1974), Blurton-Jones (1972), and Brazelton et al. (1974), demonstrates the active role the mother has in the normal child's development of social skills, including language. Ainsworth concluded that four components of a mother's sensitivity relate to the child's development of conversational skills: 1) her awareness of the signals, 2) her interpretation of them, 3) an appropriate response to them, and 4) a prompt response to them. The current treatment model gives the SO a central role in initial communicative training as a means of establishing an appropriate ecological context for learning.

Pragmatics

Recent changes in views of language acquisition have resulted in a transition from a focus on structure (Braine, 1976; Chomsky, 1959) to focus on the communicative uses of language in real-life environments (Bates, 1976; Bloom and Lahey, 1978; Brown, 1978; Bruner, 1975; Moerk, 1972; Nelson, 1980; Snow and Ferguson, 1978). Pragmatics emphasizes several characteristics of the language development process that may be translated into working principles for an intervention model. First, language is purposive; it develops from social, instrumental, and personal intentions (Bruner, 1978c; Dore, 1975; Halliday, 1975). Establishing the *function* of the communicative act is as necessary to language development as the acquisition of conventional form (syntax) and content (semantics). This implies that assessment and training must focus not on what language or meanings the child *has* but what he *does* with them.

Second, linguistic content emerges from prelinguistic communicative uses. Effective intervention should utilize nonlinguistic communication as a bridge to more conventional communication. If a language-delayed child's training involves only linguistic units, he may continue to prefer to use the nonlinguistic communication forms that function for him. Linking existing nonlinguistic forms with new linguistic forms may facilitate the use of new forms.

Third, language emerges from early parent-child joint activities. Conversation between parent and child begins in infancy and is the source of the pragmatic (use) and semantic (content) aspects of language as well as the model for the forms (syntax) that are shaped into conventional communication. Conversations include reciprocal feedback, which is posited to be the mechanism responsible for the development of communicative behavior (Watzlawick et al., 1967). Thus, conversation provides a natural forum in which appropriate form, content, and use can be programmed.

Fourth, normal language develops out of necessity in functional contexts. It is not taught didactically as academic units to be stored in a memory. Natural sensorimotor and social contingencies should be more successful in building a generalized language system than rote academic drills isolated from context.

Finally, language development requires that SOs respond to the child's behaviors noncontingently until a communicative repertoire is established, and then begin to require more conventional performance ("up the ante," Bruner, 1978a; or shaping, Skinner, 1953) as the child develops.

Functional Analysis of Behavior

In his response to Chomsky's (1959) critique of Skinner's (1957) *Verbal Behavior,* MacCorquodale (1971) included a reminder that provides a guideline for applying behavioral principles to natural language development: simple, direct S-R (stimulus-response) relations exist only in the starkest, nongeneralizable events. Language responses typically have multiple causes. Communication is a function of many personal contingencies and the situational context. Thus, intervention requires simultaneous and *incidental* application of differential reinforcement, shaping, chaining, and various forms of stimulus control.

Parents and teachers must learn to use behavioral contingencies. They must also learn that a didactic approach is not necessary for either contingency management or language development. Once SOs learn the reciprocal functional relations within their relationship with the child, they can deliberately provide strong differential cues and reinforcers for conversational behavior.

General Systems Theory

Interactive events such as communication have been described by systems theory as existing within a feedback system in which events have reciprocal and cumulative effects on each other, and, thus, cannot be adequately explained in isolation (Von Bertalanffy, 1950; Weinberg, 1975). Analysis of interactive events is facilitated by mapping the components of the system that are logically critical to the prediction and development of these events. These components are seen as repeating, occurring within a feedback loop in which they reciprocally and developmentally affect one another. Conversation is a system comprised of critical elements that can be diagnostically mapped in an educationally prescriptive format. The communication ecosystem consists of child communication components, conversation variables, and SO person strategies. Teaching any language component (e.g., form, content, or use) results in changes in others (e.g., use, mode, conversation).

Summary

These five theoretical approaches contributing to the model are consistent with the general systems principles that interactive events (such as language and communication) develop from reciprocal and cumulative effects on each other within a feedback system. Thus, if given the problem of explaining how language develops, each approach would pose its solution by describing a process that looks very much like the *conversation*.

Communication theory and operant theory define units by their effects, rather than by their structure or content. Both approaches define communication in terms of resulting behaviors, not in terms of form of the speaker's initiation (e.g., phoneme, word, sentence, or semantic rule). The view that the effect is more important than the form of the behavior defines the tandem roles of two persons in communication development.

In sum, communication theory suggests that intervention include *any* behaviors with potential communicative effect, not just symbolic language. Ecological theory views the members of the dyad (e.g., parent-child) as partners; thus both are clients in intervention. Pragmatic theory suggests establishing joint activity or conversation as the critical training process and communicative use as the goal of training. Operant theory provides a system for determining and altering contingencies between the child and the SO. Systems theory encourages an interactive mapping of the components of conversation and suggests that interaction mode, content, and use variables influence each other. These variables function within every discrete communicative act, as well as in the development of the broader process of language.

TREATMENT TARGETS AND TECHNIQUES

Conversation, child communication, and SO teaching strategies form the basis of the three-component training model described here. The first component, conversational process, ties child communication events to SO teaching strategies. Each component is discussed below in terms of treatment targets, teaching techniques, and its relationship to the other components.

Conversation: The First Treatment Target

Conversation is the locus, process, and goal of language intervention. Conversation is a joint activity in which the child and SO exchange messages in a sequence of turns, with or without words. Joint activity can be a conversation without words. For example, consider a father and son playing ball, each taking a turn. Sometimes turns include gestures, facial expressions, and a range of body movements that send a variety of messages such as "Go," "Your turn," "Mine," "Go get it," and "Ready?" Later, when the child is more linguistically skilled, a conversation with words would occur in the same father-son dyad. The later conversation might include verbal counterparts of the earlier nonverbal messages.

In the current model, behaviors and interactive processes that serve input, feedback, and monitoring functions for the child and SO are taught. First, interactive events such as turn-taking and chaining, which are required for progressive conversations, are established utilizing the child's and SO's current repertoires. After SOs establish some form of conversational exchange with the child more sophisticated communication forms are taught. The conversational interchange provides the necessary intentional (social contact reasons) and relational (turn-taking and chaining) structure in which child language and SO strategies are fostered. In the conversational taxonomy, response classes, rather than specific forms, are emphasized.

In developing the intervention model, operational definitions of specific responses and the structure of conversation were developed in order to reliably and validly observe them. Definitions were flexible enough to account for "nonvocal conversations." Studies of communication during joint action routines between mothers and infants provide some basis for a taxonomy of conversational variables (Bruner, 1977; Snow and Ferguson, 1978; Stern, 1974). In addition, our work describing parent and teacher contexts identified a progression of conversational components to use in training.

The conversational structure included social recognition events, purposive social contacts, joint activities, turn-taking, chains, initiations, responses, topics initiations, shifts, closes, and off-topic behavior. All behaviors can be verbal or nonverbal. In fact, a persistent nonlinguistic conversation system may be necessary before generalized productive language will emerge.

Social Recognition   The first set of conversation targets are behaviors that recruit social recognition. Few severely handicapped children seem to notice what others do. However, these children often later display evidence of having been very socially attentive. It is essential to increase the child's signaling of social awareness and the SO's notice of the child's signal. Once a SO notices the child signaling to her, she can use it as an opportunity for conversation. For example, if a mother sees her child watching her go to the door, she can try to make it a conversation by extending her arms or saying "Wanna come?" then responding to any response the child makes.

Social Contact Purpose   There are many natural opportunities for conversation during child-SO interactions. Social contact purposes are beginning points for conversations. They are reasons for or intentions that underly the initiation of an interaction episode. Interaction episodes may be identified by asking: "What is the communicative act intended to do?" (Dore, 1975; Searle, 1969). A social contact purpose is the pragmatic *intent* of the initiation of an interaction with another (e.g., getting help, turn-taking, giving information, playing). By observing naturally occurring social contact purposes in a dyad's interactions it is possible to assess and develop a range of language and communication learning situations. Utilizing a variety of interaction opportunities will foster the development of a range of communication functions or pragmatic uses of behavior. Training in these situations also facilitates generalization of newly learned modes, content, and use.

Several child and SO social contact purposes are used in training. Each is potentially the beginning of an interaction episode. Initially, only a small set of social contact purposes are targeted. Training begins by extending current social contact purposes into conversations, then training SOs to identify additional child behaviors that can be turned into a conversation.

Joint Activity Routine   Once a social contact is extended into a conversation, joint activity routines can be developed. The more familiar the SO is with the child's perceptual, motivational, and sensorimotor world, the easier it will be to establish the routines. Joint activities are assessed by observing dyads, preparing scripts describing their joint activities, and then analyzing the events as a communication ecosystem that includes child, conversation, and SO events.

An ecosystem analysis is useful for individualized educational planning as well as prescriptive programming and monitoring. In assessment and training, the social interaction patterns between the child and SO are considered. If the pattern is a didactic one in which the SO and child are in a question-answer and SO-controlled relation, natural conversation and its potential learning opportunities may be limited. If the interaction is cooperative, each will follow the other's lead and share the power.

During training, the social and contingent nature of the interaction is gradually increased. The child is taught to develop conversation from activities of his choosing. Joint activity is the basis for accelerating the child's communication along a continuum from solo to parallel, to associative, to cooperative, to social-didactic, and finally to social-caregiving. The SO observes the child playing alone (solo), noting his motivations, skills, and problems. She then plays beside the child (parallel) with materials, and in ways similar to the child's performance (thus setting the stage for modeling). During parallel play, the SO initiates an interesting activity with the dual intention of modeling ways to communicate about the activity and bringing the child into the activity. Whether the child does or does not join in, the SO then begins to play with him associatively. The SO performs a little above the child's level to ensure effective modeling. The SO establishes a conversation by initiating, waiting, responding, signaling turns, and chaining the child's responses into a conversation. During associative play, no formal contingencies are set. The only goal is for the SO to become an effective source of modeling and reinforcement. Subsequently, both partners will begin to share responsibility and exchange information. In cooperative play, more formal training strategies, such as "upping the ante" (e.g., increasing the child's performance criteria; Bruner 1978a) and differential attention for more complex forms are used by the SO.

After cooperative interaction patterns have been established in play situations, conversation skills can be established in caregiving and didactic interactions. When caregiving and didactic interactions are used for initial language training, the interaction can easily become one-sided and lose the balanced content, activity, and purpose of natural learning situations. Such activities often have external contingencies for the adult that limit their value as conversations and as teaching settings.

Turn-taking and Chaining   In addition to a shared topic and sufficient match of communication modes, turn-taking and chaining are two essential tools for any teaching conversation. Turn-taking and chaining permit the exchange of messages without interruption and assure that messages will have some meaningful relation to each other.

Turn-taking requires that only one member in a dyad sends a message at a time. Balanced turn-taking is the goal, wherein each partner shares about the same number of turns and neither dominates turns. Turn-taking begins with actions under the rationale that communication evolves from actions (Bates, 1977). Thus an action turn-taking habit is the context in which language is taught. There are a hierarchy of ways to signal another to take or yield his turn. Turn-taking can occur in any mode as long as the message is communicated. SOs must attend carefully to the child's behaviors as potential turns in a conversation. SOs learn to treat all productive child behavior as communicative and as turns in a primitive conversation. A primary goal in training is to increase the number of related turns during the expression of appropriate social contact purposes. SOs are trained to keep the child taking turns for increasingly longer periods of time. Maintaining the child in the turn-taking format exposes the child to more language and better conversational models than do short didactic interchanges.

Chaining is more complex than turn-taking. A communicative chain is a message that is both a response to the other person's message and a cue for the partner to communicate again. Chaining is a kind of turn-taking that keeps the other person taking turns. Untrained SOs often respond in a manner that stops the conversation rather than facilitating it. For example, a child walks by his father and waves; his father says "Hi" and ends the contact. The father could have chained the child's response into a conversation by waving, then gesturing to the child to come, saying, "Hi, look what I have," or signaling in some other way that he wanted the child to stay in the interaction. In chaining, the child is invited to participate in the conversation. Partnership in communication is fostered. The examples below contrast two conversations on the same topic with and without chaining:

EXAMPLE A: Without Chaining	EXAMPLE B: With Chaining
SO: What's that? (points to picture)	SO: I see cow (points)
C: Cow	C: Cow, I see
SO: That?	SO: You see?
C: House	C: I see house
SO: (points)	SO: Funny house?
C: Boy (walks away)	C: Cow house?
SO: Where are you going?	SO: You know that (waits with anticipation)
C: No answer	C: Barn?
SO: (follows child) What are you doing?	SO: Barn, red barn
C: Nothing	C: Me go barn
SO: Say, "I'm sitting"	SO: You leave me? (feigns a cry)
C: No	C: No, you too

Example A illustrates an unchained, dead-end contact in which a reciprocal give and take of information never gets started. Example B shows true conversational aspects that can result when an SO takes a chaining role in interactions with the child. By chaining, the SO in Example B keeps the child contributing to the conversation. Child B is learning that he can take the lead. The SO's chaining allows him to get as much from her as she does from him. Child A may know how to respond but he does not show an understanding of how to stay in the conversation. Chaining would enable him to remain in longer, more natural language-learning conversations.

Chaining is a flexible language training strategy. All the SO need remember is to respond to the child in a way that keeps him in the interaction. Chaining can be used at all behavioral levels and with any communicative mode. Any response that has the operational effect of stimulating another response from the partner is a chain. When SOs attend carefully to the child's current activities and to the logical flow of the joint activity, the problem of how and what to chain is solved by the general dictum: keep him in there.

Turn balance and turn dominance are also targets for training. SOs must take a reasonable share of turns, but neither the child nor the SO runs the communicative show. SOs should follow the child's behavioral lead and wait for the child to take a turn. Such strategies teach the child the basic communication rule that one must give in order to receive in the conventional world of interactions.

Once shared activities are established through turn-taking specific language and communicative skills can be taught. The following section describes the content of communicative components for child and SO, and the system of natural teaching strategies for SOs.

The Child: The Second Treatment Target

Language delays may be understood best if form, content, and functions of language are considered independently. Some handicapped children are most delayed in linguistic form or physical mode, whereas others show greater delays in cognitive content or pragmatic use. Adequate assessment of the child's modes (and corollary forms), content (meanings), and uses (intentions) must be a regular part of intervention.

Every communicative act has a mode, content, and use, and can be expressed nonlinguistically, vocally, linguistically, or in some combination of these means. If the purpose of language teaching is functional communication, then language must be assessed and trained along all dimensions of its communicative structure (mode, content, and use) following the developmental continuum and beginning with nonlinguistic communications.

Communicative Mode   The concept of mode is similar to Hymes' (1972) "channel." A channel or mode is the component of communication that differentiates the oral from the written, the televised, and so on. The inclusion of modes as a component in the current model allows inclusion of all the child's behaviors that effectively communicate as training targets. The goal of communication training is appropriate messages in any mode that satisfy the criteria of both effectiveness and contextual suitability. Language, in its conventional linguistic sense, is an unrealistic immediate goal for many handicapped children. However, if the primary concern is communication, almost all students can benefit from training.

One somewhat surprising set of conclusions has emerged from our evaluations of handicapped children. Frequently, the child's language (i.e., conventional symbolic referential system) and his communication (i.e., social exchange of messages) are severely delayed for his age. Surprisingly, in spite of these delays, the child's current communication system may be working quite well for him. The child may have successful idiosyncratic communication with those persons who have fine-tuned themselves to his particular communicative modes and strategies. To identify the primary targets for language training, we first determine how the child is communicating currently.

Because the basic target in training is communication, not language, SOs are taught to discriminantly observe and to differentially attend to the child's various modes of communication as a basis for arranging a closer communicative match with the child. Building new communication skills on existing nonlinguistic communication skills (rather than competing with them) is emphasized.

By including all modes of communication, treatment is directed toward three goals. First, intervention begins at the child's current stage of communicative development because the child's language competence seems to develop parallel to the continuum of his communicative competence. Language training begins with the child's current communicative behavior rather than waiting until sounds and words emerge. Second, by including mode as a formal component, any language-delayed child regardless of his modes of communication can be treated. If communication is the basis of language development, and all delayed individuals have a communicative mode, there are no children who are "not ready for therapy." Analysis of the child's communicative modes is also a way to discover the child's prelinguistic semantics (meanings) and pragmatics (uses). Children exhibit linguistic meanings and pragmatic intentions long before they begin talking. A strictly linguistic approach may miss the semantic and pragmatic aspects of communicative competence. Attention to all modes is also a more valid vehicle for exploring the child's cognitive competence than linguistically based assessment approaches.

Communicative functions emerge when SOs interpret a child's random behaviors as though he had communicative intentions. This is the perlocutionary stage of the child's communicative development (Bates, 1976). Any behavior can become communicative if it regularly has communicative effects. The child's total behavior repertoire is a potential target for communication development efforts. The SO has a primary role in determining which behaviors become communicative. If SOs do not expect the child to communicate, they miss many opportunities to shape initially random behaviors into intentional communicative messages.

The illocutionary stage follows, in which the child begins to send messages intentionally. Now SOs must notice the full range of body language the child uses. SOs must respond contingently to natural signals and movements to maintain and develop them into formal communication in which the child uses conventional signs and symbols. At any stage of development the child may perform perlocutionary and illocutionary acts in novel situations or with novel content.

Parents and teachers seem to "see" and respond to a greater range of child behaviors as communicative than do unfamiliar professionals and strangers. The distinction between idiosyncratic and conventional communication is seldom systematically considered in assessing and determining educational and therapeutic placement. A child's communicative competence can be fully known only by examining communication in all modes and including all contents and uses that are having communicative effects in his idiosyncratic relations with familiar others. Anyone experienced with cerebral palsied children, for example, will not be surprised by the notion of idiosyncratic communication. Parents of these children often develop methods of translating their children's complex body movements into predictable meanings that strangers do not understand.

SOs and professionals can apply a "stranger test" in their teaching intervention with the children. In the "stranger test," the SO or professional asks, when communicating with a child, "Would a stranger understand and accept this child's communication?" If the answer is no, the SO asks, "What can I do to our interactions to make him more communicative with me right now?" The strong influence of idiosyncratic communication as a competitor to emerging conventional communication is perhaps the most compelling argument for considering the modes of communication as basic to any ecologically valid approach to language intervention. More mature conventional communication cannot easily emerge when the idiosyncratic communication is maintained by the SOs' intermittent understanding, attention, and reinforcement. Linking existing modes to conventional ones is a straightforward and effective intervention.

The content and sequence of classes of communicative modes in the model are based on clinical judgments of the modes used by over 100 developmentally delayed children, a survey of research on the forms of early communicative performance (Bates, 1974; Dunst, 1978; Ferguson and Farwell, 1975; Mayo, 1979; Oller, 1979; Siebert and Hogan, 1980), and analyses of performance of 18 normally developing children videotaped during interactions with their mothers. Three major classes of modes (nonlinguistic, vocal, and linguistic) were defined to provide parents and teachers the distinctions needed to observe and train. The nonlinguistic mode is defined as communications "without words," the vocal mode as communications "with sounds," and the linguistic mode as communications "with words or signs." A fourth distinction is necessary to account for the obvious and desired use of multiple modes. The SO is trained to ask: what mode is affecting me as a communication? SOs are taught to identify the child's modes, their own responses to the child's modes, and the changes needed to build more progressive modes.

Table 1 illustrates a range of modes that have different communicative intentions and effects. The interaction between Chris (C) and her mother (M) in the example script illustrates the variety of physical forms (nonlinguistic, vocal, linguistic) and communicative intentions (perlocutionary, illocutionary, locutionary) of communicative modes. In the first turn, C is engaged in sound play that shows no communicative intention. However, M interprets C's vocalizations as a communication. Thus, C's performance can be coded as a vocal, perlocutionary act and M's turn performance as linguistic in mode, locutionary in intention. Notice that the mother first accepts any behavior as communicative and then builds a chained conversation that requires more advanced communicative modes.

Table 1.   Illustration of Communicative Modes and Intentions

Turns		Mode[a]			Intentions[b]		
		NL	V	L	P	I	L
1. C	LYING IN BED: "BA BA BA BA BA"		X		X		
2. M	"Want bottle?"			X			X
3. M	"No, time to get out."			X			X
4. C	REACHES TO M, "O, O, O"		X			X	
5. M	Waits with arm extended, quizzical look	X					
6. C	"OUT"			X			X
7. M	"HUH?"		X				X
8. C	"WANT OUT, MA"			X			X
9. M	"I want out, okay?"		X				X
10. M	"Here we go." Lifts child			X			X

[a]NL = nonlinguistic; V = vocal; L = linguistic.

[b]P = prelocutionary; I = illocutionary; L = locutionary.

Communicative Content   The second component of a child's communication system is the content of messages. The current model takes a pragmatic approach toward selecting the content class for training. First, the range of meanings that the child communicates with nonlinguistic, vocal, or linguistic modes is identified. These meanings are bases for selecting the content goals that would add most to the child's communication repertoire. Three vocabularies are identified—nonlinguistic, vocal, and linguistic—corresponding to the child's meanings communicated without words, with sounds, and with words, respectively. For a child who communicates frequently but nonlinguistically, the goal for the SO may be to train a "second language" by translating nonlinguistic messages into vocal or linguistic productions. The SO will teach the child sounds or words that appropriately translate nonlinguistic messages into a more conventional form. The optimal time for such training is the moment the child sends a message and is motivated enough to attend to the word and tolerate contingencies requiring it. SOs should translate the child's nonlinguistic communications into words that would be acceptable verbal messages for the given content. The example below illustrates this "second language" training strategy, which includes nonlinguistic as well as linguistic vocabulary.

EXAMPLE: "Second Language" Training

Turns	*Content Script A*		*Content Script B*	
1.	M	"Let's go."	M	"Let's go."
2.	C	SHAKES HEAD	C	SHAKES HEAD
3.	M	"No?"	M	*"Oh, yes you will."
4.	M	picks C up	M	picks child up
5.	C	WAVES TO OTHER CHILD	C	WAVES TO OTHER CHILD
6.	M	"Bye, Bye." Leaves room.	M	*"Let's go." Leaves room.

EXAMPLE: "Second Language" Training (*continued*)

Turns	Content Script A		Content Script B	
7.	C	"KA KA"	C	"KA KA"
8.	M	"Car, go in car."	M	*"I have to stop at the store."
9.	C	"DADDY"	C	"DADDY"
10.	M	"Gonna see daddy."	M	*"We need bread and milk."

Script A illustrates the second language training strategy. The mother respects the clear or potential semantic intentions of all the child's communications while translating each into a more conventional production that the child may someday use in similar situations (turns 3, 6, 8, and 10). In Script B, the mother misses four opportunities to treat her child's behavior as a communication (i.e., perlocutionary) and to teach the child a more conventional way to communicate (missed opportunities are marked with an asterick).

For another child, the goal may be to develop a broader vocabulary base within an existing mode. The vocabulary building begins by collecting a sample of the child's common social contact purposes (e.g., to help, to give information, to play). Then, functional scripts are written. The scripts include new meanings that will efficiently allow the child to build conversations in those situations. Vocabulary targets are selected from the child's current conversations and from social episodes common to developing children.

The model's content classes are based on social contact topics and semantic referent classes. A review of several major research reports (Broen, 1972; Clark, 1973; MacNamara, 1972) revealed that no classification directly outlined a communicative approach to semantic development. A review of the topics initiated in conversations between severely delayed children (from minimal communication to broad use of three-word sentences) and their parents and teachers was undertaken (MacDonald, 1978). We found that topics of conversation could be discriminated in terms of social contact purposes, that is, the pragmatic intentions of the contact. Intentions such as "getting help," "nuturing," "playing," and "getting information" were frequently expressed.

A few semantic or meaning classes accounted for a large majority of the words in children's first sentences. These classes include agent, action, object, location, and experience. Later modifier, introduction, possession, and recurrence emerge (MacDonald, 1978). These classes have been used as the basis of an assessment inventory (MacDonald, 1978), a teaching series (MacDonald and Horstmeier, 1978), and programs for total communication (Lombardino et al., 1981; Willems et al., 1982). These programs were more directly language oriented and considered linguistic communication exclusively. In the current model, semantic classes are seen as cognitively descriptive of early nonlinguistic communications as well.

Communicative Use   The preceding sections respond to the traditional questions in language intervention: "How is the child communicating?" and "What is he communicating?" When the focus in training shifts from language structure to communicative use, the question "Why is the child communicating?" becomes a primary one.

Two major pragmatic communication problems frequently characterize developmentally delayed children. First, these children often communicate for only a few reasons, using their communication skills in restricted ways. The child's communications are often limited to basic needs. Such "crisis language" affords few of the natural opportunities for conversation that declarations, requests, replies, and other communicative acts offer. Second, SOs are frequently rehetorical rather than conversational in speaking to these children; that is, SOs do not communicate for a response (Watzlawick et al., 1967).

The role of the child's significant others in increasing communicative use is critical. SOs can give the child reasons to communicate. Often, handicapped children's basic needs are so thoroughly anticipated that they have little reason to communicate. Their SOs provide few contingencies for or expectancies of broader social uses of communication.

The general nature of the child-SO relationship also determines the child's range of pragmatics. Children in primarily caregiving or didactic relations have few reasons to communicate other than to demand and to protest. Along the same continuum, if the SO and child have a playful or reciprocal relationship, SOs can make mini-conversations out of almost any contact. During these observations SOs can model and encourage the range of uses the child needs if he is to learn to play a variety of communicative roles with others.

A taxonomy of communicative use was developed for children judged to be communicating less than they know. This target population displays severe delays in the frequency and complexity of their linguistic and nonlinguistic conversations. The children seldom respond to others' communications and frequently initiate communication. The taxonomy describes both the child's and the SO's pragmatic uses. The parallel taxonomy allows analysis of appropriate match and potential modeling effects.

Three major categories were derived from the existing category systems used to describe children of varying developmental levels (Bruner, 1975; Dore, 1975; Searle, 1969; Wells, 1974). These categories are the personal, the social, and the instrumental. *Personal use* includes behaviors that express the self rather than communicate with others. The motivation for a personal act comes from the child with no apparent intention of getting something (instrumental) or contacting others (social), for example. The child may cry when he falls but not call for attention or help. However, personal acts may acquire communicative purpose if they have systematic effects (e.g., getting attention or getting help). For example, the child who cries as he falls may get mom's attention; later he may cry intentionally to attract her attention. Personal uses can be powerful perlocutionary bases for natural communication training. The personal use category also allows for attention to the sensorimotor stages of development, in which the child's "egocentric" communication (Piaget, 1971), such as practicing, accompanying action, and pretending, may dominate his communicative functions. Attending to these personal functions may offer SOs an opportunity to initially match the child's communication and to establish an effective model for later shaping of social or instrumental functions.

Instrumental uses are communications by which the child effectively or intentionally gets something or manipulates others to do something. Handicapped children's communications are often primarily instrumental and limited to crisis situations. SOs can maximize the child's need to communicate and the resulting instrumental communications can provide for advanced mode and content training. For example, a motivated child who already requests help might be trained to do so using more conventional linguistic modes or new content.

The third category in the taxonomy is social uses. Here the primary purpose of communication is to initiate, respond to, or maintain social contact. In social communication, the SO as a person, is important to the child. When social contact and attention in themselves emerge as reasons to communicate, many new communication opportunities arise for the child.

In summary, adequate language learning occurs when the child has a number of pragmatic tools to use in conversation. A child's current communicative uses are the bases for training mode and content, and for extending the child's communicative uses beyond his basic needs to social and learning exchanges. Pragmatic targets are tools for moving the child out of his egocentric world to more reciprocal social experiences.

Significant Others: The Third Treatment Target

The delayed child's parents, teachers, and other significant persons are as important in the child's language development as the child himself. Improved child communication requires that his SOs are active as students, clients, teachers, and environmental engineers of the home or classroom.

Playing the role of student is necessary in order for the SOs to learn the essential components of a communication system and their child's current performance profile in that system. Such knowledge enables the SOs to model appropriately and to relate contingently to the child in ways that have natural teaching effects. The role of client is required because the child's communication develops within primary dyads involving the child and his SOs (Bronfenbrenner, 1979). Thus changes in both members of the dyad are necessary in order for communication to develop.

The SO must also play a more deliberate role as teacher, first directly, then indirectly, by habitually applying those principles that establish a progressive communicative relationship with the child. Two classes of strategies are proposed: one directed to training mode, content, and uses of language and the other directed toward conversation training. SO strategies cannot be completely separated into distinct classes without considerable overlap.

SOs' expectations also affect the child's development, although in a more subtle way. Expectations for the child can create a self-fulfilling prophecy (Bateson et al., 1966; Watzlawick et al., 1967). Many parents of handicapped children behave as though they do not expect the child to communicate or improve his language skills. Parents and teachers who "talk for the child" or who typically have rhetorical interactions with the child are functionally teaching the child not to communicate more or differently. In the current model, expectancy is defined in terms of directly observable events. SOs' use of expectancy cues is evaluated and trained.

The taxonomy of SO variables is a parallel, integrated part of the child's total communication ecosystem. These variables are both independent and dependent. They serve many functions in the communication program.

Active Observational Knowledge   If SOs are to stimulate progressive language in the child, they must know two things about the child's communication system. First, they must have a general developmental schema of children's development of a communication system. Second, they need a map of their own child's current behavioral placement in that system. Too often, parents and teachers, anxious to train expressive language in a child, initiate formal training before the child has the conversation skills basic to natural language learning. They engage in word training with little attention to the child's nonlinguistic modes, semantic contents, pragmatic uses, and conversational strategies. Well-intentioned teachers may attempt to train language independently of the child's current communication system, without realizing that this system is necessary for training more advanced communication and is a formidable competitor to new communication.

An ecologically valid curriculum leading to a natural dyadic training relationship must include training SOs to recognize the essential components of an ecosystem, their child's current performance profile or map in that system, and the next steps for progressive development or lateral generalization. Parents and other persons untrained in language and communication can easily be taught to see the child's linguistic and nonlinguistic communications in terms of how (mode), what (content), and why (use) the child communicates. They need only a little evidence from their own child's interactions to see the crucial but ignored conversations, both with and without words, that dominate his life.

SOs do not need to learn all the discriminations within the taxonomy; those distinctions can be programmed by consultants. However, they do need to learn to identify the general pattern of the child's communication system. For example, they might notice that the child communicates primarily with mime movements and nonspeech sounds (mode) about his own actions (content), that he communicates mainly for reasons of crisis such as demand and command (use), and that he stays for as many as six turns in nonlinguistic conversations if physical interaction is involved. The SOs must be taught to observe *when* these various communication components occur, *what* the next logical treatment targets would be, and *how* to foster these components within their conversational relationship with the child.[3]

The Role of Communicative Expectance   Three independent research programs investigating mother-infant interaction (Brazelton et al., 1974; Lewis, 1974; Lewis and Lee-Painter, 1974; Stern, 1974, 1977; Stern and Gibbon, 1977; Stern et al., 1975) have described the process of engagement and disengagement between mothers and infants. Brazelton et al. (1974) reported several ways in which mothers come to have an expectancy for the child to interact with them. Through fine tuning of the rhythm, intensity, amplitude, direction, and quality of her infant-directed behavior, the mother attempts to elicit a signal from the infant confirming that he is in touch with her. All three research groups found patterns of prelinguistic conversations in which the mother's and child's behavior suggested expectancies for the other to interact.

In interactions with handicapped children, adults often behave as though they do not expect the child to communicate or to participate in the interaction. Frequently, parents and teachers provide neither the time nor the cues a child needs to respond. SOs may regularly talk *for* the child, resulting in a dominated conversation. Early in the treatment program, after SOs learn to observe key communicative behaviors, they are taught to interact as though they expect the child to initiate, respond, and share turns in conversations. They learn the strategies of waiting and signaling for the child to communicate. Waiting has proved to be a critical starting point without which communication development will be thwarted. They also learn to reduce their

---

[3]Several professionals who have trained teachers and parents report that adults change their interactions with the child as a function of learning the critical elements of the child's communication. When parents or teachers observe the child differently, their expectations and contingencies with him change accordingly. A conceptual mnemonic device—the "lonely island" test—is suggested once the SOs know what to observe. Using this strategy, the SO imagines being isolated with the child on an island and being dependent on that child for all the natural rewards of communication. Then, with the child's current communicative map in hand (and in mind eventually), the SO asks herself: What changes would I want in the child's communication in order to make me less lonely? The answers then become targets that are important enough to the SOs that they will be willing to change their interactions in order to reach those targets. By observing developmentally appropriate and inappropriate targets, SOs come to attend differentially to the child's emerging communication, thereby reaching the first step in becoming a natural communication teacher.

rhetorical communications and demonstrate through body language and differential contingencies that they generally expect the child to communicate.

SOs' negative expectancies for child communication may be related to their definition of communication in speech and language terms. Once SOs learn that the child will develop language on a continuum from nonlinguistic to linguistic communication, they expect more child-appropriate performances. They begin to recognize vocal and nonlinguistic behaviors as communicative. Subsequently, they learn to attend differentially in favor of new modes, contents, and uses by following immature responses or failures to respond with silence or reduce attention.

The example below illustrates interactions with minimal expectancy for the child to communicate (A) and high expectancy (B).

EXAMPLE: Expectancy for Communication

Script A—Minimal Expectancy

1.	C	REACHES FOR CEREAL
2.	M	"What do you want?"
3.	C	EATS CEREAL
4.	M	"Good?" "Sure, you like it." "Tell me when you want more."
5.	C	CONTINUES EATING
6.	M	"Ready for more?" "Looks like it."
7.	M	Takes bowl, fills it
8.	C	EATS AGAIN
9.	M	"You are hungry"

Script B—High Expectancy

1.	C	REACHES FOR CEREAL
2.	M	Gives quizzical look.
3.	C	"SI SI"
4.	M	"Cereal?"
5.	C	"SI UL"
6.	M	"Cereal!" Here." (pours in bowl)
7.	M	Waits
8.	C	"MUK"
9.	M	"Milk—Watch it fall on cereal."
10.	M	"Now what?"
11.	C	"SUGAR"
12.	M	"Sugar in milk, now eat."

In Script A, the mother's communication is generally rhetorical. She answers her own questions, (4, 6) allows no time for a response (4, 6, 7), and uses no signals for the child to communicate (2, 4, 6, 7). In Script B, the mother sets the stage for a more balanced conversation. She waits (2, 7) and signals both with (4, 10) and without words (2). She is conversational with the child, waiting for him to take his turn (2, 7) and chaining (4, 10) when necessary.

Language Teaching Strategies   Several strategies are used in teaching new communication skills. These strategies have overlapping effects on mode, content, and use. The strategies include direct behavioral approaches, indirect context management, and interactional approaches. These strategies are summarized in Table 2.

The following example illustrates applications of those teaching strategies summarized in Table 2. Scripts A and B contrast two approaches to communicating with a child. Script B is judged as incorporating several natural language teaching strategies whereas Script A violates several training principles.

EXAMPLE: Language Teaching Strategies

Script A		*Script B*	
1. C	FINISHES CEREAL, PUTS SPOON ON TABLE	1. C	FINISHES CEREAL, PUTS SPOON ON TABLE
2. M	"I'm not finished yet, sit."	2. M	"More cereal?"
3. C	SHAKES HEAD HORIZONTALLY	3. C	SHAKES HEAD HORIZONTALLY
4. M	"Oh, yes you will."	4. M	Shakes head; "No."
5. C	"No"	5. C	"NO MORE"
6. M	"Come on now, stay with me."	6. M	"No more cereal."
7. C	START LEAVING ROOM	7. C	TURNS TO LEAVE TABLE
8. M	"Okay, just remember that when you want something."	8. M	"Go play?"
9. C	TURNS AROUND AND LOOK AT M	9. C	"UH HUH" SHAKES HEAD
10. M	Makes no response	10. M	"Uh huh? Go play?"
		11. C	"GO PA"
		12. M	"Go play, have fun."

In Script A, the mother misses two (1, 9) opportunities to treat the child's behavior as communicative. The mother in Script B capitalizes on similar opportunities (1, 7) and interprets the child's behavior as sending a message. In Script A, the mother fails to put words to the child's nonlinguistic communications (3, 7, 9), thus failing to give the child more conventional ways to communicate those contexts. On the other hand, the mother in Script B second language–trains the child (4, 10) and leads him into progressively more advanced communication even within the script. Mother A never imitates or expands the child's performance but stays in her own conceptual and sensorimotor world, whereas Mother B follows the child's communicative lead by coding his meanings (second language training), imitating, and expanding (6, 12).

Finally, the two scripts differ strikingly in the way the two dyads are matching each other communicatively. Mother A communicates totally linguistically with an MLU of 5 words to a child who is primarily nonlinguistic. Her models, both perceptually and cognitively, far exceed the child's commu-

Table 2.   SOs' Language Teaching Strategies

Strategy	Purpose	Description
Imitation training	Provides a model for child. Provides an opportunity to give feedback.	SO names/describes objects/events of current interest to child. SO expands childs imitations.
SO modeling	Provides a "progressive match" with child's communicative level.	SO communicates a slightly more complex level than child; reduces MLU and number of adult utterances.
Reduce rhetorical communication	Allows time for child response. Includes cues for child response (communicate once, then wait with anticipation and use more non-demand intentions with child.)	SO pauses after speaking, avoids dead-end comments.
Second language training 1. Begin with child's meanings 2. Train new meanings that will be useful in making social contacts.	Translates child's existing meaning into conventional communication forms.	SO responds communicatively to child, puts words on his meanings, actions, and communications.

nicative and activity level. Mother B, however, appears finely tuned to the child's linguistic level; her MLU of 2.7 compares favorably with his 1.0, especially because she also matches his nonlinguistic communications (4, 10).

Conversation Teaching Strategies   There are also a range of strategies for an SO to use in training the child to successfully operate verbally and nonverbally in conversations. These strategies are summarized in Table 3.

General Teaching Principles   We have identified 10 natural teaching principles as basic operating procedures for SOs. These principles can be applied to establish SOs as progressive language teachers in conversations. The first four are basic assumptions relating to the premise that language develops from natural interactions. They provide general rules for structuring language intervention. The next six principles govern the behavior of natural language teachers. These principles can be integrated into the adults' everyday interactions with the delayed child.

1. *The Ubiquity Principle: all behavior communicates*   Every behavior potentially carries a communicative message. Thus, every behavior is an

Table 3.   SOs' Conversation Teaching Strategies

Strategy	Purpose
1. Engage in joint activities	Joint activities often elicit give-and-take routines similar to conversation.
2. Increase social contact purposes (SCPs).	SCPs offer opportunities for conversations.
3. Take turns with the child—nonlinguistically, vocally, and linguistically.	Maintains child participation; parallels conversations format.
4. Use chaining responses.	Chains (responses that cue a subsequent child response) keep the child in the conversation.
5. Signal and mark turns for the child.	Cues the child in order to maintain his participation in the conversation by pausing and waiting with anticipation. Marking the turn also shifts the balance of power in favor of the child.
6. Alter activity to correspond with the child's sensorimotor levels.	Participating at the child's level encourages more equal interactions. SO can follow child's lead and potentially be more interesting to child.
7. Change communication modes to progressively match the child's mode.	SO provides model of slightly more complex mode of communication.
8. Change topic and vocabulary to progressively match child's interest and current communications.	SO provides models of linguistic content that are slightly more advanced than child's current level.
9. Perform associative and cooperative roles.	SO is most frequently in caregiving, didactic, and parallel roles, expanding her roles offers more conversational opportunities.

opportunity for teaching, for translating the child's communicative message into a conventional communicative form.

2. *The Systems Principle: there are multiple members of the communication system; each must be a target for training* Both the child and his significant others receive training. The communication system has several domains (mode, content, use); each must be treated. Treatment in any single domain affects development in the subsequent level of that domain and in all other domains.

3. *The New Forms–Old Content Principle: new forms at first express old content* Training new forms will be successful if these forms map semantic content that the child already expresses.

4. *The Gradual Balance of Power Shift: there is a critical, dynamic balance of power in parent-child interactions* With the development of new communication skills, the balance should shift toward increasing the child's power in the interaction to permit equal turn-taking interactions.

5. *The Child's World Principle: teaching begins in joint action with the child* The SO must operate the child's sensorimotor world in order to accurately match the child's communicative competence.
6. *The Conversational Principle: give in order to get* This principle underlies all the training strategies described. In a functional conversation, SOs expect the child to communicate; they interpret his behaviors as communicative and respond accordingly.
7. *The Progressively Matched Modeling Principle: models should be slightly more complex that the child's current skill level* SOs must communicate in ways that match the child's mode, content, and use levels, but they must also provide models that are slightly more complex than the child's current performance.
8. *The Second Language Training Principle: translate the child's idiosyncratic communication forms into conventional communications* The SO will respond to immature communication by putting that message into a word or utterance that is appropriate for the context.
9. *The Up-the-Ante Principle: prompt and require performance that is slightly above the child's current level of communication* This principle was first expressed by Bruner (1978a) and parallels behavioristic accounts of shaping new responses through incidental prompting and differential reinforcement.
10. *The Social Contact Rate Principle: the rate of language acquisition will increase in proportion to the frequency with which the child uses language in social interactions* A high frequency of social contacts ensures many opportunities for the child to observe how language works and for the SO to provide matched modes and contingencies for mature communication. This principle is derived from the work of Hart and Risley on incidental teaching.

SUMMARY OF DEVELOPMENT PROGRESSION OF THE MODEL

Figure 1 illustrates a view of language developing progressively from interactions to conversations. Language develops as a function of the child's interactions with his significant others (Stage I). In the initial stage, child behaviors do not have distinct communicative intentions, meaning, or modes. Through interactive feedback, the child and SOs shape each other's behavior toward progressively more conventional communications. The major components of child language (mode, content, and use) begin in prelinguistic events (Stage II). At first behaviors may be idiosyncratic in their form (mode), nonlinguistic in their meaning (content), and perlocutionary in their intentions (use). As SOs contingently and progressively match the child's communicative attempts

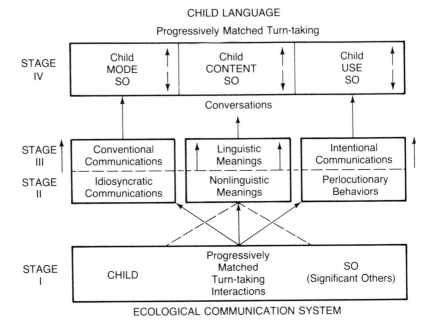

Figure 1. Model for assisted development of language from interaction through conversation.

in incidental interactions, those attempts become more conventional in form, more symbolic (linguistic) in meanings, and more intentional in functional use (Stage III).

Gradually the relationship between the child and his SOs becomes more conversational (i.e., focuses on exchange of a message) and less interactional (Stage IV). In such natural conversations, the child has many opportunities to learn new language. The appropriateness of the match between the mode, content, and use of the child's and SOs' communications will contribute to the rate of learning and quality of language learned. In addition, the SOs' language teaching strategies will determine the contingencies under which the child will establish a habit of conversational learning of language. As the child develops a rich communicative system with SOs, he can also begin to learn language in interactions with others. The model describes a course of learning for many language-delayed individual who has yet to establish a conversational habit required for natural language learning.

OVERVIEW

In this discussion we have presented a new model for early language intervention that has evolved from a convergence of several theoretical and empirical approaches with our own findings from parent and classroom-based programs. This model is based on two fundamental premises: first, that language emerges from natural conversations between the child and his significant others; and second, that intervention must involve both the child and his significant others in progressively matched and contingent conversations. Consequently, the role of the therapist in this model is that of a parent and teacher trainer and as a consultant and individual program designer, but not as a one-to-one child trainer.

In the proposed model, a set of conversation variables unifying the child and his SOs are the primary interaction targets. This conversational focus speaks to the widely accepted and logical view that language acquisition requires an active conversational milieu (Bates, 1976; Bruner, 1978; Lewis, 1972; McLean and Snyder-McLean, 1978; Moerk, 1977; Snow and Ferguson, 1978; and others) in which the child learns to be conversational through chained turn-taking and establishment of frequent progressively contingent conversations. A conversational environment differs from many therapeutic, educational, and home environments in that, in the former, the adults became conversational partners in the child's world rather than teachers or caregivers who determine the goals and dominate the interactions in the latter.

As we further develop this model, we hope to uncover some common trends that are fundamental and generalizable components across developmental classes of children and adults. Our initial clinical findings suggest that a few components are critical to teaching language to a wide range of children. First, the idiosyncratic/conventional distinction appears consistent throughout families. That is, children have one communication system that works with their significant others (idiosyncratic) and another, much narrower, one that strangers accept and understand (conventional). Based on this approach we have trained parents and teachers to attend differentially to communications that strangers would accept compared to the idiosyncratic ones that limit social and educational development. Learning to attend to the child's various communication modes differentially is one hallmark of a "communication" approach as compared to a language approach.

Second, a series of strategies involved in "being contingently conversational" seems to be essential if the child's significant others are to become natural language teachers who are fine tuned to the emerging modes, contents, and uses of their child's communication. Our almost ubiquitous finding is that parents, and often teachers, of a severely language-delayed child regularly communicate rhetorically and short circuit the child's communicative turn. That is, they expect the child not to communicate in a certain way; then, when the child fulfills their prophecy, they dominate the interaction and provide inadequately matched signals and insufficient time for the turn-taking exchanges necessary for language to emerge.

A third consistent finding is that nearly all language-delayed children offer nonlinguistic communicative acts that are rarely responded to in ways that would shape them into more conventional productions. Parents and professionals need to come to an active awareness that speech and language emerge from the child's nonlinguistic communicative acts. The finding that any behavior can become an effective communication act (Bates, 1976; Bruner, 1978b) takes the vocal-linguistic pressure off the child whose physiology or history argues against current training. Logic would argue that the delayed child needs first to develop frequent and rich communications of any form before going to a new structural level (e.g., vocal or linguistic). New forms (vocal or linguistic) will need to develop from old skills (nonlinguistic) that are thoroughly established and broadly generalized (Slobin, 1973). Training sounds and words with children who have not yet established a spontaneous communication system within other physical modes may be inappropriate. Such training may serve to erode what effective communications a child has and reinforce a form of functional social mutism.

What is next? Ongoing experimental efforts in classrooms and parent programs are attempting to determine clusters of child, SO, and conversational targets that relate to both quantitative and qualitative changes in children. This work should help us organize a taxonomy of increasingly functional and related categories. A basic question is being asked: When uninvolved but experienced judges rate a video sample as high in conversationality, conventionality, communicative expectancy, or other global goals, what is occurring in the child, significant other, and conversation events?

The proposed approach suggests an ecologically oriented solution to the problem of assisted language development. The next step must involve communicating the model to and studying it with the child's primary ecological managers—parents and teachers. Consequently, the model is being revised into three curricular approaches. First, a curriculum is being developed and tested for professional use with individual parents. Second, the same curriculum is being adapted for use by consultants who model and monitor it within infant and preschool classrooms for developmentally delayed children. A third direction has recently evolved out of our finding that parents and teachers need to learn to observe the critical components of conversations themselves before they will be sufficiently motivated and skilled to become durable change agents. To this end, we are designing a continuing education course directed to teaching parents and teachers to discriminately "see" the range of variables involved in a child's idiosyncratic and conventional communication systems. This preparatory curriculum will also train the series of events necessary for conversational prerequisites and natural teaching strategies.

Implications of the proposed model may abound for populations other than severely language-delayed children. Some corollary work has begun with adult aphasics. We will continue to address the needs of autistic, retarded, aphasic, Down's syndrome, and cerebral palsied children for now, and invite others to explore the model on their own with these and other children and their natural environments. A network of professionals interested in conversation approaches to language development has been established. Readers are invited to write to the author for the newsletter that is the focal tool of the network. Assessment tools and treatment modules are available for field testing.

REFERENCES

Ainsworth, M. D. S. 1974. The development of infant-mother attachment. *In* B. M. Caldwell and H. N. Ricutti (eds.), Review of Child Development Research, Vol. 3. University of Chicago, Chicago.

Almerico, T., and MacDonald, J. 1979. The maternal pragmatic environment of replies and declarations in non-delayed and delayed children. Unpublished Master's thesis, Department of Communication, Ohio State University, Columbus.

Bates, E. 1974. Acquisition of pragmatic competence. J. Child Lang. 1:277–281.

Bates, E. 1976. Language and Context: The Acquisition of Pragmatics. Academic Press, New York.

Bateson, G., and Jackson, D. 1964. Some varieties of pathogenic organizations. *In* D. McK. Rioch (ed.), Disorders of Communication. Research Publications, Vol. 42, pp. 270–283. Association for Research in Nervous and Mental Diseases, 1978.

Bateson, G., Jackson, D., Haley, J., and Weakland, J. 1966. Toward a theory of schizophrenia. Behav. Sci. *1*.

Bloom, L., and Lahey, M. 1978. Language Development and Language Disorders. Wiley, New York.

Blurton-Jones, N. G. 1972. Ethological Studies of Child Behavior. Cambridge University Press, London.

Braine, M. 1976. Children's First Word Combinations. The University of Chicago Press (for Society for Research in Child Development), Chicago.

Brazelton, T., et al., 1974. The origins of reciprocity: The early mother-infant interaction. *In* M. Lewis and L. A. Rosenblum (eds.), The Effect of the Infant on the Caretaker. Wiley, New York.

Broen, P. A. 1972. The verbal environment of the language learning child. ASHA Monogr. 17.

Bronfenbrenner, U. 1979. The Ecology of Human Development. Harvard University Press, Cambridge, MA.

Brown, R. 1973. A First Language: The Early Stages. Harvard University Press, Cambridge, MA.

Brown, R. 1978. Introduction *In* C. Snow and C. Ferguson (eds.), Talking to Children: Language Input and Acquisition. Cambridge University Press, London.

Bruner, J. 1974. From communication to language: A psychological perspective. Cognition 3:255–277.

Bruner, J. 1975. The ontogenesis of speech acts. J. Child Lang. 2:1–19.

Bruner, J. 1977. The role of dialogue in language acquisition. Paper presented at a Conference on the Child's Conception of Language, Max Planck Society in Linguistics, Nijmegen, The Netherlands.

Bruner, J. 1978a. Acquiring the use of language. Paper presented at the Berlyne Memorial Lecture at the University of Toronto, March.

Bruner, J. 1978b. Human growth and development. *In* J. Bruner and A. Garton (eds.), Wolfson College Lectures, 1976. Clarendon Press, Oxford.

Bruner, J. 1978c. Learning the mother tongue. Hum. Nature 2:42–48.

Chomsky, N. 1959. Syntactic Structures. Mouton, The Hague.

Clark, E. 1973. What's in a word? On the child's acquisition of semantics in his first language. *In* T. E. Moore (ed.), Cognitive Development and the Acquisition of Language. Academic Press, New York.

Cross, T. G. 1977. Mother's speech adjustments. *In* C. Ferguson and C. Snow (eds.), Talking to Children: Language Input and Acquisition. Cambridge University Press, Cambridge, England.

Dore, J. 1975, Holophrases, speech acts and language universals. J. Child Lang. 2:21–40.

Dunst, C. 1978. A cognitive-social approach for assessment of early nonverbal communicative behavior. J. Child Commun. Disord. 2(2).

Ferguson, C. A., and Farwell, C. 1975. Words and sounds in early language acquisition. Language, 51:419–439.

Haley, J. 1962. Family experiments: A new type of experimentation. Fam. Process 1:265–293.

Haley, J. 1964. Research on family patterns: An instrument measurement. Fam. Process 3:41–65.

Halliday, M. A. K. 1975. Learning how to mean. *In* E. H. Lenneberg and E. Lenneberg (eds.), Foundations of Language Development, Vol. 1. Academic Press, New York.

Horstmeier, D., and MacDonald, J. 1978. Ready, set, go talk to me. Merrill, Colombus, OH.

Hunt, J. 1961. Intelligence and Experience. Ronald Press, New York.

Hymes, D. 1972. On communicative competence. *In* J. B. Pride and J. Holmes (eds.), Sociolinguistics, pp. 35–71. Penguin, Harmondsworth, England.

Lewis, M. 1972. State as an infant-environment interaction: An analysis of mother infant behavior as a function of sex. Merrill-Palmer Q. 18:95–121.

Lewis, M. 1974. Interaction, conversation and the development of language. *In* M. Lewis and L. A. Rosenblum (eds.), The Effects of the Infant on Its Caretaker. Wiley, New York.

Lewis, M., and Lee-Painter, S. 1974. An infant's interaction with its social world: The origin of meaning. *In* M. Lewis and L. A. Rosenblum (eds.), The Effect of the Infant on Its Caretaker. Wiley, New York.

Lewis, M., and Rosenblum, L. A. (eds.). 1974. The Effects of the Infant on Its Caretaker. Wiley, New York.

Lombardino, L. 1978. Maternal speech acts to non-delayed and Down's syndrome children: A taxonomy and distribution. Unpublished Ph.D. dissertation, The Ohio State University, Columbus.

Lombardino, L., Willems, S., and MacDonald, J. 1981. Critical considerations in total communication and an environmental intervention model for the developmentally delayed. Except. Child. 47(6):142–151.

MacCorquodale, K. 1971. On Chomsky's review of Skinner's "Verbal behavior." J. Exp. Anal. Behav. 13(1):83–99.

MacDonald, J. 1978. Environmental language intervention: Programs for establishing initial communication in handicapped children. *In* F. Withrow and C. Nygren (eds.), Language and the Handicapped Learner: Curricula, Programs and Media. Merrill, Columbus, OH.

MacDonald, J., and Blott, J. 1974. Environmental language intervention: A rationale for diagnostic and training strategy through rules, context and generalization. J. Speech Hear. Disord. 39:244–256.

MacDonald, J., Blott, J., Gordon, K., and Spiegel, B. 1974. Experimental parent-assisted treatment programs for preschool language delayed children. J. Speech Hear. Res. 39:395–415.

MacDonald, J., and Horstmeier, D. 1978. Environmental Language Intervention Program. Merrill, Columbus, OH.

MacNamara, J. 1972. Cognitive bases of language learning in infants. Psychol. Rev. 79:1–13.

Mahoney, G. 1975. An ethological approach to delayed language acquisition. Am. J. Ment. Defic. 80:139–148.

Mayo, C. 1979. On the acquisition of nonverbal communication: A review. Merrill-Palmer Q. 24(4).

McLean, J., and Snyder-McLean, L. 1978. Transactional Approach to Early Language Training. Merrill, Columbus, OH.

Mechlenberg, D. 1975. Group parent language programming with retarded children. Unpublished Master's thesis, Ohio State University, Columbus.

Moerk, E. 1972. Principles of dyadic interaction in language learning. Merrill-Palmer Q. 18:229–275.

Moerk, E. 1977. Pragmatic and Semantic Aspects of Early Language Development. University Park Press, Baltimore.

Nelson, K. 1980. Children's Language, Vol. 3. Gardner Press, New York.

Nichols, 1974. Prelinguistic development of severely handicapped children: A parent training study. Unpublished Master's thesis, Ohio State University, Columbus.

Oller, D. K. 1979. Infant babbling and speech. J. Child Lang. 3:1–12.

Owens, R. 1979. Pragmatic functions in the speech of preschool-aged Down's and nondelayed children. Unpublished Ph.D. dissertation, The Ohio State University, Columbus.

Piaget, J. 1971. The Language and Thought of the Child. Humanities Press, Atlantic Highlands, NJ.

Schesinger, I. 1971. Production of utterances and language acquisition. *In* D. Slobin (ed.), The Ontogenesis of Grammer. Academic Press, New York.

Searle, J. R. 1969. Speech Acts: An Essay in the Philosophy of Language. Cambridge University Press, New York.

Seibert, J., and Hogan, A. 1980. Procedures for the early social-communication scales. A working paper. The Mailman Center, University of Miami, Miami, Florida.

Skinner, B. 1953. Science and Human Behavior. MacMillan, New York.

Skinner, B. 1957. Verbal Behavior. Appleton-Century-Crofts, New York.

Slobin, D. 1973. Cognitive prerequisites for the development of grammer. *In* D. I. Slobin and C. Ferguson (eds.), Studies of Child Language Development. Holt, Rinehart & Winston, New York.

Snow, C. 1972. Mothers' speech to children learning language. Child Dev. 43:549–565.

Snow, C., and Ferguson, C. 1978. Talking to Children. Cambridge University Press, London.

Synder, L. S. 1978. Communicative and cognitive abilities in the sensorimotor period. Merrill-Palmer Q. 24:3.

Stern, D. 1974. Mother and infant at play: The dyadic interaction involving facial, vocal and gaze behaviors. *In* M. Lewis and L. A. Rosenblum (eds.), The Effect of the Infant on its Caretaker. Wiley, New York.

Stern, D. 1977. The First Relationship; Mother and Infant. Harvard University Press, Cambridge, MA.

Stern, D., and Gibbon, J. 1977. Temporal expectancies of social behaviors in mother-infant play. *In* E. Thoman (ed.), The Origins of the Infant's Responsiveness. Erlbaum Press, New York.

Stern, D., Jaffee, B., and Bennett, S. 1975. Vocalizing in unison and in alternation: Two models of communication within the mother-infant dyad. Ann. N.Y. Acad. Sci. 263:89–100.

Van Ek, J. 1977. The Threshold Level for Modern Language Learning in Schools. Longman Group Ltd., The Netherlands.

Von Bertalanffy, L. 1950. General Systems Theory. Braziller, New York.

Watzlawick, P., Weakland, J. H., and Fish, R. 1974. Change: Principle of Problem Formation and Problem Resolution. Norton, New York.

Watzlawick, P., Beavin, J., and Jackson, D. 1967. Pragmatics of Human Communication. Norton, New York.

Weinberg, G. 1975. Introduction to General Systems Thinking. Wiley, New York.

Wells, G. 1974. Learning to code experience through language. J. Child Lang. 1:243–269.

Widdowson, H. G. 1976. An applied linguistic approach to discourse analysis. Unpublished Ph.D. thesis, University of Edinburgh.

Willems, S., Lombardino, L., and MacDonald, J. 1982. Total communication: A parent based language program. Edu. Training Ment. Retard. 17:293–299.

chapter 5

Communication in Autistic Persons
Characteristics and Intervention

Cathy L. Alpert
and
Ann K. Rogers-Warren
Department of Special Education
Peabody College of
Vanderbilt University

SPEECH, LANGUAGE, AND COMMUNICATION
CHARACTERISTICS   125
    Mutism   126
    Echolalia   127
    Use of Gesture   129
    Syntactic Development   130
    Semantic Development   130
    Pragmatic Development   133
    Summary   136

PLANNING FOR INTERVENTION   137
    Behavior Control Component   138
    Motivational Component   140
    Curriculum Component   141
    Format for Instruction   143
    Generalization and Maintenance   147

CONCLUSION   150

REFERENCES   151

In 1943, Leo Kanner, a child psychiatrist at Johns Hopkins University, published his first description of an unusual behavior disorder in children. Kanner identified behavioral features that were common to 11 children who had been brought to the clinic over a period of years. He maintained that the co-occurrence of these behaviors differentiated these children from children with other psychiatric disorders. The common characteristics noted by Kanner were profound withdrawal characterized by an inability to develop relationships with people, repetitive and stereotyped play activities, an obsessive insistence on the maintenance of sameness, a lack of imagination, a good rote memory, a skillful relation to objects, and an intelligent and pensive facial appearance. With regard to language development, Kanner noted the presence of either mutism or the kind of language that is not used for communicative purposes. A year later, Kanner (1944) published a brief paper in which he labeled the newly identified disorder "early infantile autism."

In 1946 and 1951, Kanner wrote extensively on the speech and language of autistic children. In these early descriptions, which have proved remarkably durable over the years, the following characteristics were noted: affirmation by repetition; pronominal reversal; extreme literalness; metaphorical usage; transfer of meaning through substitute analogy—through generalization (the whole for the part) and through restriction (the part for the whole); and delayed echolalia. In terms of the interpersonal communicative abilities of the children, Kanner observed that there were no fundamental differences between those children who could speak and those who could not.

In the years following Kanner's early writings, the term "autism" has come to represent a very heterogeneous group of individuals (Schopler, 1978). However, there is general agreement that disturbances in the development of social relationships, language, and communication are primary symptoms of the disorder (Creak, 1961; Kanner, 1943; Rimland, 1964; Ritvo and Freeman, 1978; Rutter, 1968, 1978).

This chapter deals with the linguistic and sociocommunicative functioning of autistic children. First, a review of the research literature on the speech, language, and communication characteristics of autistic children is presented. This is followed by a discussion on functional language training and strategies for programming generalization and maintenance of trained communication skills.

SPEECH, LANGUAGE, AND COMMUNICATION CHARACTERISTICS

Learning how to communicate may be viewed as a continuing process that typically begins during infancy. Communicative behaviors are learned through contingencies provided in the social environment, and the development of increasingly sophisticated, efficient, and conventional means of communicating are learned over time. Communicative competence is based on the acquisition of multiple and diverse prerequisite skills, including the abilities to: 1) attend to and interact with the inanimate environment; 2) participate actively in social interchanges with others; and 3) comprehend and use forms of expression (Fay and Schuler, 1980; McLean and Snyder-McLean, 1978).

It has recently been suggested that different types of prerequisite skills may differentially affect the development of various components of the communication system (Blank, et al., 1979; Curtiss, 1981). Those components dealing with form (i.e., phonology, morphology, and syntax) are said to be language specific, involving such prerequisite skills as auditory discrimination and imitative abilities. In contrast, development of the semantic and pragmatic components of the communication system is said to be dependent on conceptual learning, which requires attention to the physical environment, and the acquisition of social interaction strategies.

When the communication system is intact, forms (nonverbal and/or verbal) are systematically related to meaning and functional use. Among language-disordered individuals (e.g., aphasic and hearing impaired), however, uneven rates of development may be seen across the various components of the communication system. With regard to verbal autistic persons, the components of semantics and pragmatics are considered to be particularly impoverished as compared to the language-specific dimensions of phonology and syntax (Caparulo, 1981; Paul, 1982; Tager-Fulsberg, 1981a, 1981b).

The early writings of Kanner (1943, 1946) illustrate that the notion of asynchronous development across the components of the communication system is not new. However, research findings that now corroborate the clinical descriptions, a growing understanding that exists of the relationship between prerequisite skills and development of various aspects of the communication system, and an increased ability to identify potentially deficient prerequisite skill areas have exciting implications for intervention.

In this section, research findings on the speech, language, and communication characteristics of autistic children are presented. For purposes of discussion, the findings have been organized along the topics of mutism, echolalia, use of gesture, and syntactic, semantic, and pragmatic development.

Mutism

About 50% of all autistic children are mute (Eisenberg, 1956; Lotter, 1966, 1967; Rutter et al., 1967). The term *mute* is generally used to indicate "a lack of useful speech" (Baker et al., 1976) and has been applied to children who: 1) produce neither communicative nor noncommunicative vocalizations ("totally mute"); 2) produce vocalizations that are void of meaning and are generally used for self-stimulation and sound play ("functionally mute"); and 3) use a limited repertoire of words and word-approximations in a functional manner to express immediate desires or dislikes ("semi-mute") (Schuler, 1976). Among autistic persons, a high correlation has been reported between the lack of useful speech by age 5 and mental retardation, with both of these factors being associated with poor prognosis in language development, educational attainment, and social adjustment (DeMyer et al., 1973).

In a review of 70 studies involving operant language training with 125 autistic children, Howlin (1981) examined the relationships between training outcome and 1) language level at the onset of training and 2) age at which treatment began. She found that children who were initially mute made the least progress—23% remained mute, 60% developed a simple labeling vocabulary, and 17% developed useful phrase speech. In contrast, children who used speech when training began, including those who were echolalic, made the greatest gains—over 80% of these children used spontaneous phrase speech after treatment.

With regard to the effects related to age at which treatment began, Howlin reported that all echolalic children who began training before the age of 5 developed useful phrase speech, but the proportion declined as age at training onset increased. However, no clear relationship was found between age at which treatment began and training outcome for the mute children.

One potentially significant variable that Howlin did not analyze was the content of the training procedures used. Problems in teaching generalized verbal imitation skills to nonspeaking autistic children have been well documented (e.g., Hingtgen and Churchill, 1971; Lovaas, 1977). Whereas the age of nonspeaking children at the onset of verbal imitation training may indeed be unrelated to outcome, age at the onset of other types of operant language training procedures (e.g., nonvocal communication training and verbal and nonverbal imitation training using *functional* stimuli) may be highly correlated with the factors of absence of speech at the onset of training and training outcome. This possibility requires further investigation.

Echolalia

The prevalence of echolalia among verbal autistic children has been estimated to be approximately 75% (Baltaxe and Simmons, 1981; Rutter and Lockyer, 1967). Two types of echolalia, distinguishable on the basis of temporal latency between the original and repeated utterances, have been described. *Immediate echolalia* is the most frequently cited language abnormality of verbal autistic children (Hingtgen and Bryson, 1972; Prizant and Duchan, 1981). It has typically been viewed as nonfunctional and indicative of the child's failure to comprehend the speech of others (Shapiro and Lucy, 1978). *Delayed echolalia* is the repetition of speech after some lapse of time. Little systematic research has been done on delayed echolalia because of "the difficulty of tracing the history of usage and identifying the original occurrence of model utterances which helps to distinguish delayed echolalia from creative productions" (Prizant, 1983). Clinical observations have suggested that delayed echolalia may (although it does not necessarily) involve the repetition of whole conversations with the child alternating conversational turns, and that contextual factors associated with original utterances (e.g., setting, cointeractant, objects, and situation) may function as discriminative stimuli for its occurrence (Prizant, 1982).

Several theories exist concerning the potential role of echolalia in language acquisition by autistic persons. According to Rutter (1966), autistic children who demonstrate more adequate language functioning later in life appear to go through a prerequisite stage of echolalia. Baltaxe and Simmons (1977), Prizant (1982), and Voeltz (1977) drew similar conclusions about the potential function of echolalia as a strategy for continued language growth. They proposed that in contrast to normal language development, which is typically viewed as a "build-up" process in terms of grammar and the functional use of language, development of language in echolalic children may rely on a "breakdown" strategy in which the constituent components and functions of language are learned by analyzing larger "chunks" of repeated language. According to Baltaxe and Simmons (1981), this "gestalt language processing" (Prizant, 1982) may be related to deficits in the perception and production of prosodic features of language that make the segmentation of running speech into its constituent elements difficult.

To date, the bulk of research on echolalia has focused almost entirely on its structural properties (e.g., Buium and Stuecher, 1974; Shapiro et al., 1970). However, studies investigating the functional uses of immediate and delayed echolalia have been reported recently. Prizant and Duchan (1981) and Prizant and Rydell (1981) examined immediate and delayed echoic productions of autistic children, respectively, in terms of whether they were interactive, communicative, and produced with or without evidence of comprehension. In contrast to earlier accounts of echolalia as an undesirable and socially nonfunctional behavior (e.g., Coleman and Stedman, 1974), Prizant and his colleagues found that many echolalic responses were interactive and were produced with clear, independent, nonverbal evidence of comprehension. They further found that many echolalic productions could be categorized as serving such communicative functions as declaratives, affirmations, and requests.

Findings on the social and communicative functions of echolalic utterances have important implications for language intervention with autistic persons. In the past, the potential communicative value of echolalic utterances was largely ignored. Echolalia was primarily viewed as an inappropriate behavior that interfered with the communication process and therefore should be eliminated. Schreibman and Carr (1978), for example, taught autistic children to replace echoic responses with the answer, "I don't know." Recent findings suggest that echolalic responses may be more appropriately viewed as idiosyncratic forms of communication (Prizant and Duchan, 1981; Prizant and Rydell, 1981). Rather than extinguishing such responses irrespective of their communicative value, apparent communicative intents should be considered, and a "second language training" approach (see MacDonald, this volume) used to teach appropriate forms for expressing them.

Use of Gesture

Autistic children generally do not use gestures for the purpose of communication. This observation has support from both parental reports (e.g., Wing, 1971) and research investigations (e.g., Prior, 1977). Bartak et al. (1975) used both parental reports and observational data to compare gestural communication by 23 dysphasic [mean chronological age (CA) = 8.2 years] and 19 autistic children (mean CA = 7.0 years) matched for nonverbal IQ. In comparison to 11% (two cases) of the autistic children, 57% of the dysphasic children were reported to have used complex gestures for communication. Bartak et al. further examined the children's use of gestures by presenting object or picture stimuli and instructing the children to show (without touching the object) what one did with it. Gestural responses to verbal stimuli (e.g., "Show me washing") were also assessed. Results showed that the autistic children were significantly less able than the dysphasic children to use gestures in response to both types of stimuli.

In another study, Curcio (1978) examined the nonverbal communicative abilities of 12 mute autistic children (mean CA = 8.1 years). The children's use of proto-imperatives (nonverbal behaviors that serve instructing or requesting functions) and proto-declaratives (nonverbal behaviors that serve to show or point things to others) was assessed through teacher responses to questionnaires and classroom observations. Use of proto-imperatives was further assessed by observing the children's means of soliciting teacher assistance to obtain a desired object from a tightly closed jar.

A striking absence of proto-declaratives was observed among the children: none of them used "pointing" or "showing" to indicate the existence of properties of objects. In contrast, proto-imperative acts were observed in all of the subjects, although strategies for requesting varied considerably across children. In soliciting assistance for removing the object from the jar, for example, one subject simply banged the container, five subjects guided the teacher's hand toward it, and six subjects initiated eye contact, gave the container to the teacher, and waited. Since in young normal children the development of proto-imperatives and proto-declaratives occurs roughly at the same time (Bates et al., 1975), Curcio's findings suggest not just delayed, but qualitatively different patterns of gestural communication by autistic children.

Syntactic Development

The syntactic development of autistic children has been compared to the syntactic development of normal and mentally retarded children matched for nonlinguistic mental age. Comparisons have been made of the children's: 1) correct/incorrect production of present and past tense markers (Bartolucci and Albers, 1974); 2) syntactic complexity in free speech samples (Pierce and Bartolucci, 1977); and 3) use of functors (e.g., inflections, auxiliary verbs, articles, prepositions) in obligatory contexts (Bartolucci et al., 1980).

The results of these investigations indicated that, in comparison to the other two groups of children, the autistic children made significantly more errors in the use of past tense (Bartolucci and Albers, 1974) and showed an overall lower level complexity in syntactic development (Pierce and Barto-lucci, 1977). Bartolucci et al. (1980) found that the autistic children omitted functors in obligatory contexts more frequently than the normal children, but there were no significant differences between the autistic and mentally retarded children. The three grammatical morphemes used least often by autistic children in obligatory contexts were past regulars, present progres-sives, and articles. Bartolucci and his colleagues interpreted their findings of deficient syntactic development in autistic children in terms of deficient "semantic" development, particularly as related to deictic categories.[1] That is, the problem is thought to lie not so much in the children's ability to use syntactic forms and structures, but rather in their ability to accurately map semantic, deictic aspects of sentences with appropriate morphological inflec-tions and other grammatical markers. This theory has received support from other researchers of language development in autistic children (e.g., Tager-Flusberg, 1981a).

Semantic Development

Dale (1976) has defined the semantic component of the communication system as

. . .knowledge that a speaker must have to understand sentences and relate them to his knowledge of the world. It includes both knowledge of individual

---

[1]Deictic categories include person deixis, time deixis and space deixis. The appropriate use of these categories is dependent upon a shared understanding by the speaker and hearer of: 1) the identity of the speaker so that the pronouns *I* and *you* may be used correctly; 2) the relation-ship of events in time for purposes of adverbial (e.g., now, then) and tense selection; and 3) the proximal contrast in relation to whatever the speaker is making reference to (e.g., this, that; here, there).

lexical items and knowledge of how the meaning of a sentence is determined by the meanings of individual lexical items and the structure of the sentence. (p. 166)

Semantic functioning is also related to expressive language and has to do with use of particular lexical items to express particular relations and to serve various functions. Autistic children display deficiencies in both these aspects of semantic development.

Two early studies on semantic functioning of autistic children were reported by Hermelin and O'Connor (1967, 1970). These studies showed that, when verbal sequences of the form "blue, three, red, five, white, six, green, eight" were presented, autistic children tended to repeat the exact word order of the model, and categorized the words according to their semantic properties significantly less often than did mental age–matched normal and retarded children. In a later study, Hermelin and Frith (1971) found that, whereas normal and mentally retarded children were more proficient in repeating sentences than random strings of words, autistic children showed little difference in their ability to repeat both types of verbal stimuli. More recently, Schmidt (1976) investigated the paired associate learning of autistic children and found that, unlike matched retarded and normal children, the autistic children did not take advantage of high association values (e.g., needle–thread) in recalling paired associates.

Comparison of autistic children's use of a "probable-event strategy" versus a "word-order strategy" in comprehending linguistic stimuli has been studied by Tager-Flusberg (1981c). The probable-event strategy involves application of one's knowledge about the world to understanding linguistic input. Young normal children of 2 or 3 years of age use this strategy to interpret sentences describing semantically biased events. Sentences with positive semantic bias (e.g., "The mother holds the baby") are correctly acted out, whereas the corresponding sentences with negative semantic bias (improbable event—"The baby holds the mother") are reversed in the direction of the more probable event. The word-order strategy is used by slightly older normal children. Using this strategy, a noun-verb-noun sequence is interpreted as agent-action-object (Bever, 1970; Slobin, 1973). Children who use this strategy correctly act out semantically unbiased active sentences (e.g., "The truck hits the car"), but consistently reverse semantically unbiased passive sentences ("The truck is hit by the car") (Bever, 1970; Chapman and Miller, 1975).

Tager-Flusberg argued that the probable-event strategy has a general cognitive-semantic basis and that the word-order strategy is language specific and reflects the overgeneralization of an important syntactic device. She maintained that if, as the literature suggested, autism involves impaired semantic functioning autistic children would be less likely to use a probable-event strategy than a word-order strategy.

Tager-Flusberg (1981c) tested this hypothesis in two experiments involving autistic and normal children matched on verbal and nonverbal ability. In the first experiment, the children's use of strategies was compared using an act-out procedure in response to active and passive sentences. Results showed that the autistic group's overall sentence comprehension was significantly lower than that of the normal 3- and 4-year-old children. Moreover, and in support of Tager-Flusberg's hypothesis, the autistic children were found to generally use a word-order strategy but not a probable-event strategy in sentence comprehension.

The second experiment was conducted to determine if the strategy use results from the first experiment could be replicated using just content words as stimuli, as opposed to complete sentences. According to Tager-Flusberg, "By stripping a sentence of its grammatical morphemes, leaving only nouns and verbs, an experimenter can investigate more directly the child's strategic approach to comprehension" (1981c, p. 16). The results of this experiment supported those of the first. No significant difference was found in use of a word-order strategy by the normal and autistic subjects; both groups used this strategy for purposes of sentence comprehension. However, a significant difference was found between the two groups in regard to use of a probable-event strategy. Fifty-four percent of the normal children used a probable-event strategy with semantically biased stimuli as compared to its use by only 12% of the autistic children.

Based on the experimental outcomes, Tager-Flusberg concluded that at least some autistic children can extract and apply the language-specific rule that the order of words signals semantic relationships (e.g., agent-action-object) in English sentences. Thus, autism does not appear to involve a basic inability to use linguistic rules. The generally infrequent use of the probable-event strategy by autistic children possibly reflects deficient conceptual or semantic knowledge and/or impairment in relating conceptual or semantic knowledge to linguistic stimuli.

In addition to studies on comprehension, semantic functioning has also been examined in terms of the expressive language skills of autistic persons. Simmons and Baltaxe (1975) studied violations in semantic constraints (i.e., the rules governing the occurrence of elements of meaning) in the language of seven high-functioning autistic adolescents. The language responses were obtained in an interview situation during which the subjects were asked questions ranging from concrete (e.g., "Where do you live?") to abstract (e.g., "What would you do if you were the president?"). Various violations of semantic constraints were identified by Simmons and Baltaxe (1975); samples of each are presented here.

1. *Inappropriate antecedent reference.*
   Example: "*Mankind* is considering—*he* is considering."
   Should be: "Mankind is considering—it is considering."

2. *Opposite reference from that of target word.*
   Example: "He is getting *rarer* and *rarer* because *so many of them* are left."
3. *Inappropriate word use, where the word used belongs to the proper syntactic class, but had none of the semantic features of the target word.*
   Example: ". . .which one of the *staged* species."
   Should be: ". . .which one of the endangered species."
4. *Inappropriate word use, where the word used belonged to the proper syntactic class and had some of the semantic features of the target word.*
   Example: "The only *sport* I like is drawing."
   Should be: "The only hobby I like is drawing."
5. *Inappropriate word use, where the word belonged to the improper syntactic class, but had some of the semantic features of the target word.*
   Example: "Q: Why do you think he did it?
   A: *Questions* me."
   Should be: "Beats me."
6. *Telescoping of ideas where both syntactic and semantic constraints were broken.*
   Example: "Sometimes the foreman is—gets—and that's when—what gets the foreman angry—sometimes he asks stuff and that he couldn't get any answer out of such and such."
7. *Looseness of semantic constraints on words of emotional connotation and personal reference (tendency to avoid "I").*
   (The "you" of address in the question. . .related to singular use of pronoun.)
   Example: "Q: Is that what *you* would do when *you* get married?
   A: Yes, that's exactly what *people* would do when *they* get married."
8. *Idiosyncratic semantic usage (individual reference).*
   Example: ". . .or standing up, just like a—just like *lightning to a fireplace standing up to a fire.*"
9. *Meaningless additions and insertions."*
   Example: "Ads for different products *more or less."*
10. *Vagueness of referent.*
    Example: "Q: What are you planning to do?
    A: Just looking ahead in the future for all I care."

In sum, problems in semantic functioning have been observed in both productive and receptive language skills of autistic children. These problems may be related to impairments in conceptual development and/or in the ability to integrate real-world knowledge with linguistic stimuli. Semantic deficiencies may seriously affect the child's ability to understand language, to encode it in a manner that is intelligible to others, and to use language in socially acceptable ways.

Pragmatic Development

Bates (1976) defined pragmatics as "rules governing the use of language in context." The study of pragmatics deals with the analysis of: 1) how prelinguistic and linguistic behaviors function in communication (e.g., as requests, protests, answers, vocatives, declaratives, and so forth) and 2) social skills that tend to promote effective communication (e.g., turn-taking; maintaining the topic of conversation; relating new to old information; avoiding saying what the listener already is likely to be aware of; and using the apparent interest level of the listener as a cue for modifying one's verbal behavior). Given that autism involves both disturbances in language and the ability to form social relationships (Kanner, 1943; Ritvo and Freeman, 1978; Rutter, 1978), it is perhaps not surprising to read of reports emphasizing deficient pragmatic functioning by autistic persons (Cromer, 1981; Hermelin, 1971; Tager-Flusberg, 1981a).

Tager-Flusberg (1981b) compared the pragmatic competence of six autistic children (CA = 5 to 11 years) and six 30-month-old normal children matched for grammatical ability (mean length of utterance varied from 2.40 to 3.91 morphemes). The children's discourse communication skills in a free play situation were assessed in terms of 1) their ability to maintain the topic of conversation and 2) the semantic appropriateness of responses to questions. The possible relationship between discourse skills and levels of grammatical ability was also explored.

Data on topic maintenance were obtained by noting if child utterances were *relevant* to the preceding adult utterance, *irrelevant* to it, or simply an *imitation* of it. Whereas few differences were found in the percentages of relevant and irrelevant responses by the two groups of children, a large difference occurred in the frequency of imitative responses. At least 16% of the autistic children's utterances were imitations as compared to less than 2% of the utterances produced by the normal children. Findings of the second analysis, on the semantic appropriateness of the children's responses to questions, showed that the autistic children responded inappropriately 26% of the time compared to 14% for normal children. This difference was statistically significant.

To determine the effects of the autistic child's comparatively high proportions of imitation and semantically inappropriate responses on communicative interaction, an analysis of length of conversational episodes was conducted, a conversational episode being defined as an unbroken succession of conversationally relevant utterances. Significant group differences were found, with a mean length of episode of 2.95 reported for the autistic children and 12.98 for the normal children. The longer episodes engaged in by the normal children indicate greater ability to interact effectively in conversation.

Based on these findings, Tager-Flusberg (1981b) concluded that high levels of imitation and inappropriate responding reflect the autistic child's attempt to maintain a conversation even though he may have nothing to add to it. She further maintained that, unlike the developmental process in normal children, there seems to be little relationship between pragmatic skill and grammatical ability in the developing language skills of autistic children.

Hurtig et al. (1982) also looked at pragmatic development in young verbal autistic children (CA = 5 to 12 years), but their study investigated the relationship between question production by the children and topic maintenance. Question production by autistic children has generally been viewed as excessive and inappropriate. In his early case history presentations, Kanner (1943) observed that question production by autistic children was characterized by: 1) a high frequency of occurrence; 2) unusual content; 3) a lack of relation to the immediate context; and 4) self-response to questions. Hurtig et al. hypothesized that, rather than serving primarily to seek information from others, question asking by higher functioning autistic children may be used as a means of initiating social interactions. Maintenance of the conversation may then be dependent on the content of the listener's response and the extent to which it facilitates topic continuation by the child. Variations in listener response in terms of information conveyed and delegation of responsibility for continued conversational flow should, according to Hurtig et al., be reflected by a continuation or discontinuation of the interaction.

To test this hypothesis, responses to questions produced by six autistic subjects in a free play situation were systematically varied. Responses included *minimal* answers (just the information requested), *elaborations* (an answer to the question plus the introduction of new information), *questions* (an answer to the question plus a child-directed question on the same or a related topic), and *reversals* (a request that the child provide an answer to his own question). Results revealed that the children did indeed often know the answers to the questions they posed: 93% of reversal-type listener responses were correctly answered by the subjects. It was further found that employment of the question or reversal responses was most useful in aiding the children to make topic-related responses, whereas employment of minimal answers was least likely to do so.

Results of the Tager-Flusberg (1981b) and Hurtig et al. (1982) studies suggest that at least some autistic children do not so much seem to avoid social interactions as they seem to have ineffective strategies for initiating and maintaining them. Assessment efforts should be directed toward identifying the nature and function of such strategies so that more successful means of social interaction can be trained later on.

In addition to investigations on the pragmatic functioning of young verbal autistic children, the pragmatic skills of older autistic persons have also been examined. Baltaxe (1977) analyzed the language occurring during a structured interview situation of five highly verbal autistic adolescents (CA = 14 to 21 years; IQ = 86 to 118). Analysis of the dialogues revealed impairment in three areas of pragmatic functioning:

1. Speaker-hearer role relationships (as exemplified by the utterance, "I told my parents I'd be good at home but I feel you're too old to be at home, we feel you should be away").

2. The rules of conduct governing a dialogue (i.e., the social rules governing linguistic interchanges between older and younger speakers seemed not to have been acquired, and the subjects' language was often viewed as inappropriate, rude, or tactless).
3. Differentiating old and new information, that is, in contrast to the typical use of anaphoric pronouns to refer to old information, the subjects used nouns and fully specified noun phrases that gave their speech a sense of pedantic literalness and redundancy.

Finally, comparisons of the pragmatic functioning of autistic and developmentally language-disordered children matched for nonverbal IQ have been reported (Baker et al., 1976; Bartak et al., 1975). Analyses of spontaneous speech samples and parent responses to questions about their children's language and social development indicated that the developmentally language-disordered children were much more likely than the autistic children to engage in conversation, describe past experiences, and continue conversational topics (Bartak et al., 1975).

An additional analysis of the pragmatic functioning of 13 autistic and 13 developmentally language-disordered children from the Bartak et al. study was performed by Baker et al. (1976). In this study, a functional analysis was made of the speech produced by both groups of children during routine interactions with their mothers at home. No significant differences were found between the two groups' use of questions, answers, directives, demands, or automatic language (e.g., "hello," "please," and "thank you"). However, potential group differences may have been revealed through analyses of *qualitative* aspects of the children's productions, including the conventionality, repetitiveness, social appropriateness, and relatedness of their forms.

In sum, pragmatics involves multiple skills related to the ability to engage in functional and socially appropriate communicative interactions. Pragmatic skill is not dependent on speech production capabilities. A child may be able to produce words but be unable to use them communicatively. Alternatively, a nonspeaking child may use nonvocal forms for purposes of functional communication (e.g., McHale et al., 1980; Tager-Flusberg, 1981b). Pragmatic deficits have been observed throughout the autistic population; they affect both young and old and high- and low-functioning individuals. Because impairment in sociocommunicative functioning may be a major handicap affecting most aspects of the autistic person's life, remediation of pragmatic deficiencies should be a primary goal for intervention.

Summary

The label "autistic" has come to represent a heterogeneous group of individuals. The heterogeneity is related to the fact that impairment in social and language development and "insistence on sameness" (three of the defining features of autism; Rutter, 1978) can be manifested behaviorally in a variety of ways. The range of intellectual functioning of autistic persons (from above average to profoundly mentally retarded) and the possibility of "secondary behaviors" (behaviors often associated with autism, but that are not considered to be among its critical or defining features) such as hyperactivity, self-injury, self-stimulation, and physically disruptive behavior, contribute to the heterogeneous nature of the disorder.

Difficulty engaging in socially appropriate communication appears to be universal in autism. Problems in this area have been related to impairment in semantic and pragmatic functioning, which in turn have been associated with deficient development of prerequisite conceptual and social skills. Problems with grammatical structure that have been reported have been linked to the difficulty of linguistically mapping deficient semantic knowledge, as opposed to the difficulty of applying grammatical rules. Uneven skill level across phonological, syntactic, semantic, and pragmatic development appears to be the rule among verbal autistic persons; this extends to high-functioning and highly verbal adolescents and adults who, in spite of relatively problem-free articulatory and syntactic development, display major difficulties using semantically relevant language and adhering to social conventions indicative of "appropriate" interactions.

Behaviorally, the communication problems of autistic persons may be expressed in diverse ways. Since gestures are infrequently used for communicative purposes by autistic persons in general, the communicative skill of nonspeaking individuals is usually very limited. The linguistic forms produced by verbal autistic persons are often idiosyncratic in nature, and may or may not serve communicative functions. This relationship between form and function applies to both echolalic and nonecholalic speech. The diversity of skills and deficits that may occur within the various components of the communication system points to the necessity of assessing the language and language-related behaviors of individual children as a precursor to establishing goals for functional communication training. Once a thorough individualized assessment has been completed, treatment goals may be selected and remediation efforts begun. Specific issues related to intervention with autistic children and their significant others are explored below.

PLANNING FOR INTERVENTION

In this section the issues in teaching functional language to autistic children are addressed. Planning effective interventions includes developing an individualized intervention program that addresses five major component areas: 1) a behavior control component; 2) a motivational component; 3) a curriculum component; 4) general teaching strategies to be used during one-to-one and naturalistic training; and 5) a generalization and maintenance component. Each of these components is discussed in terms of fitting assessment information into an intervention framework that is oriented toward teaching socially useful, generalized communication skills to the autistic child. The goal of this section is to provide interventionists with guidelines derived from the existing research on teaching language to autistic children, so that they will have a firm basis for developing an individual teaching plan for an autistic child. Because autistic children vary in their skills and deficits, the guidelines are broad based and address issues rather than specific techniques.

Behavior Control Component

Autistic children, by definition, present a composite of difficult-to-handle social behaviors. This composite typically includes both disruptive behaviors and the characteristic nonresponsiveness or social isolation behaviors. Thus, the successful teacher of new skills to autistic children must also be able to manage the children's behavior in ways that allow effective teaching to occur. Language clinicians, teachers, parents, or support personnel working with this population must be skilled in applying a variety of behavior management techniques. To be "skilled" implies more than familiarity with the concept of behavior management; practice in applying the techniques with children with behavior disorders is clearly indicated if the teaching interactions are to be successful. There is a considerable body of literature documenting the primary (e.g., successful modification of target behaviors) and secondary (i.e., leading to acquisition of other skills) effects of systematic behavior management in interactions with autistic children (see Koegel et al., 1982).

Basically, the successful teacher must be able to do four things: 1) attend to and consequate appropriate behavior; 2) extinguish inappropriate behavior; 3) build new behaviors through modeling, shaping, and stimulus control techniques; and 4) masterfully engage in these behavior modification techniques while monitoring and maintaining meaningful social communication. Implicitly, the teacher must also have identified the behaviors of interest to be increased and decreased and must have control over his or her own behavior in the interaction. Since pacing and timing of contingencies will be important in establishing a smoothly functioning teaching interaction, the teacher's mastery of the behavioral techniques is critical.

Autistic children present many behavioral traps[2] for those who attempt to teach them. The traps are those related to presenting few socially soliciting and positive behaviors and many instances of nonsocial and/or disruptive

---

[2] These are not quite behavioral traps in the sense that Baer and Wolf (1970) have previously described them, but they seem to be analogous to Baer and Wolf's positive example.

behavior. The trap is the number of opportunities for the teacher to "invest" by attending to the inappropriate behaviors, in comparison to the number of opportunities to "invest" by attending to the appropriate ones. The task of the teacher in working with an autistic child is to manage, through skillful application of behavioral techniques, the child's behavior in ways that demolish the potential traps for the teacher. Put another way, behavior modification when successful not only increases the child's appropriate behavior, but decreases the probability that teachers will be trapped into investing their attention in the child's inappropriate behaviors. When children present more positive behaviors, the likelihood that these new behaviors will be consequated increases. Thus, over time, the teacher's task may become easier.

Typically, teachers will begin the intervention program by systematically prompting and consequating behaviors that contribute to effective learning: quietly attending to the task, attending to the teacher, responding, and attempting to respond. Frequently, children entering training will not yet exhibit these behaviors, and the teacher must have a strategy for teaching them that includes prompting, shaping, and systematic reinforcement. The number of behaviors that can be taught simultaneously and the intensiveness of the contingencies must be determined by the child's entry skills and behavioral characteristics. Some children will require intensive training on prerequisite skills; others can be taught to exhibit these behaviors at a higher, more appropriate rate in the context of teaching initial language content. There are numerous descriptions of procedures for shaping prerequisite behaviors available in the research and teaching literature (e.g., Harris, 1976; Hewett, 1965; Koegel and Schreibman, 1981; Lovaas et al., 1966); the reader may wish to consult these references in developing a teaching program.

Handling disruptive behaviors such as hitting, kicking, screaming, pinching, spitting, and refusing to stay seated without investing all of one's attention in these behaviors also requires skillful application of behavioral techniques. Timeout, in the form of withdrawal of the teaching task, withdrawal of teacher attention, or removal to a timeout area, is usually an effective strategy for decreasing inappropriate behaviors. However, two cautions are in order. First, for some children withdrawal of task and teacher demands may in fact be a reinforcing event in the context of a teaching session (see Solnick et al., 1977, for a discussion of the potentially reinforcing aspects of timeout). Second, for some autistic children who are extremely difficult to contact in a social interaction, withdrawal of adult attention may have minimal effects. Alternative techniques for decreasing inappropriate behavior, such as positive practice and response cost, may be more effective with children for whom social reinforcers are not strongly established. Observation of the child in his normal interactions and during brief timeout sequences will be helpful in selecting appropriate strategies for decreasing inappropriate behaviors.

Since increasing child social interaction and other positive behaviors will be a primary goal for nearly every autistic child, it is important that procedures to decrease behaviors be used in conjunction with positive techniques to increase desirable behavior. Decisions about specific contingencies should be determined prior to beginning the teaching program, and should be based on inventories of child behaviors requiring intervention and various types of behavior management procedures. In general, when target behaviors are not threatening to the child or others, techniques should be selected on the basis of their "positiveness" (i.e., less aversive techniques should be considered before more aversive ones) and their likelihood of being effective.

Effectively dealing with the self-stimulatory behaviors that are characteristic of many autistic children is one of the more difficult behavior management problems in conducting training with this population (see Koegel and Covert, 1972). Two strategies should be considered. If the self-stimulatory behavior truly interferes with the child's attention to the task, procedures for extinguishing the response should be applied. Timeout, instructions, and/or positive practice are potentially effective means for decreasing self-stimulatory behavior (Koegel et al., 1980). A second strategy may be appropriate, however. Sometimes self-stimulatory behaviors serve a communicative function or can be shaped to serve a function. For example, hand flapping might be shaped toward handwaving similar to a greeting response or hand raising to indicate that the child is ready to change activities. Selection of a strategy for dealing with self-stimulatory behavior will depend on the severity, intensity, and frequency of the particular response and its relationship to the child's attention during the task. Some frequencies of self-stimulation may be quite tolerable and noninterfering. The trainer must have a clear idea of the responses, their function, and their potentially disruptive influences, and must develop a behavior management strategy for dealing with these responses prior to initiating language training.

In sum, the behavior control component of the intervention will form the basis for the teaching interaction. Determining which behaviors will be targeted for change and establishing procedures for changing these behaviors must be done before training begins. Mastery of behavior management techniques will be equally important in one-to-one, group, or milieu teaching formats. The less formal and controlled the teaching format, the more skillful the application of management techniques demanded of the teacher.

Motivational Component

For the normal toddler learning language, gaining his mother's attention and controlling the social environment are strong reinforcers for his attempts to master the complexities of language. An autistic child, for whom social interaction is not a primary reinforcer, is handicapped not only by his language deficits but by his motivational deficits as well (Dunlap and Egel,

1982; Koegel and Egel, 1979). A primary task of the language interventionist will be designing the training program to compensate for these social deficits by identifying reinforcers that may motivate the child to learn new language.

Reinforcers are by definition individualized to the child. Any event that increases the probability of the responses that precede it is a reinforcer. For the autistic child, the events that increase the probability of preceding responses may be quite different from those teachers typically consider to be reinforcers. In particular, attention from adults, including praise and physical contact, may not be reinforcing events for the autistic child. Reinforcers must be determined by observing child interests and preferences, and by asking the child's significant others. Children may begin with a very small constellation of reinforcers. When food or manipulation of objects in a stereotypical manner are the child's only apparent reinforcers, the trainer must begin with the contingent use of these events, but must simultaneously apply a program for increasing the range of reinforcers. Pairing food with social contact, shaping manipulation of favored objects such as strings and rubber bands toward more appropriate object use, and incorporating food and objects in play sequences may be useful strategies for increasing the range of reinforcers.

The child's motivation for learning language should also be considered when selecting vocabulary or semantic/syntatic content for the teaching program. Typically, the first words normal children learn are those that name salient objects in their environment: "mom," "dad," "doggie," "cookie," and so forth (Nelson, 1973). Children also tend to generalize newly trained labels that map frequently occurring events more readily than they generalize labels for other objects (Warren and Rogers-Warren, 1983). An inventory of child interests may provide not only a list of potentially reinforcing events, but also potential training content. Children (and adults, too) talk about what interests them. Motivation for language learning can be increased if the learning relates directly to the events of interest to the child. Again, parents and others who spend time with the child may be excellent resources in cataloging the child's interests and in planning the motivational component of the program.

Curriculum Component

The curriculum for language intervention includes selecting a mode for communication, determining the general communicative functions to be addressed in short- and long-term training plans, selecting specific forms for training, and planning for integration of the linguistic component of the curriculum with the development of appropriate social interaction strategies. For the autistic child, the social interaction aspect of intervention is the primary determinant in selecting the other aspects of the curriculum because social deficits, perhaps more than any other single deficit, form the basis of the communication impairment.

The curriculum should be based on the outcome of the assessment process, and should include goals related to interacting with the environment, interacting with other persons verbally and nonverbally, and functional use of communicative forms. If the child is young or very low functioning, the individualized curriculum may emphasize developmentally early skills (e.g., establishing joint attention and activity) with relatively little emphasis on formal communication. More skilled children will have curricula that teach environmental interaction and interpersonal interaction simultaneously with the use of a complex communication system.

Development of a curriculum will begin with the selection of a communication mode. The primary consideration in selecting a mode is a social one: What mode can the child learn quickly enough to easily use it in social interaction? Young children with limited spontaneous speech or with evidence of echoic speech may be excellent candidates for verbal communication training. Older children who have not shown evidence of vocal development, or who have strong preferences for the manual mode (as evidenced by ability to write or draw, or development of gestural communication) are likely to learn a manual system more easily and are likely to generalize its use to social communication more readily than they would a more difficult-to-learn vocal system. Within the nonvocal mode several choices are possible: signing, use of communication boards, and written language. The child's emerging cognitive skills and preferences will determine which mode is most appropriate. Information from the assessment process, perhaps especially information gained from diagnostic teaching, should provide a data base for choosing an appropriate mode.

In addition to the child's preferences, the support for communication via a particular mode must be considered. When a child has a clear preference for signing, or appears to be able to use a communication board more easily than vocal language, the teacher must examine the environments in which the child will be using these modes. Effective communication depends on having significant others who understand the child's form of communication and who can respond to it verbally or in the same nonverbal form. Also, because it is impossible to teach all the language a child will need within the confines of the language intervention sessions, the child must learn additional forms from the natural environment. Unless the child's significant others are willing to learn the alternative mode and to some extent willing to teach the child forms using this mode, the child will be significantly handicapped as a communicator. Total communication programs that pair verbal and alternative modes of communication offer a partial solution, but the issue of environmental support is not easily resolved. Input of significant others (parents, teachers, caretakers) should be solicited in making this critical decision.

Most autistic children will have deficits in several areas of communication. It is likely that only one or two areas can be targeted in intervention, and the child's individualized curriculum will be developed around the areas of greatest need and those most likely to immediately impact the child's communicative functioning. Attempts to remediate the other areas of communication should be made, even if specific behaviors are not formally trained. For example, a child with limited spoken language will probably have a curriculum that includes expansion of vocabulary and combination of two words. In the context of this primary goal, the teacher may work on use of appropriate intonation and voice quality as well as using the newly trained forms to express a variety of pragmatic functions (simple question asking, acknowledgment, and question answering, for example).

If language intervention is to result in functional social language and functional use of new forms, then development of appropriate social interaction strategies must be emphasized throughout the training program. For the autistic child, language training must include lessons in contacting the social environment in ways that are reinforcing to the child. Thus, a curriculum that begins by teaching requesting forms may be appropriate for many autistic children. Verbal or nonverbal language is a more socially appropriate means for expressing needs and intentions already present in the child's repertoire than is idiosyncratic behavior. Through the process of "second language teaching" (MacDonald, this volume), the trainer can help the child bridge between existing idiosyncratic means for communicating and means that are likely to be effective with a wider range of people. Second language training requires the teacher to be an adept observer of the child. She must be able to follow the child's lead in an interaction, to determine the probable intent of the child's behavior, and, most importantly, to use these opportunities to teach the child more socially acceptable means of expression.

Ideally, the language training curriculum should be accompanied by a social development curriculum that includes not only those behaviors needed for language learning, but also other behaviors required in appropriate nonverbal interaction with adults (greeting, attending, instruction following, initiating social interchange, seeking assistance) and with peers (playing, appropriate responding to peer initiations, and so forth). A social curriculum can be critical to establishing the motivation necessary to support the child in learning communication forms. Ultimately, communication is a social behavior and without an established repertoire of interactive behaviors the development of communication and remediation of communicative deficits will be much more difficult. Since the autistic child's deficits in language are closely linked to his social behavior, attention to developing appropriate social interactions should not be considered to be outside the realm of language intervention.

Format for Instruction

Although typically one-to-one teaching and naturalistic or milieu teaching formats are presented as contrastive choices in intervention, it may be more appropriate to represent them as points on a continuum of formats for teaching. At one end is highly structured, preplanned didactic teaching in which the interaction is relatively restricted to a stimulus-response interchange in which the child's correct responses are narrowly defined and the communication context is strictly a teaching one. At the other end of the continuum is the application of incidental teaching, which follows the child's interests and uses the incidents provided by the child as opportunities to teach immediately relevant communication skills. Between these two extremes are numerous combinations of carefully planned and spontaneous teaching that include a range of levels of teacher control and prescribed child responding, and that may include peers or other significant adults in the teaching interaction.

For many autistic children, one-to-one teaching at the structured end of the continuum of formats may be needed to establish appropriate attending behaviors and to shape initial responding to adult communication. Once effective learning in this format has been established, there are several possible choices for moving to a more naturalistic teaching format. The first is to use milieu or incidental-type teaching formats as generalization settings (Hart and Rogers-Warren, 1978; Hart, this volume). Generalization and maintenance of newly learned skills can be programmed by "re-teaching" already learned skills in their more natural communicative contexts. Alternatively, a teacher might identify the sequence of viable teaching formats for a particular child and analyze them in terms of structure, social communication opportunities, and the degree of control exerted by the teaching adult. As the child shows evidence of rapid learning in more structured formats, teaching may be conducted in progressively less structured settings. Moving through the sequence of formats while monitoring child learning can be accompanied with probes to the least structured formats and generalization programming in these naturalistic settings.

An implicit goal in all language training should be to teach the child the skills that will be needed to learn from conversational interactions. Not only should training emphasize the learning of specific forms, it should also increase the likelihood that the child will be able to learn new language incidentally from those naturally occurring teaching episodes that form the basis of language learning for normally developing children. Planning to shift from highly structured to less structured formats across the course of the training period may be sufficient to program the acquisition of strategies for learning in naturalistic interactions.

Regardless of the specific format selected for training, the teacher must be adept at some basic teaching strategies. The situation should be carefully planned to increase the probability that the interaction will be a successful one. In initial teaching sessions, arrangement of the environment to encourage sitting appropriately and attending to the task and to limit distractions will be extremely important. Gradually, as the child's attentional skills increase, objects and people that might at first have been disruptive to the interaction can be introduced without distracting the child. Gradual introduction of these stimuli will be important in helping the child extend his language responses and learning strategies to natural environments that have many distractions. Monitoring the child's performance will be necessary throughout the process of introducing new stimuli. Response decrements or increases in disruptive behavior should signal the trainer that too much change has occurred too rapidly.

The environment should also be arranged to make application of behavior management procedures easy. If a timeout room or a timeout chair is used, it should be easily accessible. If withdrawal timeout procedures are applied, the room should be relatively free of "entertaining" stimuli.

The management of activities within the session is an important aspect of arranging the teaching environment. Since change can be very disruptive for many autistic children, change points will be especially critical. Applying the Premack principle (1959)—making access to a preferred activity contingent on completion of a less-preferred activity—may be a means of minimizing disruptive transitions and reinforcing the child for participating in the less-preferred activity. Also, it is important that individual activities end on a positive note. The time to change activities is while the child is still fully attending, interested, and responding to the task. It is often tempting to continue for just a few more trials when the child is working well, but shifting to another activity while both child and teacher are enjoying their interactions with the first activity may maintain a higher level of interest, avoid the disruptions associated with declining attention, and make returning to the activity in later sessions likely to be pleasant. By changing activities while the child's behavior is appropriate, the contingency for reinforcing appropriate behavior is more easily maintained. When task change occurs following child loss of attention, the child may inadvertently be reinforced for undesirable behavior. Gradually, longer periods of time can be spent with individual activities as long as the teacher continues to monitor the child's attention and anticipate the length of time that will be a positive learning experience.

Pacing within activities and across activities is critical for many children. Preparing materials in advance, planning a schedule of activities, and having data sheets ready will minimize disruptions and keep the flow of the interaction going. When additional preparations are required before a new activity can begin, the teacher should program for appropriate child behavior by providing the child with a toy or other transition material to bridge the time between activities (rather than requiring the child to sit quietly while she prepares the new activity). In general, inappropriate behavior is more likely to occur at change points within and across activities than it is likely to occur while the pace of the activity is even and the child's interest is high. By planning for smooth transitions and carefully sequencing activities, the teacher can minimize disruptions and maximize the actual teaching contact that occurs in a finite period of time (Hart, 1982).

When more naturalistic formats for training are used, many of the same considerations apply. Now, however, the teacher must be able to maintain control over the materials and to give materials contingent on the child's behavior in less structured contexts. For example, if the teacher is training the child to imitate modeled utterances in the context of a block building free play activity, she must maintain control over some desirable materials (small cars, colored blocks, plastic people, or whatever the child finds appealing) in order to ensure that she has reinforcers to provide to the child as a consequence for imitative responding. The reinforcing materials can be a means of recruiting child attention ("look what I have") and are likely to be an effective naturally occurring consequence for the child's responses. On the other hand, if the child readily accesses any material available in the activity, the teacher will either have to take the material back to gain the child's attention, or model while the child is already in contact with the materials. Neither of these options is as likely to gain the child's attention or to reinforce him for correct responding as effectively as the instance in which the teacher controls the materials.

In naturalistic teaching, the instructor must follow the child's lead and teach about the things in which the child expresses an interest. Thus, controlling desired materials is useful in recruiting child interest, but some teaching should focus on the child's needs and wants and follow his solicited or unsolicited attention. To achieve this balance, the teacher must discriminate between when it is important and appropriate to control the materials and demand child attention and responding, and when it is appropriate to reinforce child initiations. (Not all child initiations should be reinforced. Illustrative of this point are statements/questions that are produced "ad nauseum" by the child and those that are produced as a means of avoiding responding to the initiations of others.) The child's skills and communication goals should guide the teacher in determining which type of interaction is most needed at a particular point in training. As children become more effective language learners and more communicative, a shift toward following the child's lead is usually appropriate. In all interactions, almost regardless of the child's current functioning level, some mix of child-initiated and teacher-initiated teaching is desirable.

The advantage of naturalistic teaching settings is that they provide opportunities for the child to communicate functionally. For communication to be functional, the teaching adult must respond to the child's efforts in ways that permit the child to control the environment. In other words, it is usually the response of the adult that makes the child's language or behavior functional. A wide range of behaviors can be functional for the child in communicating his needs and wants and in interacting with the environment. For example, gesture, nonverbal initiations, and vocalizations can be the beginning point for social communication if the adult responds to these behaviors as if they were communicative. A "second language training" approach (Mac-Donald, this volume) in which the adult provides more culturally appropriate forms as models for the child contingent on the child's expression of communicative intent may serve the purpose of making the child's current repertoire more functional and of teaching the child the more common forms for expressing existing intentions. Such an approach is especially attractive because it optimizes the child's motivation for learning by teaching about the things in which the child has expressed an interest.

Naturalistic settings also offer opportunities to teach functional nonverbal imitation and for developing a generalized imitative repertoire. Modeling actions that assist the child in gaining desired objects or in controlling the environment in other ways serves the dual purpose of encouraging imitation and assisting the child in exploring and managing the immediate setting (Goetz et al., 1979). This approach may have the added advantage of teaching the child a strategy for learning new actions and possibly providing a means for instructing the child in more complex nonverbal behaviors.

The techniques used in naturalistic teaching are identical to those used in the more structured one-to-one settings. The only difference is that the techniques are applied in the flow of a primarily play or social interaction and that there is continuous effort toward making the child's communication attempts functional. In a sense, the teacher has released some of her control of the interaction in order for the child to take the lead. To manage such interactions in ways that lead to the child's learning of new communication skills requires knowledge of the child, mastery of behavior management techniques, skill in selecting and teaching target language behaviors, and the ability to completely attend to the ongoing interaction. Although that is a difficult order for the teacher, when such a prescription is filled, the benefits to the child in terms of learning new forms and new functional uses may be considerable.

Generalization and Maintenance

Generalization of newly learned language to social communication contexts is a difficult process for most autistic children (Lovaas et al., 1973). The lack of generalization probably arises from two sources. First, some autistic children are overselective in their response to stimuli. That is, their language responses may be controlled by aspects of the stimulus setting or events occurring in training that are not functionally related to the language-eliciting stimuli in the natural environment (see Rincover and Koegel, 1975). Formation of response classes and stimulus classes may be significantly impeded by even small degrees of overselectivity, resulting in a significant failure to generalize or maintain newly learned responses. Second, deficits in social interaction skills and lack of social reinforcers may inhibit responding in the presence of other people. Language is a social behavior, closely linked to other social behaviors and to social contingencies. Children who do not interact socially will have few opportunities to use their language or may be unmotivated to do so even when there are opportunities. Compensating for these two potential sources of a lack of generalization requires careful planning to structure training in ways that result in formation of stimulus and response classes and the development of associated social responses that will facilitate language use in other environments.

Stokes and Baer (1977) described seven techniques that can be used to actively program generalization from training to natural environments. At least five of these techniques are important to designing effective language intervention for autistic children. These techniques address the stimulus over-selectivity and lack of social responding characteristic of autistic children. Generalization programming techniques to be included in the design of the intervention program are: 1) introduction to the natural maintaining contingencies; 2) use of indiscriminable contingencies; 3) training sufficient exemplars; 4) training loosely; and 5) programming common stimuli.

Introducing the child to the naturally maintaining contingencies for language use is essential in training functional language. This generalization-facilitating procedure begins by selecting those forms that map and control the child's everyday environment. By selecting behaviors known to be functional in the settings the child inhabits, the probability of the child's responses being met with functional reinforcement is greatly increased.

Although the natural environment contains many reinforcers, the schedule on which these reinforcers are delivered for use of newly trained language is likely to be an irregular one. Thus, a second part of introducing the child to the naturally maintaining contingencies is to acquaint the child, through systematic training in similar settings or through reduction of the reinforcement schedule in didactic training, to the frequency and form of reinforcement the natural setting will provide. As the child masters basic language skills and become more adept at learning in less-controlled settings, it becomes increasingly likely that the naturally occurring contingencies will be sufficient in quality and quantity for the child's newly learned behavior to generalize and maintain in everyday settings.

By using "indiscriminable contingencies" for reinforcement in training, the child's new communicative behavior may be made increasingly resistant to extinction in the natural environment. For example, a trainer might reinforce on an intermittent basis for responses in training or might reinforce a sequence of behaviors that includes language, motor, and academic responses. Since intermittent schedules of reinforcement are particularly resistant to extinction, relative to continuous schedules (Ferster and Skinner, 1957), the child will be more likely to persist in using newly learned language after training on such schedules. The natural environment typically provides a "lean" and variable schedule of reinforcement in which consequences are more likely to follow clusters of verbal and nonverbal behavior than to be delivered contingent on specific language responses.

The formation of stimulus and response classes is essential to language learning (see Goldstein, this volume). In order for a child to form functional classes, he must have learned sufficient exemplars of the classes. Training sufficient exemplars may include training across a variety of settings so that the child is able to generalize to any setting in which language-eliciting events occur, and training with numerous examples of referents for labels (e.g., a red cup, a large blue cup, a tea cup, and a mug might all be used as exemplars of the referent "cup"). For autistic children who are overly selective in respond-ing to stimuli and who have difficulty in forming response classes that corres-pond to the classes formed by normal language users, the systematic training of multiple examples will require careful planning to ensure that the child is given sufficient opportunities to learn the defining or prototypical characteris-tics of the members of the response class. Systematic assessment of the child's generalization to other members of the response class should be conducted (see Warren, this volume).

All functional language responses cannot be directly trained. The prin-ciple of training sufficient exemplars must be applied if the child is to develop a repertoire of communication forms. The exact number of responses that must be trained in order for the child to generalize to all examples of a response class varies with the child's skill level and particular learning style.

A fourth strategy for facilitating generalization, "training loosely," is closely aligned to training sufficient exemplars. Loose training involves "teaching with relatively little control over the stimuli presented and the correct responses allowed, so as to maximize sampling of relevant dimensions for transfer to other situations and other forms of behavior" (Stokes and Baer, 1977, p. 357). For most autistic children, loose training will be a technique to be applied after a fairly extensive repertoire of responses has been developed using more tightly controlled teaching techniques. The principle of loose training shares some critical assumptions with the principle of introducing the child to the natural maintaining contingencies. After the response, or a critical subset of responses, is learned in well-controlled training conditions, training may move to conditions that more closely resemble those the child will encounter in the natural environment. By progressively increasing the varia-bility of the learning and/or talking setting, the child's tolerance for stimulus diversity may be increased. Loose training must be carefully monitored, especially with autistic children who may respond poorly to changes in the environment. Decrements in primary responding or generalization, increases in disruptive or self-stimulatory behavior, or increased latency in responding should signal the trainer that the training is "looser" than the student can tolerate and still learn new skills. The sequence of training formats discussed previously might be used as a means of introducing less formal training that incorporates more diversity while maintaining an optimal level of child learning and responding. Again, maintaining a balance between the conditions that should facilitate generalization and those that promote optimal learning by the child should be the goal.

Generalization can also be facilitated by programming common stimuli. Programming can be accomplished in two ways—by introducing stimuli from the natural environment into the training setting and by taking training stimuli into natural settings and providing the child with opportunities to talk about them in conversational contexts. Stimuli might be verbal (the kinds of questions asked of the child, the sequence of prompts used to support the child's answers), personal (the presence of the trainer in the classroom or the parent in the training session), or object-event related (presenting the same toys in both training and home play sessions). The trainer must determine, in selecting training stimuli, if the typical picture cards available for such training are appropriate for the child being trained. Although pictures are convenient in providing a wide range of stimuli for syntactic description, pictures rarely elicit language in conversational contexts. Use of more typical stimuli (e.g., the child's actions paired with trainer's questions) may offer a more limited set of opportunities for syntactic diversity, but may bridge between training and talking context in ways that are likely to promote generalization. Planning for generalization, then, will entail making training stimuli functional and salient in the child's everyday environment, and selecting from the everyday environment stimuli that can be used during more structured training. Attention to common stimuli is especially important for autistic children whose generalization is likely to be limited because of variability in stimulus conditions.

In summary, programming for generalization must begin in the early stages of planning the intervention program rather than waiting until the child learns an extensive set of responses. By systematically selecting common examples, training sufficient related exemplars, varying the reinforcement contingencies so they resemble those to be encountered in the natural environment, and adjusting the training conditions to maintain a balance that promotes generalization while maintaining optimal levels of learning, the trainer can greatly increase the probability that the autistic child will generalize newly learned language. Ideally, this level of program planning will be accompanied by facilitative development of social skills as a means of bringing the child into more frequent contact with the conversational opportunities for language.

CONCLUSION

Autistic children characteristically display deficits in a number of areas critical to development of socially appropriate, functional communication.

Impairment in attentional, discrimination, and social interaction strategies and impaired ability to generalize learned skills across persons, settings, objects, events, and time constitute major obstacles to the establishment, growth, and refinement of skills related to receptive and expressive language capabilities. Research reviewed here suggests that the learning deficits of autistic children prove particularly obstructive to their ability to: 1) obtain knowledge about the world, and/or to map real-world knowledge linguistically (semantic functioning); and 2) use language in functional and socially appropriate ways (pragmatic functioning). Assessment and intervention efforts should specifically address these deficits in the course of communication programming. In addition, behavioral control, motivation, teaching strategy (didactic versus milieu approaches), and generalization must be carefully considered and planned for as part of the intervention process. We have proposed guidelines for addressing each of these issues in this chapter.

REFERENCES

Baer, D. M., and Wolf, M. 1970. The entry into natural communities of reinforcement. *In* R. Ulrich, T. Stachnik, and J. Mabry (eds.), Control of Human Behavior, Vol. 1. Scott, Foresman, New York.

Baker, L., Cantwell, D. P., Rutter, M., and Bartak, L. 1976. Language and autism. *In* E. R. Ritvo (ed.), Autism: Diagnosis, Current Research and Management, pp. 121–149. Spectrum Publications, New York.

Baltaxe, C. A. M. 1977. Pragmatic deficits in the language of autistic adolescents. J. Pediatr. Psychol. 2:176–180.

Baltaxe, C. A. M., and Simmons, J. Q. 1977. Bedtime Soliloquies and linguistic competence in autism. J. Speech Hear. Disord. 42:376–393.

Baltaxe, C., and Simmons, J. 1981. Disorders of language in childhood psychosis: Current concepts and approaches. *In* J. Darby (ed.), Speech Evaluation in Psychiatry. Grune & Stratton, New York.

Bartak, L., Rutter, M., and Cox, A. 1975. A comparative study of infantile autism and specific developmental receptive language disorder. I. The children. Br. J. Psychiatry 126:127–145.

Bartolucci, G., and Albers, R. J. 1974. Deictic categories in the language of autistic children. J. Autism Child. Schizophr. 4:131–141.

Bartolucci, G., Pierce, S. J., and Streiner, D. 1980. Cross-sectional studies of grammatical morphemes in autistic and mentally retarded children. J. Autism Dev. Disord. 10:39–50.

Bates, E. L. 1976. Language and Context: The Acquisition of Pragmatics. Academic Press, New York.

Bates, E. L., Camaioni, L., and Volterra, V. 1975. The acquisition of performatives prior to speech. Merrill-Palmer Q. 21:205–226.

Bever, T. G. 1970. The cognitive basis for linguistic structures. *In* J. R. Hayes (ed.), Cognition and the Development of Language, pp. 279–362. Wiley, New York.

Blank, M., Gessner, M., and Esposito, A. 1979. Language without communication: A case study. J. Child Lang. 2:329–352.

Buium, N., and Stuecher, H. 1974. On some language parameters of autistic echolalia. Lang. Speech 17:353–357.

Caparulo, B. 1981. Development of communicative competence in autism. Paper presented at the National Society for Children and Adults with Autism, International Conference on Autism, Boston.

Chapman, R. S., and Miller, J. F. 1975. Word order in early two and three word utterances: Does production precede comprehension? J. Speech Hear. Res. 18:355–371.

Coleman, S., and Stedman, J. 1974. Use of a peer model in language training in an echolalic child. J. Behav. Therapeut. Exp. Psychiatry 5:275–279.

Creak, M. 1961. Schizophrenic syndrome in childhood: Progress report of a working party. Cerebral Palsy Bull. 3:501–504.

Cromer, R. F. 1981. Developmental language disorders: Cognitive processes, semantics, pragmatics, phonology, and syntax. J. Autism Dev. Disord. 11:57–74.

Curcio, F. 1978. Sensorimotor functioning and communication in mute autistic children. J. Autism Child. Schizophr. 8:281–292.

Curtiss, S. 1981. Dissociations between language and cognition: Cases and implications. J. Autism Dev. Disord. 11:15–30.

Dale, P. S. 1976. Language Development: Structure and Function, 2nd ed. Holt, Rinehart & Winston, New York.

DeMyer, M. K., Barton, S., DeMyer, W. E., Norton, J. A., Allen, J., and Steele, R. 1973. Prognosis in autism: A follow-up study. J. Autism Child. Schizophr. 3:199–246.

Dunlap, G., and Egel, A. L. 1982. Motivational techniques. In R. L. Koegel, A. Rincover, and A. L. Egel (eds.), Educating and Understanding Autistic Children, pp. 106–126. College Hill Press, San Diego.

Eisenberg, L. 1956. The autistic child in adolescence. Am. J. Psychiatry 112:607–612.

Fay, W. H., and Schuler, A. L. 1980. Emerging Language in Autistic Children. University Park Press, Baltimore.

Ferster, C. and Skinner, B. F. 1957. Schedules of Reinforcement. Appleton-Century-Crofts, New York.

Goetz, L., Schuler, A., and Sailor, W. 1979. Teaching functional speech to the severely handicapped: Current issues. J. Autism Dev. Disord. 9:325–343.

Harris, S. L. 1976. Behavior Modification: Teaching Speech to a Nonverbal Child. H & H Enterprises, Inc., Lawrence, KS.

Hart, B. 1982. So that teachers can teach: Assigning roles and responsibilities. Topics Early Child. Spec. Educ. 2:1–9.

Hart, B., and Rogers-Warren, A. 1978. A milieu approach to teaching language. In R. L. Schiefelbusch (ed.), Language Intervention Strategies, pp. 193–235. University Park Press, Baltimore.

Hermelin, B. 1971. Rules and Language. In M. Rutter (ed.), Infantile Autism: Concepts, Characteristics, and Treatment, pp. 98–113. Churchill Livingstone, Edinburgh.

Hermelin, B., and Frith, U. 1971. Psychological studies of childhood autism:

Can autistic children make sense of what they see and hear? J. Spec. Educ. 5:107–117.

Hermelin, B., and O'Connor, N. 1967. Remembering of words by psychotic and subnormal children. Br. J. Psychol. 58:213–218.

Hermelin, B., and O'Connor, N. 1970. Psychological Experiments with Autistic Children. Pergamon Press, Oxford.

Hewett, F. M. 1965. Teaching speech to an autistic child through operant conditioning. Am. J. Orthopsychiatry, 35:927–936.

Hingtgen, J. N., and Bryson, C. Q. 1972. Recent developments in the study of early childhood psychoses: Infantile autism, childhood schizophrenia and related disorders. Schizophr. Bull. 5:8–53.

Hingtgen, J. N., and Churchill, D. W. 1971. Differential effects of behavior modification in four mute autistic boys. In D. Churchill, G. Alper, and M. DeMyer (eds.), Infantile Autism, pp. 185–199. Charles C Thomas, Springfield, IL.

Howlin, P. A. 1981. The effectiveness of operant language training with autistic children. J. Autism Dev. Disord. 11:89–105.

Hurtig, R. Ensrud, S., and Tomblin, J. B. 1982. The communicative function of question production in autistic children. J. Autism Dev. Disord. 12:57–69.

Kanner, L. 1943. Autistic disturbances of affective contact. Nerv. Child 2:217–250.

Kanner, L. 1944. Early infantile autism. J. Pediatr. 25:211–217.

Kanner, L. 1946. Irrelevant and metaphorical language in early infantile autism. Am. J. Psychiatry 103:242–246.

Kanner, L. 1951. The conception of wholes and parts in early infantile autism. Am. J. Psychiatry 108:23–26.

Koegel, R. L., and Covert, A. 1972. The relationship of self-stimulation to learning in autistic children. J. Appl. Behav. Anal. 5:381–387.

Koegel, R. L., and Egel, A. L. 1979. Motivating autistic children. J. Abnorm. Psychol. 88:418–426.

Koegel, R. L., Egel, A. L., and Dunlap, G. 1980. Learning characteristics of autistic children. In W. Sailor, B. Wilcox, and Y. Brown (eds.), Methods of Instruction with Severely Handicapped Students, pp. 259–301. Paul H. Brookes Publishers, Baltimore.

Koegel, R. L., Rincover, A., and Egel, A. L. 1982. Educating and Understanding Autistic Children. College Hill Press, San Diego.

Koegel, R. L., and Schreibman, L. 1981. How to Teach Autistic and Other Severely Handicapped Children. H & H Enterprises, Inc., Lawrence, KS.

Lotter, V. 1966. Epidemiology of autistic conditions in young children. I. Prevalence. Soc. Psychiatry 1:124–137.

Lotter, V. 1967. Epidemiology of autistic conditions in young children. II. Some characteristics of parents and children. Soc. Psychiatry 1:163–181.

Lovaas, O. I. 1977. The Autistic Child: Language Development through Behavior Modification. Irvington Publishers, Inc., New York.

Lovaas, O. I., Berberich, J. P., Perloff, B. F., and Schaeffer, B. 1966. Acquisition of imitative speech in schizophrenic children. Science 151:705–707.

Lovaas, O. I., Koegel, R., Simmons, J. Q., and Long, J. S. 1973. Some generalizations and follow-up measures on autistic children in behavior therapy. J. Appl. Behav. Anal. 6:131–166.

McHale, S. M., Simeonsson, R. J., Marcus, L. M., and Olley, J. G. 1980. The social and symbolic quality of autistic children's communication. J. Autism Dev. Disord. 19:299–310.

McLean, J. E., and Snyder-McLean, L. K. 1978. A Transactional Approach to Early Language Training. Merrill, Columbus, OH.

Nelson, K. 1973. Structure and strategy in learning to talk. Monogr. Soc. Res. Child Dev. 38.

Paul, R. 1982. Language studies in autistic children. Paper presented at the National Society for Children and Adults with Autism, Annual Conference for Parents and Professionals, Omaha.

Pierce, S. J., and Bartolucci, G. 1977. A syntactic investigation of verbal autistic, mentally retarded, and normal children. J. Autism Child. Schizophr. 7:121–134.

Premack, D. 1959. Toward empirical behavior laws: 1. Positive reinforcements. Psychol. Rev. 66:219–233.

Prior, M. R. 1977. Psycholinguistic disabilities of autistic and retarded children. J. Ment. Defic. Res. 21:37–45.

Prizant, B. M. 1982. Gestalt language and gestalt processing in autism. Topics Lang. Disord. 3:16–23.

Prizant, B. M. 1983. Echolalia in autism. Assessment and intervention issues. In B. M. Prizant (ed.), Seminars in Speech Language and Hearing. Thieme-Stratton, Inc., New York.

Prizant, B. M., and Duchan, J. F. 1981. The functions of immediate echolalia in autistic children. J. Speech Hear. Disord. 46:241–249.

Prizant, B., and Rydell, P. 1981. The functions of delayed echolalia in autistic children. Paper presented at The National Convention of the American Speech-Language-Hearing Association, Los Angeles.

Rimland, B. 1964. Infantile Autism. Appleton-Century, New York.

Rincover, A., and Koegel, R. L. 1975. Setting generality and stimulus control in autistic children. J. Appl. Behav. Anal. 8:235–246.

Ritvo, E. R., and Freeman, B. J. 1978. National Society for Autistic Children definition of the syndrome of autism. J. Autism Child. Schizophr. 8:162–167.

Rutter, M. 1966. Prognosis: Psychotic children in adolescence and early adult life. In J. K. Wing (ed.), Early Childhood Autism: Clinical, Educational, and Social Aspects, pp. 83–100. Pergamon Press, London.

Rutter, M. 1968. Concepts of autism: A review of research. J. Child Psychol. Psychiatry 9:1–25.

Rutter, M. 1978. Diagnosis and definition of childhood autism. J. Autism Child. Schizophr. 8:139–161.

Rutter, M. Greenfeld, D., and Lockyer, T. 1967. A five to fifteen year follow-up study of infantile psychosis. II. Social and behavioral outcome. Br. J. Psychiatry 113:1183–1199.

Rutter, M., and Lockyer, L. 1967. A five to fifteen year follow-up study of infantile psychosis. I. Description of sample. Br. J. Psychiatry 113:1169–1182.

Schmidt, J. 1976. Relations between paired-associate learning and utterance patterns in children with echolalia. Unpublished doctoral dissertation, Boston University, School of Education.

Schopler, E. 1978. On confusion in the diagnosis of autism. J. Autism Child. Schizophr. 8:137–138.

Schreibman, L., and Carr, E. G. 1978. Elimination of echolalic responding to questions through the training of a generalized verbal response. J. Appl. Behav. Anal. 11:453–463.

Schuler, A. L. 1976. Speech and language in autism: Characteristics and treatment. Mini-seminar at the Annual Meeting of the American Speech and Hearing Association, Houston.

Shapiro, T., and Lucy, P. 1978. Echoing in autistic children: A chronometric study of semantic processing. J. Child Psychol. Psychiatry 19:373–378.

Shapiro, T., Roberts, A., and Fish, B. 1970. Imitation and echoing in young schizophrenic children. J. Am. Acad. Child Psychiatry 9:548–565.

Simmons, J. Q., and Baltaxe, C. 1975. Language patterns of autistic children who have reached adolescence. J. Autism Child. Schizophr. 5:333–351.

Slobin, D. I. 1973. Cognitive prerequisites for the development of grammar. In C. A. Ferguson and D. I. Slobin (eds.), Studies of Child Language Development. Holt, Rinehart, & Winston, New York.

Stokes, T. F., and Baer, D. M. 1977. An implicit technology of generalization. J. Appl. Behav. Anal. 10:349–367.

Solnick, J. V., Rincover, A., and Peterson, C. 1977. Some determinants of the reinforcing and punishing effects of time-out. J. Appl. Behav. Anal. 10:415–424.

Tager-Flusberg, H. 1981a. On the nature of linguistic functioning in early infantile autism. J. Autism Dev. Disord. 11:45–56.

Tager-Flusberg, H. B. 1981b. Pragmatic development and its implications for social interaction in autistic children. Paper presented at The National Society for Children and Adults with Autism, International Conference on Autism, Boston.

Tager-Flusberg, H. 1981c. Sentence comprehension in autistic children. Appl. Psycholing. 2:1–24.

Voeltz, L. M. 1977. Syntactic rule mediation and echolalia in autistic children. Unpublished manuscript, University of Hawaii.

Warren, S. F., and Rogers-Warren, A. K. 1983. Because nobody asked: Setting variables affecting the display of trained noun referents by retarded children. In K. Kernan, M. Begab, and R. Edgerton (eds.), Environment and Behavior: The Adaptation of Mentally Retarded Persons. University Park Press, Baltimore.

Wing, L. 1971. Perceptual and language development in autistic children: A comparative study. In M. Rutter (ed.), Infantile Autism: Concepts, Characteristics, and Treatment. Churchill, London.

chapter
6

Communication Intervention for the "Difficult-to-Teach" Severely Handicapped

William J. Keogh
Center for Developmental Disabilities
Department of Special Education
University of Vermont
Burlington

and

Joe Reichle
Department of Communication Disorders
University of Minnesota
Minneapolis

DIFFICULT-TO-TEACH CHILDREN   160
    Defining the Difficult-to-Teach Population   160
    An Intervention Model   162
    Overview of the Chapter   163

**TEACHING COMMUNICATION FUNCTIONS: POTENTIAL
PROBLEMS FOR DIFFICULT-TO-TEACH CHILDREN   164**
    Intentionality: Expressing Wants and Needs   165
    Relationship between Requesting and Describing   166

**CONCEPTUAL AND PROCEDURAL BASIS FOR A BEGINNING
COMMUNICATION INTERVENTION   170**
    Learning Concepts   171
    Discrimination Learning   172
    Rule-Governed Matching-to-Sample   173
    **A Generic Strategy for Teaching Beginning
      Communication Skills   175**
    The Vermont Early Communication Curriculum   176
    Developing a Rudimentary Requesting Skill   178
    Learning to Describe   181
    Learning to Discriminate between Stimuli   182
    Learning Generalized Matching-to-Sample   184
    Teaching Speech Comprehension of Object Names   186

PHYSIOLOGICAL DETERMINANTS   188
    Psychomotor Performance   188
    Vision Acuity   189
    Hearing Screening   189

CONCLUSIONS   190

ACKNOWLEDGMENTS   191

REFERENCES   191

Until the 1960s few, if any, language intervention programs were available to teachers and other service providers. Then, the prevailing issue was the nature of human language, and it was represented by two broad theoretical positions. One position presupposed an innate, uniquely human capacity to acquire language, implying that little, if anything, could be done to alter the course of language deviancy (Chomsky, 1959, 1965; Lenneberg, 1964). The other position maintained that humans were no more predisposed to learn language than they were to learn other behaviors, and it was the infant's interaction with the environment that best accounted for language development (Skinner, 1957).

As interest in applied behavior analysis and language intervention began to accelerate in the mid-1960s, the rigidity of these positions softened some-what, alternative theories were offered, and different issues became prominent (Bricker and Bricker, 1974; Guess et al., 1974; Lynch and Bricker, 1972; Staats, 1974). The new issues focused more on the language *intervention* process than on the nature of language *per se*, and the following questions seemed to dominate the field: Does language comprehension precede expression? What role does verbal imitation play in speech and language development? Are there necessary prerequisites to language learning; if so, what are they?

The tenor of these issues reflected the field's emphasis on speech and, to be sure, some of these issues remain prominent. Today, however, a visit to almost any special education classroom will show that an array of communication aids and manual signing programs has replaced speech as the major intervention mode and the pragmatic aspects of communication have replaced concerns about grammatical structure. Now, the interventionist must determine whether an early introduction of an augmentative or alternative system really facilitates speech development for some children or (perhaps) inhibits it (Creekmore, 1982). Are assessment strategies sufficiently sensitive to ensure that children are *not* being placed in signing and/or communication aid programs who could otherwise benefit from speech training? If communication aids are to be used, how should they be designed? There is even debate over a satisfactory definition of language or communication (Siegel and Spradlin, 1978). As Alpert (1980) pointed out, most of these issues still need to be resolved. For the time being, at least, it seems as though the field of language/communication intervention is accelerating so fast that scholars are unable to resolve major issues at a rate equal to their emergence.

Faced with so many unresolved issues and so many idiosyncratic forms of language deviancy, can there be one truly comprehensive language intervention strategy (see Warren and Rogers-Warren, this volume), or even one

Work reported in this chapter was supported in part by Grant 023KH10015 from the U.S. Department of Education.

satisfactory definition of language/communication? Possibly, there may be some advantage in considering an intervention strategy that is flexible enough to accommodate (or to avoid) the major language intervention issues while remaining specific enough to be useful, permitting children to reach their full (yet-to-be-determined) potential as communicators.

Given the state of the field, it was not clear what criteria were used by practitioners to select one training program over another, but nevertheless choices were made, and practitioners began teaching in an orderly step-by-step sequence. Some children began to learn as a result of direct training even though little generalization and spontaneity were exhibited. Other children failed to learn (particularly those who failed to learn to imitate vocally). Some could not even get started because they lacked the necessary physiological "entry" or prerequisite skills to produce speech sounds. Thus, language interventionists entered the 1980s encourage by the modest successes, concerned about the failure of rudimentary speech to generalize, and discouraged about the prospects for success with children who failed to learn and/or whose spasticity, speech mechanisms, and other physiological factors were so impaired that speech training was not possible. This chapter proposes a strategy for developing a beginning communication system for severely multihandicapped children who have failed to progress with or even participate in, various language intervention strategies. We refer to these children as "difficult to teach."

DIFFICULT-TO-TEACH CHILDREN

Defining the Difficult-to-Teach Population

> Severely handicapped children are those who because of the intensity of their physical, mental or emotional problems, or a combination of such problems, need educational, social, psychological, and medical services beyond those which are traditionally offered by regular and special educational programs, in order to maximize their full potential for useful and meaningful participation in society and for self-fulfillment.
>
> *U.S. Department of Education, 1982*

Difficult-to-teach children conform to the broad definition of "severely handicapped" presented above and to other similar definitions (e.g., Grossman, 1977; Sailor and Guess, 1983). Yet we know that they are unlike the severely handicapped individuals often described in many of our professional journals. For example, Peterson et al. (1979) showed that the social behaviors of three severely retarded children could be increased by using prompting and praise—rather unintrusive interventions. Similarly, Strain (1975) increased the play behavior of eight severely handicapped children by requiring them to act out behaviors that were read concurrently in story books—another rather unintrusive technique. Halle et al. (1979) taught six severely handicapped children socially appropriate requesting behavior during mealtimes (e.g., "Tray, please," "Want food") using a straightforward prompting and imitation procedure. All the subjects in these studies were considered either severely or profoundly retarded according to Grossman's definition (1977). However, the children we are describing are typically unable to acquire skills in a similar manner. What, then, is the difference between the severely or profoundly handicapped students who are "difficult to teach" and the severely or profoundly handicapped students described in the above-cited studies? What is it about the procedures described above that would inhibit the children we have in mind from benefiting from them? Essentially, the differences might be summarized along three dimensions: apparent propensity to learn, degree of motor impairment, and degree of participation.

Children Who Fail to Learn   Experience has taught us, and others (e.g., Guess et al., 1976; Zeaman, 1976), that some students seem to possess all of the motor and motivational prerequisites to enter into a teaching-learning situation (e.g., they sit still and seem to be attending, they are able to reach and point, they have unrestricted movement of hands/ fingers or gait, they voluntarily respond, and they readily accept our food and praise), yet we fail to teach them. Baer (1978) pointed out that approximately 30% of the students enrolled in imitation training programs at the Kansas Neurological Institute failed to learn after extensive and intensive training. Alpert (1980) suggested that one means of determining whether a nonspeech training approach should be used is "to consider factors such as the child's age and history of training experiences. . . ." (p.399). Children in this category are, in effect, children whose "diagnosis" or classification (i.e., "difficult-to-teach") is given after a period of treatment or intervention has taken place. These children, who fail to benefit after various intervention strategies have been tried, represent that part of the difficult-to-teach population we wish to consider regardless of formal definitions.

Children with Severe Motor Impairments   Often, children diagnosed as severely or profoundly handicapped are further handicapped because their mechanisms for motor coordination are severely impaired. Since the majority of typically used interventions prepared for teachers of the severely handicapped require that students produce voluntary discrete responses, children with severe motor impairments present a particular dilemma to the special educator. These students lack the motor prerequisites so often required for participation in typical teaching-learning situations. Do nonresponding children fail to emit a recognizable "signaling" response because of the severity of their motor problems, or has the environment taught them to be "helpless" (Seligman, 1972). Do they comprehend more than their impaired bodies will allow them to express? Would they become efficient communicators if they had some form of idiosyncratic "signaling" response available to them? These children also represent that segment of the difficult-to-teach population we want to include in our discussion.

Passive Participants   A third category of "difficult-to-teach" children includes students who may possess all of the motor prerequisites to participate in most teaching/learning situations (unlike motorically impaired children), but they fail to benefit from teaching efforts because they remain passive participants (e.g., they may sit and allow the teacher to prompt, or to put them through targeted behaviors in order for approximations of skills to be shaped or "reinforced," but they do little else). They represent that segment of the difficult-to-teach population about whom teachers say "We can't find a reinforcer!" Unlike the child who fails to learn, passive participants lack the motivation to learn, often preferring to spend their time engaged in various forms of self-stimulatory behaviors.

The best definition we have found of "difficult-to-teach" children is not a definition at all. It is a statement that describes the characteristics of children we are concerned about. It comes from Ms. Jean Garvin, State Director of Special Education and Pupil Personnel Services in Vermont (*Teaching Exceptionally Mentally Retarded*, 1976):

> . . . I think that actually there are different people who ascribe different descriptions to these children. The children I'm talking about are the most severely multiply handicapped children with all the motor, physical and language handicaps which people in special education know so well, but don't see in the severe form except in these children. So typically, they are children of all ages, with stiff muscles and limbs that don't work too well, some with high numbers of seizures per day. They are children who of course are very small for their ages, may not walk, may not sit up, may not roll over. They are children who don't have eye contact with us or turn us on particularly until we get to know them. They may be in wheelchairs. I think the picture that I would like to give you is that these individuals are children with many impairments ranging from mental to physical disabilities. (p. 84)

An Intervention Model

The intervention model proposed in this chapter has particular relevance for difficult-to-teach children. The model should be viewed more as a *beginning communication strategy* than as a "comprehensive communication curriculum." The goal is to teach the discriminative use of the *describing* and *requesting* functions of communication. An understanding of these functions is basic to all other communication/language learning. A notable characteristic of the model is the assumption that learning the rudiments of requesting and describing need not depend on an ability to produce or even comprehend an array of complex manual signs or speech. Therefore, this model enables children to progress by pointing to various visual displays.[1]

Visual arrays that display a set of symbols to represent a portion, or all, of a child's lexicon are commonly referred to as "communication boards," "picture boards," or "symbol boards." The visual display may be photographs, line drawings, or more abstract symbol-forms such as sight-words, Rebus symbols, or Blissymbols. Communication aids of this type allow some children to achieve a level of communicative competence that they might not have otherwise. A unique characteristic of this system is the possibility that children may learn to engage in simple communication exchanges without having learned to comprehend the spoken names of significant people, places, and things. This situation exists, in part, because the most salient cues used by the child are visual and his expressive competence is demonstrated by pointing to the various symbols. Because he does not need to understand or produce speech, speech comprehension is not a prerequisite to communicate two-part utterances such as "Want object" or to "answer" simple questions such as "What's this?" or "What do you want?" For example, when teaching a communication board user-to-be to express the names for common objects, the teacher typically holds an object in front of the child and asks, "What's this?" The child answers by scanning the symbol choices he has available (on his communication board) and selecting the one that best represents the three-dimensional form. This operation may be accomplished through nonidentical matching-to-sample. Because children who are being taught to communicate by using "picture boards" must process stimuli visually and use the same response topography (pointing) to request and describe, careful attention must be given to the way the teaching-learning environment is arranged.

Overview of the Chapter

The remainder of this chapter is divided into four sections. First, an overview of the describing and requesting functions of communication and how the environment can be arranged to maximize their learning is presented. Then the relationship between conceptual behavior, discrimination learning, rule-governed visual matching, and symbolic expressions is discussed. Next, a generic model for teaching beginning communication skills to difficult-to-

---

[1] Pointing need not be restricted to the extended index finger. Here, pointing is viewed as some observable signal that may be used in requests such as "I want something" or to indicate choices in a multiple-choice task. Thus, eye orientation, the use of electromechanical devices, or hand/arm orientation are considered pointing.

teach children is proposed. Finally, the assessment of physiological determinants (i.e., psychomotor performance, visual acuity, and hearing) of communication as they relate to the difficult-to-teach child are discussed briefly.

TEACHING COMMUNICATION FUNCTIONS: POTENTIAL PROBLEMS FOR DIFFICULT-TO-TEACH CHILDREN

Intervention suggests that the normal teaching environment must be changed in order to enhance or facilitate learning. The change may be directed toward any one, or all, of the following: 1) conditions that precede behavior; 2) the topography of the behavior itself; or 3) the conditions that follow behavior. Some interventions require no more than a simple adjustment to conditions that follow behavior; others require that all three of the conditions be carefully attended to. This section discusses how the teaching-learning environment needs to be arranged in order to avoid potential problems and to maximize chances of success when teaching requesting and describing skills to difficult-to-teach children.

Early in many basic language intervention curricula, children are taught to comprehend the names (usually spoken) of common objects. An assortment of age-appropriate objects is placed on a table in front of the child, and he is instructed to "Find the (object)." Correct pointing or reaching is reinforced, and errors are either ignored or corrected. As the child becomes proficient at receptively naming (pointing to) objects, he can then be taught to produce or express appropriate names for the objects. The child is shown a specific object while being asked "What's this?" and, depending on the modality selected for expression, he is taught to say and/or sign and/or point to a symbol on a communication board. Later, the child may be taught to request objects by saying something like "Want that," "Want (object)," or "I want (object)." The Guess et al. (1976) *Functional Language Curriculum* provides an excellent example of how requesting skills can be established. However, the child must develop some competence in noun comprehension and expression before being taught to make requests.[2] To teach a requesting skill, the child is shown a specific object (e.g., a ball) and asked "What want?" Through the skillful use of modeling, fading, chaining, and shaping, the child is taught to say "Want (object)" until the child's two-word utterance reliably matches the object being held up by the teacher. The child is, of course, given the object

---

[2] In the Guess et al. (1976) curriculum, instruction in noun expression precedes instruction in noun comprehension.

requested. Similar training sequences are found in most language training curricula (see Reichle and Keogh, this volume).

Intentionality: Expressing Wants and Needs

Chapman and Miller (1980) pointed out that from birth to about 8 months of age (sensorimotor Stages 1–3) infants are unable to carry out either goal-oriented actions or intentional communication. However, infants do exercise some control over aspects of the environment—whether it be intentional or incidental. Most infants are born with the ability to cry. Because an infant's cry is a powerful signal that often produces results (e.g., parent attention, food, relief from discomfort), the child's cry often functions to satisfy a want or need. Ample evidence exists to support the view that the frequency of infant crying is influenced by the consequences it produces.

Skinner (1957) used infant crying to draw a distinction between learned and unlearned responses in terms of reinforcement:

> The distinction between learned and unlearned response is much easier to make in terms of a history of reinforcement than in terms of meaning and conscious use. An important example is crying. Vocal behavior of this sort is clearly an unconditioned response in the newborn infant. For some time it is a function of various states of deprivation and aversive stimulation. But when crying is char-acteristically followed by parental attentions which are reinforcing, it may become verbal according to our definition. It has become a different behavioral unit because it is now under the control of different variables. It has also proba-bly acquired different properties, for parents are likely to react differently to different intonations or intensities of crying. (p. 45)

Observers of child behavior generally agree that crying gives way to more sophisticated forms of communicating (e.g., pointing, uttering "Juice" to request a drink). Although the topography of the behavior changes from birth to adulthood, the behavior functions to "call for specific consequences from the environment" and has been variously described as a mand (Skinner, 1957), a protoimperative (Bates, 1976), and volitional performance (Green-field and Smith, 1976).

For the benefit of children considered difficult-to-teach, the initial inter-vention target in the model presented here is to teach children a deliberate motor and/or vocal response that is directed toward others and functions (as a request) to satisfy wants and needs. This initial "communication" response need not require the discriminated use of symbols to specify what the object of the requesting response may be. Teaching a response form such as this may be viewed as a behavioral operation that increases the rate of a discrete response by contingently following it with a variety of reinforcing consequences. Whether intentional communication or not, this form of behavior does carry with it an implicit message of "I want something" or "I want more" in much the same sense that a newborn's cry serves this function.

A common strategy new parents follow to "decode" the intent of the infant's early "want" signal is to examine the environmental conditions (the context) surrounding the cry. Is it feeding time? Does the infant need to be comforted? Is the infant teething? To follow the scenario outlined by Skinner (1957), "reflexive crying" may lead to "intentional" crying, then to some sort of vocal form, and eventually into words (symbols) and multiple utterances. Some severely handicapped children get no further along that developmental continuum than the cry. Additionally, it is sometimes difficult to determine whether the child is crying because he wants something added to the environment (i.e., positive crying) or because he wants something removed (i.e., negative crying). Therefore, children with severe communication handicaps may be taught to produce a systematic intentional response (not a cry!) that serves a generalized requesting function. To accomplish this, instructors need not wait until the children have learned to comprehend or to express the names of significant people or objects.

The ability to make requests by using some sort of generalized "signaling" response allows severely handicapped children to exercise a measure of overt control over some aspects of their lives. They are able to indicate to others that they want something. However, their audience must behave in a manner similar to that of new parents. Caregivers must examine the environmental context immediately available and make a judgment about what is needed. To be more efficient communicators, however, children need to learn how to specify which objects, people, or activities they want. They must learn to attach symbolic labels to things. These labels may be photographic representations, line drawings, manual signs, and/or the spoken word.

Relationship between Requesting and Describing

Normative accounts of childrens' emerging language emphasize the importance of considering the context and content of a communicative act as an integral unit. In a frequently cited example of treating context and content as a unit, Bloom (1970) observed a child say "Mommy sock" while the mother was putting a sock on the child. At another time, the child said "Mommy sock" while the child was picking up the mother's sock. Most likely, Bloom's child knew with certainty the *meaning* of the utterances, and what the potential consequences might be for each. It is just as likely that adult observers knew also. The ability to use the words "Mommy sock" in perfectly appropriate ways in a variety of contexts requires a general understanding of the events that set the occasion for a particular response to occur and the specific consequences produced as a result of that response. What about the 11- or 12-year-old language-delayed child who points to a glass of milk and says "Milk"?

Does he want the milk? Suppose he pointed to the refrigerator and said "Frig." What might he mean if he sees a photo of milk and says "Milk," and later sees a photo of a cow and says, "Cow." Does he want the Cow? How can we be sure?

Our use of the terms *request* and *describe* may be somewhat more limited than the manner in which Skinner (1957) used *mand* (standing for demand, countermand, etc.) and *tact* (suggesting making contact with the physical world). Nevertheless, requesting and describing do represent behavioral operations that exert control over the environment. In describing tacts, Skinner remarked that "a child is taught the names of objects, colors, and so on when some 'generalized reinforcement' (for example, the approval carried by the verbal stimulus *right!*) is made contingent upon a response which bears on appropriate relation with a current stimulus . . ." (p. 84). For severely language-delayed children who are learning to match objects with one another (e.g., identify matching-to-sample) or to comprehend object names, a pointing/reaching response to the correct object functions in the same sense as Skinner's tact. Skinner described the mand as an "operant in which the response is reinforced by a characteristic consequence and is therefore under the functional control of relevant conditions of deprivation or aversive stimulation" (p. 36). His example is particularly relevant:

> In a given verbal community, certain responses are characteristically followed by certain consequences. WAIT! is followed by someone's waiting and SH-H! by silence. Much of the verbal behavior of young children is of this sort. CANDY! is characteristically followed by the receipt of candy and OUT! by the opening of a door. These effects are not inevitable, but we can usually find one consequence of each response which is commoner than any other. There are nonverbal parallels. OUT!, as we have seen, has the same ultimate effect as turning a knob and pushing against a door. Both forms of behavior become part of the repertoire of the organism through operant conditioning. When a response is characteristically reinforced in a given way, its likelihood of appearing in the behavior of the speaker is a function of the deprivation associated with that reinforcement. The response CANDY! will be more likely to occur after a period of candy deprivation, and least likely after candy satiation. (p. 35)

Skinner, of course, was describing young children whose conceptual and perceptual skills were well established. These children knew what candy was, knew its name, and knew how to request it when hungry. Their utterance "Candy," in effect, represented a shortened version of something like, "I want to eat more candy." Based upon the usual cues available to them, most listeners would interpret "candy" correctly. However, there are children whose conceptual and perceptual skills are not well developed. They may be unable to name candy, or request it. Some enter into a teaching-learning situation unaware that their behavior can exercise some control over things and people around them (Seligman, 1972). How do we teach these children requesting and describing skills so that one function does not get confused with the other?

A common strategy for teaching naming (either expressive or receptive) and requesting skills has been presented earlier in this chapter. Table 1 illustrates the typical contingent arrangement that exists for correct responding during comprehension, expression, and object requesting training, respectively. The stimulus arrangement shown for training of noun comprehension is similar for most multiple choice discrimination learning sequences or for any sort of task that requires selecting a single specific stimulus from an array of two or more. Training of expression and requesting skills shows a similar contingent arrangement.

As Table 1 illustrates, each event in the respective series is similar except for the teacher's instruction. Assuming in each case that the instruction is spoken (although it need not be), the instruction used during noun comprehension identifies which response is correct so that a point or reach toward the milk only (or cookie only) will yield reinforcement. For requesting, the child cannot be incorrect (if he responds) because selecting either yields reinforcement. In requesting tasks the child's pointing/reaching response always results in receipt of the object touched. In photo comprehension tasks the consequence is identical. During request training, he has at least a 50% chance of receiving the object touched. After months (or even years) of training on tasks such as these where an identical response topography (direct pointing/reaching) is always followed by identical consequences, it is possible that the child may have been inadvertently taught the rule "You get what you touch." Although it is true that children may eventually learn to sign "cookie," "milk," etc., or point to representative photos (symbols) on a communication board, the operating principle of the rule remains: Sign MILK and receive some, or point to a photo of Milk and receive some.

Certainly, single-word utterances (such as "Candy") best reflect the way in which normally developing children begin to describe and request things (de Villiers and de Villiers, 1982). No doubt such children have the cognitive capacity and processing strategies (Bowerman, 1978) that enable them to engage in linguistic performances of this type. At the early stages of communication training with some severely handicapped children, their cognitive capacity and processing strategies may not match well with the materials to be learned, or the task performance expected. They may not know that objects and activities share similarities and differences, that common objects and actions have names or, that their own behavior can, in fact, exercise some consistent and systematic control over people. Intervention strategies that consistently give the object to the child as a consequence for correct naming (or describing) may, indeed, succeed in teaching the child the generalized "You get what you touch" rule. To some extent this is a useful skill, but what

Table 1. Typical Arrangement of Stimulus Events during Communication Training

Training Target	Stimulus Array	Instruction	Correct Response	Consequences
Teach student to comprehend spoken names of common objects	Two objects (e.g., milk + cookie)	"Show me milk" or "Show me cookie"	Points to object	Praise and sip of milk or bite of cookie, respectively
Teach student to comprehend spoken names of common objects when depicted on photos	Two photos (e.g., milk + cookie)	Same as above	Points to photo	Same as above
Teach student to request common objects by selecting from photo array (e.g., communication board)	Two photos (e.g., milk + cookie)	"What do you want?"	Points to photo	Same as above
Teach student to express names of common objects by selecting from photo array (e.g., communication board)	Two photos (e.g., milk + cookie)	(while holding up object)"What's this?"	Points to photo	Same as above

interference will this well-learned rule have on later efforts to teach the child to indicate yes or no to questions like "Do you want some milk?", or to utter "Yes" or "No" in response to questions like "Is this milk?", or to learn the names for object characteristics such as size or color? A more prudent intervention strategy is to teach the requesting and describing functions of communication deliberately while ensuring that the antecedent and consequent stimuli surrounding each function are fundamentally different from one another. How this can be accomplished is discussed in a later section.

CONCEPTUAL AND PROCEDURAL BASIS FOR A BEGINNING COMMUNICATION INTERVENTION

Simple exposure to a nurturing environment enables most children to achieve cognitive and perceptual competence, and eventually, to become efficient and effective communicators. However, for difficult-to-teach children the same nurturing environment is inadequate and requires modification so that concepts basic to communication are learned. What are these concepts and how might they be taught? This section discusses the relationship between conceptual behavior, discrimination learning, and generalized matching-to-sample. An understanding of this relationship is the basis for the intervention strategy presented later in this chapter.

We have often heard that the teacher of the precocious preschooler must be prepared to present a lot of interesting activities, and present them for short but useful periods of time. This strategy is used to accommodate the "short attention span" of most toddlers. Thus, novelty or stimulus change may be a reinforcer over and above the overt stimulus itself, or the activity of the moment. For most normally developing children, the potential exists for heavy doses of novelty or stimulus change. As an example, suppose children enter the preschool environment for the first time. After the few days usually required for parental separation, the toddlers begin to notice an array of "potentially interesting" things around them. Because they can walk, touch and handle things, and mouth and shake things, they are able to have almost unlimited doses of novelty or stimulus change experiences adding to those already learned during the first few years at home. If, after a few mouthings, a few shakes or tosses, a particular toy loses its reinforcing value, the children are able to cast it aside and move on to the next item, and so on. Clearly, such experiences contribute substantially to the children's cognitive and perceptual growth. What about the children who are unable to walk, or who are unable to touch or mouth things, or who are unable to even drop things that have been placed into their hands?

Recognizing that the learning of language by severely delayed children may well be limited by the extent of their cognitive competence, Miller and

Yoder (1974) indicated that "The critical question here is whether or not cognitive abilities can be enhanced by careful organization of the child's experience. Specifically, can the cognitive precursors to early language be developed in children when they do not exist?" (p. 525). In a related viewpoint, Kahn (1975) hypothesized that children who are not functioning at Stage 6 of Piaget's sensorimotor period would not be expected to learn meaningful expressive language with any reasonable degree of efficiency. These children, according to Kahn "would probably benefit more from training activities directed toward raising their cognitive level" (p. 642). However, a preferred intervention effort is to structure a beginning communication strategy so as to embrace the fundamental need to attend to the severe cognitive and perceptual deficits of children while teaching a generalized and immediately useful requesting skill.

Learning Concepts

Flavell (1970) observed that a search for a satisfactory definition of the term *concept* is a "lexicographer's nightmare" (p. 983). Conceding that the term may be too elusive to be defined, Flavell suggested that concepts can certainly be described and discussed with profit. Becker et al. (1975) offered their description of concept formation, or conceptual behavior, as a special case of operant behavior brought under the control of discriminative stimuli through differential reinforcement. To teach the concept "longer," they provided the following example:

> . . .we might present two toy cars, one four inches long and one two inches
> long, and ask, "Which car is longer?" If the child points to the four inch car, he
> is told, "Right! You then present two pencils and go on through the same rou-
> tine. Other examples (both positive and negative) may be required to teach the
> general case, but the beginning discriminations have been made. Thus, the first
> requirement in teaching a concept is to use *differential reinforcement,* present
> both positive and negative concept instances and reinforce appropriate
> responses to them. This process is called *discrimination learning. . . .* (1975,
> p. 59)

Ferster et al. (1975) concurred with the Becker et al. (1975) description of concept formation but qualified their concurrence by suggesting that the process is best described as abstraction (or abstract stimulus control) because it emphasizes the controlling properties of the stimulus rather than an inner and unreadable process:

> When we say that a man has a *concept,* it implies that the concept resides in
> him and is a means by which he performs differentially to stimuli. In contrast,
> the term *abstract property of a stimulus* emphasizes that the control of behavior
> by a stimulus depends upon how reinforcement contingencies are arranged in

respect to a particular property of a stimulus. Thus, we use abstract stimulus control because it refers to the environmental events responsible for the behavior. (Ferster et al., 1975, p. 529)

Goldiamond (1962) suggested that a concept or abstraction may be defined by the explicit rules whereby elements are included and excluded from it; any element may simultaneously be a member of different sets, that is, it may also meet different definitions (p. 293). Like Becker et al. (1975) and Ferster et al. (1975), Goldiamond equates concepts or abstractions with stimulus classes that are congruent with discriminative stimuli, brought about through differential reinforcement. Whether conceptualization or abstraction is used to describe this behavioral phenomena, it may be brought about through a process called discrimination learning. Furthermore, the relationship between concepts and discrimination learning is linked. Discrimination learning is the process and the formed concept is the outcome of the process. Generalized matching-to-sample skills may be viewed as an extension of discrimination learning.

Discrimination Learning

Discrimination learning refers to how one learns to make choices between stimulus objects in the environment and to use certain features as cues for adaptive behavior (Reese and Lipsitt, 1973). The phenomenon has been examined extensively in the research laboratory. The typical experimental model for studying the discrimination learning process has been to present the subject with a two-choice array and to reinforce (or provide feedback for) selections made to one stimulus (the S+) and never to the other (the S-). This paradigm can be applied to relatively easy, moderately difficult, and difficult discriminations. A choice involving a large blue sneaker and a small piece of carrot is an example of a relatively easy discrimination. An example of a discrimination with a supposed intermediate degree of difficulty is a choice between a photo of a large blue sneaker and a photo of a large brown shoe. A choice between printed words "Daddy" and "Dandy" may be considered a difficult visual discrimination. Essentially, the research question being asked of subjects in discrimination learning experiments is something like "Can you learn to tell the difference between two objects (or photos)?" Through differential reinforcement of the subjects' selections (i.e., always reinforcing the selections of one of the objects or photos and never the selections of the other), the subject answers "Yes" by consistently selecting the object or photo differentially reinforced. Through trial and error, the subject eventually forms the appropriate discrimination.

Zeaman and House (1963) suggested that discrimination learning requires a chain of two responses. The first is a central mediating response to the relevant stimulus dimension(s) that separate the S+ (correct choice) from the S- (incorrect choice); and the second is an overt response to the relevant dimension(s). The chain of the two responses embodies what Zeaman and House have called *attention theory*. Reese and Lipsitt (1973) have provided a succinct example of how it operates:

> On Trial 1 the subject sees a red square and a green triangle, with red square the positive pattern. On Trial 2 he sees a green square and red triangle and now choice of the green square is reinforced. On successive trials the two arrays are randomly alternated, and the left-right position of the positive stimulus also varies at random. It is obvious that form is the relevant dimension, since one of the forms, the square, is consistently positive and the other, the triangle is consistently negative, but no color or position is consistently positive or negative. Dimensions are defined as ". . .broad classes of cues having a common discriminative property" (Zeaman & House, 1963, p. 168). There are two cue values on each of the irrelevant dimensions, red and green and left and right, and each of these values is reinforced 50 percent of the time on a random basis. Learning is considered to have occurred when the subject consistently selects the stimulus pattern that contains the square, whether it is on the right or left and whether it is red or green. How this consistent selection or learning occurs is the substance of attention theory. (p. 288)

Zeaman and House (1963) reported that mentally retarded individuals "have been found particularly slow in forming some single visual habits, even slower than would be expected from their low mental age" (p. 159). According to these authors, the failure of the subjects to perform the central mediating response (i.e., attending to the relevant cues) is the reason for their overall failure. To ameliorate this problem, intervention strategies should be designed that: 1) increase the attention value of relevant cues; 2) arrange discrimination tasks in an easy-to-hard progression; and 3) use the cue value contained in stimulus novelty in teaching visual discriminations.

Zeaman and House and others have examined discrimination learning in depth and have contributed substantially to our understanding of discrimination learning among severely handicapped populations. With the exception of drawing intervention implications as to how their findings might be applied, no direct effort was made by these researchers (nor was it their purpose) to integrate their findings into more comprehensive intervention curricula. We believe that the discrimination learning paradigm represents an important and necessary intervention strategy for some difficult-to-teach children and it figures prominently in our overall intervention design.

Rule-Governed Matching-to-Sample

As a process, matching-to-sample involves a response to a stimulus that is reinforced if it matches a specified sample. Typically, the child is shown an array of choices such as a cup, a ball, and a spoon along with a sample (cup) of one of the objects in the choice array. The teacher holds up the sample object and instructs the student to match it to one present in the choice array. Correct selections are usually reinforced.

The skill to discriminate between various aspects of the environment and to appropriately match what has been discriminated to relevant stimuli is necessary before severely handicapped children can be expected to benefit significantly from instruction in functional communication. At the discrimination learning level, the child must examine various stimulus cue values contained in each of the choices, and through experience (or training trials) determine which cues correlate consistently with the delivery of reinforcement. Unlike the matching-to-sample paradigm, the child must receive repeated exposure to instances of the $(S+)$ and the $(S-)$ in order for the discrimination to be formed. However, generalized matching-to-sample may be considered a level of abstraction that is rule governed. The rule to be learned involves the association of stimuli on the basis of similarity (or in special cases dissimilarity) or by function. The rule requires the child to scan the available choices and select the one that comes closest to matching the sample stimulus.

Ferster et al. (1975) indicated that the matching-to-sample procedure is especially useful for developing control over stimuli that have complex interrelationships and abstract properties. Such abstract interrelationships exist when students match the written word with appropriate referents (reading), or when they match referents with the spoken word (speech). The matching-to-sample procedure has long been recognized as a convenient and efficient strategy to use when teaching reading (Johnson and Brown, 1974; Martin, 1975; Sidman and Cresson, 1973). However, intervention programs designed to improve communication skills, especially those designed for the communication board user, often fail to incorporate matching-to-sample as an integral part of their training strategies.

Empirical evidence that delineates levels of visual matching among difficult-to-teach students is not easily found in the literature. It is assumed that matching the spoken word "Juice" with its appropriate referent requires a greater level of abstraction than matching a photograph of juice with the appropriate three-dimensional glass containing juice. However, matching behavior may be divided into matching stimuli that are identical (e.g., blue cup with blue cup) or matching stimuli that are not identical (e.g., the word "Juice" with a glass of juice).

In developing matching behavior, levels of visual matching that appear to be most relevant to the communication board user are:

1. Matching three-dimensional objects that are identical.
   Example Display a large blue sneaker and a small brown cup as two choices and present a large blue sneaker as the sample.

2. Matching two-dimensional stimuli that are identical.
   Example Display photographs of a large blue sneaker and a small brown cup as two choices and present photos of a large blue sneaker as the sample.
3. Matching three-dimensional stimuli with their photographic representations.
   Example Display photographs of a large blue sneaker and a small brown cup as two choices and present a three-dimensional large blue sneaker as the sample.
4. Matching three-dimensional stimuli with three-dimensional stimuli on the basis of function rather than on the basis of physical characteristics alone.
   Example Display a large blue canvas sneaker and a small brown cup as two choices and present a small brown leather shoe as the sample.
5. Matching three-dimensional stimuli with two-dimensional stimuli on the basis of function rather than on the basis of physical characteristics alone.
   Example Display photos of a large blue canvas sneaker and a small brown cup as two choices and present a small brown leather shoe as the sample.

Levels 1 and 2 (above) are usually referred to as "identity matching" because the sample is identical in all aspects to one of the choices. If one dimension, or characteristic of the sample is different than the correct choice, the form of matching is referred to as "nonidentity matching."

The intervention strategy presented here requires that difficult-to-teach children develop matching-to-sample skills to the same degree of proficiency that children enrolled in speech-only programs must develop skills at imitating motorically and/or vocally. Without the ability to match real objects and events with some symbol form (line drawings, photographs, spoken words, etc.), little progress toward acquiring a symbolic and rule-governed communication system can be expected.

Discrimination learning is the process through which concepts are formed. Through experience, children learn about the physical similarities and differences between things, that different things function in different ways, that things may be matched or classified according to some rule or rules, and that some things are more reinforcing than others. If exposure to the normal environment fails to provide children with the sort of experience necessary for basic concepts to be formed, it must be changed or intervened upon. The next section suggests the form the intervention might take.

A Generic Strategy for Teaching Beginning Communication Skills

Most special educators would agree that an inverse relationship exists between the severity of a child's handicapping condition and the availability of language intervention programs: The more severe a child's handicaps are, the fewer the intervention choices. The strategy discussed here embraces the fundamental need to "build concepts" by attending to severe cognitive and perceptual deficits while teaching an immediately useful way to communicate wants and needs. The most distinguishing features of the strategy include:

1. The emphasis placed on teaching the pragmatic functions of requesting and describing as separate but interrelated skills during the earliest stages of intervention.
2. Reliance upon a child's discrete pointing response as the primary response modality for using these functions in acts of expression and comprehension.

The importance of discriminating between and using the requesting and describing functions early transcends (at least initially) concern about whether a child's expressive mode should be speech, signing, or some combination. Inherent in this design is the assumption that learning to request and describe does not depend on an ability to produce an array of complex signs or speech, and that whatever progress is achieved in requesting and describing can be maintained with minimal confusion or retraining if speech or signing becomes a more efficient alternative than pointing to symbols on a communication board. This section presents a model intervention in which children initially learn to select (point to) specific stimuli from visual displays to communicate wants and needs. This strategy is appropriate to train either requesting or describing.

The Vermont Early Communication Curriculum

Much of what is presented in this chapter reflects our accumulated efforts to develop a useful curriculum for difficult-to-teach children. Although it is not within the scope of this discussion to provide a detailed account of the *Vermont Early Communication Curriculum* (VECC) (Keogh and Reichle, 1982), a brief overview is useful. In its present form, the VECC is divided into six distinct but interrelated skill clusters. The first, called *Basic Awareness,* was designed to assess and to teach (if necessary) skills ranging from tactual awareness to visual orienting. Children whose physical, perceptual, and cognitive deficits exist in their severest form may benefit from instruction in this cluster. The second cluster, *Motor Modality,* concentrates on strengthening motor performance, particularly generalized motor imitation. The third cluster, *Vocal Modality,* contains programs to strengthen vocal production, beginning with procedures to increase vocal frequency and including sound-to-object matching. The fourth cluster, *Pointing Modality,* assesses and teaches discrete pointing and reaching. Clusters five and six develop rudimentary *Expression* and *Comprehension* skills, respectively. Figure 1 represents

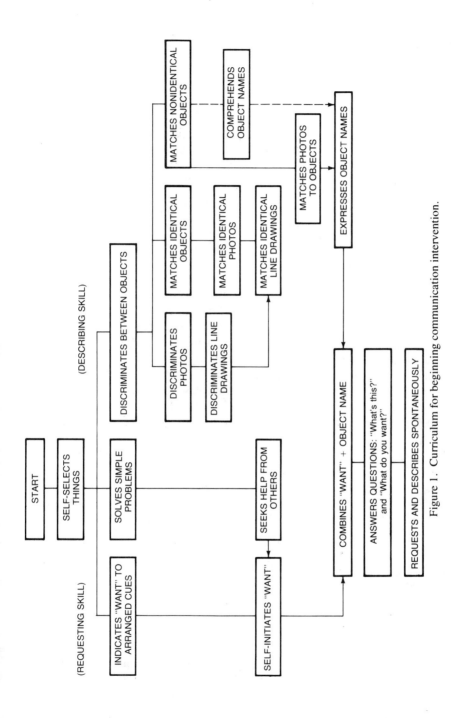

Figure 1. Curriculum for beginning communication intervention.

177

the core of the VECC through which virtually all other assessments/interventions intersect and serves as the focal point for the remainder of this discussion.

Developing a Rudimentary Requesting Skill

Figure 1 illustrates a series of interconnected interventions that begins with "Self-selects things" and ends with "Requests and describes spontaneously." It is hoped that by the time children exit they will have learned to distinguish between requesting and describing functions of early communicative acts in such a way as to eliminate or reduce any ambiguity that might be associated with their messages. To request something, the child will have learned to first point to a symbol representing "Want" and then (if he is able), point again to the symbol that best represents what he may want. To describe something, the child will have learned to point directly to an object or its representation. A test of the child's ability to differentiate between the describing and requesting functions occurs when he begins to learn to discriminate between the questions "What do you want?" and "What's this?", and respond appropriately. Once mastered, the inference might be drawn that he knows the difference between two of the basic functions of communication. Once this important inference is made, it becomes less critical that children be required to always point to a "want" symbol to initiate a request.

The sequence of intervention phases illustrated in Figure 1 shows two basic intervention tracks. One track teaches a rudimentary requesting skill; the other teaches the rudiments of describing. Each track is sufficiently independent of the other (at the outset) to allow a child to make progress in one even if progress is slow, or does not occur, in the other. In this model, children need not wait until they have learned to discriminate, match, comprehend, or express the names of significant people and objects to begin to express their wants and needs. However, progression toward a more symbolic form of requesting requires that children show some interest in people, objects, and activities around them. A first step in assessing this interest is to provide the child unrestricted access to an assortment of potentially reinforcing objects in order to determine whether they evoke a self-initiated reaching response. Are there things in the environment worth reaching for? Assuming that there are, it may be possible to teach the child that objects need not be within easy reach in order to gain access to them. The child is taught to point to a "want" symbol as a replacement for direct reaching. A three-step sequence for teaching this form of "requesting" is: 1) self-selects things; 2) indicates "want" to arranged cues; and 3) self-initiates requests.

1. Self-Selects Things   An assessment of the reinforcement value associated with common objects can be obtained by conducting a simple object reaching exercise. To conduct the exercise an assortment of potentially reinforcing objects (toys, edibles, soft drinks, etc.) is placed on a cafeteria-type tray. The tray is held within each reach of the child for about 10 seconds and he is encouraged to select an object. As soon as a selection has been made within the time period, the tray is removed and the item selected is indicated on a data sheet. If a selection has not been made, this information is recorded also. The exercise is continued until the child stops selecting (i.e., three nonselections in a row). By repeating the exercise over a 3- or 4-day period some measure of the child's "satiation" threshold can be obtained. For example, if a child repeatedly tires or becomes satiated with the task after, say, 16 or 17 trials when the only contingency involved is a self-initiated reach, this information might be used to help set the upper limits for future intervention (i.e., time and/or trials) when training contingencies become more conditional (i.e., harder). In addition, the data obtained through this exercise may suggest whether participation in the "want" exercise is necessary.

2. Indicates "Want" to Arranged Cues Assuming that the child reaches for objects at a reasonable frequency during the above exercise, the inference can be made that he *wanted* them. If such a condition exists, it may be possible to teach the child to point to an arbitrary symbol that represents the communication function "I want something." The Blissymbol for "want" might be used. This exercise is similar to the one described above except that here the goal is to teach the child to use the "want" symbol as a mediator to replace direct reaching. The "want" symbol may be fixed to a piece of cardboard and this "communication board" placed directly in front of the child. The cafeteria tray holding an array of objects is then placed in front of the child and he is asked "What do you want?" The likely response is to observe the child attempting to reach directly from the tray. If this occurs, the tray is slid well out of reach and the child is physically prompted to touch the "want" symbol first. The child is not required to point to the object on the tray to indicate what he wants (this form of behavior is not desirable here since direct selection of objects falls within the domain of the describing track). Through repeated exposure to this exercise, children learn that interesting objects need not be within direct reach in order to gain access to them. A simple touch to a "want" symbol will suffice.

The purpose of this exercise is to endow the "want" symbol with a generalized requesting function. Considerable caution must be used when selecting and presenting stimuli in order to avoid teaching the wrong rule or concept inadvertently. For example, if pointing to the "want" symbol is consistently paired with a particular food (i.e., cookies) or a single event (i.e., mealtimes), the child may come to associate the "want" symbol with the particular object (i.e., cookie) or a particular event (i.e., eating). Thus, objects selected for display on the cafeteria tray should come from four or more object classes such as edibles (e.g., cookies, soup, pudding), liquids (e.g., water, milk, juice), self-care items (e.g., hairbrush, comb, hair blow dryer), and recreational items (e.g., portable radio, wind-up toys, back massager). To avoid perseverative selecting, any item that has been selected three times in succession should be removed and replaced with another item from the same class. If the child perseverates within a particular class (i.e., selects only foods) the entire class should be omitted occasionally.

3. Self-Initiates Requests Success in the above exercise enables the child to make requests by pointing to a symbol for "want." In that exercise all of the cues are carefully arranged, a "listener" is always present, objects have been selected carefully and displayed for easy viewing, and the response-initiating stimulus has always been the question, "What do you want?" Although this arrangement may give the child a measure of control he may not have had previously, more efficient use of his requesting skill requires that he learn to self-initiate requests.

Because pointing repeatedly and spontaneously to the "want" symbol will not likely recruit an absent teacher or aide to be a "listener," the child needs a system for gaining the attention of others prior to making a request. Children who are able to walk or move about freely may learn to actively seek out a potential listener. However, nonambulatory children must have an alternative system. One alternative is to teach the child to activate a bell or a buzzer in much the same way a bedridden hospital patient must in order to call a nurse. Such a system would allow the child to: 1) ring a bell to signal for the presence of a listener; 2) wait until a listener arrives and asks, "What do you want?"; and 3) point to the "want" symbol.

There are three phases involved in teaching children to activate a bell or a buzzer to recruit listeners. An acquisition phase must be designed to teach the child to activate the device. Through the use of physical prompts, fading, and shaping, the child is taught the behaviors required. Next, an extinction phase is required. In order to teach the child to use the device as a "call signal," the novelty aspects associated with simply ringing the bell for its own sake must extinguish. During this phase, the number of bell rings per day (or per hour) are counted without attending to them. This phase should continue until bell ringing bursts are at or near zero for an extended period, say a week. In the event that bell ringing is shown to be intrinsically reinforcing and not amenable to extinction, this strategy should be discontinued in favor of a different one.

Assuming the novelty associated with bell ringing can be extinguished, the "signaling" phase of training can begin. During this phase, spontaneously occurring bell rings must be attended to immediately; if none occur, they should be prompted. The student should always be asked, "What do you want?", be required to point to the "want" symbol, and be allowed to select something from the tray. It is possible that the cafeteria tray may not contain what the child really wants, or that bell ringing, once covered, might be maintained simply by contingent adult attention. It is at this level that attending adults must behave like the parents of a newborn. Until the child learns to be more specific in making requests (through training in the describing track), listeners must examine contextual cues and make "best guess" judgments concerning what to do about perseverative responding and how to satisfy specific requests.

Learning to Describe

Eventually, children must be able to comprehend and express the names of people and objects to achieve a level of specificity in making rudimentary requests. The describing track illustrated in Figure 1 has been designed to guide the child through four "concept" levels:

1. Discrimination
2. Generalized matching-to-sample
3. Speech comprehension of object names
4. Expression of object names

Successful progression through these levels enables the child to combine skills mastered during instruction in the requesting track with those learned in this track, allowing him to express two-part utterances such as "want + (object)."

The decision to select objects (or symbols) for a beginning communication intervention depends on circumstances unique to the child. Training stimuli should include: 1) objects (or symbols) that the child wants (e.g., cookies or juice); 2) objects (or symbols) that the child may use to relieve himself of discomfort, such as a way to signal for a change in body positions to relieve himself of "fanny fatigue"; and 3) objects (or symbols) that the child's primary caregivers judge to be important, such as to request toileting. Initial training stimuli must be those that the child values as most reinforcing; later, less reinforcing stimuli, such as the toilet (object and symbol), may be introduced. In our model, objects selected for training at the discrimination level *must* be the same as those introduced later at the comprehension and expression levels.

Once objects have been selected for training it is necessary to determine what to "call" them—or what they mean. This determination should be made after examining the short- and long-term benefits a particular word may have for the child. For example, teaching the use of a photograph of a cookie to represent all foods, or a photograph of a glass of milk to represent all consumable liquids, has obvious short-term advantages, particularly when the physical dimensions of a "picture board" impose a limit on the size of the lexicon. In the long term, however, children may be deprived of the opportunity to advance in terms of the specificity of what they want to eat (e.g., a cookie, a piece of candy, a sandwich) or drink (e.g., water, juice, or milk). Some limits must be imposed concerning just how specific a particular word-object symbolic relationship should be. Words such as "candy," "cookie," or "soda" need not be further specified on the basis of taste or brand name (i.e., Oreo, M&M's, Coca-Cola); photos of an Oreo, M&M's, and a Coca-Cola cup can represent all cookies, candies, and carbonated soft beverages, respectively.

A beginning communication curriculum need not include exercises to teach words involving action verbs such as *eat, drink, play,* and *go.* In this model, the appropriate assumptions about eating, drinking, etc. are implicit in messages such as "Want milk" or "Want sandwich."

Learning to Discriminate between Stimuli

The physical arrangement for conducting two-choice discrimination learning exercises is to place one object, photograph, or line drawing directly in front of the child just to the right of midline and, the other just to the left. One stimulus item is arbitrarily designated as the correct choice and the other is incorrect. Prior to each trial an instruction is given such as "Find the (object name)." Trial-by-trial placement of the choice stimuli is varied from left to right, randomly; and child selections are reinforced differentially. The instruction "Find the (object name)" serves only as a cue to respond. In effect, the child is being asked, "Can you select the stimulus that has been correlated with reinforcement and avoid selecting the stimulus that has been correlated with nonreinforcement, or extinction?"

The discrimination learning exercises: 1) determine the extent to which children are able to distinguish between objects, photographs, and/or line drawings; and 2) assess awareness of contingency arrangements. For example, Keogh (1981) taught discrimination skills to a 7-year-old multihandi-capped, "visually impaired" girl using two-choice object, photograph, and line drawing exercises. Participation in these exercises was initiated because of virtually zero progress during her participation in two-choice (object) matching-to-sample tasks. The objects used as training stimuli during the matching-to-sample exercises were a large yellow balloon and a red and silver flashlight. These stimuli were selected because the child's parents and teachers identified them as her "toys." She rubbed the balloon with her hands, producing audible feedback, and switched the flashlight on and off repeatedly in front of her face. Sixty-trial discrimination exercises were arranged where the flashlight was designated as the correct choice and the balloon designated as the incorrect choice. By the third discrimination learning exercise the child was almost always selecting the flashlight (positive stimulus) and never the balloon (negative stimulus). Her learning curve is shown in Figure 2. Then to examine whether the contingencies of reinforcement (rather than simply showing a preference for the flashlight) were responsible for correct respond-ing the contingencies were reversed; the balloon became the correct choice (positive stimulus) and the flashlight became incorrect (negative stimulus). As the reversal condition indicates (Figure 2), the child seemed well aware of the contingencies we had imposed and was able to adjust quickly.

As this example suggests, discrimination learning exercises may be viewed as serving both an assessment and a training function. For the girl described, participation in the exercises served more as an assessment. We determined that her failure to progress during the two-choice object matching-to-sample exercises was in all likelihood *not* because of a cognitive failure to sort out the contingencies of reinforcement operating, nor was it because she lacked the visual perceptual skills required to discriminate between the two stimuli. However, other children may require a period of instruction in order to learn about contingency arrangements and stimulus differences.

Discrimination learning exercises may also facilitate matching-to-sample performance. For example, in the same project (Keogh, 1981), an 11-year-old multihandicapped girl began discrimination learning exercises because she too had failed to make progress during object-to-object matching-to-sample tasks. As Figure 3 shows, discrimination learning exercises were initiated after eight 60-trial matching-to-sample sessions. The objects used in each condition were a cream-filled cookie and a brown teddy bear. For the training phase of discrimination learning, the teddy bear was correlated with reinforcement and the cookie was correlated with nonreinforcement or extinction. This child quickly learned the initial discrimination (Sessions 9 through 14), and when contingencies were reversed (Sessions 15 through 20) she made the appropriate adjustment. During session 21, object-to-object identity

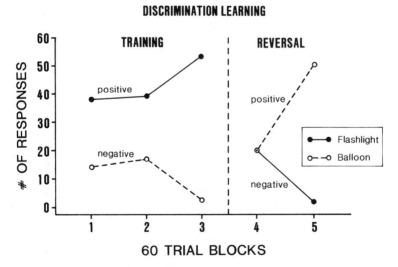

Figure 2. Number of times a flashlight and a balloon were selected by student during 60-trial object discrimination and reversal exercises.

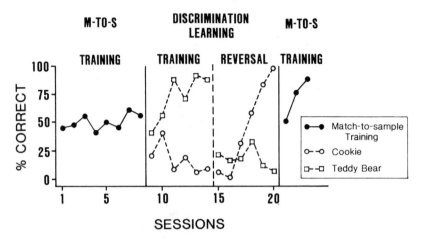

Figure 3. Correct performance during 60-trial two-choice identical object matching before and after 60-trial object discrimination exercises. During discrimination training, a teddy bear was correlated with reinforcement and a cookie was correlated with extinction. During discrimination reversal exercises, the contingencies were reversed.

matching resumed. Within three 60-trial sessions her correct responding increased to 83%. The sequence of training conditions used in this intervention sequence does not permit an empirical statement to be made concerning the facilitative function that discrimination learning exercises might have had upon object-to-object matching. However, the rapid acquisition to the matching-to-sample task during sessions 21, 22, and 23 is highly suggestive.

In any event, children must be able to discriminate between objects, photographs, and/or line drawings in order to benefit from the majority of exercises illustrated in Figure 1.

Learning Generalized Matching-to-Sample

An interesting analogy has been drawn between generalized matching-to-sample and vocal and motor imitation (Gewirtz and Stingle, 1968). Baer and his colleagues (Baer et al., 1967; Garcia et al., 1971; Peterson, 1968; Schroder and Baer, 1972) were among the first to examine the phenomenon of generalized imitative performance in previously nonimitative children. Typically the strategy for teaching a generalized imitative performance has been to present a demonstration or model of the behavior to be imitated, wait briefly for the child to approximate an imitative response, and reinforce the response. Training usually continues in this manner until the child begins to imitate new demonstrations the first time they are presented. At this point, the child is said to possess a generalized imitative skill. In referring to this generalized performance, Baer et al. (1967) suggested that the subjects in their study "were not so much learning specific responses as learning the instruction, 'Do as the experimenter does'" (p. 415). The subjects in effect had learned a "copy-cat" rule that could be easily and efficiently evoked each time the experimenters presented them with a model or demonstration (i.e., clapping hands) and said, "Do this."

Sherman et al. (1970) indicated that although children's imitative and matching-to-sample performances may differ with respect to the topography of the response required and the type of choices indigenous to each task, both tasks often involve responding on the basis of *stimulus similarity*. Thus, the goal for the matching-to-sample exercises in our model (Figure 1) is to teach the child a rule equivalent to the "copy-cat" rule: Select the choice that is most like, or best represents, the sample!

Effectively and efficiently teaching this generalized matching-to-sample rule to difficult-to-teach children remains an unresolved issue. For example, assuming that the five levels of visual matching described earlier have been ordered in an "easier-to-learn" to "harder-to-learn" sequence, then must all children progress through this sequence before Level 5 can be mastered? Must difficult-to-teach children endure training on photo-to-photo matching before a form of object-to-photo matching can be achieved? Are there stimulus boundaries in matching-to-sample across which generalization does not occur until that particular form of matching has been learned? Based on an analysis of a small sample of matching performances (Keogh, 1981), we suspect that the answer to each of these questions is both "yes" and "no." Some children may show little or no generalization across levels, requiring that they receive instruction in each level; others may show generalization to all levels after receiving instruction in only two or three. A prudent intervention strategy is to teach following the "easy-to-hard" sequence and periodically test for generalization within and across levels. Table 2 suggests a sequence by which this might be accomplished.

As soon as the child learns to match in a generalized manner at Level 5, his performance resembles a behavioral operation typically used when teaching children to use speech to label objects. For example, during matching-to-sample exercises photos of a soft drink cup, a glass of milk, a cookie, and a transistor radio may be displayed in one section of a communication board; then, the child is shown a three-dimensional sample such as a radio and instructed to "Find the radio." The correct response, of course, is to select, or point to, the photo depicting the three-dimensional stimulus. However, if the instruction is altered to something like "What's this?" while everything else is held constant, conforming to the matching-to-sample operation, the child's pointing behavior approximates an act of symbolic expression. Although the communication board user may be relying more upon what he sees to process the stimuli properly, his performance nevertheless functions in much the same way a child's speech response (i.e., "Radio") does during expressive labeling tasks.

Table 2.   Typical Training and Generalization Test Sequence

1. Train first object-to-object set to 80% criterion
2. Test the following:
    (a) 3 object-to-object sets (2 trials per set)
    (b) 3 photo to-photo sets (2 trials per set)
    (c) 3 object-to-photo sets (2 trials per set)
    (d) 3 generalized object-to-object sets (2 trials per set)
    (e) 3 generalized object-to-photo sets (2 trials per set)
3. Train second object-to-object set to 80% criterion
4. Test (a) through (e) above
5. Train third object-to-object set to 80% criterion
6. Test (a) through (e) above
7. Train first photo-to-photo set to 80% criterion
8. Test (a) through (e) above
9. Train second photo-to-photo set to 80% criterion
10. Test (a) through (e) above
11. Train third photo-to-photo set to 80% criterion
12. Test (a) through (e) above
13. Train first object-to-photo set to 80% criterion
14. Test (a) through (e) above
15. Train second object-to-photo set to 80% criterion
16. Test (a) through (e) above
17. Train third object-to-photo set to 80% criterion
18. Test (a) through (e) above
19. Train first generalized object-to-object set to 80% criterion
20. Test (a) through (e) above
21. Train second generalized object-to-object set to 80% criterion
22. Test (a) through (e) above
23. Train third generalized object-to-object set to 80% criterion
24. Test (a) through (e) above
25. Train first generalized object-to-photo set to 80% criterion
26. Test (a) through (e) above
27. Train second generalized object-to-photo set to 80% criterion
28. Test (a) through (e) above
29. Train third generalized object-to-photo set to 80% criterion
30. Test (a) through (e) above

The degree of difficulty in learning to match across various visual levels may vary, but the general teaching strategy used at each level remains relatively constant. For example, the same teaching format may be used to teach a two-choice identity object, identity photo, and nonidentity matching (object-to-photo).

Teaching Speech Comprehension of Object Names

During matching-to-sample exercises, children are presented with a number of (visual) choices and instructed to "Find the (object)" while simultaneously being shown a sample object as a visual cue. Correct performance depends upon an ability to match one visual stimulus (sample) with another (correct choice). However, the matching-to-sample format may also be used to teach cross-modal generalization where the sample is the *spoken word* and the choices are *visual* (McIlvane and Stoddard, 1981). In effect, cross-modal matching of this sort is also speech comprehension training. Because visual matching-to-sample and speech comprehension training share almost identical teaching formats, it is possible that some incidental learning (of speech) may occur during the matching-to-sample exercise as a result of consistently pairing speech (e.g., "Find cookie") with the visual stimulus (e.g., the actual cookie). Thus, care should be taken to avoid giving instructions such as "Make a match" of "Find one that's the same" to increase this possibility.

Learning to select correct choices by listening to what is *said* rather than what is *seen* is a desirable outcome of the matching-to-sample exercises. Such incidental learning should not be expected, however. A more deliberate teaching strategy must be used to transfer the cue value contained in the visual sample to the spoken word. The transfer may be brought about by increasing the time delay (Touchette, 1971) between the instruction "Find the (object)" and the presentation of object by the teacher. At the zero-delay level, the instruction and visual sample are presented simultaneously, exactly as is done during the matching-to-sample exercises. As errorless or near-errorless performance is maintained, subsequent presentations of the visual sample are delayed for 1 second following the instruction; then the delay is systematically extended or shortened depending on the child's performance. To effectively use a time-delay procedure such as that suggested here, practitioners should have an understanding of errorless stimulus control procedures. In particular, criteria for "advancing" and "backing up" need to be carefully planned and implemented. Etzel and LeBlanc (1979), Touchette (1971), Snell and Gast (1981), and Striefel and Owens (1982) provide excellent discussions of stimulus control teaching procedures, particularly with respect to time-delay fading.

Although the flow chart presented in Figure 1 allows the option to bypass teaching speech comprehension of object names, the decision to bypass should be considered more as a postponement. The potential for expanding one's communication repertoire is enhanced considerably if speech is appropriately understood. For example, in this model an immediate next step after successful exiting the curriculum presented in Figure 1 might be to learn to answer questions by using "Yes" or "No." Instead of asking "What's this?" while holding an object, the child might be asked "Is this a cookie?" Likewise, instead of asking "What do you want?" while holding a cafeteria tray containing an array of objects, the child might be asked "Do you want a cookie?" The relationship between describing and requesting may be extended to yes/no-type skills if a measure of speech comprehension exists.

Thus, the decision to include speech comprehension training immediately after the matching-to-sample exercises is a tactical one to take advantage of any incidental learning of speech that might have occurred and to enter into a time-delay procedure as soon as Level 5 matching has been demonstrated. For some students, it may be perfectly reasonable to exercise the "bypass" option.

PHYSIOLOGICAL DETERMINANTS

The communication model presented here has focused primarily upon difficult-to-teach children whose vision, hearing, and psychomotor potential enables them to participate in the suggested exercises. Because many children might also be characterized as *difficult-to-test*, carefully tailored assessments may be necessary to determine functioning level on the physiological determinants of communication. Functional approaches to determining psychomotor performance, visual acuity, and hearing are discussed below. Performance in these areas must be taken into account when developing an individual's program.

Psychomotor Performance

According to Merrill (1971), "when a student makes a muscular-skeletal reaction in the presence of some stimulus situation, he is exhibiting psychomotor behavior" (p. 196); and "the acquisition of psychomotor behavior is dependent on the basic learning processes of discrimination, generalization, and chaining" (p. 197). Thus, psychomotor behavior may be viewed as overt voluntary movement that is linked to specific (sets of) discriminative stimuli and strengthened and maintained through reinforcement. Reaching for a cookie placed on a table results in attaining the cookie and usually consumption—the reinforcing consequence. For most children, the actions of reaching and grasping present no special problems, but what about children whose musculo-skeletal organization is so impaired that even touching or pointing to a cookie seems an impossibility?

Pointing need not be restricted to the use of the extended index finger. In a broader sense, "pointing" may be viewed as a signal or a selecting response such as typically exists in multiple-choice discrimination tasks. Thus, the reliable use of electromechanical devices, head/eye orientation, or gross directional arm movements as a means by which selections are made may be considered "pointing."

If motor response topographies are identified properly, and are such that the child is physiologically capable of performance, then they can be strengthened and/or augmented to serve as functional attention-getting or selecting responses. In order to identify motor responses having the greatest potential for use as attention-getting or selecting responses, consultations with physicians, occupational and physical therapists, and others may be necessary.

Vision Acuity

The majority of screening assessments designed to test the vision acuity of clients depend, for the most part, upon client cooperation and an ability to answer the screener's questions. One notable exception is the Parsons Visual Acuity Test (PVAT; Spellman et al., 1979). The PVAT can be administered successfully to clients who are severely language delayed as long as they are able to 1) sustain correct responding during a three-choice matching-to-sample task, or 2) discriminate between a specific stimulus (S+) and two distractors (S-). Both screening methods use two-dimensional black figures on white backgrounds. Cress et al. (1981) pointed out that the PVAT also includes alternative procedures for testing clients who are unable to point or manipulate the test stimuli.

Because the PVAT screening is based upon a stimulus fading (errorless learning) procedure and because matching-to-sample and discrimination learning are the vehicles by which difficult-to-test children may be screened, the assessment is particularly compatible with the exercises presented in Figure 1. Practitioners responsible for providing educational services to difficult-to-teach (and test) children should become familiar with the PVAT (see Cress et al., 1981).[3]

Hearing Screening

Valid and reliable audiometric assessment should be considered as a critical component of the intervention process. The degree to which difficult-to-teach children respond to auditory stimuli helps to determine the parameters of the particular intervention. Essentially, two types of audiologic assessment strategies are available. Strategies that use operant responses are generally referred to as behavioral procedures; strategies that use reflexive responses are referred to as electrophysiological procedures. Cox and Lloyd (1976) suggested that, for clinical utility in assessing the actual thresholds of hearing among difficult-to-test children, behavioral audiometry may be superior. Unfortunately, many difficult-to-test children may lack the necessary behavioral prerequisites to take advantage of hearing assessments based on audiometry.

As early as 1968, Lloyd et al. (1968) provided an excellent example of the effectiveness of operant audiologic procedures used to screen difficult-to-test children. The procedural technology exists to teach most difficult-to-teach

---

[3] Currently, the PVAT may be purchased at an approximate cost of $195.00 through the Bernell Corporation, 422 East Monroe Street, South Bend, Indiana 46601.

children to respond (in some way) in the presence of a particular stimulus and to refrain from responding (in the same way) in its absence. However, the time required to identify the most appropriate motor response and conditioning procedure for some children (not to mention the actual discrimination training time) is not typically accommodated by the audiologist's busy schedule. Thus, there may be some advantage in initiating auditory discrimination exercises as part of the typical classroom routine so that the teachers and their aides can teach children the necessary test-taking skills to be screened successfully by the audiologist. Adopting such a model requires the involvement of the audiologist (or the qualified screener) at the outset.[4]

CONCLUSIONS

The generic model that has been suggested in this chapter does not represent a "comprehensive" language intervention strategy. We have identified specific communication functions to be taught and suggested specific training sequences; little has been said about generalization, or, more precisely, where training activities should take place. We have carefully avoided terms such as "comprehensive" in our discussion. We have suggested that the ability to discriminate between various aspects of the environment and to match what has been identified to other relevant stimuli is a concept formation process that must exist before many difficult-to-teach children can be expected to benefit significantly from instruction in functional communication. We have suggested that a "teaching technology" must embrace both the systematic application of errorless learning procedures and differential reinforcement, but we have said little about how to do either.

The success or failure of this (or any other) intervention model depends not so much on its degree of specificity, or upon how well it has identified teaching-learning regimens, but upon how well the skilled practitioner is able to modify or change it to accommodate circumstances unique to a particular child without violating the fundamental integrity of the model. For some difficult-to-teach children it will be perfectly appropriate to begin instruction in a rigidly controlled one-to-one teaching-learning situation and (at some point) begin to "train loosely"; for other children, the preferred milieu might be incidental teaching (Hart and Risley, 1975) from the start. In teaching object or photo matching skills, a prudent instructional sequence might include identical photo matching for some children and ignore it for others.

---

[4] For practitioners interested in learning more about the use of operant audiometric procedures with difficult-to-test children, an "old" but still relevant source is *Audiometry for the Retarded: With Implications for the Difficult-to-Test* by Fulton and Lloyd (1969). A "new" but equally useful resource is: *Auditory Assessment and Programming for Severely Handicapped Deaf-Blind Students* by Goetz et al. (1981).

Furthermore, some children will show significant progress when trial-and-error instructional procedures are followed; others will require teaching-learning strategies based on carefully designed errorless learning sequences.

We would like to conclude by recalling Siegel and Spradlin's (1978) remarks that

> The clinician should be an active partner in the task of evaluating an approach to therapy, of testing its limitations, and of modifying it to fit particular populations of children. As new understandings concerning the nature of language and communication occur, the clinician should be able to select from the old program those components that seem useful and to blend these with new insights that come from a current reading of the literature. (p. 394)

Here, we have proposed what we hope will be useful guidelines for teaching difficult-to-teach children—nothing more; nothing less.

ACKNOWLEDGMENTS

We would like to thank Wes Williams of the University of Vermont for his constructive feedback during the preparation of this chapter.

REFERENCES

Alpert, C. L. 1980. Procedures for determining the optimal nonspeech mode with autistic children. *In* R. L. Schiefelbusch (ed.), Nonspeech Language and Communication: Analysis and Intervention. University Park Press, Baltimore.

Baer, D. M. 1978. The behavior analysis of trouble. *In* K. E. Allen, V. A. Holm, and R. L. Schiefelbusch (eds.), Early Intervention—A Team Approach. University Park Press, Baltimore.

Baer, D., Peterson, R., and Sherman J. 1967. The development of imitation by reinforcing behavioral similarity to a model. J. Exp. Anal. Behav. 10:405–416.

Bates, E. 1976. Language in Context. Academic Press, New York.

Becker, W., Engleman, S., and Thomas, D. 1972. Teaching 2: Cognitive Learning and Instruction. Science Research Associates, Inc., Chicago.

Bloom, L. 1970. Language Development: Form and Function of Emerging Grammars. MIT Press, Cambridge, MA.

Bowerman, M. 1978. Semantic and syntactic development: A review of what, when and how in language acquisition. *In* R. L. Schiefelbusch (ed.), Bases of Language Intervention, pp. 97–189. University Park Press, Baltimore.

Bricker, W. A., and Bricker, D. 1974. An early language training strategy. *In* R. L. Schiefelbusch and L. L. Lloyd (eds.), Language Perspectives: Acquisition, Retardation, and Intervention. University Park Press, Baltimore.

Chapman, R., and Miller, J. 1980. Analyzing language and communication in the child. *In* R. L. Schiefelbusch (ed.), Nonspeech Language and Communication: Analysis and Intervention. University Park Press, Baltimore.

Chomsky, N. 1959. A review of Skinner's *Verbal Behavior.* Language 35:26–58.

Chomsky, N. 1965. Aspects of the Theory of Syntax. MIT Press, Cambridge, MA.

Cox, B. P. and Lloyd, L. L. 1976. Audiologic considerations. *In* L. L. Lloyd (ed.), Communication Assessment and Intervention Strategies, pp. 123–193. University Park Press, Baltimore.

Creekmore, N. 1982. Use of sign alone and sign plus speech in language training of nonverbal autistic children. J. Assoc. Severely Handic. 6:45–55.

Cress, P. J., Spellman, C. R., DeBriere, T. J., Sizemore, A. C., Northam, J. K., and Johnson, J. L. 1981. Vision screening for persons with severe handicaps. J. Assoc. Severely Handic. 6:41–50.

deVilliers, J. G., and deVilliers, P. A. 1982. Language Acquisition. Harvard University Press, Cambridge, MA.

Etzel, B. C., and LeBlanc, J. M. 1979. The simplest treatment alternative: The law of parsimony applied to choosing appropriate instructional control and errorless learning procedures for the difficult-to-teach child. J. Autism Dev. Disord. 9(4):361–382.

Ferster, C. B., Culbertson, S., and Perrott-Baren, M. C. 1975. Behavior Principles. Prentice-Hall, New Jersey.

Flavell, J. H. 1970. Concept development. *In* P. H. Mussen (ed.), Carmichael's Manual of Child Psychology. Wiley, New York.

Fulton, R. T., and Lloyd, L. L. 1969. Audiometry for the Retarded: With Implications for the Difficult-to-Test. Williams & Wilkins, Baltimore.

Garcia, E., Baer, D., and Firestone, I. 1971. The development of generalized imitation within topographically determined boundaries. J. Appl. Behav. Anal. 4:101–112.

Gewirtz, J. L., and Stingle, K. G. 1968. Learning of generalized imitation as the basis for identification. Psychol. Rev. 75(5):374–397.

Goetz, L., Utley, B., Gee, A., Baldwin, M., and Sailor, W. 1981. Auditory assessment and programming for severely handicapped deaf-blind students. Unpublished manuscript, San Francisco State University.

Goldiamond, I. 1962. Perception. *In* A. J. Bachrach (ed.), Experimental Foundations of Clinical Psychology. Basic Books, New York.

Greenfield, P. M., and Smith, J. H. 1976. The Structure of Communication in Early Language Development. Academic Press, New York.

Grossman, H. 1977. Manual on Terminology and Classification of Mental Retardation. American Association on Mental Deficiency, Washington, D.C.

Guess, D., Sailor, W., and Baer, D. M. 1974. To teach language to retarded children. *In* R. L. Schiefelbusch and L. L. Lloyd (eds.), Language Perspectives: Acquisition, Retardation, and Intervention. University Park Press, Baltimore.

Guess, D., Sailor, W., and Baer, D. M. 1976. Functional Speech and Language Training for the Severely Handicapped. Part I: Persons and Things. H & H Enterprises, Inc., Lawrence, KS.

Halle, J., Marshall, A., and Spradlin, J. 1979. Time delay: A technique to increase language use and facilitate generalization in retarded children. J. Appl. Behav. Anal. 8:431–439.

Hart, B., and Risley, T. R. 1975. Incidental teaching of language in the preschool. J. Appl. Behav. Anal. 8:411–420.

Johnson, F., and Brown, L. 1974. The use of "whole word procedures" to develop basic components of selected chart story reading skills in severely handicapped young students. In L. Brown, W. Williams, and T. Crowner (eds.), A Collection of Papers and Programs Related to Public School Services for Severely Handicapped Students. Madison Metropolitan School District, Madison, WI.

Kahn, J. 1975. Relationship of Piaget's sensorimotor period to language acquisition of profoundly retarded children. Am. J. Ment. Defic. 79:640–643.

Keogh, W. J. 1981. An experimental analysis of generalized identity and nonidentity matching-to-sample as a technique for establishing nonvocal communication for the severely/profoundly handicapped. In Nonvocal Communication Research, Publication No. 84.023K. U. S. Department of Education, Washington, D.C.

Keogh, W., and Reichle, J. 1982. Excerpts from the Vermont Comprehensive Communication Curriculum. Unpublished manuscript, University of Vermont, Burlington.

Lenneberg, E. H. 1964. The capacity for language acquisition. In J. A. Foder and J. J. Katz (eds.), The Structure of Language: Readings in the Philosophy of Language. Prentice-Hall, Englewood Cliffs, NJ.

Lloyd, L. L., Spradlin, J. E., and Reid, M. J. 1968. An operant audiometric procedure for difficult-to-test patients. J. Speech Hear. Disord. 33:236–245.

Lynch, J., and Bricker, W. A. 1972. Linguistic theory and operant procedures: Toward an integrated approach to language training for the mentally retarded. Ment. Retard. 10:12–17.

Martin, J. A. 1975. Generalizing the use of descriptive adjectives through modelling. J. Appl. Behav. Anal. 8:203–210.

McIlvane, W. J. and Stoddard, T. 1981. Acquisition of matching-to-sample performances in severe retardation: Learning by exclusion. J. Ment. Defic. Res. 25(1):33–48.

Merrill, M. D. 1971. Psychomotor and memorization behavior. In M. D. Merrill (ed.), Instructional Design: Readings, pp. 196–214. Prentice-Hall, Englewood Cliffs, NJ.

Miller, J. F. and Yoder, D. E. 1974. An ontogenetic language teaching strategy for retarded children. In R. L. Schiefelbusch and L. L. Lloyd (eds.), Language Perspectives: Acquisition, Retardation, and Intervention. University Park Press, Baltimore.

Peterson, G. A., Austin, G. J. and Lang, R. P. 1979. Use of teacher prompts to increase social behavior: Generalization effects with severely/profoundly retarded adolescents. Am. J. Ment. Defic. 84:82–86.

Peterson, R. F. 1968. Some experiments on the organization of a class of imitative behaviors. J. Appl. Behav. Anal. 1:225–235.

Reese, H. W., and Lipsitt, L. P. 1973. Experimental Child Psychology. Academic Press, New York.

Sailor, W., and Guess, D. 1983. Severely Handicapped Students—An Instructional Design. Houghton Mifflin, Boston.

Schroder, G. L., and Baer, D. M. 1972. Effects of concurrent and serial training on generalized vocal imitation in retarded children. Dev. Psychol. 6:293–301.

Seligman, M. E. P. 1972. Learned helplessness. Annu. Rev. Med. 23:407–412.

Sherman, J. A., Saunders, R. R., and Bridgham, T. A. 1970. Transfer of matching and mismatching behavior in preschool children. J. Exp. Child Psychol. 9:489–498.

Sidman, M. and Cresson, O. 1973. Reading and cross modal transfer of stimulus equivalences in severe retardation. Am. J. Ment. Defic. 77:515–523.

Siegel, G., and Spradlin, J. 1978. Programming for language and communication therapy. In R. L. Schiefelbusch (ed.), Language Intervention Strategies. University Park Press, Baltimore.

Skinner, B. F. 1957. Verbal Behavior. Appleton-Century-Crofts, New York.

Snell, M. E., and Gast, D. L. 1981. Applying time delay procedure to the instruction of the severely handicapped. J. Assoc. Severely Handic. 6:3–14.

Spellman, C. R., DeBriere, T. J., and Cress, P. J. 1979. Final Report from the Project *Research and Development of Subjective Visual Acuity Assessment Procedures for Severely Handicapped Persons.* BEH Grant #G00-76-02592, the University of Kansas Bureau of Child Research at the Parsons Research Center, Parsons, Kansas.

Staats, A. W. 1974. Behaviorism and cognitive theory in the study of language: A neopsycholinguistics. In R. L. Schiefelbusch and L. L. Lloyd (eds.), Language Perspectives: Acquisition, Retardation, and Intervention. University Park Press, Baltimore.

Strain, P. S. 1975. Increasing social play of severely retarded preschoolers with socio-dramatic activities. Ment. Retard. 13(6):7–9.

Striefel, S., and Owens, C. R. 1982. Transfer of stimulus control procedures; Applications to language acquisition training with the developmentally handicapped. Behav. Res. Severe, Dev. Disabil. 1(4):307–331.

Touchette, P. E. 1971. Transfer of stimulus control: Measuring the moment of transfer. J. Exp. Anal. Behav. 15:347–354.

U.S. Department of Education, Bureau for Education of the Handicapped. Requests for Proposals 82-020: Institutes for Education of Severely Handicapped Children. Author, Washington, D.C.

Zeaman, D. 1976. The ubiquity of novelty—familiarity (habituation?) effects. In T. Tight and K. Leaton (eds.), Habituation: Perspectives from Child Development, Animal Behavior and Neurophysiology. Lawrence Erlbaum Associates, Hillsdale, NJ.

Zeaman, D., and House, B. J. 1963. The role of attention in retardate discrimination learning. In H. F. Harlow (ed.), Handbook of Mental Deficiency. McGraw-Hill, New York.

Section

III

Facilitating and Measuring Generalization

chapter 7

Clinical Strategies for the Measurement of Language Generalization

Steven F. Warren

Department of Special Education
Peabody College of
Vanderbilt University

contents

DEFINITIONS   199

IDENTIFYING AND DEFINING RESPONSE CLASSES   202
    Lexical Classes   202
    Structural Classes and Pragmatic Classes   202

MEASUREMENT APPROACHES   204
    Probe Generalization   204
    Naturalistic Measures of Generalization   205
    Uses of Probes and Naturalistic Samples   205

CRITERIA FOR ACCEPTABLE GENERALIZATION   206
    How Much Sampling?   207
    How Much Generalization?   208
    How Much Diversity?   209
    Testing for Maintenance   210
    General Recommendations   211
    Summary: Guidelines for Establishing Effective Generalization
        Criteria   212

**DEVELOPING A GENERALIZATION
MEASUREMENT PLAN**   213
    The Plan   213
    Utilizing Probes   214
    Natural Samples   214
    Observer Training   216
    Frequency of Measurement   217
    Measurement Settings   217
    Reliability Checks   217
    Augmentative Communication Systems   218
    Data Management   218
    Incorporating Other Measures   219
    When Generalization Does Not Occur   219
    Summary: Guidelines for Measuring Generalization   221

CONCLUSION   221

REFERENCES   222

Comprehensive communication training efforts with language-delayed children may produce a range of effects. Some effects may be restricted and transitory; others may be more generalized and stable. The extent of durable generalized effects is a measure of the true efficacy of the remediation effort. Because communication is broadly based on linguistic, cognitive, and social behaviors, the range and form of generalized training effects may be varied. Thus, accurate measurement of effects is a very challenging problem.

The possible outcomes of a comprehensive language intervention program includes changes in the lexical, syntactic, semantic, and pragmatic aspects of language. Language training may affect an individual's general cognitive and social development. Furthermore, training effects may be observed along one or more dimensions of communication performance. For example, either comprehension and production or both might improve; quantity and quality of utterances may be altered; new forms may be learned and old forms may come to express new functions; the matrix of form/function covariants may be expanded, resulting in a more diverse communicative repertoire. Each of these "possible" changes might be evaluated for generalization.

This chapter discusses the evaluation of language training effects. It focuses on strategies for measuring language generalization, and not on the collection and management of training data or of standardized test results. For practical reasons, it deals primarily with language production and not comprehension.

The goal of this chapter is to provide readers with sufficient background to select appropriate generalization measures, apply them, and interpret the results. The chapter is divided into five sections. In the first section, definitions directly relevant to the measurement of language generalization are offered. The second section discusses strategies for identifying and defining functional response classes. In the third section naturalistic sampling and probe measurement strategies are proposed and contrasted. In the fourth section, acceptable criteria for generalization are discussed. Determining generalization criteria is a complex issue that has not been addressed sufficiently by research. Guidelines for establishing criterion levels are offered. Finally, in the fifth section issues relevant to developing and implementing individualized generalization measurement plans are considered. The discussion of issues is sufficiently detailed to guide readers in developing and applying their own measurement strategies. An emphasis on cost efficiency is maintained throughout because the chapter is oriented toward the needs of clinicians and teachers.

DEFINITIONS

In nontechnical terms, generalization is "an inference from many particulars" (*American Heritage Dictionary of the English Language*, 1969). For experimental psychologists interested in theoretical accounts of human learning, generalization (or transfer) represents a failure by the organism to discriminate the difference between the positive stimulus (i.e., a stimulus correlated with reinforcement) and a negative stimulus (i.e., a stimulus correlated with periods of extinction) (Rilling, 1977). In this view, generalization is placed at one end of a continuum representing degree of stimulus control, with discrimination at the other end. Applied psychologists treating disfunctional behavior have used a practical and more positive definition of generalization as the "occurrence of relevant behavior under different, nontraining conditions without the scheduling of the same events in those conditions as had been scheduled in the training conditions" (Stokes and Baer, 1977, p. 350).

Definitions of generalization applicable to the study of language are similar to the general definitions offered above. Stimulus generalization refers to the use of the trained verbal response across persons, settings, objects, or time (i.e., across different stimuli or stimulus conditions). Stimulus generalization in this case corresponds to the use of trained responses in varied appropriate communication "contexts." For example, a child might demonstrate stimulus generalization of the word "cup" by using it to request a cup at snack time in school and using it to request a cup from her mother at home while at the kitchen table. For a more detailed discussion of stimulus generalization see Goldstein (this volume). He provides many additional examples of "stimulus" classes.

Defining context by describing relevant stimulus conditions is difficult. Communicative context is more than the who, what, when, and where of a given situation. These dimensions do not exhaust the range of utterance-external variables affecting the production and comprehension of verbal behavior that must be considered among the set of potential controlling stimuli. For example, two parts of context are verbal and nonverbal behavior directed to the child and verbal and nonverbal behavior by the child immediately preceding the occurrence of the trained response. The immediate social relationship between the child and the listener (e.g., eye contact, body orientation) and the historical relationships between the child and the listener, including previous reinforcement history, are potentially controlling contextual variables as well.

The definition and measurement of response generalization is an equally complex problem. Basically, response generalization is the display of different responses similar in function to a trained response. For example, in language training a child may be taught to combine the word "want" with several different object words such as "milk," "drink," "cookie," and "ball." These object words form a response class with "want." Their use in different contexts with "want" is stimulus generalization. The substitution by the child of other "untrained" object words following "want" is response generalization. That is, if the child has the words "cup," "apple," and "car" in his lexicon and begins using these with "want" without direct training of these specific combinations, then response generalization has occurred. This recombination of learned elements of the language system into novel combinations that can describe newly encountered events is frequently referred to as "generative" behavior and is discussed by Goldstein (this volume) as "recombinatory" generalization.

Defining "similar responses" is complex because human language does not seem to be a unitary system that can be readily broken down into meaningful, exclusive subsystems. Language is composed of at least two interrelated, overlapping systems that cannot be clearly or meaningfully separated from each other nor treated as a single system. A given sentence has both structure (is it composed of syntactic and semantic rule-governed forms) and function (it does something, such as describing or requesting). It is possible to define different types of potential structure-based response classes, such as syntactic classes (e.g., all noun-verb-noun combinations) or semantic classes (e.g., all agent-action-object combinations). It is also possible to define function-based classes, such as information seeking, requests, protests, and so forth (Halliday, 1975; Moerk, 1977; Searle, 1969). Furthermore, exemplars of each of these classes can be taught and generalization to other supposed members of the class can be observed (e.g., 10 examples of noun-verb-noun combinations can be trained and the child can be observed to determine if she begins producing other nontrained noun-verb-noun combinations). However, we do not know yet how to meaningfully define and measure combined structure-function response classes (Rogers-Warren and Warren, 1981). Until multidimensional response classes are empirically defined and reliably measured (i.e., observed in natural occurrence), we must either use somewhat arbitrary definitions and classes, or study one subsystem (such as syntax) that has been defined independent of other systems.

Response generalization occurs when, without being directly informed (that is, instructed that "these responses are the same"), an individual includes a stimulus or response in a given class. Evidence of inclusion is based on the use of the response by the individual for the same function (i.e., purpose) as other members of the class. The size of a response class can be efficiently increased by generalization, and response classes are utilized efficiently by generalization across stimulus conditions. They are modified and created as needs and environmental contingencies change. Finally, a word (or gesture) can simultaneously be a member of many different response classes because it can have many different functions depending on the specific situation. For example, the word "drink" can be used as either an object (i.e., noun) or an action (i.e., verb) word in different contexts.

IDENTIFYING AND DEFINING RESPONSE CLASSES

Approaching language remediation from the standpoint of training response classes is useful because it inherently emphasizes generalization. The goal is to train not isolated responses classes, but integrated and flexible response classes that can be assimilated into an effective and functional communication repertoire (Rogers-Warren and Warren, 1981). This goal may be more or less ambitious depending on the level of the child being trained. Two general types of response classes are discussed: 1) lexical; and 2) combined structural and pragmatic classes.

Lexical Classes

A lexical response class consists of a word and all the objects, actions, or attributes that it accurately describes and that are therefore "equivalent" to the word. For example, the response "cup" represents all types of cups—coffee cups, small plastic cups, and paper cups. In training the referent *cup,* many examples of cups should be used, and their equivalence should be established. Probes of other examples of cup (e.g., tall cups, short cups, green cups, red cups, fat cups, etc.) should be conducted to ensure that the child has fully acquired the concept. Probes with other similar items might be included to ensure that the child has not overgeneralized to such items as bowls, plates, and jars.

Training lexical response classes consisting of object referents is a relatively straightforward process and so is the assessment of generalization. Other syntactic classes such as verbs and adjectives can be probed similarly. In each case, the issue of overgeneralization should be considered as well as that of undergeneralization. Lexical acquisition is primarily an association task (Moerk, 1977). Words can be taught by a simple matching-to-sample training paradigm in which the child is taught to identify the item, action, or attribute represented by the word. Even very severely retarded individuals can successfully learn and generalize a range of individual referents (see Keogh and Reichle, this volume).

Structural Classes and Pragmatic Classes

As a child obtains a basic productive vocabulary and is ready to acquire two-word combinations the issue of response classes becomes more complex. The exact relationship between form and function in language use remains unclear. Form and function cannot be meaningfully separated in actual speech (Nelson, 1981), but attempts are often made to separate them in training programs and in data analysis. Approaching the problem by defining structural classes within pragmatic classes is a possible solution. This approach is based on the assumption that form generally follows function and is dictated by it (Hart, 1980; Moerk, 1977; Skinner, 1957).

Pragmatic classes are initially very broad and originate in infancy. Bruner (1975) has traced the origin of some speech acts from early infancy. He has shown how the function of request begins almost at birth with differentiated infant crys and is slowly shaped and further differentiated into linguistic forms. From this longitudinal developmental perspective, linguistic forms may be viewed as being a more efficient and effective means for conveying already existing pragmatic functions. Therefore, it makes sense functionally to define structural classes within broadly defined pragmatic classes. For example, to train the function "request" the child would be taught a range of linguistic forms from simple to complex. These might include "want (object)" (state verb–noun), "I want (object)" (pronoun–state verb–noun), "Give me the (object)" (verb-pronoun-article-noun), and so on. Different functions could be trained concurrently; training on structures would proceed from simple to complex within each pragmatic function class. Equivalence among utterances within a class is reinforced on two levels: different words can be substituted within the same form for the same function; and different forms can be used for the same function. Some examples of linguistic response classes embedded within pragmatic classes are shown in Table 1.

Most available language training programs do not clearly identify the response classes embedded in their training sequences. Most identify the structural classes (e.g., noun-verb-noun), but not the pragmatic classes. Or they identify the pragmatic function classes they intend to be trained (e.g., self-extended control), but the manner in which these classes are trained results in the acquisition not of these pragmatic classes but of others (typically question answering). For example, you cannot effectively train a child to ask

Table 1.   Examples of Structural Response Classes Embedded in Pragmatic Response Classes

Function	Structure	Examples
Request objects	State verb–noun	"Want ball" "Want cup" "Want milk"
Request objects	First person pronoun–state verb–noun	"I want ball" "I want cup" "I want milk"
Answer questions	Third person pronoun–verb (-*ing*)	"He's running" "He's sleeping" "He's eating"
Referential questions	*Wh*-question–preposition	"What 's that?" "What's this?"

information-seeking questions with an adult-controlled rote training strategy in which the child is required to ask 20 consecutive questions in response to adult prompts. This probably only teaches the child to respond to the prompts—that is, to answer the adult's "question." The question form can only be trained functionally if the child *wants to know the answer* (Hart, 1980).

If language training is approached from the perspective of teaching structural response classes within functional response classes, generalization should be enhanced. However, most available language training programs are not organized by functional response classes, so a clinician must do one of the following: 1) search for such a program; 2) devise his or her own program with structural response classes embedded in *functionally* taught pragmatic classes; or 3) modify an existing program. In developing, modifying, or implementing a program two questions should be repeatedly asked: "What are you training the child to *do* with the forms you are teaching him?" and "Are you training forms in a context in which the intended pragmatic function is actually being accomplished?" By answering these two questions it should be possible to define and measure response classes that represent meaningful organizations of a training program. Then the tasks are to teach these classes, assess for generalization within them, and program for generalization as necessary.

MEASUREMENT APPROACHES

Generalization can be measured using either a probe or a naturalistic sampling approach. Like any measurement approach, both of these methods have certain biases (Corrigan, 1982). Probes and naturalistic sampling differ in terms of the relative structure of the response opportunity (in comparison with the training situation), the similarity of the stimuli to those utilized in training the initial response, and sometimes the length of the time between training and the response opportunity.

Probe Generalization

Probe generalization is defined as responses to artificially structured stimulus-response situations. Probes are discrete generalization tests in which some variables are similar to those encountered in training and some are different. Probes typically differ from training in that they may take place in different settings (e.g., the classroom or the home), and/or employ a different trainer (e.g., a teacher or parent), and/or utilize different stimuli (e.g., objects rather than pictures, or objects different from those used in training).

The basic format of most probes described in the literature resembles a training trial. A trainer presents a specific stimulus (an object, a picture, a question, an instruction, or some combination of these). The student makes a specific response that may or may not be reinforced by the trainer. The student's responses to a set of predetermined trials are recorded. For example, a trainer first teaches a student to produce statements of the form "want cup," "want car," or "want juice," in response to the presentation of these objects. Interspersed with reinforced trials with these objects, the trainer holds up an occasional untrained object, such as a cookie or ball, and records the child's response to these. Alternatively, a second adult might be employed to enter the training setting, hold up novel items in front of the student, ask "What do you want?", and record the student's responses. This format may also be used in other nontraining settings employing a teacher or parent as the prober.

Most reports of generalization in the experimental literature have relied on structured probes as their test for generalization (Warren and Rogers-Warren, 1980). Some examples include Guess and Baer (1973), Lutzker and Sherman (1974), and Warren et al., (1981).

Naturalistic Measures of Generalization

Naturalistic measures of generalization describe spontaneous generalizations by the child to stimulus-response variations that occur outside the training setting. Generalization is assessed by observing the child in typical, nontraining settings in which language use is frequently requisite (Warren et al., 1980). Naturalistic measures differ from probe measures of generalization in that no specific stimulus is presented to attempt to directly elicit the target response. However, observational data are collected at times when the child is likely to use the target response if it has generalized to his repertoire (e.g., when he is talking to an adult or playing with peers). Measurement of naturalistic generalization is extremely important because such measures indicate the extent to which the child is using the trained language in actual communication. Naturalistic measures are based on the assumption that "the child shows best what he knows when allowed in a familiar and unconstrained situation to express himself on a topic of his own choosing in a manner he favors" (Brown, 1973).

Uses of Probes and Naturalistic Samples

Sometimes probes and naturalistic samples of generalization may provide the same information. This is obviously true when no generalization has occurred. However, when some generalization has occurred, and the extent, nature, and sufficiency are of interest, the data derived from these two sampling approaches may give different answers. For instance, in our longitudinal analyses of language generalization with severely retarded institutionalized adolescents, we have found probes to overestimate both vocabulary generalization (Warren and Rogers-Warren, 1983a) and syntactic generalization (Warren and Rogers-Warren, 1983b). The error was minor with vocabulary words: the probes overestimated generalization by 10% compared to actual usage recorded in the natural environment. However, in the longitudinal analysis of syntax generalization, probe data suggested the subjects had generalized a large number of four-word syntactic forms, but we found no evidence of their use in naturalistic observations of each subject. Apparently the subjects could use these forms under the restricted "probe" conditions, but would not spontaneously utilize them in their actual interactive repertoires (Warren and Rogers-Warren, 1983b). In this case, if we had relied solely on the probe data (as nearly all trainers would have), we would have overestimated the effects of our training efforts.

Probes and naturalistic sampling approaches each have certain strengths and limitations in application. The primary strength of probes is their simplicity and ease of application. They are inexpensive to utilize in terms of time, effort, and resources required, and the interpretation of their results is typically straightforward. However, as noted above, they can overestimate generalization and provide a misleading view of training success. They provide no way of determining whether a form will be used at an appropriate rate in the natural environment. Their best use is determining vocabulary generalization (particularly nouns) and low-rate responses that are so context specific that they would be difficult to pick up in naturalistic sampling.

The primary strengths of naturalistic sampling are the richness of the data typically obtained and their inherent ecological validity. However, naturalistic sampling is usually expensive in terms of time, effort, and resources required, and the interpretation of the data can be very complex. If an insufficient number of observations are taken, or inappropriate situations are observed, then this approach can underestimate generalization. The best uses of naturalistic sampling are to study the effects of specific settings (e.g., home versus classroom), to determine general effects on the child's overall productive communication system, or to determine if a child is using a newly trained form at an appropriate rate.

CRITERIA FOR ACCEPTABLE GENERALIZATION

When is a response "generalized"? The answer to this question depends on the function of the response trained, how it is measured, and the "natural" or appropriate rate of the response in the target setting. With either a probe or a naturalistic approach three questions must be answered:

1. How much sampling is necessary to determine if sufficient generalization has indeed occurred?

2. How much generalization should occur in those samples?
3. How much diversity should there be among those occurrences?

How Much Sampling?

The number of samples needed depends on the probability of opportunities for the target response occurring in a given sample. With a probe, the probability is 100% because the stimulus conditions have been arranged to elicit the response. Three to five probes should provide an accurate assessment of the student's ability to generalize the trained response or response class to a situation varying on only one or two dimensions from training.

Naturalistic samples should be collected while the student is engaged in everyday activities in which the newly trained response should be functional. The presence of a listener, either an adult or a skilled peer, is essential to accurately assess generalization. The number of samples needed depends on how much the child actually talks during each sample. The more the child talks the more likely he is to display an item or form he learned in training (Hart, 1980). Thus, the probability of observing a generalized response during a single observation of a frequent talker will be much greater than it is with a child who rarely speaks.

The number of samples (or number of utterances) needed also depends on the specific target response(s). Most nouns are situation specific. The child is unlikely to use referents such as ball or milk appropriately unless he is engaged with these objects or they are at least relevant to the situation. Basic syntactic responses, such as noun-verb-noun constructions, are appropriate and probable in any interaction. Relatively elaborate constructions (e.g., third-person pronoun–adverb-verb-pronoun) may have consistently low probabilities of occurrence because their function is more specialized in normal conversation.

Our research (see Warren et al., 1980) suggests that four 15-minute observations in an "interactive situation" conducted over a period of 2 weeks should provide a sufficient sample of behavior. Alternatively, a sample containing a minimum number of utterances may be used. The student is observed until a minimum number of utterances, typically 50 or 100, is collected. This sample is then analyzed for generalized responding using a definition based on probability of occurrence in a constant sample. The time required to collect a standard sample will vary depending on the frequency of the student's communication attempts. Some children make 50 initiations in 20 minutes, others in 20 hours. For low-rate talkers we suggest using probes, and considering interventions like milieu training (see Hart, this volume) to increase the frequency of the student's speech in conversational contexts.

A third alternative is continuous monitoring of the student's productive language. A parent or teacher could record each instance of one or more target responses she observes the child using. To do this a tally of occurrences for each form must be used. The adult must keep a clipboard near at hand with a tally sheet listing each training form on it. Each time she overhears the child using one of the forms, she makes a tally of it. This method is informal and inexpensive. However, it requires an observant and well-motivated adult or it may be very inaccurate. Either the adult will need some training to utilize this method, or only very simple forms should be tallied.

Variations in the application of each of these three alternatives may also be implemented. Naturalistic samples can be made semi-structured by purposely using adult-child game formats or by using open-ended questions or other elicitation devices to increase the probability and rate of the child's talking. For example, to test the generalization of question-asking skills with severely retarded adolescents, Warren et al. (1981) utilized a probe in which an adult would approach a student with a paper bag full of items, setting the occasion for the student to ask "What's that?" Many other useful techniques are discussed by Miller (1981). The primary advantage of purposely structuring the situation is efficiency—more can be obtained in less time. However, the situation should still allow many opportunities for spontaneous child speech. Answers to questions are respondent behaviors that often take the form of sentence fragments. Typically they cannot be analyzed in the same way that spontaneous child-initiated utterances can (Corrigan, 1982).

Regardless of which approach is implemented, if a child is not using a trained form in appropriate circumstances soon after it has been taught (within 2 weeks at most), it must be assumed that it has not generalized and that additional generalization programming is necessary (for methods see Stremel-Campbell and Campbell, this volume).

How Much Generalization?

How frequently must a form be used before one concludes that it is sufficiently generalized? Few occurrences suggest the response has not yet been trained sufficiently. Frequency of occurrence is strongly related to generalization both in language (Hart, 1980) and social behavior (Warren, 1977). Furthermore, Ingram (1975) has proposed that truly productive use of a response class, not just the production of a few instances of the structure, is needed before crediting a child with knowledge of the class. The problem from any perspective is deciding how much behavior constitutes sufficient generalization.

Unfortunately, this problem cannot be addressed using a probe strategy. Probes do not provide information on natural frequency of occurrence. Therefore, we suggest estimating first an ideal average rate and then a minimum acceptable rate of occurrence for a target response. The ideal rate should be based on what a normal developmentally "matched" child (or handicapped child judged competent at the skill) might typically display under the same conditions. The best way to obtain this "normative" information is to take some baseline observations of competent children in the setting. The minimum acceptable rate might then be set as a ratio of the ideal average rate. For example, if "matched" normal children typically use or embed one noun-verb-noun construction for every four sentences they utter, a minimum acceptable rate might be set at one for every five or six utterances by the handicapped child in question. As a rule of thumb, we generally use a 2:3 ratio as a minimum acceptable rate (e.g., if the ideal average rate of a form in a representative sample is six, the minimum acceptable rate would be set at four).

If it is not possible to establish acceptable occurrence rates on the basis of observation, then an arbitrarily determined numerical criterion should be set. The observation of five occurrences of a form is a commonly accepted level (Ingram, 1975), but this could be either too high or too low because children typically emit structures with unequal frequencies (Dale, 1978). For some basic constructions like noun-verb this may be too low; for others with more specialized functions it may be too high. Unfortunately, a normative data base on frequency of use that would allow us to derive firmer guidelines does not yet exist.

How Much Diversity?

Diversity may be as important as rate of occurrence. If a student uses only a few members of a response class and has not mastered other members of the class even though he knows the constituent parts, the likelihood of him generalizing the response fully and incorporating it into his normal behavioral repertoire is lessened (Warren, 1977). Limited use of a response class (i.e., undergeneralization) implies that the child does not fully understand the parameters of the class. This is normally a transitory phenomenon common when children are acquiring language (Anglin, 1977). However, with handicapped children it can persist and limit the effects of training. The use of a multiple exemplar training format (see Stremel-Campbell and Campbell, this volume) is a good general strategy for countering this tendency. Systematic application of matrix-training approaches (see Goldstein, this volume) is an even better tactic because it can reveal when the child has fully acquired a response receptively or productively.

Probes can be used to test for diversity of responding within a response class simply by varying the stimulus conditions of the probe. For example, the trainer can test for agent-action-object responses by presenting a range of agents (e.g., *you, me, Fred*) initiating a range of actions (e.g., *run, throw, drink*) on a range of objects (e.g., *home, ball, juice*) and then recording the child's responses to these probes. The prober might say to the child "Watch me," take a drink of juice, then ask "What did I do?" The probe session might consist of several similar episodes using the child as the "agent" too. The key is to make sure the probes follow a systematic format that will reveal the extent of the child's generalization. Imagination, ingenuity, and the child's tolerance are probably the only constraints in this respect.

For naturalistic observations, calculating a type-token ratio (TTR) provides a measure of either lexical or form diversity. For example, to measure the diversity of vocabulary the number of different words (types) produced in a 50-utterance sample might be compared to the total number of words (tokens) used. This can also be done for classes of words (e.g., nouns, verbs, adjectives) and for forms (i.e., number of different noun-verb combinations versus total number of combinations). Examples of this approach to diversity can be found in studies by Hart and Risley (1974, 1975, 1980) and Rogers-Warren and Warren (1980). Rules for calculating type-token ratios are presented by Miller (1981).

How much diversity is sufficient? Again, the answer depends on what is reasonable in the setting and the child's overall level of development. There are no useful normative data on this subject. However, repetitious speech is a good indicator of restricted response class formation. A high rate of repetition or use of only a few specific utterances suggests that further training on other exemplars of the response class is necessary to facilitate generalization to the entire response class.

Testing for Maintenance

Maintenance of therapeutic gains may be viewed as a special case of stimulus generalization (Lovaas et al., 1973). However, studies by Garcia and DeHaven (1980) and Koegel and Rincover (1977) suggest that generalization across settings and across time are not the same phenomenon. In both of these studies, generalization across settings occurred but not generalization across time. These reports, in addition to those of Lovaas et al. (1973), Hall and Tomblin (1978), and Warren et al. (1981), indicate that severely handicapped children may not maintain trained communication skills on a long-term basis. However, these studies were all conducted with institutionalized children, so it is unclear whether the subjects actually "forgot" the skills or if they were simply extinguished over time by a lack of function (and therefore reinforcement) for them in the institutional environment.

If a communication or language skill is truly functional it should maintain in a student's repertoire providing it has been thoroughly trained and programmed until it generalizes to the student's actual usage repertoire. The hierarchical nature of human language provides a form of maintenance training because simple forms provide the kernals of more complex forms as acquisition proceeds. That is, individual words become the substance of sentences; verb-noun combinations become the basis of noun-verb-noun combinations, noun-verb-noun combinations become the basis of noun-verb-adjective-noun combinations, and so on. In a longitudinal analysis of generalization resulting from a comprehensive language training program with six severely handicapped adolescents, Warren and Rogers-Warren (1983b) found that, out of 73 syntactic structures trained, pronoun–state verb combinations were nested in 51%, pronoun-verb in 33%, verb-noun in 26%, and state verb–nominal in 36%. This nesting, although providing a form of ongoing maintenance programming, can also be confusing to a trainer looking for the maintenance of a form such as verb-noun. As the child progresses to more complex forms he may stop using verb-noun combinations separately and primarily use them as the kernals of longer forms (e.g., pronoun-verb-noun). So we must be careful not to confuse lack of maintenance with development, which may make an intermediate communication form no longer functional (or desirable).

Since maintenance cannot be guaranteed even when generalization has initially been observed, it should be regularly measured. This may be done using either probes or natural samples concurrently with generalization measurements. Again, probes will provide the most convenient check. This requires that the trainer predetermine which forms she wishes to check for maintenance, and then integrate probes for these with the other generalization probes. We suggest that maintenance probes be routinely integrated with all generalization probes. This procedure will also help program the maintenance of these forms by assuring some function for them in the child's repertoire. This "reactive" aspect of probes is one of their positive attributes in clinical usage.

Maintenance can be assessed in natural samples simply by noting the use of previously trained forms (or lack of them) in the samples. If a form does not appear to be maintaining, first check that it has not been nested in a longer form that the child is now using. Next use probes to make sure the child can still produce the form. If so, analyze further natural samples. If the form still is not present, institute a milieu training procedure (e.g., incidental language teaching) to facilitate generalization to the child's everyday usage repertoire (see Hart, this volume).

General Recommendations

As noted, there are advantages and disadvantages of using either probes or natural samples to estimate generalization. Probes are generally simple to design and carry out. They yield specific information and are efficient in terms of time and effort. Furthermore, if a student does not generalize in a probe situation, it is unlikely that she will generalize to the less facilitative conditions typical of the natural environment. On the other hand, probes do not indicate how the student actually performs in the natural environment.

Natural samples can be time consuming and difficult. If poorly planned or implemented, they may provide little worthwhile information. However, natural samples can indicate what the student is actually doing (or not doing) with the language she has been taught. The process of collecting naturalistic data may yield insights into how to improve training or make it more relevant. Furthermore, if teachers and parents are trained as observers, this approach can prove relatively cost efficient even for an overburdened therapist. Finally, natural samples provide the only means to assess appropriate usage rates, an important variable in programming generalization (Hart, 1980).

I recommend using both probes and natural samples as frequently as possible. Probes should be built directly into the training process. Each time a student reaches criterion on a training step, probes should be conducted across persons and settings,[1] as well as other members of the response class being taught. If the student fails these probes, additional training or generalization programming is in order. If he passes these probes, then natural environment observations should be initiated to determine if the student is using the lexical items or structures in day-to-day communication. If no solid evidence of generalized naturalistic use is observed, generalization programming should be initiated in the natural environment.

Summary: Guidelines for Establishing Effective Generalization Criteria

1. Use both probes and natural samples to estimate structure generalization. Vocabulary generalization is most cost-efficiently assessed by probes.
2. Require an 80–90% correct response rate as a minimal criterion level on probes. If this is not obtained, train further and/or introduce additional generalization programming.
3. For natural observations collect a minimum number of utterances (such as 50 nonimitative utterances) as a basis for assessing generalization. Utterances can be collected cumulatively over a few days or in a single observation.
4. A reasonable criterion for generalization of a structurally (e.g., noun-verb-noun) or pragmatically (e.g., requests) defined response class should include three to five *different* examples of the class (e.g., three different noun-verb combinations or five different requests). If sufficient diversity is not observed, or if inappropriate rates of repetition are observed, train additional functional exemplars of the class.

---

[1]When a student has a consistent history of generalizing across people and settings, these probes can be conducted less frequently. Relatively greater emphasis should then be placed on response class generalization.

5. Assess rate by recording the number of target utterances either per unit of time (e.g., per minute) or as a ratio to other utterances used. If rate is too low (e.g., one utterance per minute when matched peers are averaging five to seven, or one utterance out of every 10 when peers are averaging five out of 10) utilize milieu training techniques (see Hart, this volume) to increase it. Sufficient rate is a key to both the acquisition and generalization process and will allow the efficient measurement of training effects.

6. Require appropriate use (nonimitative) in at least two different probe situations and two different natural sample measurements over time. Periodically check for maintenance of previously trained forms. Keep in mind that as a child progresses she may cease using some simple forms and probably incorporate them as kernal structures in more sophisticated forms.

DEVELOPING A GENERALIZATION MEASUREMENT PLAN

Once response classes have been defined, training begun, and suitable generalization criteria determined, generalization measurement should begin. It is important that measurement be done systematically or the results may be misleading. An ecologically valid measurement plan should be formulated. This plan should address a number of issues including the actual behaviors to be measured, the types of measures to be taken (probe and/or natural samples), who is to do the measuring, how often, in what settings, how the data are to be managed and analyzed, and what to do when generalization is not observed. Other issues to consider include how much observer training is needed, how to assure reliability, and how to incorporate related measures of language performance (e.g., mean length of utterance). Stremel-Campbell and Campbell (this volume) provide some additional suggestions and guidelines for the measurement of generalization.

The Plan

The measurement plan should be a concisely written statement sufficiently detailed to allow others to utilize it. It should specifically address each of the issues noted above. This level of documentation will allow careful time management and later an analysis of the cost effectiveness of various aspects of the strategy. Most importantly, to be useful, the plan must be followed, so it must be a realistic approach that fits the constraints of the specific situation.

Generalization programming and assessment should be built into the individual education program (IEP) for each child. Then implementing the measurement plan does not constitute "extra work," but instead can be approached as a regular component of the child's program. This in turn will provide additional emphasis on generalization for everyone involved in the child's programming. The child's generalization goals should be specified in the IEP just as other goals are. Evidence of attainment of these goals should come from the generalization measurements.

Utilizing Probes

Probes can be conducted across responses, settings, people, or time, or various combinations of these dimensions can be tested within a single probe session. Generalization can be assessed (and programmed if necessary) either by interspersing nonreinforced discrete trials of novel examples of the training form during the training session (i.e., between reinforced training trials), or probing novel examples at another time but still in the training context.

After basic response class generalization has been established, systematic probes across people, settings, and time should be conducted. Selection of multidimensional (trainer and setting) or single dimension (trainer only) probe formats should be based on the learning characteristics of the student. Ultimately, the student must generalize across all three dimensions, but for some students multiple stimulus changes may disrupt performance. For students who are lower functioning or just beginning training, it may be advisable to first establish generalization independently across each dimension and then conduct multidimensional probes. If response class generalization has been established, it should be further assessed by incorporating novel examples of the response class into probes of other dimensions.

Across-person probes can be conducted with teachers, aids, or parents. Provision of a simple data sheet and some minimal training is typically sufficient to incorporate these individuals into the measurement process. They can either be brought into the training setting, or the probes can take place in another setting, allowing two or more generalization dimensions to be tested simultaneously.

Natural Samples

Natural samples of generalization allow the measurement of all four dimensions of generalization discussed above. That is, by observing children interacting in their natural environments, it is possible to measure response class generalization and generalization across settings, people, and time simultaneously. If settings are chosen to ensure a range of behavior and an appropriate number of utterances are obtained in the sample, then the measurement should be ecologically valid. A prerequisite for naturalistic assessments is evidence that the student has already generalized to probes. As a rule, children who fail probe tests of generalization do not use their trained language in the less structured natural environment (Warren and Rogers-Warren, 1983b).

The sampling method used in the natural environment should be based on the time available for sampling and the amount of cooperation obtainable from a student's parents and teachers. Ideally, a precise verbatim sample consisting of at least 50 nonimitative utterances should be collected cumulatively over a relatively short period of time (an hour of observation is usually sufficient). This sample can be collected by a clinician, teacher, or parent.

To collect a verbatim sample under most conditions an observer must station herself within a few feet of the child in as unobtrusive a manner as possible. The idea is to disrupt the child as little as possible, so that the observer watches the child but never makes eye contact. When the observer is suitably positioned she begins writing down in longhand everything the child says. A new line of writing is begun each time the child begins a new utterance. For each utterance a check mark is made in a ruled column at the left of the data sheet indicating to whom the utterance was directed (teacher, child, or other). The child is judged to begin a new utterance with each change of address, or after a pause of 1 second or more. At the end of each minute, the observer draws a short horizontal line after the last recorded utterance. This line is used primarily for determining rate per minute and for judging reliability. Hart (1983) has presented a detailed set of procedures for collecting and analyzing verbatim speech data.

A carefully recorded verbatim sample may contain more information about the child's productive generalization and usage than any other source, particularly if context notes are also taken. However, this can be a time-consuming process that a busy teacher or parent cannot execute satisfactorily. In this case a parent tally sheet may be the best alternative. An example of a tally sheet is provided in Figure 1. With this method, the clinician provides a one-page data sheet for the parent (or teacher). This sheet includes examples of the response class to be monitored. The parents or teacher may need training (which should require only a few minutes' time) to make sure they understand the response classes specified. Their task is to write down occurrences of target forms that they overhear the child use incidently over a specified time span (usually a week). This tally sheet method is less preferable to verbatim recordings, but it can still provide useful information (particularly if the parents or teacher are highly motivated). The tally sheet is easy to implement and manage. In addition, participating in the recording process may sensitize the parents and teacher to the child's current level of language skill, further increasing the likelihood that they will incidently engage in generalization facilitating interactions with the child.

The methods of natural sampling I described can be varied to fit the specific situation and can be used in combination. For example, a clinician might collect a 50–100-utterance verbatim sample once a month in a free play

Parent: Mary Doe   Trainer: Sid

Child: Angel   Response Classes:_____

Week of: May 10–17   1. State verb–noun _____
                                          2. First-person pronoun–
                                             state verb–noun _____
                                          3. First-person pronoun–
                                             state verb–verb _____

Response Class Examples:

1. State verb–noun:
    "Want (cookie)";   "Want (cup)";
    "Want (car)";   "Want (doll)"
2. First-person pronoun–state verb–noun: "I want (cookie)"; "I want (ball)"
3. First-person pronoun–state verb–verb : "I want (go)"; "I want (eat)"; "I want (drink)"

Tallies:

"I want milk" ////   "I want go"   ̶H̶T̶ //
"Want choo-choo"   "I want eat"   ///
"Want doggie"   "_____ want drink" ̶H̶T̶ ////
"I want _____"
"Want juice"

Figure 1. Sample parent generalization tally sheet.

setting, and the rest of the time rely on tally sheet records by teachers or parents. With very low rate speakers, milieu training (see Hart, this volume) or other specific elicitation techniques (see Miller, 1981) may be necessary to generate a sufficient number of utterances to allow an analysis.

Observer Training

The measurement techniques proposed are relatively simple. They do not require learning sophisticated observation codes or systems. They do require that the observer understands what types of utterances the child is being taught. Some training and orientation may be necessary. One training technique is to provide several examples of each response class and then assess observer accuracy in judging response class members by having the observer score utterances that fit and do not fit these classes. Recording errors that are inclusions of non-members can be thrown out by the clinician as she checks the observer's classifications. However, generalized occurrences that were not tallied are lost forever.

Verbatim recording requires almost no training, but does require some practice in order to focus on hearing utterances and quickly writing them down. Hart (1983) recommended that observers first be trained by having them practice writing down verbatim speech from a tape recording of a child narrating a story. This is typically a more difficult task than an actual live recording but it serves to quickly teach the critical skill of listening and writing simultaneously, remembering what the child is saying and catching up when the child pauses. From a clinical perspective, the more people involved in measuring generalization the better. This provides a richer and more varied data base. It also can function to facilitate generalization by promoting a better communicative match (Hunt, 1961) between the parents and/or teacher and child and by making the child's newly trained speech immediately functional.

Frequency of Measurement

From a practical standpoint, generalization measurements should be done each time the child reaches training criterion on a step of the program. Training should not actually end until the student reaches the generalization criterion. However, the emphasis in training a given structure may change to being primarily generalization or milieu programming. Each time a generalization measurement is made it should include a maintenance check on previously trained forms. If maintenance is not shown on a given form, additional measurement and/or programming may be implemented as needed. However, keep in mind that a simple syntactic form may drop of of a child's repertoire as its function is replaced by more complex forms that the child acquires.

Measurement Settings

Generalization should be assessed in those settings where language is most needed: around the dining table, during free play time or classroom preacademics time, or in a prevocational setting. If possible more than one setting should be monitored to allow a true representation of the child's skills. It is very important that the setting be a place in which the child needs to speak to control the environment. Situations in which the child is likely to simply respond to questions and instructions are not ideal because they do not provide a true test of the child's spontaneous productive skills. In general, the more "demands" there are on the child to speak the more diverse and the higher in rate his speech will be, and the more generalization will occur (Hart, 1980; Rogers-Warren and Warren, 1980; Warren and Rogers-Warren, 1983a). Free play and dining situations (e.g., snacks, lunch), in which no restrictions are placed on the child's speech and interaction, provide excellent measurement settings. Whatever settings are selected, they should be sampled consistently in order to develop a truly representative baseline on the child's skills across time. This allows an accurate determination of progress.

Reliability Checks

Reliability checks are seldom taken in nonexperimental clinical situations. However, there are reasons for checking the reliability in any behavioral measurement. Two phenomena are typical. First, people become better observers over time. Although this improvement is welcomed, it can mean that the initial observational data are inaccurate. A reliability check during the first generalization observation and then another later on can be used to determine if this has happened and if improvement in the observer's accuracy should be considered in the analysis of a child's baseline data. Second, observers sometimes develop biases about what the data should "say." For example, a teacher might be so certain that a child has few skills that she misrepresents true performance by failing to notice the child's actual use of language. This type of self-fulfilling prophecy can be limited by objective reliability checks in which "errors" are pointed out and corrected. Reliable data are important even if they are used only for "in-house" assessments. Reliability checks should be planned as a part of the generalization assessment process. Hart (1983) described how to conduct these checks with verbatim data samples.

Augmentative Communication Systems

Every principle discussed so far is applicable to children who communicate using signs, communication boards, and other augmentative systems. In such cases some modifications may be necessary for appropriate data collection, but the basic approach and most of the problems are the same. It is especially important that the observer is sufficiently familiar with the child's communication mode that she can recognize approximations (particularly in using signs) and novel forms.

Data Management

The determination of generalization assumes a comparison of training data with performance data. Accurate, written training and generalization records must be maintained. Otherwise, the validity of the generalization measurement is questionable and subjective impressions may be the only basis for making crucial decisions about training.

A well-managed and maintained data system has several benefits. First, it can indicate if the child is taking an unusually long time acquiring a form, or making systematic errors that can be corrected. Second, a good system can help identify weaknesses in training procedures. It can alert the clinician to difficulties related to the child's productive modality and indicate when alternative communication modes should be used. Reliable regularly collected data provide evidence for parents, teachers, and supervisors, documenting both the efforts being made with a child and his progress on program steps. Finally, and most importantly from the perspective of this chapter, a data base can serve as a repository for documented evidence on generalization and, therefore, of the ultimate effectiveness of treatment.

Many good data management systems have been developed in recent years; some of these are described by Carrier (1978). Within the next few years microcomputer-based systems will be available that will save time and provide a quick analysis of the data along a variety of dimensions, which might take many hours to do by hand.

Incorporating Other Measures

The primary index of generalization should be a direct comparison between training and generalization data. Overall measures of child progress can be useful but typically are not sensitive to relatively discrete changes in communication skills. Standardized tests of language comprehension and production may show progress that correlates with generalization data and may be used as a secondary validation for training efforts. However, failure to show progress on tests does not necessarily mean that training has not been effective. The tests may be too general or may measure different parameters from those being trained. Likewise, mean length of utterance (MLU) scores, speech initiation rates, or type-token ratios can be very useful as general indices of progress. Again, lack of change on these dimensions may be misleading. For example, the language of a severely handicapped child may become much more functional and directed, less repetitive, and more conventional with no apparent change in either MLU or rate of usage. Global language measures can be useful, but they are not a substitute for direct generalization measurements.

When Generalization Does Not Occur

Obviously, when generalization does not occur (or at least when we cannot detect it) we must actively facilitate its occurrence. In this case the procedures discussed by many of the authors of this volume may be utilized. Assuming we carefully select and teach a functional content, a proven technology of generalization programming is available. To appropriately implement this technology, it is necessary for our generalization measurement to feed back into our training and generalization programming. Figure 2 presents a flowchart showing how the measurement of generalization should feed back into the programming of generalization at various levels.

Inherent in Figure 2 is a hierarchy that assumes that generalization to probes across settings, people, stimuli, and responses should be established and demonstrated before we begin training the next step of a communication training program. Concurrent with initiating this training, we should measure for generalization to the natural environment. If generalization is not observed within a short time, then milieu training procedures should be implemented to facilitate it. Finally, after it is known that a form has generalized to a student's everyday usage repertoire, we should probe for maintenance while testing for

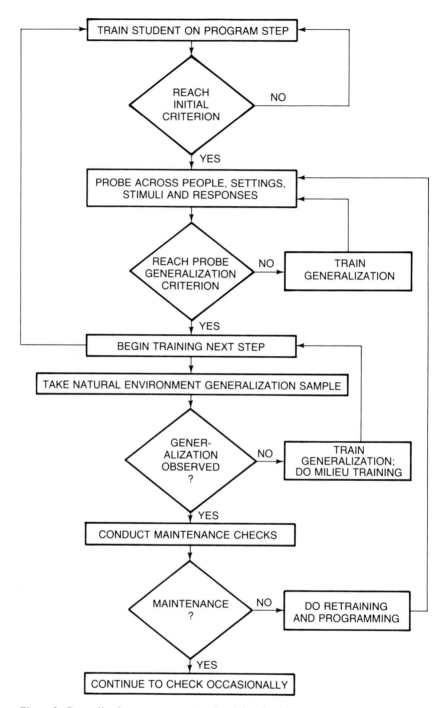

Figure 2. Generalization measurement and training flowchart.

220

generalization of more recently trained forms. If the form does not maintain, we should reprogram it as necessary.

This approach to remediation assumes that initial training of one form may overlap with the generalization training of another. Furthermore, it assumes that we do not discontinue "tracking" a form even when criterion has been met on training, on generalization probes, and once generalization has been observed to a student's usage repertoire. We still continue to check at least for a few months to see that it maintains. This approach may appear laborious, but it is the only way to assure that a student actually incorporates the training into his usage repertoire. Without this assurance, his progress in the training program may be an illusion, and therefore a tragic waste of time, resources, and perhaps the best "learning years" of the student's life. Given the large amount of data indicating the lack of generalization often resulting from training (e.g., Guess et al., 1978; Harris, 1975; Warren et al., 1980), any other approach may be unethical.

Summary: Guidelines for Measuring Generalization

1. Make a concise, detailed, realistic generalization plan. Integrate generalization goals directly into the child's individual education program.
2. Use parents and teachers as observers. Provide them with sufficient training and measure observation reliability at least once immediately after training and again after a few weeks of observing.
3. Assess generalization each time a child reaches criterion on a training step. Check for maintenance of previously generalized forms each time generalization of new forms is measured.
4. Assess generalization only in settings and situations in which there is a strong likelihood that the child will need to use the trained forms.
5. Modify the proposed strategies for assessing generalization to implement them with augmentative communication systems as necessary.
6. Maintain a data management system. This is necessary for valid comparisons of training and probe and natural sample data to determine the extent of generalization.
7. Collect standard language measures (e.g., MLU) to supplement direct generalization measures. Do not substitute these for generalization assessments.

CONCLUSION

Communication training is functional to the extent that it generalizes to the repertoire of the student. It cannot be assumed to be functional on an a priori basis no matter how much theoretical sense it makes, how perfectly it fits our own preconceptions, or how extensively its procedures have been field tested. The measurement of generalization is essential to successful remediation and should be viewed as a major component of the intervention program.

Although a considerable amount of research has gone into developing a technology of generalization, very little direct effort has been put into the development of ecologically valid measurement strategies and techniques. Much important research remains to be done. Some useful directions to proceed include:

1. Research on appropriate criteria for natural sample generalization tests.
2. Development of more efficient naturalistic sampling procedures that increase the probability of the target response without resorting to a didactic "trainer-student" interaction.
3. Development of microcomputer-based data management and analysis systems that allow the measurement of generalization effects along numerous dimensions quickly and easily.
4. The development of better predictors of generalization. We need reliable guidelines that tell us who will have problems generalizing and what techniques will work best with children who manifest different learning and generalization patterns.
5. Research on the identification of natural structure-function response classes. The relationship of form to function remains unclear in normal development. Clarification of this relationship has important implications for language remediation and generalization programming as well as measurement.
6. Development of new language and communication training curricula with generalization measurement and facilitation procedures built directly into the programs.
7. Research on more effective service delivery systems that will increase the likelihood of the most effective new procedures being used with the most students.

Many other important issues need further research and development. Despite the progress made in recent years, we are still a long way from providing optimal language training to the thousands of students who need it. Building the measurement of generalization into our remediation efforts is one of the major changes necessary to improve our efforts.

REFERENCES

Anglin, J. M. 1977. Word, Object, and Conceptual Development. Norton, New York.
Brown, R. 1973. A First Language. Harvard University Press, Cambridge, MA.
Bruner, J. S. 1975. The ontogenesis of speech acts. J. Child Lang. 2:1–19.

Carrier, J. K. 1978. Design and application of a data system for development of a set of language programs. *In* G. P. Sackett (ed.), Observing Behavior—Volume 1: Theory and Applications in Mental Retardation. University Park Press, Baltimore.

Corrigan, R. 1982. Methodological issues in language acquisition research with very young children. Dev. Rev. 2:162–188.

Dale, P. S. 1978. What does observing language mean? *In* G. P. Sackett (ed.), Observing Behavior—Volume 1: Theory and Applications in Mental Retardation. University Park Press, Baltimore.

Garcia, E., and DeHaven, E. 1980. Teaching generalized speech: Re-establishing a previously trained repertoire of functional speech in a profoundly retarded adolescent. Behav. Res. Severe Dev. Disabil. 1:147–160.

Guess, D., and Baer, D. M. 1973. An analysis of individual differences in generalization between receptive and productive speech: Acquisition of the plural morpheme. J. Appl. Behav. Anal. 6:311–329.

Guess, D., Keogh, W., and Sailor, W. 1978. Generalization of speech and language behavior. *In* R. L. Schiefelbusch (ed.), Bases of Language Intervention. University Park Press, Baltimore.

Halliday, M. A. K. 1975. Learning How to Mean: Explorations in the Development of Language. Elsevier-North Holland, New York.

Hall, P. N., and Tomblin, J. B. 1978. A follow-up study of children with articulation and language disorders. J. Speech Hear. Disord. 43:277–291.

Harris, S. L. 1975. Teaching language to nonverbal children—with emphasis on problems of generalization. Psychol. Rec. 82:565–580.

Hart, B. 1980. Pragmatics and generalization. *In* B. B. Lahey and A. E. Kazdin (eds.), Advances in Clinical Child Psychology, Vol. 3. Plenum Press, New York.

Hart, B. 1983. Assessing spontaneous speech. Behav. Assessment 5:71–82.

Hart, B., and Risley, T. 1974. Using preschool materials to modify the language of disadvantaged children. J. Appl. Behav. Anal. 7:243–256.

Hart, B., and Risley, T. 1975. Incidental teaching of language in the preschool. J. Appl. Behav. Anal. 8:411–420.

Hart, B., and Risley, T. 1980. In vivo language intervention: Unanticipated general effects. J. Appl. Behav. Anal. 12:407–432.

Hunt, J. McV. 1961. Intelligence and Experience. Ronald Press, New York.

Ingram, D. 1975. If and when transformations are acquired by children. *In* D. P. Dato (ed.), Georgetown University Round Table on Language and Linguistics. Georgetown University Press, Washington, D. C.

Koegel, R. L., and Rincover, A. 1977. Research on the difference between generalization and maintenance in extra-therapy responding. J. Appl. Behav. Anal. 10:1–12.

Lovaas, O. I., Koegel, R. L., Simmons, J. Q., and Long, J. S. 1973. Some generalization and follow-up measures on autistic children in behavior therapy. J. Appl. Behav. Anal. 6:131–164.

Lutzker, J. R., and Sherman, J. A. 1974. Producing generative sentence usage by imitation and reinforcement procedures. J. Appl. Behav. Anal. 7:447–460.

Miller, J. F. 1981. Assessing Language Production in Children. University Park Press, Baltimore.

Moerk, E. L. 1977. Pragmatic and Semantic Aspects of Early Language Development. University Park Press, Baltimore.

Nelson, K. 1981. Individual differences in language development: Implications for development and language. Dev. Psychol. 17:170–187.

Rilling, M. 1977. Stimulus control and inhibitory processes. In W. N. Hoenig, and J. E. R. Staddon (eds.), Handbook of Operant Behavior. Prentice-Hall, Englewood Cliffs, N.J.

Rogers-Warren, A. K., and Warren, S. F. 1980. Mands for verbalization: Facilitating the display of newly trained language in children. Behav. Modif. 4:361–382.

Rogers-Warren, A. K., and Warren, S. F. 1981. Form and function in language learning and generalization. Anal. Intervention Dev. Disabil. 1:389–404.

Searle, J. R. 1969. Speech Acts: An Essay in the Philosophy of Language. Cambridge University Press, New York.

Skinner, B. F. 1957. Verbal Behavior. Appleton-Century-Crofts, New York.

Stokes, T. F., and Baer, D. M. 1977. An implicit technology of generalization. J. Appl. Behav. Anal. 10:349–367.

Warren, S. F. 1977. A useful ecobehavioral perspective for applied behavior analysis. In A. Rogers-Warren and S. F. Warren (eds.), Ecological Perspectives in Behavior Analysis. University Park Press, Baltimore.

Warren, S. F., Baxter, D. N., Anderson, S. R., Marshall, A., and Baer, D. M. 1981. Generalization of question-asking by severely retarded individuals. J. Assoc. Severely Handic. 6:15–22.

Warren, S. F., and Rogers-Warren, A. 1980. Current perspectives in language remediation: A special monograph. Educ. Treatment Child. 5:133–153.

Warren, S. F., and Rogers-Warren, A. 1983a. Because nobody asked: Setting variables affecting the display of trained noun referents by retarded children. In K. Kernan, M. Begab, and R. Edgerton (eds.), Environment and Behavior: The Adaptation of Mentally Retarded Persons. University Park Press, Baltimore.

Warren, S. F., and Rogers-Warren, A. K. 1983b. A longitudinal analysis of language generalization among adolescents with severely handicapping conditions. J. Assoc. Severely Handic. 8(4):18–31.

Warren, S. F., Rogers-Warren, A., Baer, D. M., and Guess, D. 1980. The assessment and facilitation of language generalization. In W. Sailor, B. Wilcox, and L. Brown (eds.), Instructional Design for the Severely Handicapped. Brookes Publishers, Baltimore.

chapter
8

Enhancing Language Generalization Using Matrix and Stimulus Equivalence Training

Howard Goldstein

Department of Communication
University of Pittsburgh

PROMOTING GENERALIZATION THROUGH MATRIX
   TRAINING   227
      Training the Learner with No Prior Lexical Knowledge   229
      Training the Learner with Partial Lexical Knowledge   233
      Training the Learner with Extensive Lexical Knowledge   236
      Implications for Matrix Training   237

PROMOTING GENERALIZATION THROUGH STIMULUS
   EQUIVALENCE TRAINING   239
      Training Reading Comprehension Indirectly   239
      Adding an Expressive Language Component   241
      Adding a Sign Language Component   242
      Savings through the Development of Larger Stimulus
         Classes   243
      Implications for Stimulus Equivalence Training   244

INITIATING TRAINING: SOME SUGGESTIONS   245

CONCLUSIONS   246

ACKNOWLEDGMENT   248

REFERENCES   248

A primary goal of a functional approach to language intervention is to delineate the conditions that result in generative language use. Generative language use entails comprehension and production of novel, untrained utterances. This chapter introduces two useful approaches for promoting the development of such untrained behavior. The matrix training paradigm (Wetherby and Striefel, 1978) and the stimulus equivalence paradigm (Sidman, 1971; Spradlin et al., 1973) have proven useful for programming generative language use among language-deficient persons.

First, generalization within a matrix training context is discussed and recombinative generalization, a principal process responsible for the development of language, is described. Recombinative generalization is demonstrated when responding to novel word combinations is based upon learning of words in other sentences. Data collected with different populations are summarized and suggestions for implementing training to promote recombinative generalization among developmentally disabled persons are offered. In particular, it is proposed that the training conditions necessary for the occurrence of recombinative generalization vary depending upon the linguistic repertoire of the individual who is learning a new syntactic form.

Second, generalization within a stimulus equivalence context is discussed. Relationships may be derived without direct training when referents and language stimuli (e.g., words and the things that stand for words) can be substituted for one another. Suggestions are offered for understanding and teaching many functional relationships indirectly that include different domains of symbolic behavior: oral language, sign language, and written language. It is proposed that the stimulus equivalence paradigm can be particularly useful for maximizing the initial training efforts used to establish various linguistic repertoires.

PROMOTING GENERALIZATION THROUGH MATRIX TRAINING

The language systems discussed herein all include referential stimuli; they combine referents such as colors, objects, locations, and actions. Children may be required to ask for or describe referents (i.e., provide expressive responses) or they may be required to demonstrate comprehension by following instructions (i.e., provide receptive responses). An example of a basic language matrix that might be taught to a child beginning to produce two-word utterances is provided in Figure 1. Puppets or toy objects doing the

Preparation of this chapter was supported by Contract No.300–82–0368 (Early Childhood Research Institute) from the U.S. Department of Education and by BRSG Grant S07 RR07084–17 from the Division of Research Resources, National Institutes of Health, awarded to the University of Pittsburgh.

227

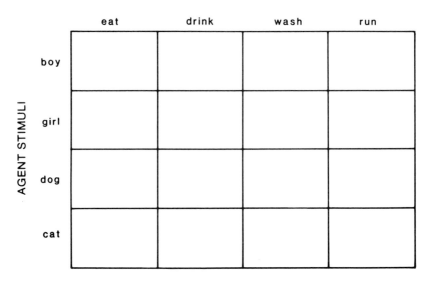

Figure 1. An example of stimuli for an agent-action language matrix.

various actions could be presented to the child. The child could be asked to describe these events. This matrix consists of combinations of four agent stimuli (rows) and four action stimuli (columns). Words are combined into two-word utterances according to a particular word order rule, stated as follows: The first word refers to the agent and the second word refers to the action. Of course, one can easily generate similar language matrices with other referents that combine stimulus components such as sizes, colors, objects, locations, and spatial prepositions. In a language remediation setting, care should be taken to select functional words for the child that can enter into combinations.

The discovery of recombinative generalization can be attributed to Esper (1925). In one of the first experimental analyses of verbal behavior, Esper taught a 4 × 4 language matrix to adults. Subjects were taught first to label 14 colored shapes with nonsense names. After they could label 14 of 16 stimuli without error, the two untrained stimuli were presented. Subjects were able to label these two stimuli accurately. This is the crux of much of the research on recombinative generalization. Generalization is demonstrated when individuals accurately label untrained combinations of stimulus components (colors and shapes, in this case) in a language system.

Recombinative generalization describes the functional relationship between environmental features and this sort of generative language behavior. Recombinative generalization refers to differential responding to novel combinations of stimulus components that have been included previously in other stimulus contexts. The stimulus components are referred to by particular linguistic constituents, such as morphemes, words, and phrases. These constituent responses are arranged in a rule-governed manner, according to specific syntactic rules, such as word rules. For example, in Figure 1 linguistic constituents comprising two different semantic classes, agents and actions, are rearranged to make up novel two-word utterances. Thus, recombinative generalization can be accomplished when stimulus components that control responding (e.g., words) are put together subsequently in a novel arrangement.

Training the Learner With No Prior Lexical Knowledge

In the first and most typical case, matrix training experiments have been conducted with subjects who have no prior knowledge of the vocabulary or lexicon being used (e.g., Foss, 1968; Horowitz and Jackson, 1959; Whitehurst, 1971; Wolfle, 1932, 1933). Researchers have determined that particular stimulus conditions must be instituted before recombinative generalization can be expected.

Useful distinctions have been made among different choices of stimuli that are trained and the extent to which recombinative generalization results (Foss, 1968). The distinction between nonoverlap (diagonal) and overlap (stepwise) training is illustrated in Figure 2. The "A" labels are six modifier-object stimuli selected from the diagonal of the matrix in a stepwise fashion with the addition of two more diagonal stimuli in the lower right-hand corner of the matrix. After children learn to label their respective training stimuli without errors, they may be asked to label each of the 36 colored objects in the matrix.

The distinction between these two training strategies is an important one. Not only do the strategies differ in the number of training items included, but, more importantly, the inclusion of nondiagonal training items provides overlap among modifier and object components. Overlap results when the modifier or object words occur in more than one two-word combination. Notice that the "B" training items share modifier and object stimulus components. In the diagonal or nonoverlap training condition, on the other hand, each modifier and object word occurs in only one of the two-word combinations designated by "A". Training the diagonal items does not ensure that subjects will learn to respond to both words in the utterance. Attention to the modifier or the object components alone would be sufficient for accurate responding to the training stimuli. Even normal adults learning foreign languages or nonsense words who are taught the diagonal stimuli do not produce novel recombinations to label the untrained stimuli (Foss, 1968; Goldstein et al., in preparation). In contrast, overlapping four modifier and four object

OBJECT STIMULI

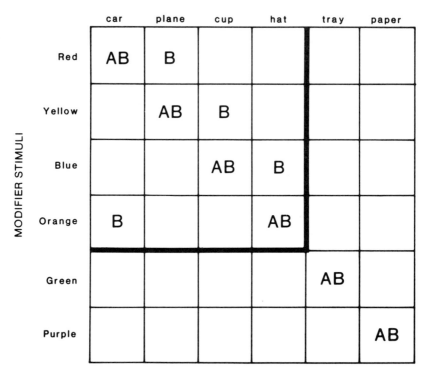

Figure 2. A 6 × 6 modifier-object language matrix. The stimuli designated "A" each combine a different modifier with a different object (nonoverlap training). The stimuli designated "B" include recombinations of four of the modifier constitutents and four of the object constituents (overlap training). Blank cells represent untrained modifier-object recombinations.

components when 10 stimuli are trained forces one to discriminate among the modifier and the object components in order to provide the correct responses to training items. Extensive recombinative generalization is demonstrated typically. Not only do children generalize within the 4 × 4 matrix for which overlap among stimulus components is explicit, they also are likely to extend their generalization to the larger 6 × 6 matrix. In doing so, children extend their use of a word order rule that they apparently induce. Generally, overlap among stimulus components is essential, apparently because it requires subjects to make the critical discriminations necessary for recombinative generalization to occur.

An alternative means of providing overlap among stimulus components has been applied with severely mentally retarded adolescents. Striefel and Wetherby (1973), attempting to systematically replicate a Whitman et al.

(1971) study, showed that generalized instruction following could not be established by simply teaching a sufficient number of commands; this tactic was based upon procedures used to establish generalized motor imitation among nonimitative mentally retarded persons (Baer et al., 1967). Striefel et al. (1976) found that overlapping the verb and noun constituents that made up instructions promoted recombinative generalization. The training sequences employed in these studies are illustrated in Figure 3.

In Figure 3, the noun words and verb words that can be combined into 100 two-word instructions are represented on the horizontal and vertical axes of a 10 × 10 matrix, respectively. The Striefel and Wetherby (1973) experiment may be conceptualized as having trained the diagonal items marked by "A" in Figure 3, with some of the remaining items in the matrix becoming the generalization items to which the subjects failed to respond. As noted above,

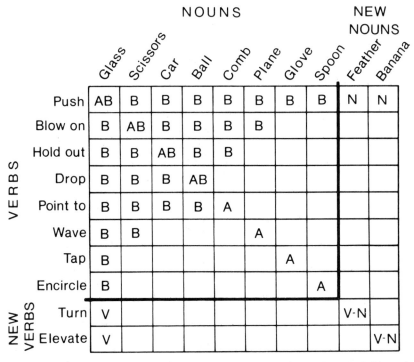

	Glass	Scissors	Car	Ball	Comb	Plane	Glove	Spoon	Feather	Banana
Push	AB	B	B	B	B	B	B	B	N	N
Blow on	B	AB	B	B	B	B				
Hold out	B	B	AB	B	B					
Drop	B	B	B	AB						
Point to	B	B	B	B	A					
Wave	B	B				A				
Tap	B						A			
Encircle	B							A		
Turn	V								V-N	
Elevate	V									V-N

Figure 3. An example of a verb-noun language matrix adapted from Striefel et al. (1976). The training stimuli designated "A" did not overlap noun and verb constituents. The training stimuli designated "B" provided overlap among noun and verb constituents. Remaining cells represent untrained verb-noun instructions. The matrix could be extended horizontally by introducing new nouns (N), could be extended vertically by introducing new verbs (V), or could be extended both ways by introducing new verb-noun (V–N) combinations.

training the diagonal items does not ensure that subjects learn to respond to both words in the instruction. In contrast, Striefel et al. (1976) trained the instructions marked "B" in Figure 3. A single verb was recombined in succession with various nouns before a second verb was introduced. As training progressed, overlap among verb and noun constituents forced subjects to discriminate among both constituents in order to provide the correct responses. Training a verb with each of the nouns before proceeding to the next verb proved to be an efficient method for teaching generalized instruction following to severely mentally retarded adolescents. Subjects exhibited generalized responding to 65–78% of the instructions in a 12 × 12 language matrix.

Most children are not limited to two-word language productions for long. Consequently, it is important to consider how matrix training principles can be applied to more complex language systems. Consider the example of a three-term language matrix shown in Figure 4. This language system was taught to a language-delayed preschooler who was beginning to produce three- and four-word utterances. A three-term utterance from this language system might take the form "The pillow is under the couch."

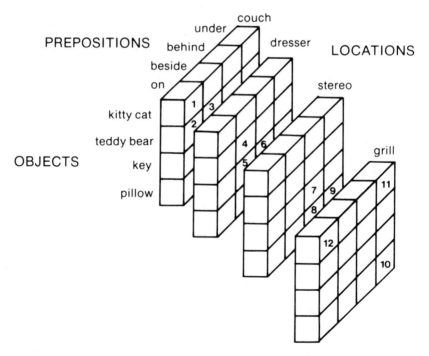

Figure 4. An example of a 4 × 4 × 4 object-preposition-location language matrix. Numbers in the cells of the matrix denote the order of introduction of stimulus items into training to maximize overlap.

If object, preposition, and location words such as those found in Figure 4 are not in the linguistic repertoires of the language-handicapped child, overlap among these stimulus components would be needed to establish recombinative generalization. Whether this would be sufficient and how one might most efficiently provide such overlap is open to question. One way of providing overlap is analogous to the stepwise training condition described earlier. This would entail introducing stimuli as training items according to the numbers shown in various cells of this language system. Notice that in Cells 1 and 2 the preposition *(on)* and the location *(couch)* are overlapped with the objects *(kitty cat* and *teddy bear)*. In Cells 2 and 3 the object *(teddy bear)* and the location *(couch)* are overlapped with the prepositions *(on* and *beside)*. In Cells 3 and 4 the preposition *(beside)* and the object *(teddy bear)* are overlapped with the locations *(couch* and *dresser)*.

Alternatively, one may choose to simplify this task. Indeed, providing overlap among three stimulus dimensions is a bit confusing. One option would be to teach a portion of the language system first, for example, either the objects alone or preposition-location utterances. Then one could recombine the objects with the preposition-location phrases. Thus, object-preposition-location utterances would include either two new constituents or only a single new constituent. First establishing part of the required linguistic repertoire before more complex recombinative forms are presented usually is a preferred approach to language programming and brings us to our second general case.

Training the Learner With Partial Lexical Knowledge

Researchers have begun to delineate the minimal stimulus conditions necessary for generative language use once subjects have been taught a portion of a language system (Goldstein, 1983; Striefel et al., 1978). For example, if children have knowledge of part of the lexicon, overlap is not always necessary for recombinative generalization to occur. This can be illustrated based on the learning of the language system depicted in Figure 1.

Part of the vocabulary used to generate agent-action utterances can be established by first teaching children to label four agent puppets (e.g., Goldstein, 1983). When children are subsequently trained to label agent-action stimuli, recombinative generalization is expected to occur in a predictable manner. For example, a child can be taught to label the agents, *boy, girl, dog,* and *cat*, shown in Figure 1. Subsequently, a child could receive training for only four agent-action stimuli drawn from the diagonal of the matrix.

Initially children do not respond correctly to new diagonal training stimuli. One diagonal item is introduced into training at a time. Recombinative generalization typically is demonstrated sequentially. Each time, generalization is evident for the three untrained stimuli that recombine the remaining agents with the newly trained action component. Many language-handicapped children may require training on more than one stimulus that includes the first action or even subsequent actions. It is advisable to continue training with one action at a time until recombinative generalization is demonstrated before moving on to the next action.

Although it is difficult to determine precisely, it seems that researchers who have successfully established generative language use among developmentally disabled individuals have employed matrix training procedures, albeit inadvertently (Baer and Guess, 1971; Guess, 1969; Guess et al., 1968; Lutzker and Sherman, 1974; Sailor, 1971; Schumaker and Sherman, 1970). For example, Wetherby (1978) illustrated how the teaching of plural morphemes demonstrated by Guess et al. (1968) could be conceptualized within a matrix training paradigm. Thus instead of combining words, words may be combined with morphological markers. Generalization also has been demonstrated by mentally retarded individuals with morphemes for marking present progressive tense versus past tense (Schumaker and Sherman, 1970) and comparative adjectives versus superlative adjectives (Baer and Guess, 1971). In the Schumaker and Sherman study, a number of verbs were combined with suffixes -ing and -ed. In the Baer and Guess study, a number of polar adjectives were taught in combination with the suffixes -er and -est.

Moreover, it appears that part of the lexicon used in the language systems often either was pretrained or already part of subjects' linguistic repertoires. Lutzker and Sherman (1974), for instance, reported that nouns and verb roots were pretaught when necessary to avoid vocabulary limitations that might have affected later generative learning of subject-verb agreement with the auxiliary verbs is and are. Based on our discussion, one would predict that overlap among constituent elements was not necessary in order for morphological and syntactic rules to be induced. Thus, it appears that recombinative generalization was demonstrated without overlap training in many prior language intervention studies. However, the lack of overlap among constituents is likely to be successful only if children have some prior knowledge of the lexical items included in the language system.

Knowledge of a linguistic system can facilitate further generalized learning. This effect is illustrated in cases when the size of a language matrix is expanded. For example, Striefel et al. (1978) found it easy to extend learning to a larger set of instructions once recombinative generalization within the original verb-noun instruction matrix was accomplished. When new objects or new actions either in isolation or in combination were incorporated into the instructions presented to subjects, further generalization was quickly demonstrated. Referring to Figure 3, the addition of new nouns extends the size of the matrix horizontally and the addition of new verbs extends the size of the matrix vertically. Alternatively, by introducing the new verb-noun combinations along the diagonal of the matrix, the size of the matrix is extended both horizontally and vertically at the same time. These alternatives allow one to expand the size of the instruction matrix efficiently and thus expand children's receptive language repertoires.

The manner in which partial linguistic knowledge may facilitate later language learning can be illustrated in the teaching of three-term linguistic systems. When the object-preposition-location language matrix shown in Figure 4 was taught, objects already known by a language-delayed child were selected. Receptive responding and expressive responding were required eventually. Receptive responses entailed following instructions, such as "Put the kitty cat on the couch." Expressive responses entailed describing similar events in response to "What did I do?" Training was accomplished using a doll house as the setting and by having normally developing classmates model either receptive or expressive responses daily. Receptive modeling of three responses ("Put the kitty cat on the couch," "Put the teddy bear on the dresser," and "Put the teddy bear beside the dresser") was sufficient for observational learning of modeled items and recombinative generalization to untrained items. Responses to all 16 possible recombinations of the four objects, two prepositions (*on* and *beside*), and two locations (*couch* and *dresser*) were demonstrated.

Only later, when classmates began to model expressive responses describing the trainer's actions, did the language-delayed child begin to exhibit appropriate expressive responding. Interestingly, the child learned modeled expressive responses but initially did not respond to the same utterances on the receptive task. However, after recombinative generalization became evident for expressive responses, transfer to receptive responding became widespread. Also, transfer to expressive responding was demonstrated for responses that were learned receptively earlier. These findings provide preliminary evidence that the level of mastery implied by recombinative generalization may be related to other forms of generalization, cross-modal generalization in this case. Expressive modeling of four responses was required ("The key is behind the stereo," "The key is behind the grill," "The key is under the grill," and "The pillow is under the stereo") before extensive recombinative generalization occurred. In sum, the learning of 64 receptive responses and 64 expressive responses was accomplished through the modeling of 7 responses. By inspecting the trained items in the language matrix (Figure 4) one may note that partial lexical knowledge made it possible to provide overlap for just two of the three constituents, the prepositions and the locations.

The first general case in which subjects had no lexical knowledge of the language system can be contrasted with this second case in which subjects had partial lexical knowledge. Only in the latter case is recombinative generalization possible when no overlap among the stimulus components is provided. By extending these findings to more complex language, we have been able to bring about recombinative generalization efficiently in response to untrained object-preposition-location stimuli.

Training the Learner With Extensive Lexical Knowledge

In this third general case, subjects with knowledge of all the content words used in a language matrix should require little or no training. Without focusing on syntax per se, Sachs and Truswell (1978) assessed children's ability to demonstrate generalization in interpreting word combinations. They studied the comprehension of two-word instructions by 1;4–2;0-year-olds whose spontaneous productions and elicited verbal imitations consisted of only single words. The instructions presented to the children formed small language matrices. For example, two verbs, *kiss* and *tickle*, were recombined with two nouns, *book* and *cat*. Thus, a 2 verb × 2 noun matrix was constructed comprising the four possible two-word instructions. A mean of 16 different instructions was presented and the average child provided correct generalized responses to 58% of them. Many of the instructions were characterized by adult raters as unusual, such as "Tickle book." Thus, it is likely that the children had never before heard many of the utterances presented to them. Nevertheless, these young children were not limited to understanding only instructions involving familiar utterances or familiar activities.

It appears that if the words used are readily understood and if the language is structured simply enough, even the single word–stage child is able to respond to novel utterances. The ability of children to interpret novel utterances based upon semantic information may enable them to induce the syntactic rules used in their language. That is, recombinative generalization might later yield syntactic learning as children discover that the order of words, for example, cues differences in the meanings of linguistic messages. When children understand all the words included in a lanaguage matrix one may question whether syntactic rather than semantic knowledge is responsible for generalized responding. Reversible sentences—for example, subject-verb-object (Goldstein, 1983) or object-preposition-object (Frisch and Schumaker, 1974) sentences—are needed to determine whether a word order rule has actually been learned and applied. Otherwise, recombinative generalization may be attributed to the use of semantic constraints rather than syntactic rules.

Expressive responding using a novel syntactic construction requires minimal training. In fact, one example of the new syntactic construction may be sufficient for recombinative generalization to be demonstrated. In a study conducted with normally developing preschoolers, an agent-action language matrix was extended to an agent-action-object language matrix in which the agent puppets also served as objects (Goldstein, 1983). Consequently, the children had prior training with the complete lexicon. This lexicon was made up of nonsense words so that non-English word order rules could be used. A number of children demonstrated recombinative generalization after training on only 1 of 64 possible agent-action-object stimuli. That is, one example of a syntactic construction used to generate reversible sentences is necessary and sometimes sufficient for children to demonstrate recombinative generalization based on syntactic rules.

When teaching more complex language systems that include function words or morphemes without any visual referents, a minimal amount of environmental input may still result in recombinative generalization. Consider a passive sentence structure language system. In response to agent-action-object stimuli, utterances like "Tony was chased by the bear" can be generated. The preschoolers mentioned earlier readily learned and generalized their labeling according to an analog to this passive construction. Training on 4 of 64 utterances was sufficient for all six preschoolers to demonstrate recombinative generalization.

Implications for Matrix Training

Language matrices and matrix training procedures provide a parsimonious conceptual basis for outlining the training conditions related to the development of generative language use. Recombinative generalization was introduced to help explain how children learn to respond appropriately to untrained combinations of morpheme and word constituents. Children learn that referents in the environment (e.g., objects, actions, modifiers) correspond to certain words or phrases. Because of the correspondence between words in utterances and referents in the environment, and the consistent use of certain words in particular linguistic contexts, children learn that certain sets of stimuli make up constituent classes. Rules for the recombination of these constituents can be induced, allowing one to interpret or produce novel recombinations appropriately.

The notion of response class has often been used to explain generalized language behavior (Guess et al., 1968; Salzinger, 1967; Skinner, 1938). Response classes exist when responses covary as a function of *similarities* in controlling stimulus conditions. In contrast, recombinative generalization stresses how *differences* in stimulus conditions determine responding. Whereas generalization is traditionally viewed as the absence of discrimination, the notion of recombinative generalization actually emphasizes the determinants of discriminative responding. That is, multiple combinations of components of complex stimulus conditions control responding.

We have begun to identify how training conditions might vary depending on the prior lexical knowledge children have of constituents in the language system being trained. A number of conclusions can be summarized:

1. In our first case, all lexical items are unfamiliar. In this case, stimuli that overlap constituents from the language matrix need to be trained to promote recombinative generalization.

2. In our second case, lexical items in all but one constituent class were known. The selection of training stimuli from a language matrix need not include overlapping constituents in order for recombinative generalization to be demonstrated. Nonoverlap or diagonal training is necessary and often sufficient to establish generalized receptive or expressive language.

3. It also is possible to take advantage of a child's knowledge when one class of lexical constituents is known and two classes of constituents are not known—for instance, objects are known, but not prepositions and locations. In this case, the amount of overlap among constituents needed to promote recombinative generalization is not as extensive as when all lexical constituent classes are unfamiliar.

4. In our third general case, all lexical constituent classes were familiar. It was not necessary in this case to select all combinations from the diagonal of a language matrix. In fact, teaching one response is often sufficient for children to learn a syntactic construction combining several constituents.

5. Knowledge of the complete lexicon used in a language system may permit appropriate responding to be accomplished through the use of semantic or lexical constraints. That is, certain word combinations have only one likely interpretation. For example, any ordering of the words "Jim," "push," and "wagon" are likely to be interpreted as "Jim pushes the wagon" in contrast to the ordering of "Mark," "Jim," and "push," which has two equally likely interpretations. Thus, recombinative generalization need not imply that a syntactic rule has been induced. Since much of language depends on syntactic rules to avoid miscommunication, it may be important to consider the use of reversible sentences. Reversible sentences may be useful for assessing whether syntactic rules have been learned and for teaching the rules when necessary.

6. Conceptualizing language training within a matrix framework allows one to determine when and to what extent recombinative generalization can be expected. As mentioned above, it is advisable to look for and facilitate recombinative generalization as soon as possible. Continuing with overlap training with a restricted set of lexical items or even a single lexical item (as Striefel et al., 1976, did) may be necessary to promote the early occurrence of recombinative generalization. Typically, however, once induction of a syntactic rule is evident through recombinative generalization, it is relatively easy to expand the language matrix.

7. Expanding a language matrix can be accomplished in a variety of ways. Striefel et al. (1978) and Foss (1968) showed that it is possible to extend a language matrix by adding diagonal items that combine two new lexical items to already established constituent classes. Although this is clearly

efficient, the most important consideration should be given to what lexical items will add functional or practical capabilities to the child's repertoire.

8. In less contrived teaching environments, recombinative generalization can be promoted through modeling. Peers, teachers, or caretakers can take advantage of consistencies in the language-handicapped child's natural environment. They can model the recombination of words from constituent classes systematically, thus providing an opportunity for observational learning as well as recombinative generalization. Observational learning seems more likely if words already in the child's repertoire are modeled in increasingly complex utterances. Modeling utterances and correcting or reinforcing relatively few of the child's attempted interpretations (comprehension) and productions may be sufficient for the child to learn to generate numerous syntactic constructions.

9. It is possible and often desirable to monitor the development of both receptive and expressive responding. As noted above, mastery as indicated by recombinative generalization may be related to when one might expect cross-modal transfer to occur. If cross-modal transfer does not occur spontaneously (a common finding), the emergence of recombinative generalization may serve as an indicator for when teaching in the opposite modality is more likely to be successful with minimized effort.

PROMOTING GENERALIZATION THROUGH STIMULUS EQUIVALENCE TRAINING

Much of language, especially referential language, involves equivalences among stimuli. Equivalence implies that one stimulus can be substituted for another. A stimulus class is a set of stimuli that control similar responses (Goldiamond, 1962). Different referents, symbols, and linguistic responses could all be substitutable members of a stimulus class, such as "car." Innumberable real cars (e.g., coupes, sedans, sport cars, station wagons), pictures of cars, photographs, emblems and trademarks, and model names all can denote "car." Although the term *equivalent* is used here, it is important to note that members of a stimulus class are not equally appropriate in all situations. Environmental contexts usually serve to specify which member of the class is called for.

Training Reading Comprehension Indirectly

The early applications of the stimulus equivalence paradigm demonstrated that severely mentally retarded persons could learn simple reading comprehension (Sidman, 1971; Sidman and Cresson, 1973; Sidman et al., 1974). In fact, these subjects evidenced reading comprehension without being directly taught these tasks. The training tasks used by Sidman are summarized in Table 1. Among the six relations described, the first two are identity matches. Whereas matching pictures is a skill often in the repertoire of language-handicapped persons, matching printed words often requires training; pre-training on identity matching is assumed to have been conducted when necessary. It was shown in these studies that learning two auditory-visual equivalences (A-B and A-C) resulted in purely visual equivalences (B-C and C-B), referred to as reading comprehension. In addition to identity matching, the two requisite skills were: 1) identifying pictures in response to dictated words; and 2) identifying printed words in response to dictated words. Without additional training, three severely mentally retarded boys were able to select printed words in response to pictures and pictures in response to printed words.

The flexibility of the stimulus equivalence paradigm becomes apparent when focusing on steps 3, 4, and 5 in Table 1. In the example described above, steps 3 and 4 (the two auditory-visual equivalences) were trained and step 5 (the visual-visual equivalence) was untrained. Upon closer examination, however, it may be noted that if any two of the three equivalences are trained it is logical that the third will emerge without direct training. For example, if a child can identify a picture that is labeled (step 3) and learns to match a printed word to a picture (step 5) then the child could identify a printed word that is named (step 4). In this case, an auditory-visual equivalence is derived without training. Children need not be taught the same content to acquire the same skills.

The flexibility of the stimulus equivalence paradigm allows one to take advantage of those equivalences already known by the child and those equivalences easier to teach to the child. In the above example, identifying pictures is seen to be less abstract than identifying printed words. Consequently, it would not be efficient to teach steps 4 and 5 in order to establish step 3 as a derived (untrained) equivalence. For a child with strengths in visual discrimination learning, on the other hand, teaching the matching of printed words to pictures (step 5) and the identification of pictures that are labeled (step 3) should be sufficient to establish identification of printed words that are named

Table 1.   Summary of Conditions Necessary to Establish Derived (Untrained) Equivalences Corresponding to Reading Comprehension in Mentally Retarded Individuals

Stimuli	Responses	
1. (B) pictures	(B) pictures	identity matches
2. (C) printed words	(C) printed words	
3. (A) dictated words	(B) pictures	trained equivalences
4. (A) dictated words	(C) printed words	
5. (B) pictures	(C) printed words	derived equivalences
6. (C) printed words	(B) pictures	

(step 4). It is clear that more work is needed to learn how to better assess important individual differences and take advantage of those differences in sequencing training tasks.

Adding an Expressive Language Component

Among language-handicapped individuals expressive language responding could entail pointing to symbols on a communication board, sign language, oral language or even written language. Any or all of these performances could be integrated within a stimulus equivalence paradigm. For example, if the names for foods are being taught, the example presented in Table 1 can easily be extended to include oral language output. Eventually the child should name and ask for preferred foods (e.g., juice, milk, hamburger, peas, spaghetti). Keep in mind that pictures, printed words, and oral labels can be taught for a number of foods together or for one food at a time. The functional use of these equivalences will not be evidenced until appropriate differential responding to at least two stimulus classes is established.

Training conditions that might result in derived equivalences corresponding to oral expression and oral reading, as well as reading comprehension, are shown in Table 2. Notice that three conditional discriminations have been added—steps 1, 6, and 7. Step 1 entails verbal imitation, step 6 entails labeling pictures, and step 7 entails reading words aloud. The learning of reading comprehension is accomplished by training picture identification and word identification (steps 3 and 4), as in the previous example. If verbal imitation has been well established in the child's repertoire then one would expect the derived equivalences in steps 6 and 7 to emerge along with steps 8 and 9 (the derived equivalences exhibited as reading comprehension in the earlier example). However, if verbal imitation has not been learned previously, then one could choose to teach any one of steps 1, 6, or 7. Teaching children to label pictures orally (step 6) might be a frequent choice, but

Table 2. Summary of Conditions Necessary to Establish Derived Equivalences Corresponding to Reading Comprehension, Oral Expression, and Oral Reading

Stimuli	Responses	
1. (A) dictated words	(A′) spoken words	identity matches
2. (B) pictures	(B) pictures	
3. (C) printed words	(C) printed words	
4. (A) dictated words	(B) pictures	trained equivalences
5. (A) dictated words	(C) printed words	
6. (B) pictures	(A′) spoken words	
7. (C) printed words	(A′) spoken words	derived equivalences
8. (B) pictures	(C) printed words	
9. (C) printed words	(B) pictures	

programs for teaching picture labeling often incorporate verbal imitation (step 1) as a correction procedure. Although teaching imitation would thus appear to be more efficient, empirical evaluation is lacking at present. Studies conducted without using the stimulus equivalence paradigm indicate that verbal imitation training should follow auditory comprehension training (step 4) if oral expression (step 6) is to be expected (Ruder et al., 1974).

As classes of substitutable or equivalent stimuli get larger the proportion of equivalent relations that need not be trained directly increases. In the reading comprehension example (Table 1), two identity matches were assumed and two equivalent relations were taught; two (of six) equivalent relations were derived for free (without training). In the second example (Table 2), three identity matches were assumed and two equivalent relations were taught; four (of nine) equivalent relations were obtained for free. Thus far in the examples, foods (e.g., *juice*) could be represented in three ways: by a spoken word (A), by a picture (B), and by a printed word (C). There are thus three substitutable members of this stimulus class, and nine equivalent relations among them.

Adding a Sign Language Component

Researchers have extended this analysis by systematically incorporating sign language into the communication training of mentally retarded individuals (VanBiervliet, 1977; Wulz and Hollis, 1979). VanBiervliet included three substitutable class members: objects, manual signs, and spoken words. In addition to the training of identity matches when necessary, producing signs in response to objects and producing signs in response to dictated words were trained. Subsequently, improved performance was shown on four other tasks. Subjects were able to: 1) identify objects in response to signs; 2) produce the words associated with signs; 3) identify objects in response to words; and 4) label objects with spoken words.

Wulz and Hollis (1979) included four substitutable members of each stimulus class: pictures, symbols or printed words, signs, and spoken words. Sixteen equivalent relations among stimulus class members were then possible. A variety of equivalent relations were selected to teach to different severely mentally retarded individuals. Generally, they found that after training two equivalent relations four relations were derived and that after training four equivalent relations eight relations were derived. Wulz and Hollis also demonstrated that two stimuli can be presented simultaneously to accomplish two steps at one time. For example, a child may be asked to respond to a picture and a dictated word presented together by selecting a printed word. Their research has shown that severely mentally retarded persons learned equivalent relations through the simultaneous presentation of an auditory and a visual stimulus at least as fast as when stimuli were presented individually.

Savings through the Development of Large Stimulus Classes

The practical savings achieved by using the stimulus equivalence paradigm are most apparent when larger stimulus classes are developed. A variety of referents and means of indicating those referents communicatively through the use of arbitrarily assigned symbols are worth considering. Substitutable members of stimulus classes might include: objects, pictures, abstract drawings or symbols (e.g., Blissymbols), gestures (sign language), spoken words, and printed words. When including six members of a stimulus class, there are 36 possible equivalent relations. In addition to six identity matches (that are assumed or trained), a minimum of five equivalent relations need to be trained. Based on these 11 equivalences, 25 equivalences could be derived without additional training. The savings in teaching time when compared to teaching all or even most of these equivalent relationships directly can be enormous. When teaching severely language-handicapped children, not all members of the stimulus class outlined will be targeted. Nevertheless, any savings possible can be easily rationalized on behalf of the language-handicapped child and the teacher.

The functional nature of equivalent relations in the preceding example is apparent in that responses in a number of modalities result (i.e., visual modality, expressive language, receptive language, sign language, written language). One should realize that large stimulus classes can be established without drawing upon many modalities of responding. Consider a case in which a common functional response is the ultimate goal. For example, stopping is a common response to members of a large stimulus class including a red light, a stop sign, a railroad crossing gate, a policeman's whistle, and the words, "stop," "halt," and "look out." Learning to respond by stopping to each of these stimuli need not be taught directly, however. Equivalent relations among auditory and visual stimuli, such as selecting the appropriate road sign related to hearing the word "stop," is an alternative to the inconvenient strategy of teaching stopping in response to each stimulus class member. (Arranging to have a policeman and a railroad crossing gate participate in a training regimen can be difficult.)

Spradlin and his colleagues (Dixon and Spradlin, 1976; Spradlin and Dixon, 1976; Spradlin et al., 1973) have pointed out the significance of the stimulus equivalence paradigm for understanding not only the development of concepts, but also the implied relationships among concepts. For example, a child may first learn to respond to members of a stimulus class containing bananas, apples, and peaches as "fruit." Later, when the child learns that peaches grow on trees, he or she may, without further training, say that fruits such as apples and peaches grow on trees. Similarly, if the child learns that apples have seeds, he or she may conclude that peaches, bananas, and fruits all have seeds.

Implications for Stimulus Equivalence Training

The stimulus equivalence paradigm provides a conceptual basis for outlining how stimulus class membership develops. This paradigm can help us to organize the training of equivalences among stimuli in an efficient fashion. This organization provides a basis for predicting and evaluating what equivalences can be derived and established without direct training.

The stimulus equivalence paradigm can appear complicated, especially when large stimulus classes are involved. Nevertheless, it is worthwhile to work with the paradigm so that generalization can be predicted accurately. Wulz and Hollis (1979) have pointed out that many researchers have instituted training procedures that should have served to establish substitutable members of a stimulus class. However, these researchers have failed to assess the performance of derived equivalent relations. Clinicians and teachers possibly have been guilty of the same oversight.

Through the application of the stimulus equivalence paradigm, a number of derived equivalences with communicative value have been taught indirectly. A number of conclusions can be summarized:

1. The stimulus equivalence paradigm has been used successfully to teach reading comprehension to mentally retarded individuals. After teaching auditory-visual equivalences, children can learn to match pictures and printed words, which are purely visual equivalences, without further training.
2. Adding spoken responses that are derived without training has also been demonstrated. The oral expressive language modality is most easily integrated among children who imitate verbally. When verbal imitation training is needed, it is recommended that it follow auditory comprehension training to maximize the chances of oral expression.
3. Advantages of including a gestural mode of communication through sign language have been demonstrated. Learning to produce signs in response to objects and dictated words facilitated subsequent comprehension of signs and dictated words. In fact, even oral expression was established indirectly.
4. Wulz and Hollis (1979) demonstrated that two equivalent relations could be taught simultaneously. Using a simultaneous communication approach, they paired auditory and visual stimuli (words and signs). Severely mentally retarded persons learned these relations at least as fast as when stimuli were presented individually. Untrained equivalent relations were derived even more efficiently in this case.
5. The flexibility of the stimulus equivalence paradigm allows one to take advantage of children's stronger learning areas. Those tasks known by children, or tasks easier to teach to individual children, can be taught first. Subsequently, one can assess whether training has been sufficient to establish equivalences that possibly could be derived.

6. By incorporating additional members of a stimulus class into training, the added savings in the learning of equivalent relations increase dramatically. With only four members of a stimulus class, there are more equivalent relations that can be learned without training than there are equivalent relations that require training.

7. The stimulus equivalence paradigm can also be used to teach implied relationships among concepts. For example, characteristics of various members of the "mammal" class can be learned within this paradigm. Although this discussion has focused on initial training efforts concerned with single words, the applicability of this paradigm could be extended much further.

INITIATING TRAINING: SOME SUGGESTIONS

Initial training efforts should be designed to facilitate immediate generalization. Typically, it is much easier to extend learning once some generalization has occurred. A number of suggestions concerning initial training efforts follow:

1. Try to teach tasks or stimuli first that will be relatively easy for the learner given their skills. Do not overlook the possibility that a learner may have difficulty with a skill despite having previously demonstrated it. For example, identity matching with pictures may have been demonstrated by a learner in the past, but different pictures or a slightly different teaching format may still disrupt performance. In this case, it may be necessary to extend the learner's repertoire with minimal intervention. Alternatively, one may face the task of trying to determine why training and generalization are progressing at an unexpectedly slow pace.

2. Make the response requirements clear and use salient and functional second-order cues when necessary. This is especially relevant to stimulus equivalence training, because stimuli can have a number of appropriate responses (e.g., pointing to pictures, pointing to words, signing, talking, writing). The matching-to-sample paradigm restricts the choices available on each trial. In other training contexts, a secondary cue often is needed. For example, a picture is presented and secondary cues are provided, such as "What is this called?" or "What is the sign for this?" or "Write the word for this." Cues that are more similar to those likely to be encountered in the natural environment (e.g., "What do you want?") are preferrable.

3. Introduce one new training stimulus at a time. After a short practice period for a new response, begin to reintroduce previously trained stimuli. As accurate responding for the new training stimulus improves, the relative frequency of presentations of new and old stimuli should become more equal. Train to a stringent mastery criterion (such as 90% correct over 2 or more days) before introducing the next new training stimulus.

4. New discriminations can be taught in any of a variety of ways. Discrete trial training programs have been instituted most often (see Wetherby and Striefel, 1978, for additional suggestions). For example, in an expressive labeling task the child may be asked to describe an event, such as "The dog is eating." Correct responses are reinforced and the next stimulus is presented. Incorrect responses may be followed by negative feedback ("No"), a model of the correct response, a request to imitate the correct response, and a repeated stimulus presentation. A number of variations of this example are possible. However, drastically different teaching techniques also can be used. For example, observational learning has been accomplished when peers have modeled correct responses. The training techniques chosen to teach discriminations involving expressive language, receptive language, matching-to-sample, and so forth should be selected on the basis of their suitability for the individual learner and trainer.

5. Avoid frequent probing of items that the learner has as yet had little opportunity to learn. It is desirable to keep generalization probes as indiscriminable from training items as possible. Probes should be interspersed within the sequence of training trials. If learners discriminate untrained items they often learn either not to respond or to respond in a stereotyped way. Such a learning history can also disrupt generalization to normal responses later on in training.

6. Reinforce initial generalized responses. Among many learners, newly generalized responses often seem tentative at first. Early reinforcement should facilitate the maintenance of such responses initially.

7. Begin training with a small matrix or with a few stimulus classes. One can develop a number of generative repertoires and then later extend the sizes of their matrices and stimulus classes. Matrices have tended to be symmetrical in the examples given here, such as the 10×10 verb-noun matrix in Figure 3. However, for individual learners it might be more functional to simply include two verbs and six nouns, for example.

8. Once generalization has been demonstrated, consider switching to a more efficient training strategy. For example, once recombinative generalization has begun as a result of overlap training it may be possible to begin using nonoverlap training. Selecting new training stimuli from the diagonal of a language matrix may allow the learner to expand two or more constituent classes of his or her language repertoire simultaneously.

CONCLUSIONS

This discussion of matrix training and stimulus equivalence training provides an organization for teaching efforts that should help teachers to maximize generalization. A conceptual basis for predicting generalization is offered. One can collect information as to the necessary and sufficient conditions for obtaining untrained responding by being aware of the logically predictable possibilities for generalization. I have begun to outline how these necessary conditions vary depending on the prior linguistic knowledge of children. The conditions that facilitate recombinative generalization and derived equivalent relations are implicit in many training programs already. However, the logic involved in predicting generalization is not recognized. Consequently, generalization usually is not maximized in available training programs. Training programs should be adapted to individuals and altered to make them more efficient by choosing training items or tasks that enhance generalization to untrained responses.

Matrix and stimulus equivalence training are approaches used to improve the efficiency of training efforts. These strategies should serve to reduce the proportional amount of direct training allotted to individual responses. Not only are more responses learned through less training, but the child is learning a generative repertoire. That is, the child is capable of providing untrained responses in appropriate contexts. The establishment of generative learning abilities should have a significant impact on our ability to teach functional communication skills, especially among severely language-handicapped children.

This chapter has focused upon preliminary steps in establishing functional communication skills (i.e., teaching linguistic responses and establishing generalized linguistic repertoires). This approach should compliment the training strategies used to promote other types of generalization (see Stremel-Campbell and Campbell, and Hart, this volume). One cannot overlook the need to provide an environment conducive to the display of language and to program for generalization across time, people, and settings.

Assessing whether derived equivalences or recombinative generalization has occurred may provide valuable information about the effectiveness of basic training procedures and mastery criteria that have been applied. It would not be surprising to find that the degree of generalization across time, people, and settings is related to the degree of mastery reflected by generalization within the training paradigms being used. That is, the mastery evident through deriving equivalent relationships and through recombinative generalization is probably a more robust predictor of the future functional use of trained language skills than is the percentage of correct responding.

Applying matrix training and equivalence training procedures to increasingly complex language is an ongoing challenge. By utilizing and adapting procedures that promote generalization, more efficient use of direct training time will continue to be realized and cumulative savings in time and effort will accrue accordingly for teachers and students.

ACKNOWLEDGMENT

The author gratefully acknowledges the helpful discussions with Dr. Bruce Wetherby that have contributed greatly to this chapter.

REFERENCES

Baer, D., and Guess, D. 1971. Receptive training of adjectival inflections in mental retardates. J. Appl. Behav. Anal. 4:129–139.

Baer, D., Peterson, R., and Sherman, J. 1967. The development of imitation by reinforcing behavioral similarity to a model. J. Exp. Anal. Behav. 10:405–416.

Dixon, M. H., and Spradlin, J. E. 1976. Establishing stimulus equivalences among retarded adolescents. J. Exp. Child Psychol. 21:144–164.

Esper, E. 1925. A technique for the experimental investigation of associative interference in artificial linguistic material. Lang. Monogr. 1.

Foss, D. 1968. Learning and discovery in the acquisition of structured material: Effects of number of items and their sequence. J. Exp. Psychol. 77:341–344.

Frisch, S., and Schumaker, J. 1974. Training generalized receptive prepositions in retarded children. J. Appl. Behav. Anal. 7:611–621.

Goldiamond, I. 1962. Perception. In A. J. Bachrach (ed.), Experimental Foundations of Clinical Psychology. Basic Books, New York.

Goldstein, H. 1983. Training generative repertoires within agent-action-object miniature linguistic systems with children. J. Speech Hear. Res. 26:76–89.

Goldstein, H., Wetherby, B., and Siewert, L. 1984. The effects of overlap among training items on adults' acquisition of miniature linguistic systems. Manuscript in preparation, University of Pittsburgh.

Guess, D. 1969. A functional analysis of receptive language and productive speech: Acquisition of the plural morpheme. J. Appl. Behav. Anal. 2:55–64.

Guess, D., Sailor, W., Rutherford, G., and Baer, D. 1968. An experimental analysis of linguistic development: The productive use of the plural morpheme. J. Appl. Behav. Anal. 1:297–306.

Horowitz, A. E., and Jackson, H. M. 1959. Morpheme order and syllable structure in the learning of miniature linguistic systems. J. Abnormal Social Psychol. 59:387–392.

Lutzker, J., and Sherman, J. 1974. Producing generative sentence usage by imitation and reinforcement procedures. J. Appl. Behav. Anal. 7:447–460.

Ruder, K., Smith, M., and Hermann, P. 1974. Effect of verbal imitation and comprehension on verbal production of lexical items. In L. V. McReynolds (ed.), Developing Systematic Procedures for Training Children's Language. ASHA Monogr. 18:15–29.

Sachs, J., and Truswell, L. 1978. Comprehension of two-word instructions by children in the one-word stage. J. Child Lang. 5:17–24.

Sailor, W. 1971. Reinforcement and generalization of productive plural allomorphs in two retarded children. J. Appl. Behav. Anal. 4:305–310.

Salzinger, K. 1967. The problem of response class in verbal behavior. In K. Salzinger and S. Salzinger (eds.), Research in Verbal Behavior and Some Neurophysical Implications. Academic Press, New York.

Schumaker, J., and Sherman, J. A. 1970. Training generative verb usage by imitation and reinforcement procedures. J. Appl. Behav. Anal. 3:273–287.

Sidman, M. 1971. Reading and auditory-visual equivalences. J. Speech Hear. Res. 14:5–13.

Sidman, M., and Cresson, O. 1973. Reading and crossmodal transfer of stimulus equivalances in severe retardation. Am. J. Ment. Defic. 77:515–523.

Sidman, M., Cresson, O., and Willson-Morris, M. 1974. Acquisition of matching to sample via mediated transfer. J. Exp. Anal. Behav. 22:261–273.

Skinner, B. F. 1938. The Behavior of Organisms. Appleton-Century-Crofts, New York.

Spradlin, J., Cotter, V., and Baxley, N. 1973. Establishing a conditional discrimination without direct training: A study of transfer with retarded adolescents. Am. J. Ment. Defic. 77:556–566.

Spradin, J., and Dixon, M. 1976. Establishing conditional discriminations without direct training: Stimulus classes and labels. Am. J. Ment. Defic. 80:555–561.

Striefel, S., and Wetherby, B. 1973. Instruction-following behavior of a retarded child and its controlling stimuli. J. Appl. Behav. Anal. 6:663–670.

Striefel, S., Wetherby, B., and Karlan, G. 1976. Establishing generalized verb-noun instruction-following skills in retarded children. J. Exp. Child Psychol. 22:247–260.

Striefel, S., Wetherby, B., and Karlan, G. 1978. Developing generalized instruction-following behavior in the severely retarded. In C. Meyers (ed.), Quality of Life in Severely and Profoundly Mentally Retarded People: Research Foundations for Improvement. American Association on Mental Deficiency, Washington, D.C.

VanBiervliet, A. 1977. Establishing words and objects as functionally equivalent through manual sign training. Am. J. Ment. Defic. 82:178–186.

Wetherby, B. 1978. Miniature languages and the functional analysis of verbal behavior. In R. L. Schiefelbusch (ed.), Bases of Language Intervention. University Park Press, Baltimore.

Wetherby, B., and Striefel, S. 1978. Application of miniature linguistic system on matrix-training procedures. In R. L. Schiefelbusch (ed.), Language Intervention Strategies. University Park Press, Baltimore.

Whitehurst, G. 1971. Generalized labeling on the basis of structural response classes by two young children. J. Exp. Child Psychol. 12:59–71.

Whitman, T., Zakaras, M., and Chardos, S. 1971. Effects of reinforcement and guidance procedures on instruction-following behavior of severely retarded children. J. Appl. Behav. Anal. 4:283–290.

Wolfle, D. L. 1932. The relation between linguistic structure and associative interference in artificial linguistic material. Lang. Monogr. 11.

Wolfle, D. L. 1933. The relative stability of first and second syllables in an artificial language. Language 9:313–315.

Wulz, S. V., and Hollis, J. 1979. Application of manual signing to the development of reading skills. In R. L. Schiefelbusch and J. Hollis (eds.), Language Intervention from Ape to Child. University Park Press, Baltimore.

chapter

9

Training Techniques That May Facilitate Generalization

Kathleen Stremel-Campbell
Teaching Research Division
Oregon State System of Higher Education
Monmouth, Oregon

and

C. Robert Campbell
Rainbows United, Inc.
Wichita, Kansas

contents

CONCEPTUAL APPROACH   254

GENERALIZATION PROGRAMMING TECHNIQUES   255
    Programming Multiple Exemplars   255
    Programming Common Stimuli   262
    Programming Natural Maintaining Consequences   265
    Programming "Loose" Training   266
    Programming Indiscriminable Contingencies   268

APPLICATION AND EVALUATION OF PROGRAMMING TECHNIQUES   270
    Development of a Generalization Plan   270
    Strategies for Applying Generalization Techniques   272
    Evaluation of the Generalization Plan   278
    Criteria for Acceptable Generalization   282

CONCLUSIONS   283

ACKNOWLEDGMENTS   283

REFERENCES   284

Generalization is one of the greatest challenges in training language and communication skills. Rapid gains have been made in programming language acquisition. However, because language does not occur in isolation, but rather in a dynamic social interaction, the interventionist must be concerned with the student's generalization of learned language skills to a wide array of social interactions. Only recently have principles been developed for formulating generalization strategies for language and communication skills. Consequently, the final goal of language training has changed form meeting a set performance criterion within an isolated setting to a more global, purposeful objective—that of achieving spontaneous usage of learned language and communication skills across a variety of language contexts, persons, and settings within the natural environment.

As these new programmatic goals for language training have emerged, so has the perception of what is involved in the process of training a student to generalize communication skills. The student, his needs and skills in understanding and using language appropriately, and specific programmatic techniques are three factors that must be considered when developing an individual treatment program. Additional factors include the opportunities that the environment provides for the student to use his language and the naturalistic consequences for the use or absence of language (Rogers-Warren, 1977). Thus, the interventionist cannot be concerned only with her ability to train the student or the student's ability to generalize. Rather, she must be concerned with other elements in the student's environment, including the major persons within that environment and the student's activities within the environment.

This chapter discusses the specific generalization techniques that may be used to develop a student's individual language training program. The examples in this chapter are oriented primarily toward severely and moderately handicapped students. However, most of the suggestions are applicable to mildly handicapped students as well. Furthermore, these techniques should not be used in isolation without programming other aspects of the student's environment (see Hart, this volume). Generalization is an interactive process between the student, his language and communication skills, and the totality of the student's environment. In order for the treatment process to result in generalization there must be an interactive process. Additionally, decisions should address the student, his language system, and the appropriateness of what is being targeted in relation to the student's current level of interaction with the environment.

Two aspects must be considered in the development of an "active" generalization program: 1) the specific skill area or activity that is the focus of

This paper was written while the second author was affiliated with the Teaching Research Division, Oregon State System of Higher Education, Monmouth, OR.

training (self-help skills, motor skills, academic skills); and 2) the generalization techniques that can be applied in training those skills. Language training often includes a broad category of subskills, such as communication functions, the language modality, receptive language, vocabulary development, semantic relations, and syntactic relations. All of these subskills must be considered in the development of a communication intervention and in the application of the generalization techniques.

CONCEPTUAL APPROACH

The theoretical basis of language programming has moved from that of a syntactical approach, which encompasses vocabulary development and the ordering of words, to a more semantic approach. The work of Bloom (1970), Brown (1973), Schlesinger (1974), and Bowerman (1978) places an emphasis on the development of semantic relations (meaning) in child language. Many language training programs of the early 1970s reflected these developments. More recently, language training programs have been directed to the social aspects involved in language interactions (MacDonald, this volume; McLean and Snyder-McLean, 1978).

The focus of the communicative functions of language is extremely important in programming language for the severely handicapped student. The aspects of communication functions, meaning, and syntax must be considered whether language is programmed through speech, signing, or communication board modes. These considerations may also be necessary in the measurement of language generalization (Warren et al., 1980). The assessment of generalization, based on the goals of the language program, is critical to determine the effectiveness of the "active" generalization programming techniques across a large number of students and language behavior.

During the early phases, the major goal of training may be oriented to basic communication behaviors. Consequently, generalization may be actively programmed and measured across a wide range of components: communication functions, meaning, structure, and vocabulary. If communication functions are the major goal of training for an individual student, then the application of generalization strategies and a measurement system should include features of communication functions before training is initiated. Once the student is expressing different communication functions, either nonverbally or verbally, the maintenance of these communication functions is critical while the student learns to express the semantic intents of notice, recurrence, greeting, etc. After the student's two- and three-word utterances are used to express numerous semantic relations, such as action-object or agent-action (e.g., "Get coat" or "I play"), syntactic features also become important. The student must learn to discriminate and correctly use pronouns, prepositions, and other syntactic elements. For example, the student may initially learn to express locative utterances by saying "Put cup table"; later, the use of the preposition ("Put cup *on* table") will make his communication more effective.

The majority of research studies investigating language generalization have focused on the reception and expression of syntactic classes. Detailed reviews of this research have been presented by Harris (1975), Guess et al. (1978a), and Warren et al. (1980). Even though additional research across other language components and student populations is needed, this research has laid a foundation for the development of generalization strategies and measurement systems that may be applicable across a wide range of communication and language behaviors.

GENERALIZATION PROGRAMMING TECHNIQUES

Five of the major types of generalization programming techniques outlined by Stokes and Baer (1977) are discussed here as they relate to communication and language training: 1) programming multiple exemplars; 2) programming common stimuli; 3) programming natural maintaining consequences; 4) programming "loose" training; and 5) programming indiscriminable consequences. These five approaches are divided into subcategories of specific techniques that are related to language training. If generalization is to be a planned outcome of training, these generalization techniques must be "actively" programmed as part of the language training process.

The sequence of techniques discussed within this section does not imply prioritization, nor are the individual procedures to be considered as isolated techniques, with no relationship to one another. It should be pointed out that a specific programming technique may be implemented in isolation or in combination with other techniques. This section describes the techniques in relation to language training and provides examples specific to language behaviors. Guidelines for applying these techniques are outlined in the following section.

Programming Multiple Exemplars

The multiple exemplar technique (e.g., Anderson and Spradlin, 1980; Garcia, 1974; Hupp and Mervis, 1981) can be applied across three main subcategories: 1) aspects of the behavior, 2) persons, and 3) settings. That is, in order to achieve the overall objective of language generalization, the student must display the trained behavior across different (but related) examples of that behavior, across different persons, and across different settings. This technique can best be defined as the selection and application of multiple examples of the behavior, persons, and/or settings. Research data suggest that training with a single example of a behavior, with a single trainer, and/or within a single training setting may limit generalization (Guess et al., 1978a). The multiple exemplar technique may be used to prevent rote responding to a specific stimulus condition and to facilitate generalization to new and untrained examples of that behavior. With this technique a number of examples are trained until the student demonstrates generalization to untrained examples under appropriate conditions. At this point it can be said that sufficient exemplars have been trained. The specific number of exemplars sufficient for generalization will vary across students, responses, and type of exemplar conditions being probed.

Multiple Behaviors   The specific types of "behaviors" that one may consider in actively programming multiple exemplars will depend upon two aspects of the language program: the specific language behavior being trained and the overall goal of the language program being implemented. The multiple exemplar technique is discussed across three aspects of communication programming: 1) communication functions; 2) linguistic classes or vocabulary; and 3) language response classes.

Communication Functions   An individual can use a single word to communicate different things. A listener will respond to the same utterance differently based upon the intonation pattern of the utterance, the context of the utterance, and the gestures that are used. An utterance paired with gestures can be used as an answer, a request for permission, a request for another person to act, a protest or rejection, a request for information, or a description or statement. The example below demonstrates different communication functions or uses of the word "music."

EXAMPLE: Types of Communication Functions

Student Says	Gesture/Context	Listener Responds	Function
1. "Music."	In response to the question "What do you want?"	Listener gives music box.	Answer
2. "Music."	Points to record player.	Listener gives permission.	Request for permission
3. "Music."	Hands peer music box.	Peer turns on music box.	Request another person to act
4. "Music."	Hands box to listener while shaking head.	Listener takes music box away.	Rejection
5. "Music?"	Looks for music box, says, "Music?" with question inflection.	Listener answers "Music box is over here."	Request for information
6. "Music."	Music coming from hallway.	Listener says, "I hear music, too."	Statement or comment

If the goal of language training is to develop a variety of communication functions, then the interventionist may want to train a specific language skill across multiple communication functions. This training will involve arranging the activity and context differently for the various communication functions being trained.

EXAMPLE: Programming Multiple Communication Functions

Functions Targeted	Contextual Arrangement	Consequence
1. Answer (response to question), "Cracker."	Choice items are presented. Question is asked, "What do you want?"	Students gets cracker.
2. Requests another person to act— "Cracker."	Choice items are presented to peer. Trainer says, "Tell Joey what to take."	Peer takes cracker.
3. Requests "Cracker."	Choice items are presented to student. Indirect cue is presented: "It's your turn."	Trainer gives cracker to student.

The communication functions may be programmed in a serial sequence (training the first function to criterion before initiating the second) for a severely handicapped student. If a student is demonstrating the use of different communication functions for words or utterances that he is already using, at least two communication functions should be trained concurrently as new words are trained.

Linguistic Classes or Vocabulary   Language utterances also can be classified as a type or as an example of different semantic and syntactic classes.

EXAMPLE: Types of Semantic and Syntactic Classes

Class	Type	Examples
Semantic	Agent-Action	"I go"
		"I eat"
		"Mary come"
		"You play"
	Action-Object	"Eat cracker"
		"Eat apple"
		"Drink juice"
		"Get milk"
		continued

EXAMPLE: Types of Semantic and Syntactic Classes *(continued)*

Class	*Type*	*Examples*
	Action-Location	"Put here"
		"Go outside"
		"Walk bus"
Syntactic	Nouns	"Cookie"
		"Milk"
		"Kitchen"
		"Bathroom"
		"Mary"
	Verbs	"Go"
		"Play"
		"Eat"
		"Drink"
	Article-Noun	"A Kleenex"
		"The store"
		"Some coffee"

Once a sufficient number of nouns or verbs or specific linguistic class exemplars have been trained, the student should learn that objects and actions have certain names. At some point the student should begin to acquire untrained vocabulary from incidental teaching episodes (see Hart, this volume), because every potentially functional vocabulary word cannot be specifically trained. Trainers typically determine only a general "set" of nouns or verbs to be trained for every student.

EXAMPLE: Programming Multiple Exemplars of Linguistic Classes

Behaviors targeted: Nouns that represent things, persons, and locations.
Selecting multiple exemplars:
   Things—cracker, apple, puzzle, car, light
   Persons—Mary (teacher), Susan (aide), Grandma, Carol (babysitter)
   Locations—home, school, bathroom, outside

Selecting and training multiple examples of each linguistic class will not automatically result in generalization. Probe data should be used to demonstrate when sufficient examples have been trained to result in generalization of untrained examples.

Language Response Classes   Stokes and Baer (1977) operationally defined a response class as "a class of responses that are organized in a way that operations applied to a subset of responses in the class affect other members of that class in the same manner."

EXAMPLE: Potential Response Classes

Types of Classes	*Members of the Class*
1. Motor imitation (actions visible to student)	Waving goodbye
	Clapping hands
	Holding out hand
	Tapping table
	Putting hand to cheek
2. Vocal imitation of vowel sounds (vowels are phonetic symbols)	"a"—as in f*a*ther
	"e"—as in m*a*ke
	"i"—as in *ea*t
	"ɪ"—as in s*i*t
	"u"—as in sh*oe*
	"o"—as in h*o*me
3. Object matching-to-sample	Cup to cup
	Apple to apple
	Pencil to pencil
	Washcloth to washcloth
	Book to book
4. Plurality	-*z* ball*s*
	shoe*s*
	pencil*s*
	-*s* book*s*
	cup*s*
	plant*s*
	-*es* bus*es*
	hous*es*
	box*es*
5. Auxiliary verbs	*is* Mary *is* coming.
	She *is* eating now.
	Bob *is* working.
	are They *are* sleeping.
	The fish *are* eating.
	Mom and Dad *are* coming.

The last two examples represent syntactic elements that form a response class. Additional syntactic response classes include articles (*a, the,* and *some*), future verbs, regular past-tense verbs (*-ed*), and comparatives (*bigger, longer*). The objective in programming multiple exemplars is to train enough examples that generalization to untrained members of the response class occurs. Thus, it is necessary to probe after training multiple examples to determine if generalization has occurred or if more items need to be trained.

EXAMPLE: Programming Multiple Response Exemplars

Response Class	Multiple Exemplars Trained	Untrained Exemplars Probed
Plurality	-z—apples, cards,	Games, shoes, cookies,
	-s—snacks, cups	Coats, plates, chips,
	-es—glasses, boxes	Sandwiches, pieces, dishes

If the student does not generalize to untrained probes, additional examples are trained and the probe is repeated. If the student generalizes the plural ending to appropriate untrained exemplars, the student has demonstrated generalization. The number of exemplars that need to be introduced into training before generalization occurs will depend upon the behavior being targeted and the individual student being trained.

Many of the words or concepts taught in language training represent not one specific item or activity, but a variety of objects. Objects are therefore categorized or labeled based on perceptual or functional features. A "cup" can be of different colors and shapes, and made from a number of different materials. However, it is restricted to functioning as a container that can be used for drinking hot or cold liquids.

EXAMPLE: Object Class Exemplars

Language Target	Word(s) Represented by Object/Action	Examples of Objects/Actions
Nouns	Cracker	Soda cracker
		Graham cracker
	Cup	Paper cup (white) without handle
		Plastic cup (red)
		Glass mug
Verbs	Eat	Eating apple
		Eating cheese
	Drink	Drinking water
		Drinking milk

The trainer may need to present many different "cups" or examples of cups to the student during training before the student is able to make a similar response to cups that have not been trained. The student's response may include matching, identifying, requesting, or labeling, depending on what is being trained. By training multiple object exemplars, the number of irrelevant stimulus dimensions of the object (color, size, etc.) are limited.

EXAMPLE: Programming Multiple Object Class Exemplars

Response Being Targeted	Multiple Objects Trained	Objects Probed
Identification of objects	Cookie	Sugar cookie on plate
	small lemon cookie	(Box of) animal cookies
	large chocolate chip cookie	Oatmeal cookie
	Ball	Small white ball
	large red ball	Basketball
	small blue ball	Green tennis ball

Again, a train-probe-train strategy of introducing multiple exemplars may be used to determine when generalization to untrained exemplars has occurred. When generalization has occurred, it can be said that sufficient examples of objects have been trained.

Multiple Trainers   The use of only one trainer to teach a behavior often results in the student demonstrating that skill only to that specific person. This lack of generalization to other persons may result from irrelevant stimulus cues that are specific to that trainer. The lack of generalization may also be based on the fact that the one trainer serves as a consistent reinforcing agent whereas other persons do not. Consequently, it may be necessary to use multiple trainers before generalization to persons not involved in training will occur.

Multiple Settings   A student's language response cannot be limited to a specific setting; it should occur across all appropriate settings. However, some language responses are usually appropriate only in a few specific settings. For example, saying "Juice" may be consequated positively in a snack setting or in a dining setting, but may not be consequated positively during a free play period. Therefore, it may be necessary to assess which language responses are functional across multiple settings to determine the similar skills that will be consequated positively within similar settings and to determine the skills that will not be positively consequated across certain environments.

EXAMPLE: Programming Multiple Settings

Behaviors Being Targeted	Training Settings	Probe for Nontraining Settings
"Eat"	One-to-one training setting, snack setting	Lunch setting (in school)
		Breakfast setting (at home)
		Dinner setting (at home)
		Restaurant
"Play"	One-to-one training setting, morning free play setting	Afternoon free play
		Home setting
		Outside on playground

Programming Common Stimuli

The common stimuli technique (e.g., Rincover and Koegel, 1975; Walker and Buckley, 1972) involves determining the salient stimuli or cues that are present in the student's natural environment and then programming these stimuli within the training settings so that the training stimuli are common to or highly related to one another in both the generalization settings and the training setting. Common stimuli can be programmed across the behavior being targeted, across persons who will be present when the behavior occurs, and across settings in which the behavior should occur.

Across Behaviors   Stimuli and responses selected for training may be common across communication functions, words, and the specific physical stimuli used for training. The common stimuli technique may be described as one of selecting functional language targets. For example, a student is observed in his natural environment to assess how he is currently requesting objects or actions or describing objects or events. The first task is to determine if the student is communicating and to determine the function or use of the communication response. His current communication level may be one of pointing, gesturing, and reaching to request objects and actions, and/or one of pointing and showing objects to comment or describe what he sees. If the student is not communicating in any way, it must first be determined if the environment is requiring the student to make his needs known, since a trained response (such as a sign or word) will not generalize unless the student has the opportunity to use it.

EXAMPLE: Programming Common Communication Functions

Natural Environment Settings	*Communication Functions Demonstrated*	*Responses Trained within the Communicaton Function*
1. Home setting Free play setting Snack setting	Joe points, grunts, gestures to request specific objects.	Train nouns (representing objects) through a requesting function.
2. Group home setting Vocational setting	Mary says two-word utterances to: request permission, ask questions, make statements, and request other persons to act.	Train three-word utterances across a request for permission, and a statement communication function.

These examples demonstrate how communication functions can be trained to facilitate actual usage. It is also important that the specific words or examples being trained are common to those that are prominent in the student's natural environment. Words or language structures being trained should have a clear function for the student in the natural environment.

If specific syntactic elements (such as articles—*a, the,* and *some*) are being trained, they should be taught in combination with other words. The words or structures selected for training can be those that the student is already frequently using, such as "I want peanuts," "I need spoon," and "Bus coming." However, these examples are only common stimuli if the utterances "I want/I need" and the words "peanuts," "spoon," and "bus" are things that the student frequently talks about.

The use of common physical stimuli is an extremely important feature in a student's program. Physical stimuli would include the salient stimuli that are used directly in programming. These should be identical or very similar to those prominent in the natural environment. The following example shows training stimuli that were selected because they are identical to the physical stimuli in the natural environment.

EXAMPLE: Selecting Common Physical Training Stimuli

Student's Response in the Natural Environment	*Specific Word Being Targeted*	*Stimuli Selected for Training*
1. Student points to bus whenever he sees it.	"Bus"	Any actual bus, not a toy.
2. Student requests container for milk.	"Glass" or "cup"	The actual glass or cup used in school/home or a similar one.
3. Student requests "play" by pointing to toys.	"Play"	A number of the toys that the student is indicating by pointing.
4. Student says "Two cracker" when requesting multiple items.	Plurals	Select objects/words the student is currently using, such as "cracker," not ducks, purses, etc.

Thus, the selection of the common content or objects for training requires the examination of the student *and* his interactions within the natural environment.

Across Adults and Peers   The use of peers as common stimuli is important for two reasons: 1) peers or siblings are often involved in many home, work, or school environments; and 2) peers can be utilized as models and as reinforcing agents. Moderately and severely handicapped students often do not communicate with their peers in the natural environment. Therefore, using peers as common stimuli in training may facilitate generalization only if the teacher or parent are concurrently using specific techniques to increase peer/sibling interactions (see Paul, this volume). The following example suggests uses of peers as common stimuli.

EXAMPLE: Programming Peers as Common Stimuli

Specific Peers in Natural Environment	*Programming with Peers*
1. Student H.J. passes food to Mary during snack time and plays with Joey during free play.	1. Mary and Joey are working on skills similar to H.J.'s and group training involves Mary, Joey, and student H.J.
2. Nonhandicapped students are present in the preschool classroom with student B.G.	2. A nonhandicapped student is used as model and as a reinforcing agent within the training setting.
3. Student K.B. has an older sibling whom he interacts with at home.	3. The older sibling is involved in training one day a week to reinforce the correct language responses being targeted.

Because communication is an interactive process involving reciprocal responses between a speaker and a listener, peers can be programmed to take an active role in the training process, in which the student and the peer take turns requesting (expressive language skills), responding to a request (receptive language skills), and acknowledging the response (expressive/social language skills).

Both the student's teacher and the student's parents are usually prominent persons in his or her natural environment. Involving them in the training setting allows them to serve as common stimuli. The result is twofold. First, the student has the opportunity to direct language skills to a listener (or speaker) who is involved in a number of natural settings. Second, the teacher or parent learns what language to expect from the student and what specific cues and consequences control those language behaviors. Specific programming involvement may require a teacher or parent (or both) to observe and conduct training within the setting on a daily basis, or on a more intermittent basis.

In the past students were often taken from the classroom to an isolated room for language training by a specialist. With this type of training strategy the trainer is not common to the classroom or home setting. A language strategy that utilizes the communication specialist as a consultant to the teacher or parent so that the teacher or parent actually conducts the language training programs is probably more functional (see MacDonald and Campbell et al., this volume). This strategy permits the teacher, aide, or parent to be common to both the training settings and the generalization settings. Furthermore, it may be ideal for increasing the probability of generalization because the trainer can deliver similar cues and consequences across both settings.

Across Settings   The majority of activities that occur in our lives are somewhat specific to an environmental setting. We cook and often eat in the kitchen, small children play on the floor when a variety of toys is present, and adolescents may work at a large table in a work activity setting. The specific environmental setting can be defined by its physical dimensions, furniture, and other necessary objects. Therefore, unless training can actually occur in one or more of those settings, the training environment should simulate the natural environment as much as possible.

EXAMPLE: Programming Across Common Settings

Natural Settings	Behaviors Being Targeted	Training Setting
1. Free play setting	Using nouns to request toys.	Train on floor, having a number of toys available.
2. Snack time setting	Using nouns to request foods.	Train at a table similar to the one used in the snack setting, or use the actual setting for training.

Programming Natural Maintaining Consequences

Language use should be naturally reinforcing to a child or youth because he can use language to more efficiently and effectively control his environment. However, the environment often anticipates a student's needs or responds to gesturing and pointing. Therefore, the environment may consequate "Juice" and "I want juice please" in the same manner. In this case, both the student and the environment may require concurrent programming.

If we select training objectives that provide the highest level of natural, positive consequences, then the consequence should be directly related to the stimulus and response. If an apple is a motivational object and the student says "Apple" to request an apple, then a piece of an apple would be the natural consequence. The research data (e.g., Williams et al., 1981) suggest that these natural maintaining contingencies should be applied in the training setting also.

EXAMPLE: Programming Natural Maintaining Consequences

Behaviors That Are Reinforced within the Natural Environment	*Stimuli*	*Response*	*Consequence*
1. Holding out hand to request	Cracker	Student signs CRACKER.	Student given cracker.
2. Other students are reinforced for signing or talking	Milk Yogurt	Student signs MILK. Student signs YOGURT.	Student given milk. Student given yogurt.
3. Pointing to objects or show-ing object	Bus	Student signs BUS.	Teacher says "Right, here's the bus."
	Completed drawing	Student signs FINISH.	Teacher comments, "Good, you're finished."

An example of *not* programming natural maintaining consequences would be to use one consequence (such as a piece of cereal) to consequate the labeling of different objects. In the natural environment the student's label of a specific object is typically consequated with a related comment, not by giving a piece of cereal. Nor are each student's utterances consequated by saying "Very good" or "Good talking." Rather, either tangible or social consequences that are related directly to the language utterance and communication function made by the student should be provided.

Programming "Loose" Training

The "loose" training strategy (e.g., Campbell and Stremel-Campbell, 1982) permits variation of irrelevant stimuli and also allows for a broader range of relevant stimuli to be selected for training. The technique of "loose" training should not be applied as an unsystematic approach to training, but rather as a systematic application of consistent and yet varied stimulus conditions that may operate within the student's natural environment. For many severely and profoundly handicapped students, the variation of stimulus conditions may need to be a gradual process in order for the student to acquire the targeted behavior. The final application of this technique would reflect variations of the stimuli being presented and the responses being accepted by the trainer. In the language learning process, it is critical that the student learn to respond similarly to a range of instructions or cues and also learn to respond differently to similar cues or conditions. Consequently, we do not want to train "rote" language responses. By programming variation in both the stimulus cues and the responses accepted, restricted responding may be prevented and generalization facilitated.

Three basic types of "loose" training techniques are described: 1) programming behaviors concurrently; 2) programming variations of verbal and nonverbal cues; and 3) programming response variation. The use of these techniques to "loosen" the control over the stimuli presented and the responses allowed may need to be gradual, depending upon the language responses to be trained and the level of the student.

Concurrent Training   One example of loose training is to teach responses concurrently so that the student can demonstrate that his response is controlled by a relevant stimulus. For example, if a student is learning to sign CRACKER in a serial training sequence, there is a high probability that the sign will overgeneralize to other food items as well. However, if CRACKER and APPLE are trained concurrently the student is more likely to respond to the specific stimulus (i.e., cracker/apple) than to the consequence (i.e., eating). Once a student has learned a sufficient number of actions and objects, a range of examples of action-object utterances may be trained concurrently. Figure 1 displays a training and generalization matrix similar to one developed by Striefel et al. (1976), which proposes a 2 × 2 level of training to promote generalization of untrained action-object combinations. Initially one verb is trained with at least two different nouns (e.g., eat *cookie*, eat *apple*) and each noun is trained with at least two verbs (e.g., *eat* apple, *cut* apple).

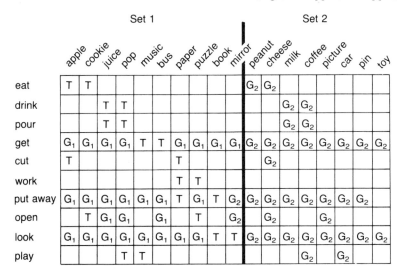

| | \<— Set 1 —\> | | | | | | | | | | \<— Set 2 —\> | | | | | | | |
	apple	cookie	juice	pop	music	bus	paper	puzzle	book	mirror	peanut	cheese	milk	coffee	picture	car	pin	toy
eat	T	T									G₂	G₂						
drink			T	T									G₂	G₂				
pour			T	T									G₂	G₂				
get	G₁	G₁	G₁	G₁	T	T	G₁	G₁	G₁	G₁	G₂	G₂	G₂	G₂	G₂	G₂	G₂	G₂
cut	T						T					G₂						
work							T	T										
put away	G₁	G₁	G₁	G₁	G₁	G₁	T	G₁	T		G₂	G₂	G₂	G₂	G₂	G₂	G₂	G₂
open		T	G₁	G₁		G₁		T		G₂	G₂			G₂				
look	G₁	G₁	G₁	G₁	G₁	G₁	G₁	G₁	T	T	G₂	G₂	G₂	G₂	G₂	G₂	G₂	G₂
play				T	T							G₂		G₂				

Figure 1. Action-object training and generalization matrix. T = training; G₁ = generalization probe for Set I; G₂ = generalization probe for Set II.

Untrained combinations (G_1) (e.g., get apple) are probed and, if generalization does not occur, a limited set of new action-object combinations are included within the original training until the student is able to use trained verbs and trained nouns in untrained combinations. Additional generalization probes (G_2) include assessing untrained combinations of new verbs and nouns that are within the student's vocabulary but not used in the original action-object training.

Varying Verbal and Nonverbal Cues The type and presence or absence of verbal and nonverbal cues can also be used to loosen stimulus control. For example, at some point in training, the student should make similar responses to various cues (e.g., "Show me _____, Give me _____, Find _____, Where is _____?"; "What do you want?" or "Tell me what you want"). Variations of verbal cues should be programmed if necessary. Verbal cues can be faded to encourage spontaneous initiations with familiar and routine situations. A focused attention cue plus a delay is often effective in facilitating generalization. Students can become dependent on a specific verbal cue and thus not respond unless that specific cue is presented. The presentation of multiple cues should discourage such stimulus-bound responses.

The student must learn that he can make a choice. Training can occur with the student being trained to respond when only one object is presented, yet there are often competing choices within the student's natural environment. Additional objects may serve as competing stimuli and therefore may be programmed into training. Furthermore, in training the student to request or talk about objects that are not always visually present in the environment (a critical function of language), objects may be removed from the student's view. Displacing objects within a training program should occur during the final steps of training.

Response Variations In order to inhibit rote responding, it may be necessary to train the student to respond in different ways to achieve the same goal. This "loose" training technique is usually implemented across programs. First, the student may learn to say, "I want juice, please," then "Please give me juice." Later, "Can I have juice?" may be targeted as a variation. The trainer's expansion of the student's response may be sufficient to increase the student's variation, especially for specific language forms. However, if the student does not learn response variations through indirect training techniques, the variations may need to be presented with more structured training techniques.

Programming Indiscriminable Contingencies

The use of indiscriminable contingencies (e.g., Kazdin and Polster, 1973; Koegel and Rincover, 1977) suggests a programming strategy involving the arrangement of schedules of reinforcement such that the student may find it difficult to discriminate between reinforced and nonreinforced stimuli. Generalization may be facilitated if the responses taught are less likely to extinguish. Two different types of indiscriminable techniques can be "actively" programmed in the training process: 1) programming delayed reinforcement, and 2) programming intermittent schedules of reinforcement.

Delayed Reinforcement   A delayed reinforcement technique consists of providing a latency period between the student's response and the delivery of reinforcement. During the initial phases of training, the delivery of immediate reinforcement may be very important for acquisition. For example, the minute the student says or signs "Juice," the trainer immediately presents the juice. As training proceeds, the delivery of the reinforcer can be delayed. The trainer first pours the juice, then presents it. Later, the trainer gets the juice, opens it, pours it, and gives it to the student. In this manner, the time between the student's response "Juice" and the actual drinking of the juice (the reinforcement) is gradually delayed in a natural manner.

Intermittent Schedules of Reinforcement   Initially in the training program, social reinforcement may be paired with the natural reinforcer ("Good, you said, *juice,*" as juice is delivered). However, the natural environment will not always provide high levels of social reinforcement. It may be necessary to gradually fade reinforcement so that it is not given on a continuous schedule and instead is delivered intermittently. The student may receive social reinforcement for every two trials [fixed ratio (FR) of 2] and then every five trials (FR5), such as, "Good for you, you asked for juice and cracker every time."

EXAMPLE: Building a Response Chain Using One Reinforcer

Level I	*Level II*	*Level III*	*Level IV*
			(levels of training)
"Drink juice."	"Open juice."	"Get juice."	"Open cupboard."
	"Pour juice."	"Get cup."	"Get juice."
(juice given)	"Drink juice."	"Open juice."	"Get cup."
		"Pour juice."	"Two cup."
	(juice given)		"Open juice."
		(juice given)	"Throw away (lid)."
			"Pour juice."
			"Give juice Mark."
			"Drink juice."
			(juice given)

Thus, the student must use longer chains of individual responses before receiving the juice, or advancing to the next trial.

An additional strategy for using functional intermittent schedules includes the use of peers. For example, on a FR2 schedule, the student may be required to request juice for a peer before he can request juice for himself. This strategy is more appropriate than having the student simply say "Juice" two times before he receives it. The peer can also be requested to say "Thank you" to the student to provide natural social consequences.

APPLICATION AND EVALUATION OF PROGRAMMING TECHNIQUES

The final outcome of language training should be the student's spontaneous use of trained and related language behaviors across a wide range of conditions, persons, and settings. It is necessary to determine through measurement whether generalization has occurred as a result of training and/or the use of specific generalization programming techniques. The following sections discuss the development of a generalization plan, the measurement of classes of generalization, and strategies of evaluating if the generalization techniques that were applied were sufficient to result in generalization of a trained skill.

Development of a Generalization Plan

The generalization techniques discussed in the preceding section may be applied in total or in parts. A "cookbook" approach to the application of these techniques is not appropriate. Rather, strategies for developing a generalization plan for each student are presented. The resulting individual plan will be based on decisions regarding appropriateness and feasibility. The utilization of every conceivable generalization technique will not be necessary for all students. Also, it may not be possible for one person to apply a range of generalization techniques without the cooperation of other persons (e.g., the teacher and the parents). It is critical that teachers, parents, the communication consultant, and other relevant persons function as a team to develop and implement the generalization plan.

Determining Functional and Appropriate Objectives   The basis of the generalization plan is the selection of functional language objectives. These objectives should be based on assessment data in conjunction with parent and teacher input. Once functional and age-appropriate objectives have been selected, these target objectives should be observed in the natural environment. The functionality and appropriateness of the targeted objectives may be assessed by using systematic spontaneous language samples and/or an informal report. The language sample shown in Figure 2 presents the verbal utterances and nonverbal gestures demonstrated by student A.G. (column 2)

Name __A.G.__   Teacher __J. Doe__

Classroom __A__   Activity __Snack__

Key:

R — response	
I — initiation	
Imit — imitation	

Min.	Utterance	Sign	Type	Peer	Gloss/Errors
1	juice/	X	R		"I want juice"
	cracker/	X	R		held up 2 fingers
2	more/	X	R		"More juice"
	(pointed to carrot)		R		carrot
	me/	X	I		"I open"
3	cheese/	X	R		"I get cheese"
	me/	X	I		"I pour juice"
4	(shook head no to peer)		R	X	"No"
5					
6	cheese/	X	R		"More cheese"
7	yes/	X	R		
8	(showed plate to teacher)				look/finished
9	(pointed to play area)		R		"I go play"
10	bathroom/		R		"I go bathroom"
	go/	X	Imit		"I go bathroom"
	(pointing at peer)				look at Joey

Figure 2. Language sample for student A.G. Note: if the samples are taken from observation of videotapes, grammatical glosses "I want *some* juice" or "I want *more* juice" are recorded in the gloss/error column.

as well as the modality of these utterances (column 3), the type of utterance (coded as responses, initiations, and imitations; column 4), the utterances directed to a peer (column 5), and the possible gloss (column 6). The gloss is a sentence or phrase that another person might use in the same contextual situation. The initial objectives for this student included two-word utterances.

An informal teacher or parent report can also be used to determine the student's language use in the natural environment. The information gathered from a number of spontaneous language samples and/or the informal report should provide answers to two questions:

1. Is the language behavior to be targeted occurring at a low frequency in the natural environment?

2. Are prerequisite skills or component behaviors being demonstrated by the student in the natural environment?

In some cases, formal assessment results may not be indicative of the student's actual performance in the natural environment. For example, a student may demonstrate noun labeling in a structured testing environment but may not be using any nouns in other settings. Based on formal assessment data, two-word phrases were originally included as individual education program (IEP) objectives. However, language samples and informal reports of this student's language within his natural environment would indicate that initial training should concentrate on increasing one-word utterances prior to targeting two-word utterances. Another student's observational data may reveal that he is frequently using appropriate one-word utterances in familiar settings with familiar persons even though formal assessment results suggest the student is essentially nonverbal. It is hoped that this type of problem will not occur if parents and teachers are encouraged to discuss the student's current language performance during the IEP conference.

Determining Features of the Student's Natural Environment   Once functional and appropriate language objectives have been developed, it is necessary to determine the features of the student's environment that are relevant to the generalization techniques. Before multiple exemplars or common stimuli are selected for training, the persons involved in planning the intervention need to analyze what exemplars or stimuli are available for programming. These can be outlined informally with parent and teacher input. Figure 3 presents an analysis of a 16-year-old student's major environments, the typical activities within those environments, the time spent within those environments, and the persons who are prominent within the activities and settings. A further breakdown would include the relationship of the activities and the language training behaviors. More specifically, the interventionist needs to determine what content is appropriate to those activities. Once this information is gathered, the individual student's generalization plan can be outlined by specifying the appropriate generalization techniques.

Strategies for Applying Generalization Techniques

The approach taken in developing a student's generalization plan is based on the application of one or more programming techniques. Each technique and application must be carefully considered in relation to the level of the student, the student's environment, and the available resources within that environment. Based on this information, a decision is made as to whether to "actively" program each specific technique for training. The following example presents the application plan for a moderately handicapped sixteen-year-old student who is learning plurals.

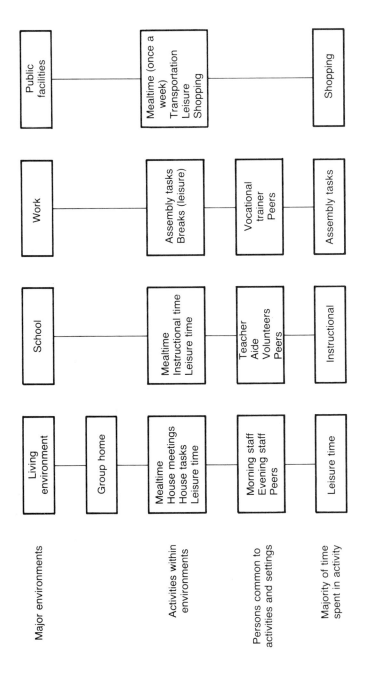

Figure 3. Analysis of environmental settings and activities for a 16-year-old student.

273

EXAMPLE: Application of Generalization Techniques for a 16-Year-Old Student

Language Objective—Plural Endings

Techniques	Types Available	Active Programming
Multiple Exemplars		
Across behavior	Communication functions	Yes
	Linguistic class exemplars	Not applicable
	Response class exemplars	Yes
Across settings	Mealtime in group home	Yes
	House meetings	No
	House tasks	No
	Leisure time in group home	Yes
	Mealtime in school	Yes
Across persons	Morning staff	No
	Evening staff	Yes
	Peers	Yes
	Teacher	Yes
Common stimuli		
Across behaviors	Communication functions	Not applicable
	Words	Yes
	Physical stimuli	Yes
Across settings	Common mealtime activities	Yes
	Common leisure activities	Yes
Across persons	Teacher available for training	Yes
	Evening staff available for training	Yes
	Peers common to all settings	Yes
Natural maintaining consequences		
	Direct relationship (train persons in the environment)	Yes
Loose training	Concurrent training	Yes
	Varying cues	Yes
	Response variation	Yes
Intermittent schedules	Social reinforcement	Yes

The programming plan for this student includes the use of multiple exemplars, common stimuli, natural maintaining consequences, loose training, and intermittent schedules. The combination of generalization techniques applied in this example could logically result in generalization across response classes, settings, persons, and time. The specifics of this generalization plan as they would be applied in training are presented below.

EXAMPLE: Specific Generalization Plan

1. Training will occur in multiple settings by training at the group home during the evening mealtime activity and at the school during leisure activities.
2. Both an evening staff person and the teacher will conduct training.
3. Two peers will be present during training.
4. Because the student is currently using various communication functions, plurals will be trained across multiple communication functions (e.g., "Give me some carrots," "Look at the cars," "I don't want these shoes," "I'll have two hamburgers").
5. Multiple examples of noun +/-s, *noun* +/-z, and noun +/ez will be trained. Plural nouns will also be trained in different syntactic phrases, such as "The apples are good," and "I like apples." Even though multiple object class exemplars will be used, the presentation of multiple object classes is not critical because the student already labels various exemplars of the nouns being used for training.
6. Because the evening mealtime training setting in the group home is identical to the breakfast setting and is also a setting where leisure skills (e.g., card playing) occur, the training setting will be common to the generalization setting. Also, the leisure activity setting in the school will be common to other activities (vocational breaks and instructional activities).
7. The teacher (trainer) will be common to other settings within the classroom, school, and community. The group home staff will also be common to other settings within the group home and community. However, neither trainer will be common to the vocational setting.
8. The peers that are included in each training setting will be common to all of the generalization settings.
9. The behaviors selected for training will be based on nouns that the student currently uses in all environments:

Nouns trained in groups home	*Nouns trained in school*
hambugerz, chips, dishez, potatoez, carrots, sandwiches, applez, cups, glasses	moviez, bolts, boxes, magazinez, cokes, pieces, cardz, plants

Therefore, the nouns taught in the training setting are common to all the generalization settings.

10. Different examples of the training stimuli will be common across environments. For instance, magazines identical to those in the group home will be used in the school training setting.
11. Natural maintaining contingencies will be used. For example, if a student says, "Pass potato please," only one potato (or piece of a potato) will be passed, so that the trainers will be responding to what the student *says* and not what the student means.

continued

EXAMPLE: Specific Generalization Plan *(continued)*

12. The stimuli selected for training will be taught concurrently (hamburgers, pota-
toes, etc.) by randomly presenting the objects or verbal cues to evoke those
responses across trials in each training setting. Also, other social skills will be
trained concurrently with language training.
13. Verbal cues will be varied to correspond to questions and responses typically
made in social communication interactions.
14. Any response containing a plural noun will be reinforced. Initially, correct and
incorrect responses will be consequated on a continuous schedule by visual feedback (plus and minus codes recorded on paper) and verbal feedback.
15. Once the student has reached training criterion, intermittent (variable ratio; VR)
schedules of reinforcement (VR2, VR5, VR10) will be used in the training-
maintenance phase of the program if generalization has not occurred at that point.

The application of all these techniques will not ensure that generalization will occur across different exemplars, sentences, persons, or settings.
However, the probability of generalization may be increased if a number of
generalization techniques are used.

An example of a generalization plan for a moderately handicapped 5-
year-old child is presented below. This example reflects a less comprehensive
and intense application of generalization techniques. It is presented to demonstrate how one strategy can be applied and result in very different types of
programming. The decision for using certain generalization techniques and
not others should be based on the available resources and parent cooperation.

**EXAMPLE: Application of Generalization Techniques for a Moderately
Handicapped 5-Year-Old Student**

Language Objective—One-Word Sign Utterances

Techniques	*Types Availability*	*Active Programming*
Multiple exemplars		
Across settings	Day care playtime	No
	Day care snack time	No
	Home mealtimes	No
	Home self-care	No
	Home interactions	No
	Clinic setting (1/2 hour daily)	Yes
Across persons	Father	No
	Mother	No
	Siblings	No
	Day care staff	No
	Grandparents	No
	Speech clinician	Yes

EXAMPLE: Application of Generalization Techniques for a Moderately Handicapped 5-Year-Old Student *(continued)*

Techniques	*Types Availability*	*Active Programming*
Across behaviors	Communication functions	Yes
	Linguistic class exemplars	No
	Response class exemplars	No
	Object class exemplars	Yes
Common stimuli		
Across settings	Home	No
	Day care	No
Across persons	Mother	No
	Siblings	No
Across behavior	Communication functions	Yes
	Words	Not applicable
	Physical stimuli	Yes
Natural maintaining consequences		
Loose training	Concurrent training	Yes
	Varying cues	Yes
	Response variation	Not applicable at this level
Intermittent schedules		No

The generalization programming plan for this student includes only those aspects of the generalization techniques that the speech clinician can program considering her job requirements and the available resources. The combination of the generalization techniques results in a minimum level of generalization programming. The specific intervention procedures for the student are outlined below.

EXAMPLE: Specific Generalization Plan

1. Training will occur only in the clinic setting; therefore, multiple settings will not be programmed.
2. Because only the speech clinician will serve as the trainer, training will not occur across multiple persons.
3. The communication functions—requesting and labeling—will be programmed.
4. Multiple examples of the objects will be used across different training sessions.
5. Since the clinic setting is dissimilar to the home and day care settings, the training setting will not be common to the generalization settings.
6. The trainer will not be common to either the home setting or the day care center.
7. Because the student is currently gesturing, pointing, and showing objects to request and to point out things within his environment, the communication functions will be common to both the generalization settings and the training setting.

continued

EXAMPLE: Specific Generalization Plan *(continued)*

8. Objects that the student is nonverbally requesting and labeling will be used to train the one-word signs.
9. Real objects common to those prominent in the student's home and to the day care setting will be used for training stimuli. The reinforcement will be directly related to the student's response.
10. At least two nouns will be trained concurrently.
11. The training cues will vary in targeting the different communication functions:
    "What do you want?" JUICE
    "What's this?" JUICE

A training session for this student may be arranged as follows:

EXAMPLE: Training Session

Trial-Teacher Behavior	*Student Response*	*Reinforcement*
1. Graham cracker presented. Teacher asks "What do you want?"	Signs CRACKER.	Gets cracker.
2. Grape juice presented. Teacher asks "What's this?"	Signs JUICE.	Trainer says, "Right, juice."
3. Large can of apple juice presented. Teacher asks "What do you want?"	Signs JUICE.	Gets juice.
4. Soda cracker presented. Teacher asks "What do you want?"	Signs CRACKER.	Gets cracker.

The training sequence demonstrates how common physical stimuli and communication functions may be programmed. Multiple examples of objects are used in a concurrent training sequence. The student's responses are those that should be maintained by the natural environment only if persons in those environments understand the student's signs. Therefore, signs would be a functional language system only if persons in the generalization setting were trained to use signs.

Evaluation of The Generalization Plan

The effectiveness of the generalization plan can be assessed only by the occurrence of generalization. Warren (this volume) discusses the major types of measurement systems that can be used to determine if generalization has occurred. These systems include structured probe measurements and observations in the natural environment. Warren et al. (1980) suggested that a student may demonstrate generalization within structured probe conditions before demonstrating the trained behavior within the natural environment.

Structured Probes   A structured probe can be used to test for generalization across response classes, settings, persons, and time. An example of summarized structured probe data across all the generalization conditions is presented in Figure 4.

The data presented are an example of the generalization probes for the 5-year-old moderately handicapped student whose program was previously described. Two objects were trained in each training set (juice and cracker) with two different examples presented for each object trained. The techniques that were used are indicated under "Generalization Plan." Systematic probes were conducted when training criteria were met for each set of nouns. Two examples of untrained objects were presented in the probe condition. The student demonstrated 100% correct responding to the response probe and

Name: J. Doe   Date Initiated 2/10

Training Objective: One-word signs   Date Completed 3/21

GENERALIZATION PLAN

Active Program	Response exemplars (multiple objects)	Settings	Persons	Time
Yes	X			
No		X	X	

GENERALIZATION PROBES

Training				Percentage measures of generalization to untrained exemplars								
Trials to criterion				Response objects (two new examples)			Settings (#2)			Persons (#2)		
Dates	2/10	3/3	3/21	2/10	3/3	3/21	2/10	3/3	3/21	2/10	3/3	3/21
Set I	210			100%								
Set II		120			100%		50%			40%		
Set III			60			100%		60%			48%	
Final maintenance probe after training across 3 sets				100%	90%	100%			55%			45%

Figure 4. Structured probe generalization summary. Note: for the generalization probe, criterion is 90% across two training blocks (two blocks of 10 trials).

maintained correct responding across time (1½ months). The structured probes to an untrained setting (home) and to an untrained person (mother) taken after Sets I and II were trained showed that the student used the trained signs at levels of 50% correct responding (10 out of 20 probe trials) to the untrained setting and 40% correct responding (8 out of 20 probe trials) to the untrained person. Probes after criterion was met on each set indicated that the student met the generalization criterion to untrained object exemplars, but that generalization to settings and persons did not increase significantly across time or additional training (Sets II and III).

Because generalization was not demonstrated across persons and settings within a structured probe, observation of the trained behavior within the natural environment would not be taken until additional training across persons and settings occurred. For example, additional training (i.e., sequential modification) might include the use of the student's mother as a trainer both in the clinic and in the home setting. Once training is completed with a second trainer and across a second setting, the structured probe would be administered again. If generalization occurred across all potential probe categories of generalization, observations in the natural environment could then be used to determine if the student was using the trained language behavior within a natural communication context.

Observations in the Natural Environment   The observations within the natural environment may include a verbatim record of all language utterances or simply a frequency count of only the language behavior being trained. Fifteen-minute verbatim records could be collected across all or some of the generalization settings to determine if the student is using trained language skills in the natural environment and how frequently these skills are being used. Verbatim samples also provide baseline data for language behaviors to be taught at a later point of training. However, many language practitioners will not have the time or the resources to collect verbatim samples.

Measuring frequency of occurrence is a practical alternative to verbatim sampling. A frequency measurement may be a simple occurrence tally of the language behavior(s) that have been trained. These measurements can be collected by the parent or the teacher in the generalization setting. Figure 5 presents an example of a simple observation record that could be completed by a parent or teacher. The words that are relevant to a specific generalization setting are listed for the parent. Persons common to that setting are also designated. The frequency of the student's use of the target language behaviors and the person to whom each target utterance was directed are recorded by a tally mark. In this example, the data show that the student used each trained sign during the 15-minute period and that the utterances generalized to persons who were not involved in training. If children are speaking infrequently, a similar tally could be used for syntactic forms (verb-noun) or semantic forms [action-object ("Eat cracker"), action-location ("Go home"), or state verb–pronoun ("Want that")].

SAMPLE DATA SHEET

Name __J. Doe_____   Setting__Home_____

Date	Nouns requiring plural endings	Plurals used correctly	Percentage correct
2/15	ℋℋ	/	20
2/17	////	//	50
2/19	///	/	33
2/23	///	//	67

Figure 5. Sample data sheet for generalization of trained nouns. Tally marks show the frequency of utterance of trained language objectives during 15-minute observations, and persons to whom the utterance was directed.

Some language elements, such as plurals, are obligatory. If the student is referring to multiple objects, a plural ending should be used. Data records for these language forms should include correct and incorrect use columns so that a percentage of correct responses can be determined. It is recommended that these generalization forms be developed according to the behavior being targeted. Figure 6 shows a completed data form for plurality.

If the observation data show that the student is not generalizing across settings and persons in the natural environment, it is suggested that sequential modifications be added to the student's program until generalization does occur. The modifications that are made should relate to the probe and the observational data. For example, if the student demonstrates that he does not

SAMPLE DATA SHEET

Name_____J. Doe_____   Setting_____Home_____

Date	Trained language			Utterance directed to person			
	juice	cracker	apple	Mom	Dad	Siblings	Grandmother
4-10	//	/	/	///	/		
4-11		/	//				///
4-12	/	//		//		/	
4-13	/	/	/	/		//	
4-14	/		//	//		/	

Figure 6. Sample data sheet for generalization of plurals in spontaneous speech during 15-minute observations.

generalize to new examples of objects but does generalize training items to different settings and persons, the program modification would consist of adding more object exemplars to training. However, if the student demonstrates generalization across settings when the original trainer is present, but does not display generalization to other persons, modifications would include adding a second and possibly a third trainer. Consequently, the relationship between the generalization techniques utilized and the generalization data is extremely important.

Criteria for Acceptable Generalization

Generalization can occur in isolation within any one situation or it can occur across a combination of conditions. For example, a student may demonstrate generalization to new examples of objects used in training and demonstrate generalization to an untrained subset of a response class (new imitative behaviors), and yet not demonstrate generalization of the trained behavior across different persons or settings or time. Therefore, generalization should always be assessed across all four of these dimensions.

To assess response class generalization, similar but untrained objects may be used to determine if the student will generalize a trained response to untrained examples of that object, such as saying "Cup" when new examples of cups are presented. An additional response class measurement would be the assessment of behaviors that were not trained but that are members of a larger response class in which a subset of the behaviors was trained. Generalization is said to occur if the student responds correctly to new members of the response class, such as using plural endings with nouns that have not been used in plurality training. To measure setting generalization, the trained behavior is assessed across new but appropriate settings. It is important to assess the trained behavior in natural settings in which it may be expected to occur. To determine person generalization, measures should be taken with persons not involved in training. It is suggested that the initial "person" generalization probe include person(s) who are familiar to the individual (e.g., father, sibling, grandmother, or aide). From our perspective generalization across time does not mean the maintenance of the trained behavior within the training condition, but rather the durability of generalization in the natural environment.

Based on its presence or absence within any one condition (i.e., response class, settings, persons, and time), the extent of generalization can be determined. However, an acceptable criterion level must also be determined, which is a difficult and subjective process. When has sufficient generalization occurred that programming can cease? Warren (this volume) suggests that a criterion for each generalization target be established prior to training. These criteria should be based on "natural" rates of occurrence and on the number of opportunities provided by the natural environment (i.e., the student has the opportunity to request three items during snack time).

CONCLUSIONS

The effectiveness of any training program should be determined not by the trials necessary to reach the acquisition criterion, but rather by the occurrence of generalization across behaviors, settings, persons, and time. Because the research data indicate that generalization is not an automatic outcome of programming, it should be "actively" programmed as part of each student's individual program. Types of programming techniques were discussed and specific examples were provided. Although the examples given were specific to language training, these techniques are applicable to many other skills.

The application of the generalization techniques cannot be made "in total" for every student. Strategies for applying the techniques can be systematic and specifically designed for each student, the language behavior being targeted, and the available resources. Once a plan has been developed and implemented, its effectiveness can be measured by the occurrence or nonoccurrence of generalization. Modifications can be made based upon the resulting generalization data. However, it is important to ask two questions before making modifications on the student's program:

1. Has the student learned the task sufficiently to result in generalization?
2. Is the natural environment providing opportunities for the student to use his trained language?

If the student has not learned the task sufficiently, further training is necessary. If the environment is not providing opportunities for language to occur or is not consequating the language that is occurring, further training probably would not increase generalization. In this case modifications must be made in the environment. That is, prominent persons in the student's environment should be trained to increase both the opportunities they provide for language responses and the consequences delivered for those language responses. Training persons in the natural environment is especially critical if the language modality being used is not common to the natural environment (i.e., manual signs or communication boards). In this case adults and peers must learn and demonstrate the use of the student's modality (such as signs) so that the language system itself becomes common to the natural environment.

ACKNOWLEDGMENTS

The authors wish to thank Jeannie Parker, Ethel Wetzstein, and Kelly Spellman for their dedication to data collection and analysis, and Colleen

Eisenhart and Mary Miller for their excellent skills in training. Their contributions to this chapter are greatly appreciated.

REFERENCES

Anderson, S. F., and Spradlin, J. G. 1980. The generalized effects of productive labeling training involving common object classes. J. Assoc. Severely Handic. 5:143–157.

Bloom, L. 1970. Language Development: Form and Function in Emerging Grammars. MIT Press, Cambridge, MA.

Bowerman, M. 1978. Semantic and syntactic development: A review of what, when and how in language acquisition. In R. L. Schiefelbusch (ed.), Bases of Language Intervention. University Park Press, Baltimore.

Brown, R. 1973. A First Language: The Early Stages. Harvard University Press, Cambridge, MA.

Campbell, C. R. and Stremel-Campbell, K. 1982. Programming "loose training" as a strategy to facilitate language generalization. J. Appl. Behav. Anal. 15:295–301.

Garcia, E. 1974. The training and generalization of a conversational speech form in nonverbal retardates. J. Appl. Behav. Anal. 7:137–149.

Guess, D., Keogh, W., and Sailor, W. 1978a. Generalization of speech and language behavior. In R. L. Schiefelbusch (ed.), Bases of Language Intervention. University Park Press, Baltimore.

Guess, D., Sailor, W., and Baer, D. 1978b. Functional Speech and Language Training for the Severely Handicapped. H & H Enterprises, Inc., Lawrence, KS.

Harris, S. L. 1975. Teaching language to nonverbal children with emphasis on problems of generalization. Psychol. Rec. 82:565–580.

Hupp, S. C., and Mervis, C. B. (1981). Development of generalized concepts by severely handicapped students. J. Assoc. Severely Handic. 6:14–21.

Kazdin, A. E., and Polster, R. 1973. Intermittent token reinforcement and response maintenance in extinction. Behav. Ther. 4:386–391.

Koegel, R. L., and Rincover, A. 1977. Research on the difference between generalization and maintenance in extra-therapy responding. J. Appl. Behav. Anal. 10:1–12.

McLean, J. E., and Snyder-McLean, L. 1978. A Transactional Approach to Early Language Training. Charles E. Merrill, Columbus, OH.

Rincover, A., and Koegel, R. L. 1975. Setting generality and stimulus control in autistic children. J. Appl. Behavior Analysis, 8:235–246.

Rogers-Warren, A. 1977. Planned change: Ecobehaviorally based interventions. In A. Rogers-Warren and S. Warren (eds.), Ecological Perspective in Behavior Analysis. University Park Press, Baltimore.

Schlesinger, I. M. 1974. Relational concepts underlying language. In R. L. Schiefelbusch and L. L. Lloyd (eds.), Language Perspectives: Acquisition, Retardation, and Intervention. University Park Press, Baltimore.

Stokes, T. F., and Baer, D. M. 1977. An implicit technology of generalization. J. Appl. Behav. Anal. 10:349–367.

Striefel, S., Wetherby, B., and Karlan, G. R. 1976. Establishing generalized verb-noun instruction-following skills in retarded children. J. Except. Child Psychol. 22:247–260.

Walker, H. M., and Buckley, N. K. 1972. Programming generalization and maintenance of treatment effects across time and across settings. J. Appl. Behav. Anal. 5:209–224.

Warren, S., Rogers-Warren, A., Baer, D., and Guess, D. 1980. Assessment and facilitation of generalization. In W. Sailor, B. Wilcox, and L. Brown (eds.), Methods of Instruction for Severely Handicapped Students. Paul H. Brookes Publishing Co., Baltimore.

Williams, J. A., Koegel, R. L., and Egel, A. L. 1981. Response-reinforcer relationships and improved learning in autistic children. J. Appl. Behav. Anal. 14:53–60.

Section IV

Utilizing Significant Others

chapter

10

Programming Peer Support For Functional Language

Linda Paul

Assistant Director of Education
Suffolk Child Development Center
Smithtown, New York

CHILDRENESE VERSUS THERAPESE   292

PERFORMANCE DEFICITS   295

SKILL DEFICITS   298

PEERS AS INTERVENTION AGENTS   300
    Peer Assembly   301
    Peer Confederates   303

SUMMARY AND RECOMMENDATIONS   304

REFERENCES   305

A young child's language skills reflect a combination of linguistic, cognitive, and social skills. The competent speaker uses the correct form of language within a context. Language use is tied to a number of social, communicative functions. Social context shapes language use.

> Language, as we have seen, is essentially a form of action: social growth. The child—perhaps innately, certainly very early in life has manipulative and declarative needs. He also enjoys making and listening to vocal noises; he enjoys the give-and-take of vocal interchange with others. All these incentives combine to impel the child to become more widely and more deeply skilled in both speaking and understanding. He finds that language is the indispensable means of social cooperation. We know that social cooperation is the indispensable means of the development of infant speech into the mother tongue. (Lewis, 1951, p. 261)

The social process involves reciprocity. Ultimately, functional language is language that enables interaction with other people.

The child who is delayed in developing language needs to learn skills that are useful in real situations. Technical skills alone are not sufficient. The child's learning of syntax and semantics must be embedded in meaningful social interactions. A valid criterion for the determination of language training objectives is the usefulness of the target behaviors in the child's day-to-day interactions.

Three basic and interrelated dimensions of language use are:

1. The *reason* for using language
2. *Where* the language is used
3. *To whom the language is addressed*

Analysis of a child's typical interactions and communicative needs leads to the selection of functional, realistic language learning objectives. Training within naturalistic settings (e.g., MacDonald, this volume; Hart and Rogers-Warren, 1978) further supports the acquisition of functional language. Traditional approaches to training do not fully consider who the child talks with because the general focus is on adult-child interaction. But, what about peers?

> Peers are the life of people—not only of children. With the exception of brief infancy and toddler years, the individual is likely to be with near-age mates for very considerable portions of his time and for widely varying relationships. (Yarrow, 1975, p. 299)

Functional language training should enable the child to interact with both adults and peers.

Social contact between children during their typical play contributes to a child's cognitive and social development (Garvey, 1977). Normally developing young children are able to sustain interactions with one another, using a combination of verbal and nonverbal behaviors (Lee et al., 1974; Mueller,

291

1972; Spilton and Lee, 1977). The language used by the child is comparatively less complex than that of adults. Although peers are not generally exemplary language models or teachers (Bates, 1975), interactions between children do provide valuable learning experiences. The mutuality of interests, similarity of skills, and egalitarian relationship result in qualitatively different interactions between children than between an adult and a child. Not only are children able to practice learned behaviors while playing with peers, but such interaction also promotes acquisition of behavior. Peers create opportunities for the development of skills such as sharing, maintaining possession of toys, and imaginative, dramatic play. In the absence of an adult, children have increased opportunities to control and structure their own activity.

The expectation that a child *should* interact with peers, and the acknowledgment that peers contribute to a child's development, result in the referral of children who are "isolate" or "socially withdrawn" to guidance clinics. A review of demographic data indicates that from 14% to 30% of the children with behavior problems have low rates of social interaction (Strain et al., 1976). The long-term impact of social withdrawal in young children has not been conclusively determined, but there is evidence that poor peer relations during childhood can be a predictor of later neurotic and psychotic behavior (Hartup, 1976).

This chapter considers ways in which peers contribute to language learning and identifies ways in which peers can and should be part of language programs. The focus is on children who do not talk with other children. Analysis of such children's abilities in terms of performance and/or skill deficits is described. Using peers to remediate such deficits is suggested via simple manipulation of grouping or peer assemblies, and by employing peers as confederates. The chapter closes with some teaching recommendations related to the notion that peers support functional language skills.

The child who is language-delayed may have difficulty interacting with peers. Such a child may lack critical communicative skills. Having problems in initiating or responding to verbalizations places limits on the child's frequency of peer contact. Other children's contacts with the language-delayed child may be discouraged by the lack of response and thus further increase isolation. Analysis of preschooler's patterns of interaction (Greenwood et al., 1977; Kohn, 1966) indicates high correlations between child initiations and responses. Remediating the socially withdrawn child's language deficits should include teaching socially valid, effective peer approach and response behaviors.

CHILDRENESE VERSUS THERAPESE

In teaching language to children a distinction should be made between typical adult and child behavior. Reliance on an adult model of skills reflects adult competencies, not child competencies. Our current model of language development is firmly anchored in viewing progressions in child competency rather than in constant comparison with adult competency.

Child language characteristics such as early use of grammatically incomplete but semantically valid utterances or semantic over generalizations are not errors. They are a stage in development. Holland (1975) asserted that language training must reflect characteristics of children's language. Language training should involve the teaching of "childrenese."

Selection of lexical content and the teaching sequence of syntactical-semantic forms on the basis of typical children's language is a component of most language training programs. However, the social aspects of language training create conditions that limit a child's learning to respond to childrenese. Adult-child interaction is the prime social context of training. Ideally, the language learned in adult interactions will generalize to child interactions. Observation of a child's interaction with a skilled speaker of "therapese" as compared to an interaction with a speaker of "childrenese" suggests that generalization may be limited.

Consider these segments of interactions between a language-delayed child and an adult:

(reading a book)

Adult: What's this?
Child: Play guitar
Adult: Say girl
Child: Girl
Adult: Play
Child: Play guitar
Adult: Now, say it again for me
Child: Play guitar
Adult: Who's playing the guitar
Child: Mommy
Adult: No, is that mommy?
Child: (m)
Adult: Girl, girl play guitar
Child: Play guitar

(hearing the telephone ring)

Child: Hi, who who.
Adult: I thought you said it was Jason's mother awhile ago.
Child: Jasie mommy.
Adult: Is he gonna go to school today?
Child: No [?] who who [?].
Adult: Oh no. Not Jason Hoover, Jason Smith.

The speaker of therapese (in this case, mothers) elicits, clarifies, and expands the child's responses. The child's limited or unclear responses are used to increase the tutorial aspects of the interaction. Also, the adult is persistent in maintaining the interaction.

Now, compare the following interactions between normally developing preschoolers:

(playing with markers)

Child 1:   A leaf is a meef. A leaf is a meef. Meef meef meef meef beef. I got pe I got pes Jenny.

Child 2:   What?

Child 1:   I got pe. Ya dummy [*?*] marker [*???*] popcorn goes in here.

Child 2:   Not pencils.

Child 1:   No popcorn.

(playing with markers)

Child 1:   Uh oh muffin man, uh oh muffin man.

Child 2:   Uh oh muffin man. Ya know what a muffin man is? He's a muffin and sometimes when I find muffin man I eat muffin man. Muffin man is a silly.

Child 1:   I yea. Punch muffin man, punch muffin man, punch muffin man.

Child 2:   Punch muffin man. Punch, punch, punch, punch, punch, punch, punch.

Conversations between two children are often relatively incoherent because of unintelligible articulation, unclear referents, and idiosyncratic words or combinations of words. Specific cues in the form of questions or directives may be lacking. Topics may shift erratically and turn-taking rules are readily broken. In addition, there may be conflict in the activity and inattention to one another's utterances. The challenge provided by a peer conversational partner is considerable.

Qualitative differences in child-child and adult-child conversations are described in Table 1 with reference to characteristics of childrenese and therapese. Given the relative lack of child competence and the often idiosyncratic characteristics of child language, child-child interaction differs on many dimensions from adult-child interaction. Expecting or predicting generalization of behavior requires consideration of these differences.

The pessimistic hypothesis is that conversational skills learned through adult-child interaction will not generalize to child-child interaction. The child who does not verbally interact with peers may not:

1. Generalize learned skills *(performance deficiency)*.
2. Have the requisite skills to initiate, respond, and maintain conversation with peers *(skill deficiency)*.

Remediation of either set of problems or a combination of problems involves establishing criteria or performance objectives and training procedures.

Table 1. Conversational Characteristics

	Childrenese	Therapese	Conversational Impact
Lexicon	May be limited in range; may include nonsense words	Full range of vocabulary options	Clarity of reference Range of topics Range of responses
Syntax	May not use all grammatical forms or combinations; word order may be unconventional	Able to correctly combine words in a conventional manner	Meaning of a given utterance
Semantics	May not use all relationships; may have idiosyncratic meanings for words	Uses words and combines and relates them in a conventional manner	Meaning of a given utterance Expression of ideas Comprehension by a listener
Phoenetics	Intelligibility of particular words and sounds hampered	Speech is intelligible	Comprehension of speaker's utterances
Topic	Egocentric reference may prevail; focus on the here and now; frequent shifts; object orientation common	Nonegocentric reference prevalent; can focus on abstract as well as here and now; coherence maintained	Comprehension of speaker's utterances Maintenance of interaction Content limitations
Turn-taking	Monologues and joint turns may occur; cues for a response may or may not be provided	Provides clear cues for a response; one speaker at a time common	Reciprocity of interaction Clarity of topic

PERFORMANCE DEFICITS

A child's low rate of interacting with peers is relative to what is considered typical behavior. Developmental scales provide age-correlated norms for developmental milestones as compared to a sizeable sample of other children. Such standardized behavior guidelines enable one to determine the extent of a child's delayed development and provide criteria for acceptable performance. However, such norms do not provide very detailed analyses of social verbal interaction. Normative frequencies of peer interaction must be generated on the basis of existing, scattered data or specially collected data.

A review of research describing young children's patterns of peer interaction provides data of the former sort. Table 2 summarizes data describing

Table 2. Rates of Peer-directed Verbal Interaction

Reference	Age of Subjects	Number of Subjects	Situation	Rate (% in 25 min)
Slater (1939)	2–4-year-olds	40	Free play in preschool	
	2			44
	3			50
	3			56
	4			66
Garvey and Hogan (1973)	3–5-year-olds	18	Dyads; free play	59
Salzinger et al. (1975)	2 years, 7 months	13	Free play in preschool	66
	3 years, 7 months			70
Mueller (1972)	3–5-year-olds	24	Dyads	62
Van Alstyne (1932)	2–5-year-olds	112	Free play in preschool	30–48
Robinson and Conrad (1933)	2–5-year-olds	50	Free play on playground	31 Social contact 56
Rubin (1976)	Mean age 4–6 years	34	Free play in preschool	63
Greenwood et al. (1977)	3 years and 7 years	457	Free play in preschool	Mean 0.627 interactions per minute (verbal and nonverbal)

normally developing children. Based on this information, a realistic expectation would be that children should talk to peers from one-third to two-thirds of the time during unstructured or free play time. Setting characteristics such as the teacher-child ratio and activities available account for a wide range of behavior across different children and classrooms. For example, Greenwood et al. (1977) found that peer interaction rates ranged from 0.275 to 1.054 interactions per minute. Determining that a particular child or classroom of children has an inadequate rate of peer interaction requires not only a sufficient sample of behavior, but allowance for fluctuation and a range of typical behavior.

Specifically collecting data to establish a norm is a simple and socially valid strategy. Walker and Hops (1976) provided an example of this approach. Target elementary school children were referred to a special classroom because of low rates of acceptable classroom behavior. Their peers who remained in the regular classroom provided a normative comparison group.

Through baseline, intervention, and follow-up, data were collected on target children and peers who were not involved in the intervention. Follow-up data collected in the regular classroom demonstrated that the target children's behavior was now within normal limits as established by peer behavior rates. The peer comparison data provided a standard that was appropriate to the real situation. It also was useful in evaluating generalization and maintenance of behavior that had been learned in another setting.

Selection of an appropriate peer group depends on the setting in which you want the child to function. Peers remaining in the classroom where the target children were expected to return to were a logical comparison group for Walker and Hops (1976). Peer verbalizations in a child's current classroom (e.g., a class for handicapped children), a potential classroom (e.g., an integrated classroom of handicapped and nonhandicapped children), or an ideal classroom (e.g., a classroom of nonhandicapped peers) might provide norms. It is important to remember that the child who talks with peers effectively in classroom X may still not be as skilled as the child in classroom Y.

Equating behavior across different settings is difficult because behavior reflects the characteristics of the environment as a whole. Particular activities (Parten, 1933; Quilitch and Risley, 1973; Updegraff and Herbst, 1933; Van Alstyne, 1932) may elicit differing levels of social behavior. The number of adults and their behavior is another critical variable. The rate of teacher interaction with children and teacher attention to peer interaction (Allen et al., 1964; Goetz et al., 1975) create different levels of child behavior. A sufficient sample of behavior collected in a setting will reflect natural variability.

Observation of the target child in different classrooms may reflect the situational nature of a performance deficit. A child's performance may differ considerably depending on the behavior of peers and the other setting characteristics. For example, observations of the same children in different classrooms will reveal clear differences in their rates of interaction. Two language-delayed children observed in a classroom with primarily language-delayed children and in a classroom with primarily normally developing children were found to talk with peers 15–20% more often in the classroom containing primarily normally developing peers (Paul and McQuarter, 1979). If behavior is at an acceptable rate in the classroom with language-proficient peers, the performance deficit in a special classroom may indicate a need for classroom restructuring. Furthermore, intervening within the special classroom possibly requires focusing on all of the children rather than on a particular child who is viewed as being socially withdrawn.

Determining a standard or criterion level of peer-directed verbal interaction establishes guidelines. The method of collecting the information, the peer group used as a comparison, and the target child's relative ability in different situations require careful attention.

SKILL DEFICITS

Increasing the rate at which a child talks frequently results in a subsequent increase in language complexity (Hart and Risley, 1980). Measures of numbers of new words, lengths of utterances, or kinds of utterances can readily be monitored. Additional quality considerations in the case of language as interactive behavior would be the responsiveness of peers and the duration of interactions.

If increasing a child's rate of peer-directed verbal interaction does not enhance the quality or success of interactions, or if behavior does not increase, a child's conversational skills should be analyzed. Table 3 provides some suggested behavior categories to assess. Mueller's (1972) and Spilton and Lee's (1977) analyses of successful and unsuccessful interactions provide further data concerning specific behaviors that are likely to elicit a listener response. Assessing a child's nonverbal, verbal, and interactional skills and/ or particular key behaviors will indicate instructional objectives. Training of speaker and/or listener skills may be necessary.

Parallel to the strategy of determining a normative level of performance, social validation can be used to assess a child's skill deficiency. Analysis of successful peer conversationalists not only indicates what skills to train but also provides standards for evaluating the success of training. Minkin et al. (1976) remediated conversational deficiencies of delinquent adolescents using a form of normative social validation. Their procedures are applicable to intervening with younger children. Observers first watched videotapes of typical junior high school and college students conversing. The tapes were scored in terms of the occurrence of questions, positive feedback, and time talked. A panel of adult judges watched the same tapes, rating each student's conversational skill on a 7-point bipolar scale. The correlations between ratings of skill and behaviors observed were: .70 for questions, .56 for feedback, and .43 for time talked. These data provided some content validity for selection of instructional targets. Minkin et al. (1976) then taught the delinquent adolescents to ask questions and provide feedback. Adult judges' rating of the adolescents' conversational skills averaged 2.8 prior to training and 4.7 after training. These judgments validated the increase in the subjects' conversational skills. The skills taught were based on behaviors displayed by typical peers.

Both the assessment of a child's conversational ability and the selection of critical target behaviors are facilitated by analysis of the skills of competent peers. Such an analysis can be used to determine what behaviors are typically displayed and/or what behaviors are most successful in eliciting a response from a peer, maintaining an interaction, and so forth. Alternatively, after selecting particular target behaviors, analysis of peer performance provides a measure of validity. Skills chosen for training should be those that will be

Table 3.   Conversational Skills

Skill	Definition
Nonverbal	
1. Interpersonal distance	a. The child maintains a distance of no greater than 5 feet between himself and the listener.
2. Nonverbal attention	a. The listener visually attends to be the speaker.
	b. The speaker visually attends to the listener. (Visual attention refers to directed gaze for a descernible duration—probably about 3 seconds or longer.)
3. Nonverbal contingent responses	a. The listener provides feedback such as nodding the head when the speaker is talking.
	b. The child complies with speaker verbalizations that request a nonverbal response or for which a nonverbal response is appropriate.
Verbal	
1. Vocal quality	a. The child's utterances are articulated clearly enough for listener comprehension.
	b. The child can repair unclear utterances.
	c. Utterances are loud enough to be easily heard by the listener.
2. Content	a. The child talks about the listener or the listener's activity or objects.
	b. The child talks about mutual activities.
	c. The child can maintain the topic introduced by the preceding speaker.
	d. The child indicates a change in topic.
	e. The child talks about present referents.
	f. The child talks about nonpresent referents.
	g. The child can attract the listener's attention by using utterances such as- -*hey, look, see, watch*, the listener's name, etc.
	h. The child can ask questions.
3. Contingent	a. The listener verbally responds to the speaker's utterance.
	b. The listener's response is related contextually to the speaker's utterance.
	c. The listener seeks clarification of unclear utterances.
	d. The listener provides short verbal feedback, such as *ok, uh-huh, yea* to speaker utterances.
Interactional	
1. Turn structure	a. Only one child speaks at a time.
	b. Each participant has a turn, i.e., turns alternate.
	c. The child in some way signals that a turn has ended (e.g., pausing, asking listener a question, gesturing), and may also select the next speaker.
	d. Each participant produces a similar number of utterances.
2. Social rules	a. The speaker's utterance is informative and relevant to the conversational context.
	b. The child demonstrates an awareness of the listener (by talking about the listener, by repairing unclear utterances, etc.).
	c. The speaker's communicative intentions are recognized by the listener.
	d. The participants in some way establish a common basis for conversing.

maintained by the behavior of other children in the group. The skills also should reflect actual communicative needs.

PEERS AS INTERVENTION AGENTS

Baseline data collection on the frequency of peer interaction and the conversational skills involved in interactions ideally involves a target child plus other, more competent children. This process is instrumental in setting functional training objectives, determining behavior norms, and providing evaluation standards. The social context in which the child needs to function is the focus of attention.

In determining a strategy for intervention, the social context should also be considered. Verbal interaction with peers is characterized by peers providing stimuli, responses, and feedback. Other children's verbal and nonverbal behavior provides discriminative stimuli, and their responses also provide reinforcement. Using adults as the primary trainers is likely to establish adults as discriminative stimuli and reinforcers. Transfer of stimulus control from the adult-child social context to the child-child social context may require additional intervention. Furthermore, if the child does display the trained behavior with peers, assurance that peers will provide feedback sufficient to maintain the behavior is not guaranteed.

Peer support for the acquisition and maintenance of a child's verbal skills is a component in the generalization of behavior. However, assuming that behavior elicited by adults and/or initiated to adults will also occur in contact with other children may be insufficient. In effect, one is training behavior in a given context and hoping that it generalizes (Stokes and Baer, 1977). Promoting language use in all social contexts requires consideration of the stimulus differences between "therapese" and "childrenese," the relative unpredictability of how peers will respond to another child's behavior, and the differences in training and talking environments (Hart and Rogers-Warren, 1978).

Peer involvement in the intervention process may be an effective means to establish training conditions that share common elements with the performance setting. Intervention that involves creating particular opportunities for interaction and modifying the behavior of peers can assure that a child uses language in peer- as well as adult-oriented interactions. Language-promoting characteristics of typical play interactions can be heightened by enlisting the aid of children. A peer may already be a source of reinforcement for the target child, or may become a reinforcing agent as a result of intervention. Hooking the child into the natural community of reinforcement will support maintenance of behavior.

The way in which a child or group of children is used as an intervention agent reflects the needs of the target child. The role of peers in the remediation of a child's performance or skill deficit is influenced by issues such as:

1. Do peers provide appropriate models of behavior?
2. Do peers provide sufficient opportunities for the child to interact?
3. Do peers provide reinforcement for the child's initiations?

Enhancing or establishing peers as models, peers as eliciting stimuli, and peers as reinforcers can be accomplished in a number of ways. Utilizing peer assemblies and peer confederates are described here as potential strategies for using peers as intervention agents.

Peer Assembly

Structuring of a peer group to provide language models and opportunities for interaction can be accomplished by grouping or assembling children in particular ways. The size and composition of a group are variables influencing the amount and quality of interaction. Creating an assembly to promote a desired rate or form of behavior is a way to use the typical behavior of skilled children in a therapeutic fashion.

A heterogeneous assembly provides a less skilled child with access to more skilled models. Fairly routine dialogue patterns in the course of play activities with telephones, dishes, puppets, and so on may readily be imitated. Such patterns are linguistically simple but do provide a turn-taking model and experience with reinforcing interactions. Peers also routinely model behaviors such as ways to attract another person's attention, appropriate interpersonal distance, and ways to seek clarification of utterances. The target child's response to such modeling may not always be immediate. Devoney et al. (1974) found that handicapped children's play contact with nonhandicapped children had a delayed effect. When the nonhandicapped children were *not* present, the play of the handicapped children was more advanced than it had been prior to exposure to the more skilled children. A child's inclusion in a group where peers model verbal interaction has potential for immediate display of behavior as well as later imitation.

The probability that observation of peer models will result in some form of imitation can be facilitated. Research on imitation learning suggests that imitation can readily be established as a response class (Baer and Sherman, 1964). Reinforcing peer behavior also promotes imitation (Bandura, 1965). Directing a child's attention to particular behaviors could also be used to prime observation of behaviors to imitate. Oden and Asher (1977) applied a coaching procedure that, with adaptations, might capitalize on models provided by peers in particular interactions. With third and fourth graders, they discussed examples of behaviors effective in interacting with peers. The children were then told to practice these behaviors. Coached observation of socially adept peers would provide more concrete examples for younger children.

Placing a less skilled child in a group with more skilled peers also increases the opportunities available for interacting. A language-delayed child in the company of other language-delayed children may not have opportunities to respond to verbal initiations and/or may not receive a response to his verbal initiations. In comparing triads of normally developing preschoolers and triads of language-delayed preschoolers, Paul (1979) found dramatic differences in the number of utterances children produced. For a 10-minute play session the normally developing children averaged 2–47 utterances, in contrast to an average of 0–3 utterances in triads of language-delayed children. After placing three language-delayed children in triads with two normally developing children, verbalizations increased for two out of the three children. Also, there was a dramatic increase in the number of utterances directed to a language-delayed child in the heterogeneous triad.

The therapeutic aspect of a particular assembly of children may not necessarily involve placing a less skilled child with more skilled peers. Furman et al. (1978) paired children with low rates of social interaction with a same-age peer or a younger peer for five play sessions. The children who played with a younger peer showed levels of behavior similar to that of their typical peers in the posttest observation. Children who participated in the play sessions with same-age or younger peers interacted twice as much as they did during pretest observations, with the greatest change in behavior occurring for children paired with a younger peer. A younger peer provided opportunities to initiate behavior and experience successful interactions. Imitation or modeling were perhaps not as operative as were opportunities to engage in particular behaviors.

Dyadic and triadic play sessions may create a situation that is particularly conducive to verbal interaction. The distraction provided by other children's play activities is reduced, as is the noise level. Also, a gregarious child might not normally seek out the quieter child in a larger group. Somewhat "out of necessity" the talkative child will be least likely to attempt interactions with the target child. Finally, attention and turn-taking behavior are simplified with fewer participants. Conversational interactions involving more than two participants can quickly become very complex.

For the child who is successful in verbally interacting only in a small group setting or only with particular people, a gradual fading in of other children may be an effective approach. Wulbert et al. (1973) modified a 6-year-old's verbal responsiveness by gradually fading in other adults to replace the child's mother. Finally, children from the potential first-grade classroom were faded in as a way to encourage the target child to speak in class.

Systematic modifications in the size of a group and/or in the skills of group members are potential ways to engineer peer support for behavior.

A cautionary note as to manipulating peer assembly to promote verbal interaction is warranted. Physical assembly does not assure social integration. Cross-group interaction does not always occur in preschool classrooms integrating normal and handicapped children (Cooke et al., 1977; Devoney et al., 1974; Guralnick, 1976; Porter et al., 1978; Snyder et al., 1977). Additional procedures may be necessary. However, the extent to which a particular peer assembly influences acquisition, maintenance, and generalization of behavior and contributes to the success of other procedures should be considered. Establishing homogeneous classrooms may place limitations on the extent to which a child's peers support and enhance behaviors. Peers who demand limited communication from other children and who do not respond to initiations can create conditions that extinguish behavior. Heterogeneous groupings of children with varied ability levels are more likely to provide models for less skilled children, as well as opportunities and reinforcement for social interaction.

Peer Confederates

Peer confederates or accomplices can be instrumental in modifying a socially withdrawn child's behavior. The success that children of varied ages and abilities have had as reinforcement agents or contingency managers (McGee et al., 1977) is impressive. Instructing another child to provide particular stimuli or to reinforce particular behaviors can be a means of increasing the verbal interaction of a target child.

Contingent peer attention may be particularly functional for a child with a performance deficit but adequate skills. Wahler's (1967) use of peer attention as a means to modify rates of doll play, aggressive behavior, cooperative behavior, speech, and passive behavior documents the effectiveness of differential peer attention. Proximity, joint or cooperative use of materials, nonverbal compliance, and so forth can be reinforced by peers as behaviors corollary to the actual verbal interaction. Promoting more parallel and cooperative play via differential attention may be the first goal of the peer confederate. In this way opportunities for interaction are provided that may subsequently elicit verbalizations. The peer reinforcement paradigm may require shaping of the target behavior. Or, the peer confederate can provide extrinsic reinforcement via tokens or edibles to increase a peer's existing low rate of verbal behavior. Alternatively, consistent or continuous reinforcement can be provided. A child's behavior may be occurring at a low rate because of inadvertant extinction.

Using a child as the contingency manager eliminates the need for one-to-one teacher involvement. The reinforcement value of peers is enhanced, and prior negative consequences (e.g., no response) for interacting with other children can be altered. A history of not receiving reinforcement from peers may typify the child whose speech is difficult to comprehend. The peer confederate who is given a special role and/or additional reinforcement may also find interacting with the target child more positive.

Child confederates can be instructed to provide particular stimuli. Strain et al. (1977) gave one member of a triad the role of initiating behavior at a high rate. The positive social behavior of the other members of the triad increased, with the greatest change occurring in verbal behavior. Initiations increased as well as responses. Strain (1977) successfully replicated the procedure. Finally, in comparing using peers to initiate social interaction with using peers to prompt and reinforce interaction Strain et al. (1979) found both procedures equally effective.

An extension of Strain and his colleagues' use of peer confederates would be to instruct peers to initiate particular kinds of behavior. A specific question form, mand for a response, or model of a language response may be presented by a peer as effectively as by an adult. This use of a peer confederate is parallel to using a peer as a trainer. Peer presentation of stimuli in a tutoring situation may promote generalization of behavior beyond the intervention situation. Teacher time spent in training the peer confederate or prompting the peer's behavior may not represent a savings in teacher one-to-one training time. However, the peer confederate can become a cue or discriminative stimulus for behavior. Stokes and Baer (1977) found that the physical presence of the peer tutor promoted the target child's display of the learned behavior in probes occurring outside of the training situation. The extent to which a peer confederate actively participates in language training and then functions as a discriminative stimulus for behavior is subject to empirical demonstration. Small-group language training sessions provide an effective, efficient alternative to one-to-one training. In addition the group experience can be designed so as to include structured practice in interacting with peers. The similarity between training interactions and naturally occurring classroom interactions is thus heightened.

The use of peers as confederates provides a means to engineer modeling of behavior, provision of particular stimuli, and the presentation of feedback. For children with limited histories of reinforcement for interacting with peers, such an approach helps establish positive reinforcement conditions. The target child-peer confederate relationship will ideally lead to an expansion in general peer contact as a result of spillover effects.

SUMMARY AND RECOMMENDATIONS

Teaching technology, and operant methods specifically, is not lacking in ways to teach language skills to children. However, the determination of content is a critical issue. A child may learn to use the proper syntactical form and learn to express a variety of semantic relations and still not be a competent speaker. A child must be able to express a variety of communicative functions in various situations. The social demands embedded in communicative situations point to the need to teach peer-directed and not just adult-directed language.

The child who is not interacting with peers sufficiently may not generalize behavior from adult-child to child-child interaction. Or, different behavior may be critical in different contexts. The intervention process in either case should include:

1. Assessment of normative or typical child-child interaction in terms of rate and content.
2. Evaluation of the target child's behavior as compared to the norm.
3. Selection of target behaviors.
4. Establishment of a training or talking environment where the target child is given opportunities for positive interaction with peers.
5. Evaluation of training impact on the target child with reference to normative child-child interaction.

Utilizing children in the intervention process assures that there is social validity to instructional content. Maintenance of behavior is supported by concomitant changes in nontarget children's behavior when they are given active roles in the remediation of peer behavior.

REFERENCES

Allen, K. E., Hart, B., Buell, J. S., Harris, R. F., and Wolf, M. M. 1964. Effects of social reinforcement on isolate behavior of a nursery school child. Child Dev. 35:511–518.

Baer, D. M., and Sherman, J. A. 1964. Reinforcement control of generalized imitation in young children. J. Exp. Psychol. 1:37–49.

Bandura, A. 1965. Influences of model's reinforcement contingencies on the acquisition of imitative responses. J. Pers. Soc. Psychol. 1:589–595.

Bates, E. 1975. Peer relations and the acquisition of language. In M. Lewis and L. A. Rosenblum (eds.), Friendship and Peer Relations. Wiley & Sons, New York.

Cooke, T. B., Apolloni, T., and Cooke, S. A. 1977. Normal preschool children as behavioral models for retarded peers. Except. Child. 43:531–532.

Devoney, C., Guralnick, M. J., and Rubin, H. 1974. Integrating handicapped and nonhandicapped preschool children: Effects on social play. Child. Educ. 50:360–364.

Furman, W., Rahe, D. F., and Hartup, W. W. 1978. Rehabilitation of socially withdrawn preschool children through mixed-age and same-age socialization. Unpublished manuscript, University of Minnesota, Minneapolis.

Garvey, C. 1977. Play. Harvard University Press, Cambridge, MA.

Garvey, C., and Hogan, R. 1973. Social speech and social interaction: Egocentrism revisited. Child Dev. 44:562–566.

Goetz, E. M., Thomson, C. L., and Etzel, B. C. 1975. An analysis of direct and indirect teacher attention and primes in the modification of child and social behavior: A case study. Merrill-Palmer Q. 21:55–65.

Greenwood, C. R., Walker, H. M., Todd, N. M., and Hops, H. 1977. Normative and descriptive analyses of preschool free play social interactions. Report No. 29, Center at Oregon for Research in the Behavioral Education of the Handicapped, Eugene, Oregon.

Guralnick, M. J. 1976. The value of integrating handicapped and nonhandicapped preschool children. Am. J. Orthopsychiatry 40:236–245.

Hart, B., and Risley, T. R. 1980. In vivo language intervention: Unanticipated general effects. J. Appl. Behav. Anal. 13:407–432.

Hart, B., and Rogers-Warren, A. K. 1978. A milieu approach to teaching language. In R. L. Schiefelbusch (ed.), Language Intervention Strategies. University Park Press, Baltimore.

Hartup, W. W. 1976. Peer interaction and the behavioral development of the individual child. In E. Schopler and R. J. Reichler (eds.), Psychopathology and Child Development. Plenum Press, New York.

Holland, A. L. 1975. Language therapy for children: Some thoughts on context and content. J. Speech Hear. Disord. 40:514–523.

Kohn, M. 1966. The child as a determinant of his peers' approach to him. J. Genet. Psychol. 109:91–100.

Lee, L. C., Brody, L., Matthews, W. S., and Palmquist, W. 1974. The development of interpersonal competence: Strategies of social exchange. Symposium presented at the annual convention of the American Psychological Association, New Orleans.

Lewis, M. M. 1951. Infant Speech. Humanities Press, New York.

McGee, C. S., Kauffman, J. M., and Nussen, J. L. 1977. Children as therapeutic change agents: Reinforcement intervention paradigms. Rev. Educ. Res. 47:451–477.

Minkin, M., Braukmann, C. J., Minkin, B. L., Timbers, G. C., Timbers, B. J., Fixsen, D. L., Phillips, E. L., and Wolf, M. M. 1976. The social validation and training of conversational skills. J. Appl. Behav. Anal. 9:127–140.

Mueller, E. 1972. The maintenance of verbal exchanges between young children. Child Dev. 43:930–938.

Oden, S., and Asher, S. R. 1977. Coaching children in social skills for friendship making. Child Dev. 48:495–506.

Parten, M. B. 1933. Social play among preschool children. J. Abnorm. Soc. Psychol. 28:136–147.

Paul, L. 1979. Social language and assembly effects. Unpublished Ph.D. dissertation, University of Kansas, Lawrence.

Paul, L., and McQuarter, R. W. 1979. A comparative analysis of peer directed talking of normal and language delayed preschoolers. Poster presented at the Annual Convention of the Association for Behavior Analysis, Dearborn, MI.

Porter, R. H., Ramsey, B., Tremblay, A., Iacobo, M., and Crawley, S. 1978. Social interactions in heterogeneous groups of retarded and normally developing children: An observational study. In G. P. Sackett and H. C. Haywood (eds.),

Observing Behavior, Vol. 1: Theory and Applications in Mental Retardation. University Park Press, Baltimore.

Quilitch, R. H., and Risley, T. R. 1973. The effect of play materials on social play. J. Appl. Behav. Anal. 6:573–578.

Robinson, E. W., and Conrad, H. S. 1933. The reliability of observations of talkativeness and social contact among nursery school children by the "short time sample" technique. J. Exp. Educ. 2:161–165.

Rubin, K. H. 1976. Social interaction and egocentrism in preschoolers. J. Genet. Psychol. 129:121–124.

Salzinger, S., Patenaude, J. W., and Lichtenstein, A. 1978. A descriptive study of the effects of selected variables on the communicative speech of preschool children. In D. Aaronson and R. W. Reiber (eds.), Developmental Psycholinguistics and Communication Disorders. Academic Press, New York.

Slater, E. 1939. Types, levels and irregularities of response to a nursery school situation observed with special reference to the home environment. Monogr. Soc. Res. Child Dev. 4:21.

Snyder, L., Apollini, T., and Cooke, T. P. 1977. Integrated settings at the early childhood level: The role of nonretarded peers. Except. Child. 43:262–266.

Spilton, D., and Lee, L. C. 1977. Some determinants of effective communication in four-year-olds. Child Dev. 48:968–977.

Stokes, T. F., and Baer, D. M. 1977. An implicit technology of generalization. J. Appl. Behav. Anal. 10:349–367.

Strain, P. S. 1977. An experimental analysis of peer social initiations on the behavior of withdrawn preschool children: Some training and generalization effects. J. Abnorm. Child Psychol. 5:445–455.

Strain, P. S., Cooke, T. P., and Apolloni, T. 1976. Teaching Exceptional Children: Assessing and Modifying Social Behavior. Academic Press, New York.

Strain, P. S., Shores, R. E., and Timm, M. A. 1977. Effects of peer social initiations on the behavior of withdrawn preschool children. J. Appl. Behav. Anal. 10:289–298.

Strain, P. S., Kerr, M. M., and Ragland, E. U. 1979. Effects of peer-mediated social initiations and prompting/reinforcement procedures on the social behavior of autistic children. J. Autism Dev. Disord. 9:41–54.

Updegraff, R., and Herbst, E. K. 1933. An experimental study of the social behavior stimulated in young children by certain play materials. J. Genet. Psychol. 42:372–390.

Van Alstyne, D. 1932. Play Behavior and Choice of Play Materials of Preschool Children. University of Chicago Press, Chicago.

Wahler, R. G. 1967. Child-child interactions in free field settings: Some experimental analyses. J. Exp. Child Psychol. 5:278–293.

Walker, H. M., and Hops, H. 1976. Use of normative peer data as a standard for evaluating classroom treatment effects. J. Appl. Behav. Anal. 9:159–168.

Wulbert, M., Nyman, B. A., Snow, D., and Owen, Y. 1973. The efficacy of stimulus fading and contingency management in the treatment of elective mutism: A case study. J. Appl. Behav. Anal. 6:435–441.

Yarrow, M. R. 1975. Some perspective on research on peer relations. In M. Lewis and L. A. Rosenblum (eds.), Friendship and Peer Relations. Wiley, New York.

chapter 11

Programming Teacher Support for Functional Language

C. Robert Campbell

Rainbows United, Inc.
Wichita, Kansas

and

Kathleen Stremel-Campbell

Teaching Research Division
Oregon State System of Higher Education
Monmouth, Oregon

and

Ann K. Rogers-Warren

Department of Special Education
George Peabody College
Vanderbilt University

LEGISLATIVE AND TECHNICAL DEVELOPMENTS   311
    Legislative Contribution   312
    Technical Contribution   312

**THE TEACHER'S ROLE IN SERVICE DELIVERY
MODELS   314**

**THE TEACHER'S RESPONSIBILITY FOR COMMUNICATION
LANGUAGE INSTRUCTION   315**
    Teacher as Communication/Language Facilitator   320
    Teacher as Primary Trainer   324
    Teacher as the Only Trainer Without Supportive Services   326

STRATEGIES FOR TEACHER TRAINING   329
    Analysis of Teacher and Student Evaluations   330
    When Direct Training is Necessary   332

SUMMARY AND CONCLUSIONS   338

REFERENCES   338

The previous chapters have introduced the reader to the functional elements of teaching language-deficient students. The authors included identification of appropriate programs, implementation of specific acquisition and generalization strategies, and systematic measurement of the effects of intervention on each student. In addition, the importance of parents, peers, and significant others who may impact on the student's communication environment has been emphasized. The focus of this chapter is the role of the teacher in delivering language and communication instruction to the handicapped student. For the purpose of this chapter, a teacher is any professional or paraprofessional engaged in the delivery of instruction in the student's home, school, work, or other living environment. Thus, the "teacher" may be a classroom teacher, workshop supervisor, group home trainer, teaching assistant, or any significant other whose interaction with the handicapped student provides opportunities for the student to learn or practice language or communication skills.

This chapter emphasizes the importance of the teacher's role as a language and communication trainer utilizing the techniques and strategies proposed in other chapters. A number of strategies for increasing the teacher's competencies as a communication trainer are examined. The chapter is divided into four sections focusing on:

1. The legislative and technical developments that have changed the teacher's role in communication training.
2. A framework for determining the teacher's role in specific service delivery models.
3. The teacher's responsibility in implementing the instructional and measurement techniques described in this text.
4. Strategies for training teachers, including identification of resources and specific training procedures.

LEGISLATIVE AND TECHNICAL DEVELOPMENTS

The teacher's role in language and communication intervention has changed dramatically in the past 10 years. Historically, language and communication intervention focused more on clinical delivery (in one-to-one settings) than on teaching in natural environments, more on the development of language content than on its integration in social interaction, and more on acquisition of language than on extension of new communication skills under nonacquisition conditions. Two key factors have served to refocus the teacher's role in communication: legislation and increased technology.

This paper was written while the senior author was affiliated with the Teaching Research Division, Oregon State System of Higher Education, Monmouth, OR.

Legislative Contribution

Public Law 94-142 is by now a well-established force in securing the educational rights of the handicapped student. Two regulations within this law have had particular impact on the teacher's role in providing communication instruction to the handicapped: the Least Restrictive Education (LRE) clause and the provision for related services (e.g., speech and language services) in meeting the specific needs of handicapped students.

The LRE requirement of P.L. 94-142 has resulted in the placement of many handicapped students in integrated or mainstream environments. A recent report to Congress on the implementation of P.L. 94-142 (U.S. Department of Education, 1981) indicated that, across all handicapping conditions, approximately 96% of all handicapped children and youth ages 3–21 were served in regular or special classrooms. In addition, nearly 99% of those students identified as speech impaired were being served in regular or special classrooms. Such data demonstrate the need for teachers to have specific competencies in speech and language therapy. Furthermore, the LRC clause has effected delivery of speech and language as a related service, thus increasing the probability that these services will be provided under less restrictive conditions (i.e., in classrooms).

Individual Educational Plan (IEP) data presented in the U.S. Department of Education report revealed that, of those IEPs containing performance information about specific academic or functional areas, 33% described needs in the area of speech/language. Twenty-eight percent of IEPs with performance information contained short-term objectives in the area of speech/language.

Whereas legislative mandates have set the stage for increased teacher responsibility for communication programming and a less clinically oriented view of related services, recent technical advancements greatly facilitated the functional implementation of the LRE clause and related provisions of P.L. 94-142.

Technical Contribution

The role of the teacher in programming and facilitating speech, language, and communication training has increased as a result of several technical advancements. Compelling arguments for the importance of teaching communication skills in the context of their subsequent use have been made (see Mahoney, 1975; McLean and Snyder-McLean, 1978). Empirical evidence for context-oriented instruction is emerging (e.g., Campbell and Stremel-Campbell, 1982). In addition, studies describing the acquisition of language and communication in context have suggested a need for more functional training in everyday communication settings (Warren and Rogers-Warren, 1980). A number of authors have stressed systemically programming generalization as a part of the acquisition process (see Stremel-Campbell and Campbell, this volume). Training communication in the context of its subsequent use increases the probability that the student's language will be functional and will generalize to other persons, settings, and similar behaviors. Functional use and generalization are much less likely when language and communication objectives are not functional or when training is conducted under isolated conditions.

The teacher's role in programming language and communication is both functional and pragmatic. First, the teacher is likely to have the most information concerning the functional opportunities for communication during the student's instructional day. Second, it may not be possible to duplicate these functional opportunities in an isolated training setting. From a pragmatic point of view, the teacher is the professional most likely to have time to conduct language and communication in a functional context. From an economic point of view, it may be impossible to provide a speech pathologist to deliver the type and amount of individual instruction mandated by current best-practices literature. Often, adequate personnel are not available for traditional one-to-one training, even if they were desirable.

To summarize, the teacher is critical in language and communication intervention. The reasons are numerous:

1. More children are being served than ever before in less restrictive environments.
2. Speech, language, and communication needs of the handicapped individual are among the most frequent IEP objectives (over 25% of all IEP objectives are communication oriented).
3. The teacher is most likely to know the students' functional needs and the appropriate context for programming.
4. Clinical or isolated training settings are unlikely to duplicate the natural conditions that promote acquisition, maintenance, and generalization of language and communication skills.
5. Adequate numbers of language and communication specialists are not available to provide the intensity of individual instruction indicated as necessary in recent empirical studies.

These factors present considerable challenge to those concerned with ensuring that teachers are prepared to provide communication training. Sailor and Haring (1977) addressed this issue, proposing that evaluation systems must be developed to determine: 1) the presence or absence of speech, language, and communication services; 2) the model in which services are to best be delivered; and 3) the extent to which personnel need and demonstrate competencies for teaching speech, language, and communication skills. The remainder of this chapter proposes a functional framework to respond to these issues.

THE TEACHER'S ROLE IN SERVICE DELIVERY MODELS

Several approaches to the delivery of related services have been proposed. In general, these approaches fall into two broad categories: 1) models that isolate services and professionals; 2) those that integrate the various services and professionals delivering instruction to the handicapped student. Sternate et al. (1977) have examined both types in relation to occupational and physical therapy services.

In terms of service delivery, the isolated model assumes that:

1. Assessment information gained in isolated settings (i.e., a therapy room) validly represents the student's performance in more natural settings.
2. Episodic therapy will result in substantial skill gains.
3. Skills acquired in a setting isolated from the settings where those skills are to be used will generalize to those settings.

In contrast, the integrated approach assumes:

1. Assessment yields more functional information about skills if conducted in the context of subsequent skill use.
2. Training should be conducted throughout the day when the need for newly learned skills naturally occurs.
3. Generalization is promoted when skills to be used in classroom, home, play, or work environments are taught in those environments.

Just as Sternate et al. advocated using the integrated model with students with a motoric handicap, a similar approach for handicapped students with speech, language, and communication deficiencies is recommended here.

The integration of related services into the total instructional plan for a handicapped student can be accomplished through either an interdisciplinary/multidisciplinary or a transdisciplinary approach (McCormick and Goldman, 1979). Both models emphasize student assessment and development of a coordinated plan. However, only the transdisciplinary model addresses the issue of instructional delivery. In interdisciplinary/multidisciplinary models, students leave the classroom for instruction by several professionals from different fields. The transdisciplinary model prescribes the assignment of one individual to deliver instructional programming, after assessment and consultation from professionals in other disciplines has occurred. The person most likely to assume responsibility for instructional delivery in a transdisciplinary model is the classroom teacher (Wilcox and Sailor, 1980). Instruction is conducted by the teacher in the classroom. When a specialist other than the teacher works directly with students, this work also occurs in the classroom. A teacher must have considerable expertise as a manager and have skills in several related service areas to assume responsibility for transdisciplinary services (Bricker, 1976; Lyon and Lyon, 1980).

The role of the teacher is one of an educational synthesizer (Bricker, 1976). The educational synthesizer is an individual who can select relevant input from specialists in a variety of instructional domains and integrate this information into an instructional plan for a given student. Bricker describes the functions of the educational synthesizer as:

> . . . acquiring, organizing, evaluating, and implementing (in a practical sense) inputs from disciplines that either are not or cannot be included as daily, integral parts of an intervention program. The educational synthesizer becomes the pivotal force in the overall educational program by seeking and coordinating the necessary resources to produce growth and change in the severely impaired child. (p. 88)

In Bricker's approach to transdisciplinary service delivery, the educational synthesizer is typically the classroom teacher because teachers have the most contact with individual students. To play this role, teachers must have considerable cooperation from other specialists. Lyon and Lyon (1980) proposed an approach to this cooperative team planning and delivery called "role release." The role release concept suggests the sharing of some roles and responsibilities by related service personnel. For example, if the speech pathologist has implemented a program to increase question-asking, the teacher, the physical therapist, and the occupational therapist might be expected to prompt question-asking from the student as well. Role release may be as simple as sharing general information about schedules or routines, or as complex as training professionals in other disciplines to conduct a specific program.

Implementing a transdisciplinary approach requires careful planning by each professional responsible for the student's total program. To ensure adequate service delivery, there must be cross-training of personnel. In planning integrated speech, language, and communication training, it is necessary to evaluate the assessment, the program implementation, and the instructional needs of the student, teacher, and related service professionals who may be asked to train the student.

THE TEACHER'S RESPONSIBILITY FOR COMMUNICATION LANGUAGE INSTRUCTION

Three models of "teachers as language trainers" are presented. Each model is defined in relation to the activities that the teacher and the speech/language clinician must perform to meet the communication/language needs of the language-deficient student. The three models are:

1. The teacher as facilitator, with the clinician as the primary trainer.
2. The teacher as primary trainer, with the clinician as consultant.
3. The teacher as primary trainer without functional resources.

Selection of a model usually is based on a school district's resources, the teacher's training, and the speech clinician's preferred therapy plan. However, choice of a model should be based on the skills and needs of the student as well.

Table 1 outlines some general areas of language/communication delay and suggested models of intervention. Selection of a model should be based on specific needs of each individual student in order that the teacher's and speech clinician's time and skills are used most effectively and efficiently. Irrespective of the model selected, either the teacher and/or the speech/language clinician must have the following information: 1) what to train (content); 2) how to train (procedures and strategies); and 3) how to measure the effects of training.

Figure 1 summarizes the critical components in communication/language development and intervention. The emphasis of any one component depends upon the functional level and the age of the student. The relationship of a student's cognitive skills and social interaction skills to communication and language development are well documented (Bruner, 1975; Mahoney, 1975; McLean and Snyder-McLean, 1978; Miller et al., 1977; Nelson, 1974). Both the teacher and speech/language clinician must have an awareness and understanding of these components, regardless of who serves as the student's primary trainer. Parents and teachers must also understand that a child learns to communicate (by pointing, showing gestures) prior to learning

Table 1.   Specific Model of Training Based upon the Individual Student

Critical area of intervention	Handicapping condition	Suggested model
Communication	Severely handicapped	Teacher as primary trainer; speech clinician as consultant
	Mildly handicapped	Teacher as primary trainer; speech clinician as co-trainer or consultant
Language	Severely handicapped	Teacher as primary trainer; speech clinician as consultant
	Moderately handicapped	Teacher as primary trainer or as facilitator; speech clinician as consultant or as co-trainer
Speech	Severely handicapped	Teacher as primary trainer
Speech (articulation)	Mildly handicapped or speech delayed	Teacher as facilitator; speech clinician as primary trainer

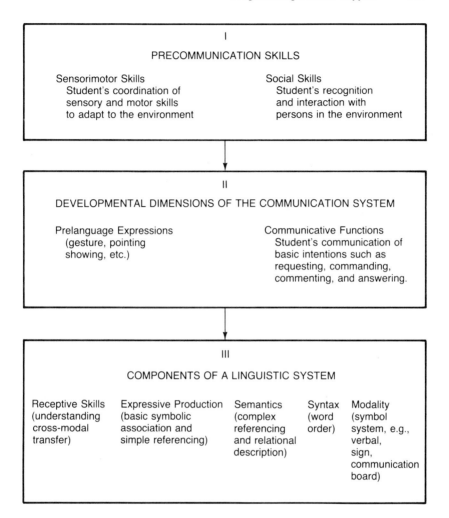

Figure 1. Critical components for communication and language interventions.

a formal language system (such as speech, signs, communication boards) and that a child can demonstrate the use of language without speech. Parents and teachers should have input into what is being trained regardless of the training model selected.

Once the basic needs of an individual student have been determined, it is important for the administration, the teacher, and the speech/language clinician to have a clear understanding of who has the responsibility for the major activities that should be carried out for each individual student or group of students. Table 2 outlines these activities according to the three basic models of training communication and the responsibilities of completing

Table 2. Activities Necessary for Communication Programming

Activities necessary	Teacher as facilitator		Teacher as primary trainer		Teacher as only trainer checklist	
	Teacher	Clinician	Teacher	Clinician	Teacher skills	Teacher needs
Assessment						
1. Conduct assessment in the critical areas for communication.	minor	major	minor	major		
2. Send assessment summary to parents/teacher prior to IEP conference.		major		major		
3. Get information from parents/teacher relative to communication functioning within the natural environment.		major		major		
4. Use assessment results for organizing possible objectives for IEP development.	minor	major	minor	major		
Individual Educational Plan						
1. Develop long-term IEP objectives based on assessment data and parent input.	minor	major	minor	major		
2. Develop short-term IEP objectives that are directly related to long-term objectives.	minor	major	minor	major		
3. Prioritize (with parents) short-term objectives based on skill area and student need.	major	major	major	major		

4. Determine evaluation criteria, type of programming, type of data to be collected, and schedule of programming.

Implementation/Evaluation

Task				
4. Determine evaluation criteria, type of programming, type of data to be collected, and schedule of programming.	minor	major	major	major
1. Select type of training format (one-to-one, group, incidental, combination).	minor	major	major	major
2. Select content for program based on functionality.	minor	major	major	minor
3. Determine activities for training.	minor	major	major	minor
4. Select sequence of content for programming based on specific discriminations involved.	minor	major	minor	major
5. Write/select individualized programs.	minor	major	minor	major
6. Implement programs as written in IEP.	minor	major	major	minor
7. Facilitate generalization to natural environments.	major	major	major	minor
8. Collect ongoing data.	minor	major	major	daily
9. Monitor student progress.	minor	major	major	regularly scheduled
10. Modify program based on student data and generalization outcomes.	minor	major	major	major
11. Assist parents in setting up home programs.	minor	major	major	minor
12. Report student progress to parents on a regular basis.	minor	major	major	minor

those activities. The responsibilities listed under each model are provided only as examples because each model is somewhat flexible. Table 2 can be used as a checklist by administrators, teachers, and speech/language clinicians in determining who is responsible for each specific training activity. If the teacher is solely responsible for the individual student's communication and language programming, Table 2 can be used as a simple needs assessment for the teacher to determine what type and level of in-service training is necessary before he or she can implement and complete these activities. Each of the models is described and examples are provided according to the level of the student.

Teacher as Communication/Language Facilitator

The speech/language clinician has the major responsibilities for programming communication and language in this model. These responsibilities include assessment, IEP development, and program implementation and evaluation.

Assessment The speech/language clinician will conduct an educational assessment for the purpose of IEP development and program implementation. It is important to thoroughly evaluate the student in each critical communication area (see Figure 1) in order to recommend to the administration, the parents, and the teacher the best training model based on the student's needs and skills. The speech/language clinician often will obtain information from the parents and teacher to determine the student's communication and language functioning in natural environments (i.e., home and school). More formal assessments may include gathering spontaneous prelinguistic (gestures, pointing, showing) and linguistic samples within the home and school environments. The speech/language clinician should summarize the results of the assessment for parents and teacher prior to the IEP conference and encourage the parents and teacher to provide input into developing long-term communication and language objectives.

Once the student has been assessed, recommendations should be made concerning the type of model for a specific student. For example, if the results of an assessment indicate that a student is using intelligible one-word utterances to communicate requests, statements, protests, and questions ("Cracker," "More," "Book," "Mine," "No") and is demonstrating age-appropriate cognitive skills, the clinician's summary of possible IEP objectives and training suggestions may include the following:

1. Expand noun and verb vocabulary.
2. Train adjectives, adverbs, and possessive pronouns (in receptive and expressive modes).
3. Train different two-word utterances that reflect different meanings ("Eat cracker," "My cracker," "No cracker") for different communication functions (as requests, as statements, as questions).
4. Facilitate generalization of training objectives to the natural environment.

This student's primary delay or deficit at this point is not communication or speech but language (including vocabulary, semantics-meaning, and syntax-word order).

Individual Educational Plans   The speech/language clinician is the major representative of the student's communication skills and needs in this model. The clinician's responsibilities include sharing assessment information with parents, teachers, and other resource personnel, synthesizing the information and their input into clear and concise long-term and short-term objectives, and facilitating setting priorities among overall academic objectives and communication objectives. The teacher also plays an important role in prioritizing communication goals in relation to the student's other educational or vocational/living skills goals.

The evaluation criteria (acquisition and/or generalization), the type of programming, the type of data to be collected, and the scheduling of the training program should be discussed by the clinician, teacher, and parent. For example, the parent and teacher may feel that the evaluation criteria should include generalization of the trained skill to the home and school environments even though this may mean that they would be responsible for collecting data in those environments. Also, if language training were a priority objective and the clinician's caseload allowed her to conduct one-to-one programming only once a week, the teacher may take a more active role in facilitating language by conducting additional one-to-one or group programs.

Implementation/Evaluation   The assessment of activities in the two training models "teacher as facilitator" and "teacher as primary trainer" vary once initial assessment and initial IEP planning is completed. When the teacher is the facilitator of language in the classroom setting, the speech/language clinician determines the direct training format (one-to-one or group instruction) and the context of training. After the training content (the specific structures and/or words) has been selected with teacher and parent input, the clinician must train the teacher to facilitate language training and generalization.

To be a facilitator, the teacher must be able to answer three basic questions:

1. What classroom activities will serve as the best facilitating activities?
2. Specifically, what type of language/communication utterances will be targeted within those activities?
3. Which procedures or strategies are appropriate to facilitate the student's language?

The speech/language clinician should train and determine if the teacher demonstrates the specific competencies necessary to facilitate the student's language. For example, if the teacher is facilitating a student's use of two-word utterances and the expansion of the student's basic vocabulary, the teacher and the clinician would decide which activities would provide the most opportunities for communication in regard to the student's training needs. The clinician may also provide a list of specific vocabulary words and two-word utterances to be targeted within the activity.

EXAMPLE   Facilitating Language for a Preschool Student

Occasion	*Expand Vocabulary*	*Training Two-Word Utterances/Phrases*
During snack time	"Pour"	"Want (noun)"
	"Get"	"Want more"
	"Throw away"	"More please"
	"Put away"	"Cracker please"
	"Clean"	"Eat cracker"
	"Dirty"	"Drink juice"
	"Napkin"	
	"Knife"	
During free play	Names of peers	"Want _____"
	"Hat"	"Go play"
	"Shoe"	"Play (with) hat"
	"Sand"	"Play (with) Mark"
	"Light/Bright"	"Get doll"
	"Make"	
	"Get"	
	"Put away"	
	"Pour"	
	"Put on"	

The strategies and procedures used for facilitating language depend on the theoretical approach of the educational program and speech/language clinician's and teacher's preferences as well as the level of the student (see Hart, this volume). At a minimum, the teacher must have mastered several basic principles for language facilitation:

1. Arrange the environment so that the student *needs* to communicate.
2. Provide the cues that the student has been trained to respond to.
3. Provide cues that support the student's response, without pre-empting or "helping" the student too much.
4. Provide general positive feedback to the student that reinforces communication attempts.
5. Provide specific feedback to the student that supports use of the targeted structures.
6. Expand the student's responses within the immediate communication context as a model of more complex language (e.g., "*More* crackers").
7. Arrange the daily classroom routine to promote language use.

8. Arrange the environment so that the student must communicate with peers.
9. Consequate the student's communication/language in a natural, communicative, and conversational manner.

The following example illustrates a "minimal assist" strategy for training a teacher to facilitate a preschool student's use of two-word utterances during a snack-time activity.

EXAMPLE   Sequence of Hard-to-Easy Cues

1. *Situation only—focused attention*   Hold up the juice; look at the student. Wait approximately three seconds. If the student does not initiate saying "Want juice," provide an indirect cue.
2. *Indirect cue*   Say "Kim, it's your turn," or "We have juice today." If the student does not respond within 3 seconds, present a more direct cue. If the student is acquiring the specific utterance, different types of support prompts may be utilized.
3. *Direct cue without a prompt*   "Kim, what do you want? Say the whole thing"; the student says "Want juice." One- and two-word responses are "natural" responses to many questions [e.g., "Do you want milk?" ("Please"), "What do you want?" ("Milk")]. The teacher must let the student know that a longer response is required.
4. *Direct cue with prompts*   "Kim, tell me what you want." The teacher uses a gesture prompt for ". . . want _____." The student is required to complete the teacher's sentence ("You _____ _____") and say or sign "Want juice."
5. *Model the response*   The teacher models a two-word response ("Kim, tell me what you want; say, *want juice*"). If the student does not respond with a two-word utterance, the teacher provides more support: "Say, *want*" (student signs or says "Want"; teacher then says "Juice" and the student signs or says "*Juice*."
6. *Physically assist the student*   For students who are using signs or communication boards; the teacher assists the student in making the correct response if the student is having difficulty imitating the sign or pointing to the correct picture of symbol.

Once the teacher is familiar with the student's level of responding in particular situations, the teacher provides a cue (support) one step above the one in which the student can respond. For example, if the student usually uses a two-word response only when a direct cue is provided, the teacher will initially provide an indirect cue. This provides the student with the opportunity to respond with less support. It is important that the teacher learn to provide cues that facilitate the student's initiation of communication/language as well as responses.

Teachers who do an excellent job of facilitating a student's language demonstrate three major skills: 1) arranging the environment within all activities to promote the student's use of language; 2) communicating with the student in a normal manner for a speaker-listener interaction; and 3) observing and utilizing a student's prelinguistic (gesture, pointing, showing) and linguistic initiations and responses to extend and expand the student's language.

Teachers are often the primary contact between parents and the student's educational program. Thus, teachers can also serve as facilitators by suggesting ways parents can provide opportunities for language to occur at home and by encouraging parents to observe programming in school.

Many speech/language clinicians who conduct direct language programs will not have the time to measure the effects of training (i.e., the generalization of trained language to the classroom and home environment). Teachers and parents may be requested to measure generalization to these environments. Measurements may include intermittent language samples, frequency counts for targeted language objectives, and a simple checklist to determine if the student is using trained words or utterances in the natural environment (see Stremel-Campbell and Campbell, this volume). When teachers and parents collect generalization data, the speech/language clinician is responsible for developing the data collection forms and procedures and for training the use of those forms and procedures.

If teachers are to be effective facilitators, the speech/language clinician and teacher must have regular, open communication about the student's program and progress. Such communication may involve a written system and/or regularly scheduled meetings or phone calls. Student programs should be reviewed at least biweekly. It is critical that the speech/language clinician frequently observes the student and teacher in the classroom to: 1) provide positive feedback to the teacher; 2) determine if additional programming suggestions are necessary; 3) determine if modifications need to be made; and 4) answer any immediate questions that the teacher may have. Teachers who facilitate language use the classroom can also provide the speech/language clinician with information about the student's skills and needs that may improve the clinician's programming for that child.

Teacher as Primary Trainer

For the most part, the assessment and IEP activities and responsibilities of the teacher who serves as a primary trainer do not differ from those previously described for the teacher who serves as a facilitator. The teacher who is familiar with the student, the student's language needs, and language development may provide more input into the assessment and IEP process. The major difference between the first model (teacher as facilitator) and the teacher-as-primary-trainer model occurs at the level of program implementation and evaluation.

The teacher and the speech/language clinician as a team should make decisions concerning the type of training format and the content for the program. For example, the speech/language clinician may review the teacher's word list for initial vocabulary for a particular student and provide feedback to the teacher. The clinician may suggest additions or revisions based on her knowledge of programming communication or the student's particular needs and skills.

EXAMPLE   **Initial Functional Vocabulary (Signing) Determined by Teacher and Parent**

Signs	*Speech Clinician's Feedback*
1. CRACKER	
2. JUICE	
3. APPLE	Signs look too much alike for initial vocabulary
4. ORANGE	
5. COOKIE	Sounds too similar to cracker; also may be confusing conceptually
6. PLAY	May be too difficult in terms of sign movement
7. HELP	
8. MORE	
9. MOM	
10. FINISH	

The speech/language clinician should serve as a consultant to the teacher to provide guidelines for content selection and determining acceptable approximations of initial speech or sign acquisition. For example, in planning the initial content for a student's "Identifies Common Objects" program, the speech consultant's guidelines could include: 1) do not select words/objects that look alike (*apple* and *ball*); 2) do not select words that sound alike (*comb* and *coat*); 3) do not select signs that are similar (*paper* and *cheese*); and 4) do not select words that are used for similar purposes (*spoon* and *fork*). At some point, the student will need to identify (discriminate) objects and actions that sound similar, look similar, and are used for similar purposes, but initially similarities may confuse the student and result in more errors.

The speech/language clinician is responsible for selecting an appropriate language curriculum for the student or for writing an individual program, and for demonstrating to the teacher how the program is to be conducted. Once the teacher demonstrates the competencies necessary to conduct the program, she becomes responsible for implementing the program and conducting training according to the schedule outlined in the student's IEP. The teacher who serves as the primary trainer usually is responsible for collecting data as a basis for programming decisions.

Because programming decisions (e.g., continue program, modify program, program completed, drop program) should be made on a daily basis, the teacher must assume responsibility for most decisions. The speech/language clinician serves as a consultant by providing guidelines or rules for the teacher to use in making these decisions and by regularly reviewing students' progress in their overall communication program. Communication between the teacher and clinician should include both systematic data review by the clinician and a "red flag" convention that the teacher can use when she needs immediate input from the clinician concerning programming modifications. The speech/language consultant's role should include observing the teacher on a regular basis and ensuring that: 1) the language objectives are actually functional and appropriate; 2) the program is being conducted as written and demonstrated; 3) the student is making adequate progress; 4) data are being collected correctly; 5) data-based program decisions are being made; 6) programming decisions are appropriate; and 7) the teacher is being supported and reinforced for conducting the direct programming.

The teacher who serves as the primary trainer must also serve to promote generalization to nontraining settings. Thus, the teacher in the second training model is both generalization facilitator and primary trainer. The teacher must determine how to utilize the speech/language consultant most effectively to meet each student's needs. Frequently, the speech/language consultant is responsible for assessing students, providing long-term language objectives, and assisting with programming decisions for the teacher when requested. However, teachers may have difficulty deciding exactly when assistance from the language consultant is needed. Table 3 provides a checklist for teachers and speech/language consultants to use in pinpointing when and what type of consultive support is needed. This checklist should be reviewed for each student because teacher needs are likely to be linked to individual programs reflecting skills and needs.

The teacher who is the primary language trainer may prepare and implement home training programs as well as report student progress to parents. The teacher may also develop probe or checklist systems to determine if home training is effective. Most teachers will usually need support and feedback from their speech/language consultants in preparing home programs. The development of guidelines for assessing parent skills and for preparing home programs should be provided by the speech/language consultant. A sample of guideline questions is given in Table 4.

Teacher as the Only Trainer Without Supportive Services

Some teachers will be solely responsible for a student's communication and language program without the benefit of a regular speech/language consultant. Teachers responsible for programming for the severely/profoundly handicapped student may find that available speech/language clinicians do not have the skills for programming for that student. Teachers "on their own" are

Table 3. Questions to Ask—Where Is the Problem?

Are IEP goals based on assessment data?
Are short-term goals directly related to long-term goals?
Do the assessment data reflect the demonstration of prerequisite skills?
Can the IEP objective be met by the program objective?
Does the program objective reflect the next goal of training?
Can the trainer express the rationale for the program?
Does the teacher/trainer know "where" she is going?
Does the individual program take into account the student's limitations?
Does the program utilize the student's strengths?
Is there a relationship between program objectives?
Is the program (steps, reinforcers, stimuli) written for that individual student?
Is there a rationale for selecting the specific program content?
Is the program conducted at a prime time (if it is a priority)?
Is the program conducted consistently?
If programming is conducted in the natural environment, is the trainer taking advantage of a "teachable moment"?
Is the student placed (physically) in a position to facilitate increased responding?
Is the teacher placed in a position to facilitate increasing student responses?
Is the program sequenced (for each individual student) so that more than correct/incorrect responses can be observed?
Are data (probe or continuous) being collected?
Do the data being collected lend themselves to making modifications?
If the program is not working, have modifications been made?
Do the data reflect: a) no correct responses?
b) inconsistent responses?
c) incorrect responses?

responsible for primary language training, facilitating, generalized language use, and pinpointing their own skills and needs in the area listed in Table 2. These teachers must conduct their own "needs assessment" to determine what type of in-service training they need. At times, teachers may recognize that they need more extensive training in communication/language programming. If the administration does not conduct regular staff needs assessments, it becomes the responsibility of the teacher to state his or her needs to the administration and to negotiate ways in which these needs could be best met. Teachers who find themselves asking the questions "What are my skills? What are my limitations? How do I find out?" may use Tables 2, 3, and 4 as informal checklists. Regardless of the training model adopted, it is important that the teacher has adequate skills and resources to conduct instruction. On a long-term basis, specific in-service strategies are necessary to ensure that teachers are fully prepared for the task of training language.

Few teachers are fully prepared to be the sole language trainer for their students and it is unreasonable to expect that teachers will have the extensive knowledge base regarding phonetics and syntax that is part of the speech

Table 4.   Guidelines for Preparing Home Programs

Parent Assessment

1. How interested are the parent(s) in conducting a home program?
2. Does the parent understand the child's general speech/language goals?
3. Has the parent had any training in behavior management or simple teaching procedures?
4. Does the parent typically attempt to teach the child new skills?
5. How much time can the parent commit to teaching speech/language skills?
6. What are the parent's priorities for the child to learn in terms of speech/language skills?
7. Has the parent ever conducted a home program before?
8. Has the parent ever collected home data before?
9. Does the parent prefer to run sessions or teach incidentally?
10. Does the parent accept feedback from professionals comfortably?
11. If there are two parents or other adult family members, is there support from others in the household for conducting home training?
12. In terms of the child's overall program, is speech/language the area most in need of home programming?

Teacher/Program Assessment

1. Do you have time to develop and monitor a home program for this child?
2. What specific skills should be targeted at home?
3. Are you sufficiently familiar with the teaching procedures/generalization procedures for this set of skills to teach them to the parent?
4. Do you have sufficient rapport with this parent to work successfully with him or her? If not, what is necessary to develop that rapport?
5. Do you have a data collection system that can be used at home? Can you design one that is simple enough to be manageable yet yields the needed data?
6. Do you know how to teach the parent to run the program you design?
7. Do you have a strategy for monitoring and supporting the parents during the time they run this program?
8. Are you open to parent input regarding skills and methods of teaching?
9. Do you have a clear set of decision rules regarding program changes? Can you communicate these rules to the parent?
10. How often will you meet with the parent to review the child's progress?
11. How long do you anticipate that the home programming will continue? What will be your criteria for termination?
12. What is the goal of this home programming? How will you determine when you have met that goal?
13. What special materials are needed for this program? Can you provide them for the parent?
14. What assistance do you need from the speech/language consultant in developing this program?

clinician's training. Thus, a few practical suggestions seem in order for teachers who find themselves in this role:

1. In assessing and planning programs for students, consider their needs for functional communication as primary targets for training. Teach skills the student can immediately use to control his or her environment.
2. It will probably not be possible to run individual sessions with each stu-

dent. Consider grouping students according to their needs or according to their ability to serve as models for one another.

3. Teach skills in their functional context, integrating language teaching into other curriculum areas.

4. Although data collection is extremely important, it must be managed in a way that will ensure that it occurs regularly and the data are used in decision making. Fewer data, collected carefully and analyzed in depth, may prove to be more useful than daily data that are not integrated into the decision-making process. Design data collection systems that will be manageable when implemented with an entire classroom of children.

5. Program design should address the communication priorities of the students. It will not be possible to teach every needed skill to each child; select a set of priority skills to be programmed thoroughly and a secondary set of skills that may be taught informally. Setting modest goals and meeting those goals is a better long-term strategy than setting comprehensive goals which simply cannot be met in a given context. An emphasis on functional communication skills should form the basis for selecting priority skills.

6. When a consulting speech/language therapist is not readily available, seek advice and support from other teachers who are sole language trainers. Sharing ideas, data systems, and problem-solving strategies should be an integral activity of staff who are responsible for language training.

7. Administrative support, in the form of materials, in-service training, extra planning time, paraprofessional assistance and recognition for exceptional efforts, is requisite to maintaining teacher performance over time.

STRATEGIES FOR TEACHER TRAINING

Defining appropriate strategies to increase the teacher's skills in delivering communication/language instruction is a dynamic process. The process involves environmental conditions that change in synchrony with teacher and student development. Selecting appropriate strategies for training teachers requires assessing needs and skills of both the student and the teacher, the availability and skill of the training specialist, and access to resource materials. The resulting dynamic interface is illustrated by several levels of a continuum, as shown in Figure 2.

For example, a student may need a systematic program involving differential reinforcement for successive approximations to teach new vocal responses. A teacher with limited operant conditioning skills may conduct this instruction with direct assistance from the training specialist. The specialist would provide direct instruction to the student and act as a model for the

330   Campbell et al.

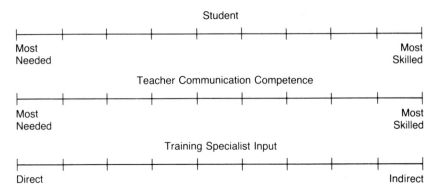

Figure 2. Continuua of teacher/student learning needs in relation to the specialist's input.

teacher. Another teacher may have developed and mastered a very substantial cognitive curriculum sequence. If a student's needs are within this area, the training specialist would provide only indirect service, possibly in the form of limited consultation with the teacher.

Some teachers may begin their participation in communication training at the lowest component of the service continuum. At that point, the training specialist would provide assessment, written programs, and instructional materials. She would demonstrate the program and teaching techniques, and would provide systematic teacher training on these techniques, if needed. At this level, there is short-term, direct service by the specialist with the teacher initially observing the training program. Next, the training specialist would use a step-by-step procedure to train the teacher to administer the communication program. A teacher's success in communication programming depends on her comfort with the specific communication program and adeptness at applying the procedures. If teachers are confused about the program's content or how to implement the procedures, they will not administer the communication program effectively and eventually they may not administer the program at all.

The training specialist must provide considerable support for the teacher with limited skills. Analysis of the teacher's communication skills training is essential in determining the amount of training and type of support needed.

Analysis of Teacher and Student Evaluations

The analysis of the teacher and student evaluations will place the student at some point (or several points) along the need/skill continuum. In addition to the student's needs, the results of each component of the teacher evaluation must be considered.

The following example illustrates the outcome of a teacher-student evaluation analysis:

EXAMPLE   Teacher-Student Evaluation Analysis

Teacher Analysis

Area	Evaluation
1. Classroom organization	
a. Physical arrangement	Appropriate storage
	Limited materials
	Limited access to materials
b. Management arrangement	Schedule defined
	Schedule followed
	Appropriate time allowed for communication
	Behavioral control only during scheduled programs
2. Program delivery	
a. Structured program	Simple data system
	One-to-one instructional pattern
b. Semistructured programs	Routines not well established
	Behavior control breaks down
	Opportunities for establishing routines exist
	Free time activities seemingly have no objectives
	Small amount of teacher-student interaction
3. Specific communication needs	
a. Social interactions	Primarily in structured programs
	High degree of request for student action and protest by students
b. Semantic relations	Classroom does not afford many language contexts
c. Receptive language	Inconsistent directives repeated
	No consistent follow-through
	Teacher understands that direction-following is part of receptive language
	Good directives in structured programs
d. Expressive language	Teacher realizes student knows some signs and wants to learn signs and use them in classroom

Student Analysis

Area	Evaluation
1. Modality of communication	Signs
2. Receptive skills	Understands simple verbal instructions with/without signs

continued

EXAMPLE   Teacher-Student Evaluation Analysis *continued*

Student Analysis

Area	Evaluation
3. Expressive skills	Consistent vocabulary across stimulus conditions (nouns—25; verbs—7)
4. Social interaction	Protest function
	Request action
5. Semantic	Uses noun or verb to express recurrence, existence, nonexistence
	Hits others in protest
6. Cognitive	Interacts appropriately with objects
	Explores environment
	Imitates complex motor movements

The student described in this analysis has acquired a communication response topography (i.e., he has a basic repertoire of signs). His needs are: 1) strengthening the verb class; 2) maintaining the noun class; 3) extending signs to different stimulus control; 4) generalizing signs to other persons and settings; and 5) initiation of signs for communication.

When Direct Training is Necessary

Regardless of the model used to program teacher support for teaching functional language and communication, the teacher cannot be expected to be as competent as a language facilitator or as a primary trainer without specific training. Student progress depends on the competencies of the teacher, and changes in teacher skills will, in turn, depend on the skills of the in-service trainer.

Training may be provided on a number of levels. There are seven levels of instruction applicable to training personnel in the area of language and communication (Baldwin et al., 1982). These levels, in terms of their outcomes are: 1) awareness; 2) change in attitude; 3) change in knowledge; 4) change in skill; 5) implementation of the skill in the classroom; 6) skill generalization; and 7) change in student skills as a result of training. Even though instruction may include each of these levels, the training specialist must train the teacher so that the *student's language and communication skills change as a result of the teacher's training.*

Awareness   The awareness training introduces the teacher (or person being trained) to "what will be trained" (content) and "how it will be trained" (procedures and strategies). Specific topics covered by the in-service trainer include: 1) the difference between communication, language, and speech; 2) appropriate assessment instruments; 3) how to select functional training objectives; 4) the importance of social skills and the student's interaction in the environment; and 5) the importance of the teacher as the language trainer.

Training may include lectures and selected readings. The purpose of the training is to present information to make the trainees more "aware" of what is expected of them. It is often difficult to measure awareness other than by a self-report. A number of scales are available to evaluate in-service training (Brookfield, 1982). Teachers may also complete pre-posttests to measure their understanding and recall of information presented during awareness training.

Change in Attitude   If the teacher and the trainer have different philosophies of training children (for example, one may prefer a cognitive approach and the other a behavioral approach), the in-service training may be difficult and result in few changes in teacher performance. If the teacher is opposed to the type of procedures being trained, she is unlikely to implement these procedures in the classroom. The training specialist must determine if the teacher-to-be-trained has different perceptions about the way in which language should be taught. If there are widely differing philosophies, the training specialist must either change the attitude of the teacher or change the instruction so that the important points are presented in a way that more closely approximates the teacher's theoretical bases (if this is possible).

For example, a teacher may be opposed to teaching nonverbal students to use manual signs as an augmentative language system. In this case, the in-service trainer could present data demonstrating the student's accelerated progress resulting from using signs, have the teacher observe students who are using signs, or have the teacher talk to teachers and parents who have found that sign training has been effective as a primary language system or as a speech facilitator. However, if the teacher is opposed to the use of signs simply because she does not know signs, training the teacher in manual communication would be necessary. The instructions' effectiveness in changing the teacher's attitude may be evaluated informally or formally. Formal measures may include pre-posttest measures. Informal measures could be as simple as asking the teacher for verbal feedback.

Change in Knowledge   One way to determine if a person (student or teacher) understands the information being presented, and to determine if the in-service trainer has presented the material clearly, is to have the teacher demonstrate her comprehension in some observable manner. In-service training intended to change a teacher's knowledge of communication training content or procedures may need to include more than lectures and selected readings. Observations of videotapes, training demonstrations, individual or group exercises or assignments, and role playing are effective training strategies. The training specialist may measure the trainee's change in knowledge in either formal or informal evaluations. Formal evaluations may include written assignments or rating exercises. Informal evaluations may consist of trainee-trainer discussions. These evaluations are not meant to measure "how much the teacher has learned," but rather "how well the training specialist has taught." The in-service trainer should use these evaluations as feedback to make modifications in the in-service training program.

Change in Skill   This level of instruction requires that the teacher demonstrates new skills or competencies with trainer support and feedback. Once the teacher or trainee has an awareness and knowledge of what is expected, she should have an opportunity to practice these skills and to receive immediate feedback. Practice sessions should include role-playing activities, observations of the trainer demonstrating new procedures with students, and the teacher demonstrating the newly trained skill with the students.

The training specialist may approach training (for either facilitation or structured training) using a shaping procedure in which the teacher gradually learns more and more skills for training communication. The following sequence is an example of systematically training a teacher to conduct a structured communication program:

1. The teacher observes the specialist conducting direct training:
    a. The visual aspects of the stimulus are clearly defined for the teacher.
    b. The verbal aspects of the stimulus are clearly defined for the teacher.
    c. The level of physical support is clearly defined for the teacher.
    d. The correct responses are defined.
    e. The consequences and contingencies are clearly defined.
    f. The specific recording procedure is clearly defined.
2. The teacher records data while the training specialist conducts training.
3. The teacher conducts training while the training specialist records data; the specialist provides immediate feedback.
4. The teacher conducts training and records data with the training specialist providing immediate feedback.
5. The teacher conducts training while the training specialist takes data on the stimulus presentation, response reliability, and consequences delivered by the teacher. (Figure 3 shows an example of an observation form the training specialist may use to determine the skill level of the teacher.) The specialist provides feedback.

Once the teacher can conduct structured communication training on a one-to-one basis, additional training is necessary for the teacher to learn to facilitate communication in semistructured programs. For example, the teacher must learn when to run probes for generalization and how to conduct communication training with a group of children. Since communication training programs for the severely handicapped should include training children to communicate about objects, persons, events, and relations, the teacher must learn to organize the stimulus materials in order to provide for maximum responding.

TEACHER: _____   TRAINING: _____

CHILD: _____   DATE: _____

GROUP: _____   PROCEDURE: _____

Trial	Stimulus					Response	Consequation					Nontraining			Data		
	Attending	Visual	Verbal	Temporal	Physical		Immediate	Primary	Verbal	Tactile	Correction	Maintain seat	Interfering	SR + for sitting	Correct	Tabulated	Graphed
1																	
2																	
3																	
4																	
5																	
6																	
7																	
8																	
9																	
10																	

Figure 3. Observation form for determining teacher skill level.

The skills to be demonstrated by the teacher are broken down into small steps and the training specialist records whether the skill was performed correctly or incorrectly. When the training session is completed, the training specialist provides positive feedback for those skills that were correct and provides additional or modified training for those skills that require more practice. The observation procedure helps the training specialist determine which skills require additional training.

Strategies used to train teachers should also include active generalization techniques. Multiple language skills or behaviors, different students, different settings, and delayed feedback should be incorporated into the training so that the teacher has the opportunity to program across responses, students, and settings and thus facilitate her generalization of the training techniques.

Once the teacher is familiar with the student's language modality, the training program, and the student's level of responding, communication training can be extended so that it is targeted concurrently with preacademic and self-help programs. Concurrent programming can be used to expand the student's vocabulary, and to provide opportunities for the student to use trained language functionally. For example, if the student is learning to use the words "spoon" and "napkin" to express various functions (e.g., request, comment), training should occur at mealtime when the functions are probable and the vocabulary is appropriate. When the student learns that he can use a word to request an object, give information, or regulate another's behavior, he is learning to use language to communicate with people in his environment.

Teaching the teacher to train language concurrently with other programs may require additional demonstrations, feedback, and practice presented in sequential steps. Again, the amount of training needed depends on the student's skills and needs, and the teacher's skills. Teachers who claim to "know nothing about language" may provide ample opportunities for students to use language, but still need to learn to target specific language behaviors (that have been trained). A variety of methods for prompting specific language behaviors, correcting incorrect responses, and consequating correct responses should be demonstrated by the training specialist and mastered by the teacher.

Initially, a minimum of language responses should be required in one or two programs. The teacher should be taught to fade the verbal prompts to help the student learn to initiate language responses with a minimum of support. At this point, the teacher should be trained to expand the student's vocabulary by teaching novel words or structures in a meaningful context.

The teacher must be trained to use nontraining settings, such as routines and free play, to teach the student how to use language as social communication. Because generalization of training language does not occur automatically and must be programmed as carefully as structured training, the teacher should be familiar with generalization techniques such as programming common stimuli and sequential modification. In nontraining settings, the stimuli that evoke communication are not strictly controlled. If the teacher learns and uses the principles of environmental language facilitation, she will be able to arrange settings, and she may be able to promote requesting and commenting. For example, the physical environment may be arranged so that preferred objects may be out of reach or out of sight, so that the student is required to use language to request them. The teacher should be taught to vary the context of the free play setting so that a wide variety of functional language can occur (see Hart, this volume). The teacher must also learn to cue the students at various levels and to emphasize the communicative function of language. Hart and Rogers-Warren (1978) described a "milieu approach" for teaching children to use language as communication. In this approach, the teacher's goal is to get the child to comprehend and produce more language and to learn that language has consequences. Newly trained teachers should be introduced to the milieu approach and should practice applying its principles in their classrooms. Feedback and assistance from the training specialist should support the teachers' applications.

Forms to be used in observing the teacher in a "facilitation" role should be developed to quantify teacher behavior and to provide a basis for specific feedback and shaping new skills. The types of cues presented by the teacher (instuctions, *wh*—questions, yes/no questions, demands for verbalizations, models, prompts) and teacher consequences for student responses or initiations should be recorded regularly.

Implementation of Skills To be truly effective, the teacher must implement his or her newly learned skills and programs in the classroom for each student even when the in-service trainer or consultant support is not available. The observation forms (and feedback) discussed previously and open channels of communication will assure that the teacher has the skills to implement the programs and maintain her or his programming skills. Student programs need to be conducted frequently and consistently for the student to progress and show generalized acquisition of new skills.

Skills Generalization Training is not complete until the teachers can demonstrate and apply the learned skills under a variety of conditions and program levels. Therefore, use of strategies to promote generalization of the teachers' learned skills is a critical final step in the acquisition process. Many of the generalization programming strategies for children (outlined by Stremel-Campbell, this volume) may also be applicable for increasing teachers' skill generalization. Such strategies as programming sufficient exemplars, programming common stimuli, programming "loose" training, and training to generalize should be considered in designing the teachers' instructional programs.

For example, the teacher should have an opportunity to work with several examples of instructional programming formats. Instructional delivery should be implemented with several children who demonstrate a range of instructional needs. Common elements should exist between the training setting and the teacher's own classroom. If possible, training should be conducted in the teacher's instructional setting. A basement classroom and a lab school facility may have few common elements. The teacher who is able to apply language and communication training techniques across the widest variations of setting, programs, and children is most likely to succeed in increasing his or her students' language and communication skills.

Change in Student Skills The final evaluation of in-service training must be evidence of positive changes in student skills. If the trainer has done an adequate job of training, the teacher will be able to demonstrate new skills and implement those skills in the classroom, and the student data is critical because it provides information required in making modifications of the student's program, and in determining what additional in-service training is needed. Collecting data on both the teacher's implementation of a program (or facilitation) and the student's responses during training will assist the in-service trainer in identifying and remediating program and instructional delivery problems.

SUMMARY AND CONCLUSIONS

To meet the communication needs of an increasing number of handicapped children, teachers must assume new roles in programming language and communication skills in the classroom. A variety of roles are possible, from that of facilitator of language programs designed and delivered by a speech/ language therapist to primary trainer and implementer of home training programs. To fulfill these new roles, teachers must be trained in the design of programs, direct teaching techniques, generalization strategies, and environmental arrangement principles. Most often, training in these areas is provided by the speech/language therapist serving as a consultant to the teacher or by an in-service specialist working with the teacher.

Training teachers as language trainers and facilitators is a task demanding sophisticated task analysis and behavioral management procedures. This chapter has described some strategies that can be used to train teachers and has integrated teacher training and the definition of teacher roles in language and communication intervention into a curriculum to be applied by in-service training specialists or speech clinicians serving as consultants to classroom teachers.

Sometimes, the teacher must be her own trainer. When the speech clinician available to the classroom teacher lacks sophisticated procedures for training children or for teaching auxiliary personnel, and when no outside trainers are available, acquiring the specific skills required for classroom-based language intervention may become a "do-it-yourself" endeavor. The sequence of training steps described here may be applied as a self-managed curriculum for interested and highly motivated teachers. Cooperative training by two teachers or a teacher and a speech/language clinician may be a means of providing support for the acquisition of new skills and for improving the programming provided for children in an educational setting.

The role of the teacher in language and communication intervention is an expensive and critical one. Teachers hold the key to functional communication for many handicapped children. Their efforts to learn new communication and language training skills, to apply them creatively, and to support both their students and their colleagues in learning new behaviors may open new doors to remediating language deficiencies.

REFERENCES

Baldwin, V., Campbell, B., and Fredericks, H. D. 1982. The application of inservice training technology. *In* B. Campbell and V. Baldwin (eds.), Severely Handicapped Hearing Impaired Students: Strengthening Service Delivery. Paul H. Brookes Publishing Co., Baltimore.

Bricker, D. 1976. Educational synthesizer. *In* M. A. Thomas (eds.), Hey Don't Forget about Me! Council for Exceptional Children, Reston, VA.

Brookfield, J. 1982. Staff Development: A Systematic Process. WESTAR, Monmouth, OR.

Bruner, J. S. 1975. The onotogenesis of speech acts. J. Child Lang. 2:1–19.

Campbell, C. R., and Stremel-Campbell, K. 1982. Programming "loose training" as a strategy to facilitate language generalization. J. Appl. Behav. Anal. 2(15):295–301.

Hart, B., and Rogers-Warren, A. 1978. A milieu approach to teaching language. *In* R. L. Schiefelbusch (ed.), Language Intervention Strategies. University Park Press, Baltimore.

Lyon, S., and Lyon, G. 1980. Team functioning and staff development: A role release approach to providing integrated educational services for severely handicapped students. J. Assoc. Severely Handic. 5(3):250–263.

Mahoney, G. 1975. An ethological approach to delayed language acquisition. Am. J. Ment. Defic. 80:139–148.

McCormick, L., and Goldman, R. 1979. The transdisciplinary model: Implications for service delivery and personnel preparation for the severely and profoundly handicapped. AAESPH Rev. 4(2):152–161.

McLean, J. E., and Synder-McLean, L. K. 1982. A Transactional Approach to Early Language Training. Merrill, Columbus, OH.

Miller, J. F., Chapman, R. S., and Bedrosian. J. L. 1977. Defining developmentally disabled subjects for research: The relationship between etiology, cognitive development and language and communication performance. Paper presented at the Second Annual Boston University Conference on Language Development, Boston, October.

Nelson, K. 1974. Concept, word and sentence: Interrelations in acquisition and development. Psychol. Rev. 81:267–285.

Sailor, W., and Haring, N. 1977. Some current directions in education of the severely/multiply handicapped. AAESPH Rev. 2:67–87.

Sternate, J., Messina, R., Nietupski, J., Lyon, S., and Brown, L. 1977. Occupational and physical therapy services for severely handicapped students: Toward a naturalized public school service delivery model. *In* E. Sontag (ed.), Educational Programming for the Severely and Profoundly Handicapped. The Council for Exceptional Children, Reston, VA.

U.S. Department of Education. 1980. "To assure the free appropriate public education of all handicapped children." Third annual report to Congress on the implementation of Public Law 94–142: The Education for All Handicapped Children Act. U.S. Department of Education, Washington, DC.

Warren, S. F., and Rogers-Warren, A. 1980. Current perspectives in language remediation. Educ. Treatment Child. 3:133–153.

Wilcox, B., and Sailor, W. 1980. Service delivery issues: Integrated educational systems. *In* B. Wilcox and R. York (ed.), Quality Education for the Severely Handicapped: The Federal Investment. U.S. Department of Education, Washington, DC.

Acquisition level of learning, 8
Activities necessary for communication
    programming, 318–319
Adult speech to children, communication
    characteristics of, 45–46
Apraxia, 43
Attention theory, 173
Audiologic assessment strategies, 189
Autism
    characteristics of, 125–137
        echolalia, 127–129
        mutism, 126–127
        pragmatic development, 133–136
        semantic development, 130–133
        syntactic development, 130
        use of gesture and, 129–130
        violations in semantic constraints,
            132–133
    intervention planning and, 137–150
        behavior control component,
            138–140
        component areas of, 137–138
        curriculum components, 141–143
        format for instruction, 143–147
        generalization and maintenance,
            147–150
        motivational component, 140–141
Autistic persons
    behavior traps set by, 138–139
    communication characteristics of,
        125–137
        echolalia, 127–129
        mutism, 126–127
        use of gesture, 129–130
    format for instruction, 143–147
    generalization and, 147–150
        techniques to program, 148–150
    impaired areas of pragmatic function-
        ing, 135–136
    intervention planning and, 137–150
        behavior control component,
            138–140
        curriculum components, 141–143
        format for instruction, 143–147
        generalization and maintenance,
            147–150
        motivational component, 140–141
    "loose" training and, 149–150
    pragmatic development, 133–136
    semantic development of, 130–133
    syntactic development of, 130

use of "probable-event strategy" ver-
    sus "word order-strategy,"
    131–132
violations in semantic constraints, 132
    examples, 132–133

Behavior
    as communicator, 94
    functional analysis and, 96
Behavior modification, manipulation of
    the environment and, 36
Behavior traps, autistic persons and,
    138–139
Behavioral procedures of audiologic
    assessment, 189–190
Bidirectional generalization, 41, 48

Chaining, 100–101
    defined, 100
    significant others and, 101
Channel defined, 102
Child development, ecological theory of,
    94–95
    mother's sensitivity and, 95
Children
    characteristics of conversations
        between, 294–295
    communication systems of, 102–108
        content, 105–106
        mode, 102–104
        semantic classes of, 106
        significant others and, 108–115
        use, 107–108
        vocabularies of, 105
    difficult to teach
        communication intervention and,
            159–191
        conceptual intervention and,
            170–188
        physiological determinants,
            188–190
        defined, 160–162
        intervention model, 162–163
        teaching communication functions
            and, 164–170
        types of, 161–162
    interacting with peers
        performance deficits, 295–297
        skill deficits, 298–300
    severely handicapped, defined, 160

Child's World principle, 115
Cognition, and language acquisition, 29–31
Common settings, programming across, 265
Common stimuli, programming of
  across adults and peers, 263–265
  across behaviors, 262–263
  peers, 264
Communication
  acquisition of, prerequisites for, 28–31
  by autistic persons, characteristics of
    echolalia, 127–129
    mutism, 126–127
    pragmatic development, 133–136
    semantic development, 130–133
    syntactic development, 130
  development of
    illocutionary stage, 103
    perlocutionary stage, 103
  dyadic feedback as a function of, 94
  prerequisites for, 28–31
    cognitive, 29–31
    social, 29
Communication boards, 40–41, 163
  direct selection, 40
  electronic scanning, 41
  see also Picture boards
Communication chain, defined, 100
Communication functions
  programming common, 262
  programming multiple, 257
  teaching difficult-to-teach children, 164–170
  types of, 255–256
Communication intervention
  comprehending objects and actions, 42
  curriculum for beginning, 177
  difficult-to-teach children and, 159–191
    conceptual and procedural basis for, 170–188
    physiological determinants, 188–190
    teaching communication functions, 164–170
  pragmatics defined, 27–28
  production versus comprehension, 41
  programs, 27–54
    behavior modification through
      environmental manipulation, 36
      establishing a discourse topic, 34
      establishing multiword utterances, 36–39
      establishing word use, 31–36
      guidelines for selecting word constructions, 37
      integrating structured and incidental teaching formats, 49–50
      prerequisites, 28–31
      reinforcement through stimulus conditions, 44
      sequencing communication objectives, 39–52
      teaching strategies, 43–52
      three-term semantic functions, 37
    questions facing researchers, 53
    relationship between comprehension and production of words, 41
    "stranger test," 104
    teacher's role in, 313
Communication mode choices and significant others, 142
Communication objectives, sequencing of, 39–54
Communication problems, developmentally delayed children and, 107
Communication programming, activities necessary for, 318–319
Communication skills
  age of acquisition in normal children, 40
  developing rudimentary requesting, 178–182
  generic strategy for teaching, 175–176
  learning to describe, 181–182
    concept levels, 181
Communication systems of children,
  content, 105–106
  idiosyncratic, 92
  mode, 102–104
  semantic classes of, 106
  semantic component defined, 130–131
  significant others and, 108–115
  use, 107–108
  vocabularies of, 105
Communication theory, 93–94

principles for an intervention model,
    95–96
principles of, 94
Communication training
    goals of, 102, 103
    sign language and, 242
    stimulus events during, 169
Communicative expectance, 110–111
Communicative referencing, 28–29
Competency level of learning, 8
Comprehension and production of
        words, relationship
        between, 41
Concept, defined, 171–172
Concurrent training, 51, 267–268
Content, defined, 200
Conversation
    establishment of discourse topic, 34
    language development and, 91–119
        experimental and clinical basis,
            93–97
        treatment targets and techniques,
            97–115
        treatment targets and, 98–102
        joint activity routine, 99–100
        significant others, 108–115
        social contact purpose, 99
        social recognition, 98
        turn-taking and chaining, 100–102
Conversation teaching strategies, signifi-
        cant others and, 114
Conversational characteristics of chil-
        dren, 295
Conversational Principle, 115
Conversational skills, 299
Conversational teaching strategies, 113,
        114
Cross-modal generalization, 48, 187

Delay process in language acquisition,
        72–74
    sequence of steps in, 72–73
Delayed echolalia, 127
    studies of, 128
Delayed reinforcement, 269
Describing and requesting, 163
    relationships between, 166–170
Developmentally delayed children, com-
        munication problems of,
        107
Didactic teaching, preplanned, 144

Difficult-to-teach children
    communication intervention and,
        159–191
        conceptual and procedural basis,
            170–188
        physiological determinants,
            188–190
    communication problems and, 107
    defined, 160, 162
    initial intervention target, 165
    intervention model, 162–163
    teaching communication functions
        and, 164–170
    types of, 161–162
Direct selection communication board,
        40
Direct training, 332–337
Discourse topic, establishment of, 34
Discrimination learning, 172–173,
        182–184
    defined, 175
    exercises, 182–183
Down's syndrome, cognitive and com-
        municative skills in, 29
Dysarthria, 43

Echolalic verbal behavior, 42–43,
        127–129
    theories concerning, 128
Ecological theory of child development,
        94–95
    mother's sensitivity and, 95
Education
    content of, 8–9
    content organization, 12–13
    determining results, 13–14
    parent's and teacher's role in, 9–10
    setting for, 12
    student reinforcement, 10–12
Educational synthesizer,
    defined, 315
    teacher's role as, 315
Electronic scanning communication
        board, 41
Electrophysiological procedures of
        audiologic assessment, 189
Environmental aspects of language
        acquisition, 14–15, 79–83
    adult-child ratio, 79–80
    function, 82–83
    imitation, 81–82

Environmental aspects of
            language—*continued*
    models, 81
    prompts, 82
    rate, 83
    routines, 80–81
    stimulation, 79
    topic, 80
Environmental interventions, 66–68
    advantage of systematizing, 68
    goals of, 66
Environmental Language Intervention
            (ELI) Program, 91
Environmental manipulation and behav-
            ior modification, 36
Establishing a discourse topic, 34
Evaluations, analysis of teacher and stu-
            dent, 330–332
Expressing wants and needs, 165–166

Functional analysis, behavior and, 96
Functional language
    child versus adult, 292–295
    defined, 6–7
    legislative contributions to, 312
    peer support programming and,
            291–305
    programming teacher support for,
            311–338
    teacher's role in, 313
    technical contributions to, 312–313
Functional Language Curricula, 164

General teaching strategies, 113–115
Generalization
    aspects of active programs, 253–254
    autistic persons and, 147–150
        techniques to program, 148–150
    bidirectional, 41, 48
    criterion for acceptable, 206–213
    cross-modal, 187
    defined, 47–48, 199–200
    evaluation of plan, 278–282
        natural environment observations,
            280–282
        structured probes, 279–280
    guidelines for measuring, 221
    language measurement
        approaches to, 204–206
        clinical strategies for, 199–222

criterion for acceptable, 206–213
    diversity, 210–213
    maintenance testing, 210–211
    sampling, 207–208
level of learning, 8
maximization tactics, 13
measurement and training flowchart,
            220
measurement plan, 213–221
    see also Language generalization
            measurement
measurements, 324
naturalistic measures of, 205
    uses of, 205–206
plan development, 270–272
probe, 204–205
    use of, 205–206
programming techniques, 255–270
    application and evaluation of,
            270–283
    application of for a 16-year-old,
            274
    common stimuli, 262–265
    criteria for acceptable, 282–283
    indiscriminable contingencies,
            268–270
    "loose" training, 266–268
    multiple exemplars, 255–261
    natural maintaining consequences,
            265–266
    specific plan, 275–278
    strategies for applying, 272–278
prompting through matrix training,
            227–239
prompting through stimulus equiva-
            lence training, 239–245
recombinative, 228–229, 233–234
response, defined, 47–48
test training sequence and, 186
training techniques to facilitate,
            253–284
    conceptual approach, 254–255
    training test sequence and, 186
Gesture use by autistic persons, 129–130

Handicapped, communication interven-
            tion and, 159–191
    see also Severely handicapped
Hearing screening, 189–190
Home programs, guidelines for prepar-
            ing, 328

Iconicity in signs, 33
Idiosyncratic communication as a com-
        petitor to conventional com-
        munication, 92, 104
Illocutionary stage in communication
        development, 103
Immediate echolalia, 127
    studies of, 128
Incidental teaching, 144
    combined with structured teaching,
        49–50
    defined, 44
    goal of, 77
    language acquisition and, 74–79
    model of, 44–45
    sequence of steps in, 75
Indiscriminable contingencies, program-
        ming of, 268–270
Individual education program (IEP), 18,
        213, 312, 321
Infant-mother interaction, 110–113
Instruction-following skills, 38
Interactional conversational skills, 299
Intervention
    communication
        comprehending objects and
            actions, 42
        curriculum for beginning, 177
        difficult-to-teach children and,
            159–191
            conceptual and procedural
                basis for, 170–188
            physiological determinants,
                188–190
            teaching communication func-
                tions, 164–170
        pragmatics, defined, 27–28
        production versus comprehension,
            41
        programs, 27–54
            behavior modification, 36
            establishing a discourse topic,
                34
            establishing multiword utter-
                ances, 36–39
            establishing word use, 31, 36
            guidelines for selecting word
                constructions, 37
            integrating structured and inci-
                dental teaching formats,
                49–50
            prerequisites, 28–31

reinforcement through stimulus
    conditions, 44
sequencing communication
    objectives, 39–52
teaching strategies, 43–52
three-term semantic functions,
    37
questions facing researchers, 53
"stranger test," 104
critical components of, 317
environmental, 66–68
    advantage of systematizing, 68
    goals of, 66
"stranger test," in teaching, 104
teacher's role in, 313
Intervention agents, peers as, 300–304
    peer assembly, 301–303
    peer confederates, 303–304
Intervention decisions, using develop-
        mental data questioned, 39
Intervention model, 95–96
Intervention planning, autistic persons
        and, 137–150
    behavior control component,
        138–140
    component areas of, 137–138
    curriculum components, 141–143
    format for instruction, 143–147
    generalization and maintenance,
        147–150
    motivational component, 140–141
Intervention programs, 27–54

Language acquisition
    cognitive landmark skills and, 29–30
    contributing factors of, 67
    delay process, 72–74
        sequence of steps in, 72–73
    environmental aspects of, 79–83
        adult-child ratio, 79–80
        function, 82–83
        imitation, 81–82
        models, 81
        prompts, 82
        rate, 83
        routines, 80–81
        stimulation, 79
        topic, 80
    environmental assistance to, 68
    incidental teaching, 74–79
        sequence of steps in, 75

Language acquisition—*continued*
    mand-model, 69–72
    processes for, 68–79
    sequence of steps in, 69
Language development
    characteristics of, 95–96
    through conversation, 91–119
        experimental and clinical bases,
            93–97
        treatment targets and techniques,
            97–115
Language facilitating skills, 323–324
Language facilitation
    basic questions for, 321
    principles for, 322–323
Language facilitators, teachers as,
        320–324
Language, functional
    child versus adult, 292–295
    defined, 6–7
    legislative contributions, 312
    peer support programming and,
        291–305
    programming teacher support for,
        311–338
    teacher's role in, 313
    technical contributions to, 312–313
Language generalization, 48
    see also Generalization
Language generalization measurement
    approaches to, 204–206
    clinical strategies for, 199–222
    criterion for acceptable, 206–213
        diversity, 210–213
        generalization, 208–209
        maintenance testing, 210–211
        sampling, 207–208
    plan for, 213–221
        augmentative communication sys-
            tems, 218
        data measurement, 218–219
        frequency of measurement, 217
        measurement settings, 217
        natural samples, 214–216
        observer training, 216–217
        reliability checks, 217–218
        utilizing probes, 214
    response classes, 202–204
Language instruction, model of teacher's
        responsibility for, 315–329
    as communicator/language facilitator,
        320–324

as only trainer without supportative
        services, 326–329
    as primary trainer, 324–326
Language intervention
    curricula, 164
    functional social language and, 143
    goals of, 98
Language programming, theoretical
        basis of, 254
Language remediation
    goal of, 7–8
    technology for, 20, 21–22
Language teaching strategies, 111–115
    significant others and, 111–113
Language training
    content of, 8–9
        organization of, 12–13
    goal of, 253
    parent's role in, 9–10, 16–17
    program administrator's role in, 18
    reinforcers for, 10–12
    superstructure of, 15–19
    teacher's role in, 10, 17
    techniques for, 10
    therapist's role in, 18
    university training programs, 18–19
        see also Training
Language use
    child versus adult, 292–295
    conversational characteristics, 295
    dimensions of, 291
    function of, 82
    social context of, 291
Learned and unlearned responses, 165
Learning
    concepts defined, 171–172
    criteria for, 13–14
    environment and, 14–15
    levels of, 8
    variables affecting outcome of, 8–15
Least Restrictive Education, 312
Level of learning response, 8
Lexical knowledge, 229–237
Lexical response classes, 20
Linguistic vocabulary, 105
"Loose" training, programming of,
        266–268
    autistic persons and, 149–150

Mand defined, 167
Mand-model of language acquisition,
        69–72
    sequence of steps in, 69

Matching-to-sample
    aided by discrimination learning exer-
        cise, 183
    exercises, 186–188
        objects used in, 182
    goal of, 185
    learning generalized, 184–186
    levels of visual matching, 174–175
    procedure, 173–175
Matrix training, 12
    implications for, 237–239
    prior lexical knowledge for
        extensive, 236–237
        none, 229–233
        partial, 233–236
    promoting generalization through,
        227–239
Mean length of utterance (MLU), 219
Measurement of effects of training, 4
Measurement of language generalization,
        199–222
    criterion for acceptable, 206–213
        diversity, 209–210
        generalization, 208–209
        maintenance testing, 210–211
        sampling, 207–208
    measurement approaches, 204–206
    plan for, 213–221
        augmentative communication sys-
            tems, 218
        data management, 218–219
        frequency of measurement, 217
        measurement settings, 217
        natural samples, 214–216
        observer training, 216–217
        reliability checks, 217–218
        utilizing probes, 214
    response classes, 202–204
Minimally Discrepant Modeling Princi-
        ple, 115
Model defined, 102
Mother-infant interaction, 110–113
Motor imitation programming, signing
        programs and, 32–33
Multiple exemplars, programming of,
        255–261
    linguistic classes, 258
    multiple behaviors, 256–261
    multiple settings, 261
    multiple trainers, 261
Multiple response exemplars, program-
        ming of, 260
Multiple settings, programming of, 261

Multiword utterances, establishing,
        36–39
Mute defined, 126–127
Mutism, 126–127

Natural maintaining consequences, pro-
        gramming of, 265
Naturalistic language training tech-
        niques, 65–86
Naturalistic measures of generalization,
        205
    uses of, 205–206
Needs, expressing, 165–166
New Forms–Old Content Principle, 114
Nonlinguistic vocabulary, 105
Nonverbal conversational skills, 299

Object class exemplars, 260
    programming of, 261
Operant conditioning, 66–67
Operant responses strategy in audiologic
        assessment, 189–190

Parent's role in language training, 9–10,
        16–17
Parsons Visual Acuity Test (PVAT), 189
Peer-directed verbal interaction, rates of,
        296
Peer support programming, functional
        language and, 291–305
    child versus adult, 292–295
    performance deficits, 295–297
    skill deficits, 298–300
Peers as intervention agents, 300–304
    peer assembly, 301–303
    peer confederates, 303–304
Perlocutionary stage in communication
        development, 103
Physiological determinants, 188–190
    hearing screening, 189–190
    psychomotor performance, 188–189
    visual acuity, 189
Picture boards, 163
    see also Communication Boards
"Pointing," defined, 188
Potential response classes, 259
Pragmatic functioning in autistic per-
        sons, impaired areas of,
        135–136
Pragmatic response classes, 202–204

Pragmatics
   defined, 27–28, 133–134
   communication interactions and,
      27–28
   language development and, 95–96
Premack principle, 145
Preplanned didactic teaching, 144
Prerequisites of communication interven-
      tion programs, 28–31
"Probable-event strategy" versus "word-
      order strategy," 131–132
Probe generalization, 204–205
   uses of, 205–206
Production and comprehension of words,
      relationship between, 41
Programming
   across common settings, 265
   common stimuli, 262–265
   communication, activities necessary
      for, 318–319
   generalization techniques, 255–270
      application and evaluation of,
         270–283
      application of for 5-year-old,
         276–277
      application of for 16-year-old, 274
      common stimuli, 262–265
      criteria for acceptable, 282–283
      indiscriminable contingencies,
         268–270
      "loose" training, 266–268
      multiple exemplars, 255–261
      natural maintaining consequences,
         265–266
      specific plan, 275–278
   indiscriminable contingencies,
      268–270
   language, teacher's role in, 313
   multiple exemplars, 255–261
      linguistic classes, 258
      multiple behaviors, 256–261
      multiple response, 260
      multiple settings, 261
      multiple trainers, 261
   natural maintaining consequences,
      265
   object class exemplars, 260
   peer support, functional language
      and, 291–305
   theoretical basis of language, 254
Programming teacher support, 311–338
   guidelines for preparing home pro-
      grams, 328

strategies for teacher training,
   329–337
Programming techniques of generaliza-
      tion
   application and evaluation of,
      270–283
   application of for 16-year-old, 274
   common stimuli, 262–265
   criteria for acceptable, 282–283
   indiscriminable contingencies,
      268–270
   "loose" training and, 266–268
   multiple exemplars, 255–261
   natural maintaining consequences,
      265–266
   specific plan, 275–278
Programs, home, guidelines for prepar-
      ing, 328
Proto-declaratives, absent among chil-
      dren, 129
Proto-imperatives, defined, 129
   observed in children, 129
Psychomotor behavior, defined, 188
Psychomotor performance, 188–189
Public Law 92–142, 15
   Least Restrictive Clause, 312

Reciprocity of behavior in dyads, 95
Recombinative generalization, 228–229,
      233–234
Reflexive responses strategy of audiolo-
      gic assessment, 189
Reinforcement
   delayed, 269
   intermittent schedules of, 269–270
   learned and unlearned responses, 165
   of student, 10–12
   using naturally occurring events for,
      11–12
Reinforcers, use in language training,
      10–12
Relational terms defined, 32
Requesting and describing, relationship
      between, 166–170
Response classes
   identifying and defining, 202–204
      lexical classes, 202
      pragmatic classes, 202–204
      structural classes, 202–204
   potential, 259
Response generalization defined, 47–48,
      200–201, 206, 282

Response level of learning, 8
Responses, learned and unlearned, 165
Request training, 168, 170
Requesting and describing, 163
  relationship between, 166–170
Requesting skills
  developing, 178–181
  establishing, 164–165
  sequence for teaching, 178

Scanning boards, 40
"Second language" training, 105, 143,
  147
  principle of, 115
Self-fulfilling prophecy communication
  principle, 94
Semantic and syntactic classes, types of,
  257–258
Semantic constraints violations by autistic persons, 132
  examples, 132–133
Semantic development of autistics,
  130–133
Sequencing communication objectives,
  39–54
Serial training, 51
Service delivery models, teacher's role
  in, 314–315
Severely handicapped,
  communication intervention,
  159–191
  defined, 160
    see also Handicapped
  intervention program, 176
  limited intervention choices, 175–176
Shaping as a technique, defined, 50–51
Sign language and communication training, 242
Significant others
  as intervention agents, 300
  child's communication and, 108–115
  communication mode choices and,
  142
  conversational teaching strategies
    and, 114
  defined, 92
  language teaching strategies, 111–113
  role as teacher, 109
  teaching principles and, 113–115
  treatment targets and, 108–115
  use of chaining, 101

use of "stranger test" by, 104
  utilizing, 291–338
Signs, iconic, 33
Similar responses defined, 201
Social Contact Rate Principle, 115
Special education teacher's role in language training, 17
Specific generalization plan, 277–278
Speech/language clinician, 324–326
  observation of teacher by, 324
  responsibilities of, 325
  role of, 326
Stimuli
  discriminating between, 182–184
  training, 181
Stimulus control
  defined, 50
  transfer of, 50
Stimulus equivalence training, 13
  adding expressive language compo-
    nent, 241–242
  adding sign language component, 242
  implications for, 244–245
  promoting generalization through,
    239–245
  savings through large stimulus train-
    ing, 243
  training reading comprehension indi-
    rectly, 239–241
Stimulus fading strategy
  errors resulting from time delays, 50
  procedures poorly documented, 50
Stimulus generalization, 47–48
  defined, 47
Stimulus prompts defined, 50
"Stranger test" in teaching intervention,
  104
Structural response classes, 202–204
Structured program, criticism of, 47
Student reinforcement, 10–12
Symbol boards, see Communication
  boards
Syntactic and semantic classes, types of,
  257–258
Syntactic development of autistics, 130
System principle of teaching, 114
Systems theory, 96–97

Tact, defined, 167
Taxonomy of communicative use,
  107–108

Teacher training strategies, 329–337
    analysis of teaching and student eval-
        uations, 330–332
    conduct a structural communication
        program, 334
    direct training, 332–337
        awareness training, 332–333
        change in attitude, 333
        change in knowledge, 333–334
        change in skill, 334–336
        change in student's skill, 337
        implementation of skills, 337
        skills generalization, 337
Teachers
    attributes of successful, 138
    models of responsibility for language
        instruction, 315–329
        as communication/language facili-
            tators, 320–324
        as only trainer without supportive
            services, 326–329
        as primary trainer, 324–326
    programming support, 311–338
    role as educational synthesizer, 315
    role in intervention, 313
    role in language training, 10, 17
    role in programming language, 313
    role in service delivery models,
        314–315
    significant others and, 109
Teaching
    defined, 10
    environment changed to aid difficult-
        to-teach children, 164
    goals of functional language, 5
    incidental, 144
        combined with structured teach-
            ing, 49–50
        defined, 44
        language acquisition and, 74–79
        model of, 44–45
        sequence of steps in, 75
    language goals, 66
    preplanned didactic, 144
    setting for, 12
    significant others principles and,
        113–115
    speech comprehension of objective
        names, 186–188
    techniques of, 10
    variables of, 8
    see also Language training; Training
Teaching strategies, 43–52

    conversational, 113–115
    discrimination learning, 172–173
    integration of structured and inciden-
        tal, 49–50
    less intrusive, 44–47
    matching-to-sample, 173–175
    more intrusive, 47–49
    significant others and, 111–113
    time delay procedure, 187
    see also Language teaching strategies
Teaching targets, significant others and,
    108–115
Therapist's role in language training, 18
Time delay stimulus fading strategy, 50
    errors resulting from, 50
Training
    based on individual student, model
        of, 316
    conceptual approach, 254–255
    concurrent, 51
    content of, 8–9
        organization of, 12–13
    criteria for, 13–14
    determining results, 13–14
    generalization test sequence and, 186
    and generalization, 13
    goal of, 254
    language
        goal of, 253
        lessons of, 11
        parent's role in, 16–17
        therapist's role in, 18
        university training programs,
            18–19
    "loose," programming of, 266–268
    matrix, 12
        implications for, 237–239
        learner with extensive lexical
            knowledge, 236–237
        learner with no prior lexical
            knowledge, 229–233
        learner with partial lexical knowl-
            edge, 233–236
        promoting generalization through,
            227–239
    measuring effects of, 14
    parent's role in, 9–10, 16–17
    process defined, 68
    program administrator's role in, 18
    programs
        change in, 18–19
        importance of process in, 68
    "second language," 105

serial, 51
setting for, 12
social context of, 293
stimuli, 181
   selecting common physical, 263
stimulus equivalence, 13
   adding expressive language component, 241–242
   adding sign language component, 242
   promoting generalization through, 239–245
   savings through large stimulus training, 243
   training reading comprehension indirectly, 239–241
strategies, 329–337
   analysis of teaching and student evaluations, 330–332
   conducting a structural communication program, 334
   direct training, 332–337
      awareness training, 332–333
      change in attitude, 333
      change in knowledge, 333–334
      change in skill, 334–336
      change in student's skill, 337
      implementation of skills, 337
      skills generalization, 337
      for teacher, 329–337
   student reinforcement, 10–12
   suggestions on initiating, 245–246
   teacher's role in, 10, 17
   techniques, 10
      facilitating generalization, 253–284
      naturalistic language, 65–86
      reason for, 65
   therapist's role in, 18
   see also Language training; Teaching
Training and generalization test sequence, 186
Treatment targets, 98–115

child as, 102–108
conversation as, 98–102
   joint activity routine, 99–100
   significant others, 108–115
   social contact purpose, 99
   social recognition, 98
   turn-taking and chaining, 100–102
significant others as, 108–115
Turn-taking, 30, 100–102

Ubiquity principle, 113
Up-the-Ante Principle, 115
Use of language
   child versus adult, 292–295
   conversational characteristics, 295
   dimensions of, 291
   social context of, 291

Verbal conversational skills, 299
Verbal interaction, rates of peer-directed, 296
Vermont Early Communication Curriculum (VECC), 176–178
Visual acuity testing, 189
Vocabularies, types of, 105
Vocabulary comprehension tasks, skills utilized in, 35
Vocabulary
   methods of selecting, 51
   selection of
      for augmentative systems, 32–33
      for early comprehension training, 31–36
      redundant vocabulary avoided, 32
Vocal vocabulary, 105

Wants, expressing, 165–166
Word use, establishing
   initial, 31–36
   multiword, 36–39